The Essential Guide to Lesbian Conception, Pregnancy, and Birth

The Essential Guide to Lesbian Conception, Pregnancy, and Birth

Kim Toevs and Stephanie Brill

alyson books
los angeles | new york

THIS BOOK IS INTENDED AS A REFERENCE VOLUME ONLY. IT IS NOT A MEDICAL MANUAL. THE INFORMATION CONTAINED IN THIS BOOK WAS WRITTEN TO HELP READERS MAKE INFORMED DECISIONS ABOUT CONCEPTION, PREGNANCY, AND BIRTH, AND HEALTH ISSUES ASSOCIATED WITH CONCEPTION, PREGNANCY, AND BIRTH. IT IS NOT DESIGNED AS A SUBSTITUTE FOR ANY TREATMENT THAT MAY HAVE BEEN PRESCRIBED BY YOUR PERSONAL HEALTH CARE PROVIDER. IF YOU SUSPECT YOU HAVE A MEDICAL PROBLEM, SEE A COMPETENT HEALTH CARE PROVIDER TO DISCUSS YOUR CONCERNS.

© 2002 BY KIM TOEVS AND STEPHANIE BRILL. ALL RIGHTS RESERVED.

MANUFACTURED IN THE UNITED STATES OF AMERICA.

THIS TRADE PAPERBACK ORIGINAL IS PUBLISHED BY ALYSON PUBLICATIONS,
P.O. BOX 4371, LOS ANGELES, CALIFORNIA 90078-4371.
DISTRIBUTION IN THE UNITED KINGDOM BY TURNAROUND PUBLISHER SERVICES LTD.,
UNIT 3, OLYMPIA TRADING ESTATE, COBURG ROAD, WOOD GREEN,
LONDON N22 6TZ ENGLAND.

FIRST EDITION: FEBRUARY 2002

02 03 04 05 06 **a** 10 9 8 7 6 5 4 3 2 1

ISBN 1-55583-626-7

CREDITS

ILLUSTRATIONS BY SUZANN GAGE (PGS. 260-261) FROM *A NEW VIEW OF A WOMAN'S BODY* (1991),
  COURTESY OF THE FEDERATION OF FEMINIST WOMEN'S HEALTH CENTERS.
KNOWN-DONOR HEALTH SCREENING QUESTIONS (PGS. 118-122) ADAPTED FROM DOCUMENTS
  PROVIDED BY RAINBOW FLAG HEALTH SERVICES.
SAMPLE KNOWN-DONOR CONTRACT (PGS. 123-127) ADAPTED FROM A DOCUMENT CREATED
  BY PROSPECTIVE QUEER PARENTS (WWW.QUEERPARENTS.ORG)
COVER DESIGN BY MATT SAMS.
COVER PHOTOGRAPHY BY PHOTODISC.

I dedicate this book to the Goddess.
I place the book, and all it brings forth, into Her heart of Love.
—Stephanie

Each of us may come to some point on the path of queer parenting where we feel afraid that we stand alone, but what comfort we receive when we remember that we aren't the firsts or the only's! I honor those who have walked before us, for they, along with our own children, are often our best inspiration. I dedicate what I have learned writing this book to Meg and Jane.
—Kim

Acknowledgments

Many wonderful people have helped us bring this book into being. First and foremost, we would like to thank the hundreds of women and their families who have shared their journey to parenthood and family with us. This is your book. We would like to acknowledge Limor Inbar-Hansen, Cathy Cade, and Jean Weisinger, our stellar photographers. Visual imagery of our families is essential, and we deeply appreciate our photographers for their artful eyes. We are indebted to our apprentices and interns for their enthusiastic research and writing over the past six years, especially Fiona Procheppin, Cecily Arenas, Rachel Lanzerotti, Kimberly Christiansen, and Sarah Bly. We appreciate the time Jane Magid and Rebecca Kutlin took out of early motherhood to so helpfully review the manuscript, and the time Kenna Lee-Ribas took away from her midwifery practice to do the same. The staff at the National Center for Lesbian Rights, the staff at the Sperm Bank of California, and Leland Traiman at Rainbow Flag Health Services have all been most generous in taking their time to provide us with informational resources, as well as to do such dedicated work in general within the community. We'd also like to thank all of the people who have shared pictures of themselves for this book—we love all of you. Angela Brown, our editor at Alyson Publications, has been unfailing in her enthusiasm about this project. Her dedication to such a big undertaking, along with her encouragement to each of us, has been invaluable. Now we'd like to individually thank those who have helped in the creation and completion of this book.

Stephanie

I would like to thank Kim for our many years as a team. There's nothing like working with a woman with a brilliant mind and an ever-opening heart. We covered so much ground together and opened many doors that may not have been opened otherwise. You are definitely power-packed! I would also like to thank Elizabeth Wyatt and Joan Rose for support and encouragement throughout the writing of this book. I also need to thank Robin Winn, Lisa Arellano, Terry Boland, Nathan, Wendy, and my parents for their unwavering belief in me. And most of all, I would like to honor my family for supporting me throughout the seemingly endless process of writing this book. Colleen, my partner, is the song of my heart. Gitanjali, Namaya, and Prana, my children, are the light of my soul. My part of this book is what it is because of you.

Kim

I want to thank Stephanie for being such a revolutionary teacher, midwife, friend, colearner, critical thinker, fellow adventurer, big dreamer, and business partner.

I'd like to gratefully acknowledge all the people who have given us encouragement to take on (and finish!) such a big project: our Maia clients, my public health peers at San Jose State University, and my community of family and friends (especially my mom and Percy).

Special thanks go to my sister Gwen for confidence in my creativity and for her incredible illustration assistance.

Thanks to my coparent Paul and to my parenting support team/extended family, who so generously enabled me to be a mother, midwife, and writer all at once: David, Anne, Suegee, Manuel, Susie, and Heather.

Thanks to my kids Wilson (almost not a kid!) and Denali (who wants it to be known she is named after a mountain) for giving my life deep meaning and lots of laughter. I have been so inspired to watch each of you struggle and succeed at navigating the world as righteous and proud members of queer family.

Finally, I want to thank Susan for her tireless and joyful contributions to this project and to me as writing instructor, ardent fan, daily support person, coparent, best friend, and lover. For your confidence in me I will forever be indebted.

Contents

Part Six: Pregnancy, Birth, and Beyond

Introduction

In autumn 1998, members of the childbirth preparation class we teach were meeting over a potluck dinner for their final session. Everyone was taking a moment to reflect back on the nine achy and exciting months of their pregnancies and on the long personal journeys that had brought them all here. They were all wondering how birth could be "just the beginning" when it seemed they had already come so far. Kate and T.L. were due sooner than the rest of their classmates and were thinking a little further ahead. Out of the blue, Kate asked us, "Would the two of you consider expanding your book to cover not just conception, but all the other stuff about pregnancy and birth we talked about in class?" Everybody laughed. "Our book" was an in-joke among our clients, friends, and colleagues, because at that point we hadn't yet committed to writing a book based on our work. Apparently, we were the only ones who seemed unsure that such a book was in our future.

We met Kate and T.L. in 1996 at a community forum we facilitated for gay, lesbian, bisexual, and transgender people considering parenthood. In 1997 they came to us for preconception counseling, discussing with us sperm-bank options, how to track fertility signs, and how to do a hundred other things you might need to do if you wanted to get pregnant but didn't have a male partner who was fertile. They told us then that it would be really convenient to have a book that covered all the topics we discussed in the counseling sessions, and asked us if we'd ever thought about writing one. We'd heard that often, actually, as we did community presentations and saw an increasing number of queer clients in our private preconception and midwifery practice. People were always asking us for the book where we found the information we were giving out. "There isn't one yet," was our reply. "Then write it!" we'd hear. But our work lives and family lives were so full, and we had never undertaken a project as big and complicated as a book.

By the beginning of 1998 we were helping Kate and T.L. get pregnant by performing at-home intrauterine inseminations for them. We shared with them the joys of their pregnancy, watched as they grew their baby, and provided them with prenatal care. Little did we know, even in 1998, how close we were getting to writing the book everyone said we should write.

We started Maia Midwifery and Preconception Services only four years earlier, in 1994. We offered a full range of traditional home-birth midwifery services as well as counseling for lesbian and bisexual women who wanted to start a family. Initially much of what we told these women about increasing their fertility came from our traditional midwifery training in herbs, diet, and fertility awareness. We also shared insights based on our own personal experiences as queer moms. Mostly, though, we simply listened and tried to apply what we knew to individual situations. We heard many different stories and came to appreciate the incredibly wide range of women's conception experiences. While we expanded our understanding of the field through our own research and consulting, we had the honor of learning a tremendous amount from our clients.

Since 1994 we've constantly incorporated what we learn, as we've continued to expand our services in response to our community's needs. For two years we ran the gay parenting program at the nation's only lesbian health clinic. Through Maia we now teach classes on insemination and run support groups for pregnant and new moms, single moms, nonbiological moms, and people who've been trying unsuccessfully to conceive. We teach childbirth preparation classes for queer women and also provide in-home insemination services. We continue to offer fertility and infertility care to the lesbian and bisexual community. After the first year and a half of focusing on queer women's parenting issues, we began to train other health care and mental health professionals to provide culturally sensitive care to lesbian and bisexual women and their families.

In 1998, Kate and T.L. finally had their baby. They, and a lot of other people in our lives, eventually persuaded us that it was time for us to write our book, the book that would contain the wisdom we had gathered from our community. We made the commitment to write it, and Alyson Publications made the commitment to publish it. This book is the greatest gift we know how to give to lesbian, bisexual, and single women who want to be mothers.

Who Is This Book For?

There are estimated to be anywhere from 1 to 5 million lesbian parents in the United States, and the number is growing. Many of these women have children from previous relationships with men, while more and more are becoming parents as single women or within partnered lesbian relationships. There aren't statistics available, however, for the additional numbers of bisexual women not in male-female relationships—as well as single heterosexual women—that are planning pregnancies. Of those who choose to conceive instead of adopt, some get pregnant easily; others must overcome a variety of monumental obstacles. We wrote this book for all of you—lesbian, bisexual, and single women of any sexual orientation—not only to help you reach your goal of conceiving children, but also to help you celebrate your experience along the way and to remind you that you are not alone.

Many lesbian women want to become pregnant and raise families but never do. Why? The list is long. Women without male partners rarely get pregnant by accident. Lesbians, bisexual women, and single women of any sexual orientation must reconfirm their commitment to parenting at each step of an often-long road to pregnancy. A lack of role models, a lack of familial and societal support, and—most significantly—internalized homophobia can erode a woman's commitment to become a mother. If she doubts her right to parent, she may never find the courage to take the practical steps required to conceive. She may dream of pregnancy without planning for it or actively moving toward her goal. If this is you, this book is for you too. Perhaps you aren't yet ready to call a sperm bank, or to ask a friend to be a donor, or even to sit in a support group. Reading *The Essential Guide to Lesbian Conception, Pregnancy, and Birth* can be that first step you've been waiting to take.

Perhaps you've been actively formulating a plan to conceive but live in an area where resources are not available. One of our goals in writing this book was to make a wealth of information available and easily accessible. Whether you've always wanted to be pregnant or just recently started to explore the possibility, this book is a useful resource guide for the entire process of becoming a gay parent—from trying to conceive through the first stages of babyhood.

Finally, this book is also for single heterosexual women who want to get pregnant and raise a baby. If you're a single straight woman, you have a remarkable number of issues in common with lesbian and bisexual women, including trying to conceive without having a male partner. You won't suffer the homophobia, or fear of it, through your process, but you'll find the vast majority of the information in this book relevant to your experiences with conception and pregnancy.

Why We Wrote This Book

Our deep belief in a woman's fundamental right to make personal choices about her role in reproduction led both of us to work in the field of birth and reproductive health. We want women to have the information and tools they need to follow their own unique path to creating a family.

As midwives, we value not only the outcome of pregnancy, but also the transformational process of becoming pregnant and growing a baby. We want you to keep in touch with your capacity to share big, open-hearted love, which is the original inspiration to parent. Through the exercises provided and our discussion of the emotional aspects of each part of the pregnancy process, we focus on self-love and self-understanding as the foundation for loving others. Self-love is the most fundamental tool lesbians and bisexual women have to combat external and internalized homophobia, and the subsequent self-doubt and low self-esteem that homophobia can cause. A healthy love of self helps each woman celebrate her power to conceive, birth, and raise children, without falling victim to the message that she is unfit to parent.

We emphasize communication skills and exercises throughout the book, to help you clarify your desires and foster closer relationships with your partners, coparents, and other family members. Communicating clearly increases joy and happiness, and improves the stability and longevity of the family unit. Skills that support your family's emotional health and integrity are important in light of the additional strains a homophobic world can place on queer families.

The themes woven throughout the entire book are pertinent not only to the conception and birth processes, but also to parenting in general. Many mothers realize that the myriad challenges of getting pregnant and giving birth are not suffered in vain, but bring experience and wisdom that create fundamental parenting skills.

How to Use This Book

To get the most out of this book, read it from front to back, then use it as a reference guide. Use the exercises and questions we pose as tools for discussions with partners, donors, or coparents. Bring *The Essential Guide to Lesbian Conception, Pregnancy, and Birth* to an appointment with your fertility specialist as a reference guide for asking questions. Read it for inspiration to remember that others have walked down this path before you. Despite the uniqueness of your own individual circumstances, we each share some remarkably common fears, doubts, and challenges. Even if you feel you're past making your initial decisions, the exercises and ideas in the book's first section provide a good opportunity for you to take a step back and survey the decisions you've made thus far.

Our book begins where you do, with a section titled "Many Choices, Many Decisions." Our goal is to lay out the available options, give you the appropriate decision-making tools, and help you envision your unique path through this maze as you work to create your family. Part Two, "Sperm Options," tackles the topic most women find to be the greatest hurdle to pregnancy, providing in-depth information on the multitudes of ways women choose sperm donors or fathers for their children. In Part Three, "Optimizing Your Health and Fertility," we supply otherwise hard-to-find information about increasing your chances of conceiving and growing a healthy baby.

Part Four, "Conception," covers the specifics of how, when, and where to inseminate, with a discussion of relevant emotional issues that may affect your ability to conceive. "Challenging Conceptions," Part Five, is crucial reading for anyone who has inseminated for more than a few months. It gives support and offers new ideas you may not have tried in the past. Part Six, the final section, "Pregnancy, Birth, and Beyond" is not intended to be a complete medical guide to all aspects of pregnancy but rather a primer for pregnancy, birth, and postpartum issues specific to lesbian, bisexual, and single parents.

Even if your choices have changed over time, we hope you find that the essence of your original ideals about creating your family remains with you now. If not, we invite you to revisit how you arrived at the place you are now and whether you want to be there. If you've rushed through or been pressured about decisions regarding family structure or infertility, take the time to reevaluate whether these decisions feel right and true for you personally. We also encourage you to read Part 3 on health and fertility, even if you've already started inseminating or are currently pregnant. The ideas you'll find there can benefit anyone's health, including new parents and children.

Our Background and Experience

Kim Toevs

At age 16, I developed an overwhelming urge to become pregnant, which came to fruition in my early 20s after asking my best friend Paul to donate sperm to me. I was intending to parent as a single woman, within the support of a collective group household and a fairly new love relationship with a woman who had an older child. Over time and changing circumstances, Paul became an actively involved coparent who lives in the same city but not the same house. My lover Susan developed a co-parenting relationship with my daughter Denali over time as well, though I remain the primary parent. I've been deeply involved in raising Susan's son, Wilson. Denali and Wilson are siblings, and the four of us are a family. Denali includes her dad in her family, and Wilson includes his other mom. A number of other adults who have lived in our group household, along with a couple of longtime friends, are our extended family. Our kids are now 18 and 8, and we may have one more! As this book goes to press, though, Susan and I are ending our journey together as lovers. I respect her close relationship with Denali, and I'm happy she'll continue her parenting role.

For the last 13 years I have been involved in a variety of ways with women's and men's sexual and reproductive health. Between being a home-birth midwife specializing in queer conception work and being a jill-of-all-trades for many years at Planned Parenthood in abortion, family planning, and prenatal clinics, I've had the opportunity to hear a wide range of stories about reproductive and parenting experiences. Listening to these stories has tremendously broadened my understanding of how many ways there are to create and raise loving families.

Stephanie Brill

In addition to being a midwife, I bring 11 years of motherhood to my work. As Kim and I have written this book, I have conceived and been pregnant with my third child. By the time this book goes to press, I will have given birth as well. My oldest daughter was born at home in a cabin in the woods. As a young mother I knew I wanted to be a mom, but I didn't spend much time thinking about the process—I just jumped into it. I had planned to actively coparent with two men I knew. We were all going to live communally and raise my first child and future children communally. Our thoughts were not well developed, though, and by the time my daughter was born it was clear that I would be a single mother. Even though my plans went awry, I found that I absolutely loved single motherhood and wasn't actively looking for someone with whom to share my parenting responsibilities.

Surprisingly, when my daughter, Gi, was almost five we met Colleen and all fell head over heels for one another. A few years later, after blending our family, we decided to have a second child, and Colleen wanted to be pregnant this time. After 11 months of inseminating with frozen sperm from a sperm bank, we switched to an anonymous fresh-sperm donor and got pregnant with one try. Namaya is now two and a half, and we await the birth of our third child. This baby was conceived with the sperm of a different known donor.

In addition to being a mom and a midwife, I have cofounded an elementary charter school based on antibias principles. I have provided teacher and staff training on issues of cultural sensitivity in the classroom and have helped to develop gay-friendly elementary curriculum. I have also led workshops for parents and students about overcoming homophobia and heterosexism. And most recently I authored *The Queer Parent's Primer*, a book for current queer parents that covers the day-to-day issues we face raising our children in a straight world.

My work is dedicated to making the world a better place for us and our children. There is nothing better than being a mom. My kids are the highlight of my life. I wish you all the same joy!

■ ■ ■

Congratulations! What an exciting journey you are on. We wish you all the joy and personal growth that children can bring into your life, and hope your family will be filled with love and pride.

Part One
Many Choices, Many Decisions

Chapter 1 Creating New Family Models

Because lesbian and bisexual women must reach beyond mainstream models and definitions of family, we have the opportunity to create profoundly new models of family. Traditionally, adults who parent together are usually biologically related to their children, and sexually and romantically linked to each other. The very nature of how lesbian and bisexual women make family debunks the myth that these relationship components are inextricably linked, thereby liberating each of us to create family structures best suited to our needs and ideals.

Children and parents alike are well served by a woman's ability to choose the number of parents in a family as well as how the roles of parenting, home keeping, and income earning will be divided. All may benefit as well from creative decision making about the nature of extended family and the structure of community support networks. The multitude of ways in which queer people are building families speaks to how unique each of us is. Along with our diversity, we are fundamentally united in knowing that, ultimately, love is indeed what makes a family.

Creating Our Family Relationships

If you're just beginning to explore the possibility of parenthood, now is the perfect time to look more closely at your ideas about various family structures. In this chapter we give you some new ideas and ask some essential questions to help you clarify your vision, even if you've already made some decisions about how you would like to create a family. Most of us retain some assumptions and unexamined ideas about the concept of family that may subconsciously restrict the choices we make. Take this opportunity to explore the different components of parenting relationships and look at some examples of how we can incorporate them into our families.

3

Although most lesbian and bisexual women considering motherhood either plan to be single mothers or partnered mothers, there are many additional options for including other parents and coparents in families that step outside these more traditional models. Many of us who are currently parenting didn't realize or didn't choose from the more nontraditional scope of options when we became parents. Ten years into parenting—and through breakups, new relationships, and other life changes—we've found that our respective families are more complex and less "nuclear" than when they began. No matter what your initial parenting vision may be, it's helpful to carefully examine the nature of the bonds that are traditionally associated with family. In so doing, you can give more thoughtful attention to your choices about your family in the making.

Biological Relationships

An adult can be biologically related to a child, whether by providing the sperm or egg for conception or by carrying the child in utero and giving birth. This adult may or may not be an active parent, if we define "parent" as someone who takes on daily primary responsibilities for the child. Conversely, a biological relationship isn't necessary for one to be considered a parent.

Limor Inbar-Hansen, Indelible Images

Hopefully you can see, through the following examples, the multitude of possibilities that exist for creating family. When we break apart the connections between the building blocks of biology, love, sex, and parenting that society often suggests are inseparable, we can form an almost infinite number of new family models by recombining them. To our great benefit, the many choices we have allow us to create families that suit our individual needs and lifestyles.

Example: Tanya and Leslie choose to parent together. Tanya conceives with sperm obtained through a sperm bank that will release information about the donor when the child turns 18. Although the child may have a relationship with the donor after he or she reaches that age, the donor will have no contact with the child previous to that time and therefore no parenting role. Both Leslie and Tanya equally and fully identify as mothers, even though only one of them is biologically related to the child.

Another example: Jill and Tamika have always wanted their close friend Andre to donate sperm to them and be actively involved in their child's life in a coparenting capacity. When he tests positive for HIV, however, they initially lament the loss of his involvement in their family. Over time, though, they realize that his special role as their best friend and the baby's key male role model isn't contingent upon his biological relationship with the child. They choose an anonymous donor and invite Andre to become a coparent.

"We were so relieved when we realized we could stay together and Maria could still have a baby! We had thought we both were supposed to want to parent equally, which we didn't. One day we realized we were basing our idea of family on models that were irrelevant. We love each other dearly. Maria wants to parent. I like kids, but I don't want that kind of day in, day out commitment that parenting requires. We've now decided that she'll be a single parent and I'll be the baby's auntie. With this realization we've decided to formalize our commitment to each other. We're getting married this summer!" —Tammy, age 44, Modesto, Calif.

Romantic Relationships

Often a romantic relationship between two adults is a key element in their decision to parent together. Two people, from their love for each other, can choose to raise a child together, regardless of their respective biology or gender. Although this frequently is accompanied by an equal desire to raise children, sometimes one partner has a much stronger interest in being a parent than the other. It is quite common for two women to enter into parenting together with unequal interests because they want to stay together as a couple and one of the women decides to have a child regardless of the other woman's lack of desire to parent.

Some lesbian and bisexual women have difficulty believing that two people who are romantically involved can raise a child together while having different levels of commitment to parenting. Perhaps this unequal level of responsibility too closely resembles stereotypical heterosexual models of parenting, where, regardless of how much both partners profess to want children, the woman finds herself in the obligatory role of primary caretaker, with little option to prioritize her career or other personal needs. In contrast to the stereotypical heterosexual model are the thoroughly explored and clearly communicated arrangements that queer families have the opportunity to consent to before pregnancy. These involve the division of labor and responsibility surrounding raising a child that otherwise falls primarily on the shoulders of the woman wanting to give birth. This ends up being a meeting ground for women who want to stay together. Sometimes the more reluctant mother-to-be finds that she wants more parental involvement over time, and sometimes she does not.

Example: Peggy and Yolanda live together as romantic partners, but only Yolanda is fully committed to parenting a child. Peggy decides that although her life will be affected by having a baby in the house, she doesn't want to take on the primary responsibility of raising the child. She is past her own childbearing years and feels her life has a different focus now. Although partnered with Yolanda, Peggy plans to act more as a supportive secondary parent than a primary parent. Yolanda conceives with sperm from a gay male friend. He and his male partner, who live nearby, also actively parent the child. As the child grows older, she spends a substantial amount of time at both homes.

Occasionally, none of the people involved in parenting a child are romantically connected.

Example: Ellen, who is straight, and Jim, who is gay, are parenting together. She self-inseminated at home with his sperm to conceive, and they share a home.

Example: Barb and Anne are good friends who share parenting responsibilities. Barb is the primary parent, while Anne is an active coparent who spends slightly less time with the kids and defers to Barb for primary decisions, such as those concerning the child's health and education. Barb and Anne don't live together, but when Barb and the children relocate to a new town, Anne moves with them to continue her involvement in the family.

Sexual Relationships

A sexual relationship initiated for the purpose of conceiving doesn't necessarily imply a desire to share parenting responsibilities.

Example: Dana, a lesbian, has sex with her male friend Mateo to get pregnant. She becomes a single parent, and he doesn't have an ongoing partner relationship with her or a parenting relationship with the child.

Many bisexual women coparent with men they're sexually involved with, whether or not other parents are also present in the family. Sometimes conception occurs between queer-identified people who share both a sexual relationship and a parenting relationship.

Example: Inez is a male-to-female transsexual. She and her bisexual partner Akiko conceive a baby together before Inez completes her sexual reassignment surgery and loses her ability to make sperm, and they both parent their child together.

The Challenges of New Family Structures

There are many inherent challenges to creating new and different models of family. One of the primary struggles is finding in others the recognition and validation of the legitimacy of our families. When we step outside of the culturally familiar to such extremes, we also need to create new language to define our family relationships. This requires ongoing awareness. Because our models of family are often new and different, we may find very little social support for our family structures. This can be quite stressful on the family unit as a whole. Breakups in "alternative" families caused by pressures from an unsympathetic culture are truly tragic.

If you plan to have a family that is considered "alternative"—and we assume that includes most readers of this book—it's valuable to plan ahead as to how each of you individually, and as a family unit, will get the support you need to be a family outside of, and sometimes against, the mainstream. Regular counseling for all relevant

Photo © Cathy Cade

family members often helps to keep lines of communication open and strong. Personal self-reflection will also help you to deepen your own commitment to parenting. Additionally, finding other lesbian and gay families to connect with helps to break feelings of isolation. And perhaps most importantly, a carefully thought-out vision that is honestly shared by all involved will go far in helping you to feel confident in your choices. Crafting such a vision and gaining clarity about mutual desires and goals can take many, many months or even years to develop.

If you don't wish to take that much time to clarify your desires and goals in the planning stages, it's all the more important for you to establish mechanisms for keeping decisions and emotions clear among all adults involved throughout the process of parenting.

> **"I'm a bisexual woman who wants to be a mom. I've never been in a long-term romantic relationship and would be fooling myself to think that I'm ready for one now. I don't even want one. However, I live close to my parents and siblings, and we all want to raise my children collectively. So, although I'll be a single mom, I feel like I actually have more support than most partnered parents I know." —Terri, age 37, Las Vegas, Nev.**

Naming Our Family Relationships

Crucial to our parenting identity is the language we use to identify our relationships to our children and the rest of our family. We also are greatly affected by how we are named by our children, our community, and the broader culture.

Because, as queer parents, we are at the edge of a cultural frontier, many terms haven't yet been created or standardized for our family-structure concepts and definitions of family members. It's vital and empowering to claim our own language and find ways to make our names accurately reflect our relationships. Because language is so fluid, careful clarification of exactly what you mean by a term will help prevent miscommunications and misperceptions.

Language and the Needs of Children

Explore, from your child's perspective, the language you use for naming your family relationships. The language you choose should help to clarify donor negotiations, discussions with your partner, and how you identify yourself to coworkers, your families of origin, and neighbors. Likewise, the language you establish before your child is born provides the initial framework within which your child will understand his or her family and relationships.

What follows is an accounting of the more common titles we at Maia have heard from women. There is great diversity in how lesbian and bisexual women identify themselves and their kinship relationships. Pay attention to your reactions as you read; they will give you a lot of insight into your own philosophies and assumptions.

Mom

"Who's the mother?" If you're a partnered lesbian parent, once you've heard this question one or 20 times, you'll start to understand what a vested stake people have in fitting our personal relationships into the familiar heterosexual paradigm. Depending on who asks this question and why, you may give a number of different responses. But what's most important is how you answer the question to yourself, your partner, and your children.

Most women who are parenting the child they birthed self-identify as "Mother" or "Mom." If their female partner is also the child's parent, they're in a unique parenting category, which the dominant culture may struggle to recognize. Some call themselves "Second Mom," "Other Mom," or "coparent." Some go by "Mama," "Ima," "Mommy," or simply their own first name. Some women are fully parents but haven't been able to find any title that rings true for them. Some butch women who are nonbiological parents identify more with the term "Dad," feeling that the image invoked more accurately reflects the image of themselves as parents. Additionally, some butch women who give birth also identify more with the term "Dad." Most nonbiological mothers we've worked with, however, identify themselves as "Mom," just like the mom who gave birth, but often with a subtle distinction (for example, "Mama" or "Mommy"). When both women choose the same title, they confront our culture's inability to conceptualize a "nuclear family" with two moms and children instead of one with both a mom and dad.

All lesbian couples raising children are confronted by one question from strangers as well as new friends: "But who's the *real* mom?"—meaning, "Who gave birth?" For lesbians, who gave birth doesn't define this reality. Both moms are real. The use of the word *real* in place of *biological* demonstrates how difficult it is for many people, even those with the best intentions, to step outside the heterosexual model of procreation. Many people meeting a lesbian couple with children feel the need to identify for themselves who is "more the mom." This identification, if not made based on biology, is often made on the basis of which partner stays home more with the kids, which partner is more femme, or some other concept rooted in heterosexual stereotypes.

Choosing family names you feel accurately reflect your family relationships, and wearing those names with pride, are the first steps in communicating to others that their use of your chosen titles is important, not only to you but also to your children.

Dad

At Maia Midwifery we've seen tremendous variation in the definition of "Dad." If women choose an anonymous donor through a sperm bank, they often use the title "donor" to describe him. "Biological father" works for some women who want to specify a man's connection to the child, implying that he isn't taking on additional aspects of fatherhood. When working with a donor they know, some women refer to him as the father of the baby, whether or not he'll have a parenting role. Some men are called "known donors," some "uncles," "special uncles," or "super uncles." Some are called "coparents."

Although all these titles in some way reflect the nature of the relationship the man has with the child, what exactly these titles reflect isn't always obvious to someone outside the family. For example, some children's donors become key family members. These donors hold a unique position in the childrens' lives different from that of other men; they regularly see the children and provide child care. Their only title is "donor," which in other families may refer to the man who donated sperm but has no relationship with the child. In other families, the men may be called coparents, though they may see the child just once a month.

"I know some lesbians feel compelled to have a man involved in their family so that the child can have a male role model. Whatever. We really want nothing to do with men in our immediate family. We have enough love between us to nourish a small country. We're not lacking anything. Our family is complete with the two of us and any kids we have."
—Angela, age 36, Culver City, Calif.

Occasionally we'll hear a story about a known donor without parenting responsibilities who self-identifies as "Dad" to family and friends, to the great consternation of the moms, who would never dream of calling him that. Having a more thorough initial discussion with the donor about names and their power helps to avoid this type of unexpected, and sometimes messy, situation.

The titles women choose for the men involved in their family often speak to some deep desires they have about family ties—regardless of how day-to-day parenting logistics work out. Whether consciously or not, many of us are greatly influenced by our feelings about the presence or absence of our own fathers and/or stepfathers in our upbringings. Bringing these feelings into the light can help you to communicate more clearly exactly what you mean when you use these different words. Communicating about this is vital initially within your partnership, then in your negotiations with a known donor, and finally directly with your child.

Exercise

In a journal, write about who, if anyone, occupied the father role in your life. What was his biological relationship to you? What kind of parenting did he provide? How was he related to your other family members? What did he add to your life? Did your friends or cousins have different relationships with their fathers or stepfathers? If you didn't have a participatory father, how did this make you feel? How do you feel about this now? Do you feel there's an ideal image of "father" that benefits children the most? How consciously do you carry these old feelings and memories into your present decisions about creating a family?

Family

Exercise

Do some writing or thinking about your reactions to the titles we've discussed. Explore the titles family members had when you were a child and what these symbolized to you. Then, with your partner or a friend, do some role-playing experimenting with different titles. Role-play or imagine telling your potential donor your thoughts about what you'll call him to friends, family, and your child. Role-play explaining to extended family or your child's schoolteacher or your pediatrician who you all are and what your child calls each of you. Discuss in your role play why your choice of titles feels accurate and important to you, if you imagine people involved in your child's life being confused. Role-play or imagine discussing the topic with your child at different ages. Hopefully you'll gain insight into both your logical rationale and your sometimes "illogical" gut reaction to the important topic of naming. This will help you clarify what's important, why it's important to you, and how to communicate it to others. As you—and your partner, if you have one—discuss your insights, you'll gain a better understanding of the emotional intensity each of you potentially brings to this topic.

"Family" has many meanings in the queer community. At pride events we often hear the recording of Sister Sledge singing "We Are Family" as our unofficial anthem. In this context, the lyrics ask us to celebrate the adult kinship systems that queer people form, especially those of us who are distanced from our own biological families by homophobia and our sexual orientation. Gay people often use a question such as "Is your coworker family?" to mean "Is he or she queer-identified?"

When we include children in our families, we again recognize the malleability of language. Family may have a nuclear family connotation, meaning two adult partners and their children. It may refer to the people who sleep under the same roof and have an interconnected living arrangement, regardless of their kinship to each other and their children. Family may refer to the extended biological family.

11

To some, family includes all of the people who have unique relationships with the children, perform regular and committed child care, and actively participate in either daily or weekly life with other family members.

Although laws in many countries limit the notion of family to relationships of blood or marriage, unless specifically contested, many cultures (both inside and outside the U.S.) are more flexible. For example, some cultures identify special child-to-child relationships with the term "cousin," and special nonmaternal female adult-to-child relationships with the term "aunt." These inclusions are also common among lesbian families, especially in single-parent households.

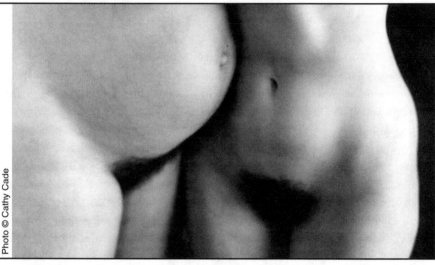

Photo © Cathy Cade

Besides needing names to refer to their primary parents, children often need special names or titles to give to other important people in their lives, especially for relationships they don't see reflected or valued in popular culture. Examples we've heard of are "stepmom," referring either to a mom who comes into the family when the child is older; or "my lovee" and "my special," referring to a mom's partner, former partner, or housemate who doesn't identify as the primary parent. Friends and family members need to understand that supporting your child's sense of family means recognizing and participating in using the names you and your child use for important family members.

The use of these names may be crucial to a 2- or 3-year-old who is just learning how to describe his or her world in concrete terms, but may be different for a 13-year-old who is making her or his own decisions about how to come out to friends. Our children may answer the question "Who's in your family?" differently according to their developmental stage. Sometimes their answer will include all the important adults in their lives, such as preschool teachers and baby-sitters, sometimes just biological relatives, sometimes just playmates, siblings, and fairies (no grown-ups al-lowed!). In any case, the solid foundation of your family is created from the work you do before your baby's birth. When you're as clear as possible in your own vision and choices, you'll be able to maintain inner confidence that will naturally allow for more flexibility and acceptance of your child's creative expressions of family.

The Big Exercise: Your Vision

To create the family of your dreams, it's important to identify your unexamined, ingrained beliefs about family. This exercise will help you distinguish between your underlying belief system and what you would choose to create freely in your ideal world. You probably can't tackle these questions all at once; they aren't merely an item on a to-do list, but are instead tools for ongoing discussion and reflection. As you write or discuss your answers, ask yourself what has influenced your beliefs over the course of your life. Your own family experiences? Images from TV? Opinions of other lesbians who are already parents in your community? Notice the opinions you cling to most rigidly, since they may point to your unspoken fears. Notice also the opinions you feel most passionate about, since they may point to your heart's truest yearnings.

- What, from your childhood memories, was beneficial about your family structure?
- What was challenging about it?
- What seemed to work or not work in terms of roles for each parent?
- As a child did you have friends who had alternative family structures? What were the benefits and drawbacks to their models, both for the children and the parents?
- How many people, ideally, should parent a child? How many people should parent two or more children?
- Does a child need both a male and a female parent?
- Should a child have male and female role models who aren't primary parents?
- Does a child need access to information about who s/he is biologically related to?
- Does a child need the opportunity to have a relationship with the people he or she is biologically related to?
- Can people actively involved in parenting live in more than one household? Does this necessarily mean the child should live in more than one household?
- Can you imagine sharing an intimate and lifelong parenting relationship with someone with whom you aren't romantically partnered?
- Can you imagine sharing an intimate and lifelong parenting relationship with someone with whom you are romantically partnered?
- Can you imagine people who are committed, connected participants in a

child's life who aren't primary parents? Would you consider these people family members?

• What would an adequate support system for a single parent encompass?

Inherent in families is the concept of change. Our families are similar to heterosexual families in that after five or 10 years they don't necessarily look like they did at the beginning. Households may evolve as people redefine their relationships. New lovers connect and blend their families, including stepparents and ex-lovers. While keeping this in mind, remember that you have the power to thoughtfully choose your initial family structure. When you've answered the above questions, summarize by describing your vision of the ideal family, whether in writing, drawing, or doing some other method of recording, such as tape recording. You'll probably want to be able to refer back to your ideas at a later date.

After you're finished with this exercise, come together with relevant family members and compare your answers. Can you take your visions one step further by combining them? If you decide to do this, save it: It's your family's mission statement and probably contains some of your most heartfelt beliefs.

Keep this document available as your own personalized family template. Hold clear the essence of your vision and why it's important to you. As you move along your pathway to parenthood, you may lose sight of not only what you're trying to achieve, but also why. When you're at an impasse while making decisions about all the various details, or feel overwhelmed, pressured, or uninspired, return to this original vision. Let it rekindle your passion to parent.

Change the vision as you grow, if it seems appropriate. Expand it and clarify it as your understanding of your goals deepens. Use it to ensure that the decisions you make are aligned with your truest intentions. This is a living document that reflects your hearts' desires. Keep it updated, and it will continue to inspire you for years to come. Share it with your children as they grow.

Sample Family Mission Statement

We are committed to raising our children in a loving and nurturing home. Alice, Cathy, Manuel, and Jeff are planning to parent our incoming child equally. To us that means we will support Alice throughout the pregnancy and early newborn period. When the baby is old enough we all eagerly look forward to being with our child for as much time each week as our respective schedules permit. We know that time isn't the only requirement of being a parent. Some of us earn more money and will put this toward supporting our child. Some of us will have more time to be with our child in his or her formative years. We are committed to parenting together even if Alice or Manuel turn out to be infertile. We will try together all of the various options that we can come up with in order to make a baby. This may include using another man's sperm or even considering adoption. If our couples should break up in the future, each of us remains committed to parenting this child throughout his or her life. As four loving parents we welcome our baby.

Resources

Books

The Complete Single Mother, Andrea Engbar and Leah Klungness, Adams Business Media, 2000

Considering Parenthood: Choosing Children, Cheri Pies, Spinsters Ink, 1988

Gay Parents/Straight Schools: Building Communication and Trust, Virginia Casper and Steven B. Schultz, Casper Teachers College Press, 1999

Home Fronts: Controversies in Nontraditional Parenting, Jess Wells (ed.), Alyson Publications, 2000

A Legal Guide for Lesbian and Gay Couples, Hayden Curry (ed.), Nolo Press, 1999

The Lesbian and Gay Parenting Handbook, April Martin, Harper Perennial, 1993

Lesbian Parenting: Living With Pride and Prejudice, Katherine Arnup, Gynergy Books, 1995

Love Makes A Family: Portraits of Lesbian, Gay, Bisexual, and Transgender Parents and Their Families, Gigi Kaeser, Peggy Gillespie, and Kath Weston, University of Massachusetts Press, 1999

Politics of the Heart: A Lesbian Parenting Anthology, Sandra Pollack and Jeanne Vaughn (eds.), Firebrand Books, 1987

Reinventing the Family: Lesbian and Gay Parents, Laura Benkov, Ph.D., Crown Trade Paperbacks, 1994

Queer Family Values, Valerie Lehr, Temple University Press, 1999

The Queer Parent's Primer, Stephanie Brill, New Harbinger Press, 2001

Single Mothers by Choice, Jane Mattes, CSW, Random House, 1997

The Single Mother's Book: A Practical Guide, Joan Anderson, Peachtree Publishers, 1990

The Single Parent Resource Book, Brook Noel and Art Klein, Champion Press Limited, 1998

The Single Mother's Survival Guide, Patrice Karst, Crossing Press, 2000

Organizations and Programs

ACLU Lesbian and Gay Rights Project
125 Broad St., 18th Floor
New York, NY 10004
(212) 549-2627

Center Kids: The Family Program of the Lesbian and Gay Community Center
208 W. 13th St.
New York, NY 10011
(212) 620-7310
www.gaycenter.org

COLAGE (Children of Lesbians and Gays Everywhere)
3543 18th St., #1
San Francisco, CA 94110
(414) 861-5437
www.colage.org

Family Pride Coalition
P.O. Box 34337
San Diego, CA 92163
(619) 296-0199
www.familypride.org

Gay and Lesbian Advocates and Defenders
294 Washington St., Suite 740
Boston, Ma 02112
(617) 426-1350
www.glad.org

Lambda Legal Defense and Education Fund (offers many free documents and publications on their Web site)
120 Wall St., Suite 1500
New York, NY 10005-3904
(212) 809-8585
www.lambdalegal.org

Lesbian, Gay, Bisexual, and Transgender Family and Parenting Services
Fenway Community Health Center
7 Haviland St.
Boston, MA 02115
(617) 927-6243
www.fenwayhealth.org

National Center for Lesbian Rights (Along with other information and resources, NCLR offers a packet of helpful documents titled "Partnership Protection Documents.")
870 Market St., Suite 570
San Francisco, CA 94102
(415) 392-6257
www.nclrights.org

PFLAG (Parents, Families and Friends of Lesbians and Gays)
1726 M St., N.W., Suite 400
Washington, DC 20036
(202) 467-8180
www.pflag.org

Web Sites and Periodicals
Gay Parent magazine (available in print and online)
www.gayparentmag.com

Lesbian Moms Web Page (One of many, this site keeps a referral list of recommended service providers such as doctors, lawyers, and sperm banks.)
www.lesbian.org/moms/index.htm

Proud Parenting magazine
www.altfammag.com

Chapter 2 Making Decisions

As you start out on your path to parenthood, you'll face many decisions unique to lesbian, bisexual, and single women. The sheer number of these decisions, as well as their importance, may make you feel simultaneously powerful and intimidated. Whether you struggle through these decisions or make them with ease, you're creating your unique approach to parenting that will carry you through the years ahead. Most of us experience at least a few instances when we can't seem to make a decision, doubt a decision we thought we had firmly made, or can't reach a mutual decision with a partner. This chapter will help you develop specific decision-making tools and skills. It will advise you on how to create your own plan and time line for your journey to pregnancy. This time line and the information included on what to do when you're stuck making a decision are the essential tools you'll need to keep yourself moving forward toward your goal of creating a family.

The first part of this chapter discusses **why** some decisions seem so difficult to make. The second section focuses on **how** to make decisions well. The third part guides you through creating a personal plan and time line, describing **when** to make each decision. The final section outlines ideas about **what** to do if you're procrastinating or can't seem to move forward with your decisions.

Self-Love

By the time your child is growing up, you'll be used to making many daily decisions, both big and small, about his or her life. Some you will undoubtedly agonize over; most you'll make easily. Right now you may feel overwhelmed about the fact that parenting involves making decisions that may permanently affect another person's life. Sometimes, especially in the beginning, the staggering weight of this responsibility immobilizes people. "What if I don't make the best decision about something very important?" is a fundamental question parents ask themselves again and again.

You'll parent most successfully and joyfully when you approach decisions from a place of self-love instead of fear or guilt. Learning to trust and believe that you'll make the best possible decisions you can at the time, with the best intentions for your family and self, is a crucial element of self-love. Self-love includes acknowledging that some of your decisions may seem like mistakes later. If you can commit to being as honest as you can in your self-reflection and communication, you'll do well. Women who approach the many parenting decisions ahead of them from this perspective more easily avoid becoming burdened by regrets or immobilized with indecisiveness.

If you've made many other important decisions in your life, you may feel awkward now if you find yourself challenged by the decisions before you. Don't worry: This awkwardness is a sign that you're on the right track; feeling awkward is a natural part of learning and growing. We honor growing babies with love instead of judgment as they learn to walk, hesitatingly, taking clumsy tentative steps, falling, and trying again. We need to honor ourselves in this way as we learn to make parenting decisions, because we not only grow our babies, we also grow our parent-selves.

Internalized Homophobia and Other Kinds of Shame

Due to cultural homophobia, internalized homophobia, and the lack of easy access to sperm, women without male partners have to claim their right and renew their commitment to have children at each step toward getting pregnant. They constantly must call upon their courage to go forward, in the presence of many messages that say they shouldn't. When women internalize society's homophobia, self-doubts can take on a life of their own, carrying an emotional charge that's sometimes difficult to recognize and understand.

Often lesbians feel they must be perfect before they parent, not only to provide the best for their children, but also to prove to everyone who may wonder whether lesbians and bisexual women can be excellent mothers. This self-expectation of being 200% perfect can reveal itself in various forms.

In the early stages of deciding to parent, women appear to be especially vulnerable to the effects of both homophobia and single-parent prejudices. Women who spend many years wanting to parent but not taking the necessary steps to start inseminating are often immobilized by unprocessed internalized homophobia. Homophobia is insidious because it's often invisible. It's important to examine whether you're experiencing internalized or external homophobia when you're unable to take the necessary steps toward becoming a parent. Sometimes therapy or counseling is needed to help you explore these issues, as their impact on your life can feel paralyzing.

Internalized homophobia and external homophobia can arise once you begin to inseminate as well as when you're pregnant and parenting. Therefore, it's important to actively address these influences now and begin to dismantle their power over you. You do a service to yourself and your children when you eradicate shame and move into pride.

Donor Decisions

Donor decisions are the most common area in which women reach an impasse in their decision-making process. The foundational and often subconscious reasons for this phenomenon usually involve homophobia and single-parent shame. Only some of the influences of homophobia stem from its internalized forms; many arise from the external structures of society's homophobia. For example, societal homophobia has created a legal system that greatly affects how women make decisions about donors and sperm, in that the system doesn't automatically protect queer women's parenting relationships.

If you want to use sperm from a known donor, you may choose to inseminate in a doctor's office or freeze your donor's sperm at a sperm bank solely for legal protection. If making decisions about sperm isn't easy for you economically or philosophically, you may get stuck at this decision-making point, unable to reconcile your fear of unsecured custody with your desire to conceive with sperm that doesn't come from an anonymous donor.

Internalized homophobia may also affect you at this juncture. You may feel secure in your decision to conceive with sperm from a sperm bank. Yet as you look at the lists of potential donors at a sperm bank, you may feel suddenly sad. Some women feel sad or disappointed at the thought that their child won't have a father in his or her life. Others feel sad at the realization that they've been considering their own female household to be less valid because there is no father. It's important to reframe these forms of thinking from a perspective of lack to an appreciation of all you have to give your child. Exploring your own issues surrounding men, fathers, and society's expectations may be necessary in order for you to find the donor you wish to use.

Single Women

Single women—straight, lesbian, or bisexual—who are at an impasse in their journey to parenthood often need to sort out a variety of internalized messages. If you're single and waiting for a partner to arrive before you parent, try to disentangle your parenting needs from your ideas about the stigmatization of single moms so that you can truly consider different arrangements of feasible parenting that suit your situation. If you have a clearly articulated understanding of which resources you specifically bring to parenting, not just in comparison with a two-parent family, you'll be less likely to make decisions about donors and other issues based on internalized feelings of inadequacy or shame.

Is It Desirable to Remain Closeted?

Lesbian and bisexual women choose many different strategies of being out or closeted about their sexual identity. Often someone will choose to express her identity in different ways depending on the situation. In some situations you may choose to disclose your sexual orientation. In others you may choose to "pass" as heterosexual. Many lesbians are afraid to parent while they are closeted but are also afraid to come out. But being closeted to feel safer isn't necessarily something you want to continue to do as a parent. Still, finding the courage and strength to come out may seem overwhelming. The desire to remain closeted often stems from a combination of internalized homophobia and perceived risk of external homophobic actions.

When you picture yourself at various steps in your journey, from preconception through pregnancy and parenthood, think about how feasible it will be for you to be either out or closeted in different environments. Are you tempted to make decisions about donors and family structure and conception based, in part, on a desire to remain closeted? Try to specify your actual fears: What would happen if you came out in a given situation? What would happen if you were to remain closeted in that same situation? This exercise can assist you in separating your internalized homophobia from your actual risk.

Before pregnancy, fears of homophobia may make it difficult for you to interact with sperm-bank employees or health care providers who offer services you need, especially if you don't have an active plan for how you'll present relevant information about yourself, your partner, or other family members. Deciding whether to come out is always a personal decision. Give this issue attention from the beginning, and if you're partnered, make sure that you both share an approach that feels inclusive yet safe for both of you. Deciding in advance how you'll present yourself to others will reduce homophobia's power over you, which would otherwise cause you to delay entering potentially uncomfortable situations.

When deciding whether or not to come out, be aware that many people will assume you're straight when you mention planning a family, even if they don't assume so already. If you're partnered, how you respond to questions about the father is always an opportunity for you to come out. If you're partnered and you don't come out—whether or not your partner is with you at the time—you negate her importance in your life and family.

Examining Your Internalized Homophobia

Exercise

It's helpful to become more consciously aware of the impact internalized homophobia has on you. As you read the following section, examine what you think you need in your life before you're ready to parent. You may realize you hold yourself to a standard you wouldn't expect others to maintain. Or perhaps you'd expect other lesbians, but not straight women, to match your standards. These expectations are unfair both to yourself and to other lesbians. Holding yourself to impossibly high standards, however, is understandable, since many of us are asked by others to justify our decision to parent in ways that heterosexuals are not. You may not even be consciously aware that heterosexual women are not often asked to validate their parenting choices in the way lesbian, bisexual, and single parents often are.

Explore these questions in your journal or through discussion with a friend or partner: Is it fair to give birth to a child who may be stigmatized because of his or her family members? How much homophobia will my child suffer because of my choices? Will my child be gay? How would I feel about that? When I'm a parent will I lose control of who I'm out to? Do I necessarily have to lose my dyke identity to gain a motherhood identity? Do I have the right to have children? Can children be healthy if raised by lesbians? Can children be healthy if raised by one gay woman? Can I be a good parent?

These are reasonable questions, and how we answer them is influenced by how each of us grapples with homophobia. If you find that your answers reflect a strong level of internalized homophobia, you may find the resources listed at the end of the chapter very helpful. At Maia we've found that as a necessary part of the journey to parenthood, women need to explore the impact of external and internal homophobia on their decision to parent. Women who don't address these issues often get delayed in their decision-making process.

Decision-Making Styles

Time spent actively reflecting on how you make decisions will not be wasted. You have so many decisions ahead of you: some small, some large, some reversible, some permanent. Stress over making decisions often stems from a fear of the consequences of your decisions. Stress may also stem from the fact that your style of decision making isn't the healthiest for you.

If you're partnered, making big decisions can place a strain on your relationship. It's valuable to explore together how each of you makes important decisions and how you've made decisions together in the past. Such reflection will give your relationship a much more solid footing for parenting discussions to come. After reading through the following descriptions of some common approaches to decision making, try the accompanying exercise to help you determine your decision-making style.

Analytical: You create budgets, time lines, and lists of pros and cons. Your approach strictly adheres to cost-benefit analysis, meaning you balance the potential cost of decisions against their potential benefit. You may focus on the probabilities of risk.

Intuitive: You take a spiritual approach to decision making, perhaps through prayer, tarot, or your own intuition. You may write in a journal stream-of-consciousness style to clarify your feelings and ideas. You may sit by a stream or in a temple or church or wherever you go to ponder and listen to your soul.

Body-Based: Your approach is visceral, on the "gut level." You're aware when decisions make you feel peaceful and calm or agitated and unsettled. You get information from whether a choice you make leads you to relaxed deep breathing versus shallow breathing. You notice if your decisions cause an upset stomach or headache.

Default: Your fear of decision leads you to make no decision. You think often about worst-case scenarios. Perhaps you procrastinate until your lover decides for you, or you're forced to make a last-minute decision, or you miss the opportunity entirely. Most commonly your decisions are made by default.

Experimental: You try things on for size and don't hesitate to change your mind and try again. You gather information about what works and doesn't work for you through the experiential process.

External-Input: You ask for opinions from your community, your friends, therapist, your parents, and/or spiritual guides. You organize an "advisory committee" or "board of directors" of friends, coworkers, and family members. Perhaps you generalize from anecdotal stories you read or hear about, or people you interview.

Exercise

Take some time to contemplate or write in a journal your responses to the following questions: What decision-making style or combination of styles do you employ? Does it suit you? Is it effective? Has making decisions in the past caused you a lot of stress?

If you aren't sure how you make decisions, think back in time. What big decisions have you made in the past? Have you been happy about how you made them? Have the decisions you've made given you a feeling of achievement or confidence? Have you rushed through the process of making a decision because it was uncomfortable for you? Do you feel you took an unreasonably long time to make your decision? What feedback have you gotten from others about how you make decisions? Has their feedback been useful or rung true?

A sophisticated decision-maker can consciously employ a mix of the above styles to any one decision, with the balance dependent upon the type of decision. How would you like to make decisions?

Decisions in a Partnership

So often lovers fall into the habit of speaking in emotional shorthand. You may assume your partner knows you well enough that she isn't obliged to fully articulate her thoughts, needs, and desires. She may feel, in return, that the familiarity she has with you allows her to take for granted many aspects of communication. Moving into parenthood, though, means moving into a completely new territory of life. You may discover things about yourself and each other that you hadn't yet realized. Who your parents were to you, what family means to you, and how you want to create new life are some of the biggest, deepest, and most personal topics you can explore. What you learn through this exploration—and how you integrate the influence of your upbringings into your joint parenting choices—may require levels of communication and skill that your relationship hasn't yet needed.

Clear decisions within a partnership support greater intimacy. A relationship is strengthened when both partners feel included and invested in making decisions. Creating a unified vision of your intentions and plans to parent will help you not only negotiate each of your roles and expectations throughout the process, but also negotiate clearly with potential coparents or donors.

Roles in Decision Making

You'll probably notice, if you haven't already in your relationship, that each of you occasionally falls into predetermined roles, whether consciously or unconsciously. Perhaps one of you is the worrier, so the other becomes the reassurer. The worrier doesn't get to feel her own confidence and trust, and the reassurer has no room to name her own fears. Perhaps one is the initiator, more aggressively pursuing information and pushing for making decisions, while the other holds back. The initiator feels unsupported and alone in manifesting the parenting vision, and the one holding back feels rushed or even guilty for not doing her share of the work. Perhaps one of you expresses passion and intuitiveness about your decisions, so the other plays the role of the rational thinker to maintain a sense of balance.

When you have set roles, it's common for neither of you to feel completely whole in your approach to the decision at hand. Be aware of who takes on which role, name it, and bring it into the conscious realm. When making decisions, choosing roles that balance each other is often helpful. If you don't want the role you find yourself in, remember that you can change that. Look for other ways to find balance within the partnership, or even try out some new roles as an exercise for expanding your perspectives. Evaluating each of your decision-making styles and how they mesh will give you valuable insight into the dynamics of your relationship roles.

Honoring Different Discussion Styles

Often one partner will want to discuss the baby-making process more frequently than the other. Perhaps one of you prefers to set aside a block of uninterrupted time during the weekend to update each other and share feelings, while the other calls at work a number of times a day to share late-breaking news and thoughts on the subject. If this is the case, you may need to set aside times for baby-free discussion as a way to keep space for the other aspects of your life together. You may also need to create some structure for the baby discussions you do have, to make sure each of you gets a chance to express your feelings fully.

Many women find the following listening practice helpful. For five minutes at a time, take turns actively listening to each other without interrupting. At the end repeat to your partner what you heard her say, without her interrupting to correct you. This practice will reveal the subtle differences between what you say and what your partner hears. This fine attention to clear communication will lead to more harmonious conversations and a deepening of your relationship.

Partner Exercise

Review your answers and insights from the exercise on page 25 that helped you clarify your decision-making style. Share your insights with your partner. Next, explore and discuss the following: Think about a few important decisions you've made together in the past, one at a time. For each decision, reflect on how you think the decision-making process went. Thinking about it now, do you notice any unresolved feelings? If so, why? How did your partner communicate (or not) what she wanted? Did the process of making this important decision elicit a feeling of greater intimacy? What style of decision making did you use in each situation? What style of decision making did your partner approach the decision with? How would you describe the style of decision making that you ultimately used together to come to your final decision?

Next, make some active and explicit commitments with your partner about how you'd both like to approach making decisions about having a baby. If you feel your current communication style is effective, discuss with your partner what in particular works for you. If you feel you'd like to improve or try a new approach, articulate specifically how you intend to change your communication style and in what way you'd like to see hers change. Ask her to tell you in her own words what she heard you say, to make sure you're both clear. Ask her to let you know if she shares these intentions, then ask her to tell you her own intentions so that you can repeat them back to her.

Positive feedback about the specific successes of your communication together will not only make each of you feel appreciated for your efforts, but also will help reinforce what works in your communication together. Making difficult decisions together can be some of the most challenging yet rewarding work in your relationship.

Embodied Decisions

Conception, pregnancy, and birth are body experiences. Our bodies hold ancient wisdom in the form of instinct about how to conceive, grow, and birth a baby. Learning to notice your body responses will help you access a lot of important information. When you have trouble implementing a decision you've made, notice how your body feels when you think about that decision. If you hold ambivalence about your decision, you should reexamine it: You may notice your body feeling tense, closed up, or uncomfortable instead of soft, relaxed, or open. Your body speaks for your heart, not your mind. Your heart is where you hold your truth about what is most important to you. Your mind can get caught in details and limited options that may hinder your ability to solve problems creatively.

The specific type of information that your body can best give you is regarding whether you feel safe. The following exercise will help you discover how safe you feel about a certain decision, both consciously and subconsciously. If you commit yourself to doing something that feels unsafe, whether it's working with a specific sperm donor or trying an infertility treatment, you'll eventually have to disconnect or numb yourself from your body's discomfort/danger signals in order to continue with your choice. Disconnection is a powerful coping mechanism for dealing with difficult situations. Unfortunately, many of us use disconnection in challenging situations that we actually *could* change. Making decisions that are validated by your body—embodied decisions—allows you to make strong choices. Such choices support you in being present rather than employing patterns of disconnecting or "checking out." When you prioritize choices that make you feel embodied, your process of becoming a parent will feel much more rewarding, and you'll be able to model this embodiment for your own children.

Exercise

No matter how you make decisions, it's helpful to use a body "check-in" to confirm your decision. Sit where you won't be distracted and picture yourself in a scenario in which you've made a decision. Notice your breathing and your muscle tenseness or relaxation in your neck, shoulders, and jaw. Are your hands relaxed or fists clenched? Are your arms open or crossed in front of your chest? Does your stomach feel relaxed, tense, painful? Do you feel any of these things or does your body feel numb and disconnected from you? This form of deep self-reflection can give you insight into whether or not you're making decisions with which you feel comfortable and aligned.

Past Influences on Decision Making

Sometimes when we make decisions solely from external information or pressure, we make choices that aren't appropriate to us as individuals. To make a decision that's right for you, you may find it helpful to take into account your past experiences. Recognizing and acknowledging what has been particularly joyful or painful about your experiences with men, your reproductive cycle, and the medical system will help you understand what makes you feel safe or unsafe about the process of getting pregnant and giving birth. We encourage you to try the above body check-in exercise while thinking about any of these past experiences. Using your body to gather information about your past experiences is time well spent, as they will affect your decisions both consciously and subconsciously. Our life experiences greatly affect our sense of safety and comfort—both positively and negatively.

Making Your Plan

The following section outlines specific areas in which decisions often need to be made in order to help you devise a personal pre-insemination plan that includes a time line. As you read through these topics, take notes on which issues are pertinent to you, which decisions you've already made, and any additional things that arise that you need to make decisions about. The next step is to create a working plan and time line for making these decisions and moving toward your goal of getting pregnant.

For many women, breaking down a pregnancy plan in this way makes the process much more manageable. Working with a checklist can help to greatly shorten the time it takes to move from wanting to parent to actually getting pregnant.

Preparing for Pregnancy Checklist

❏ Have I thought about homophobia and its role in my decisions?
❏ Do I need to come out to people in my life?
❏ Do I need more support structures in place before I begin inseminating?
❏ Am I clear about my family vision?
❏ Do I have a workable financial plan or budget?
❏ Do I need to research insurance plans and maternity leave benefits?
❏ Do I need to change jobs?
❏ Is my housing situation adequate?
❏ Do I have personal issues I'd like to resolve before inseminating?
❏ Do we need to do anything to strengthen our partner relationship?
❏ Are we clear about which one of us will get pregnant first?
❏ Do I have a plan for improving my health and fertility?
❏ Have I started to monitor my fertility?
❏ Do I need to make any health-care appointments or have tests performed?
❏ Do I need to research how legal issues in my state affect my donor and parenting choices?
❏ If I'm using a sperm bank, have I completed all preliminary registration steps, including having health tests performed and sent to the bank? Have I selected my three donors?
❏ If I'm working with a known donor, have we negotiated expectations, reviewed his health history, received sperm-count results and the results of other necessary tests, and written a contract?

Family Structure

Having read through the information in Chapter 1, you've been exploring your visions of ideal family and the support structures you'll need to be a good parent. How you envision your family will not only affect your sperm options, but also may affect some of the issues covered in the following sections, such as work and housing options. It's crucial to clarify your desired family structure before you make any permanent decisions. Take your time thoroughly exploring your own family history, personal motivations, and ideals. If you're partnered, communicate with each other clearly so that you'll understand each other's needs and desires.

Finances

Women often feel great pressure to guarantee financial security for their children before they conceive. As you may guess, a lot of variation exists as to how much is adequate. You may choose to plan a budget for conception costs, prenatal care costs, and even the first months of parenting. We include information about sperm and insemination costs, as well as applicable legal fees later in the book; as you read on, though, you may decide funds to add to your conception budget for nutritional supplements, acupuncture visits, and ovulation test kits. An awareness of your financial limitations will be helpful in making decisions further down the road, but also remember that creative financing for women has included everything from taking out loans, throwing insemination fundraising parties, and sharing child care responsibilities with others.

Work

Some women have concerns relating to their job that they would like to resolve before getting pregnant. These concerns can usually be addressed by creating a task list. Work-related tasks may include exploring your insurance and maternity leave options. Your list may include wanting to find a job that pays more or gives you adequate health coverage, or negotiating better maternity benefits. You might discuss working part-time from home or job sharing for a few months after the baby is born. Consider how difficult it may be to stay at your current job while you're pregnant if your workplace isn't gay friendly and/or you aren't out to your coworkers or boss. If loyalty to your company means remaining in the closet to employees or clients, know that being closeted and pregnant in the workplace is a daunting challenge for many women.

You may initially choose not to let your boss know that you're trying to conceive. You may choose not to share your baby plans with your boss because you're aware of the discrimination women face in some work environments when they're perceived as being on the "mommy track" instead of the "career track." Unfortunately, pregnancy discrimination, combined with homophobia, can make job stability shaky at a time when you want and need to count on stability.

Some women feel that becoming perfect at their job is the only action that will provide adequate security in the face of such discrimination, and thus they delay pregnancy indefinitely in their quest for perfection. If this is your case, it will be most helpful to give yourself a definite time line to follow in order to make your work environment feel stable enough for you to move forward with having a baby. In Chapter 17 we'll give you information about being an out pregnant lesbian in the workplace. If this is a significant concern for you, you may want to read ahead before you make a work task list as part of your overall baby plans.

Housing

Creating an action plan for housing issues is important for many women. Will your current housing situation be adequate or appropriate after you give birth? If you feel you need a lower mortgage payment or rent, enough room to grow into with a child, good schools, child-friendly roommates, or a smoke-free environment, what is your action plan? Consider carefully if it's essential that you move before starting to inseminate. Financial reality and financial dreams are often separated by many long years. Include only the necessary steps in your overall plan and time line.

Personal Emotional Growth

Some women feel they need to break a pattern of addiction or stabilize their depression or other mental health issues before they can conceive. Others feel they haven't had all the experiences they need and want for personal growth as child-free adults, such as traveling or dating. Having children doesn't preclude you from pursuing your personal endeavors, but it certainly changes the focus of your life.

It's unrealistic to think you'll have completed your personal emotional growth before parenting. Sometimes this desire to be "issue free" is related to the internalized-homophobia "perfect parent" pressure discussed previously. Sometimes it stems from wanting to be fully healed from issues of abuse or dysfunction that you're afraid to repeat in the next generation. Parenting is a process of personal growth; you grow while your children grow. If these issues are pertinent to you, do the necessary reading, therapy, or self-reflection you need to be able to move forward. Creating emotional milestones that you must pass before you get pregnant may be important to you; realize, however, that emotional work rarely agrees to follow a given time line. In fact, feeling a sense of pressure, deadline, or urgency often hampers emotional growth and change. Therefore, consider your goals carefully and decide whether it seems reasonable to consider your life a work in progress rather than to force yourself to wait indefinitely to move forward toward parenthood.

Partner Issues

If you're in a committed relationship with someone who isn't sure she wants to parent, you're in a tricky—and common—situation. There are a number of approaches to this challenge. You may choose to keep discussing it with your partner, hoping for a clear solution to arise. You may choose to leave the relationship in order to start a family. You may start inseminating anyway, with a "wait and see" approach but no guarantee from your partner that she'll necessarily stay and participate in the process. If you're in this situation, it may be helpful for you to review some of the models of creating family discussed in Chapter 1. Explore in depth your partner's concerns about parenting as well as your desires. A couples counselor may be able to assist you in sorting through these issues and establishing a realistic time line for doing so.

Perhaps you need to decide whether you or your partner will get pregnant first. If only one of you is able to conceive or doesn't want to get pregnant, no discussion is needed. If you both want to conceive at some point, however, there are a variety of factors to consider. Many women feel the older partner should try to conceive first, if both would like to give birth. If your age difference is great, this can be a key factor in your decision. Some couples decide that if one woman has chronic health issues, only her partner should conceive. If a couple thinks they'd like to have more than one child and they'd both like to conceive, the woman with greater health issues might be well served by trying first so that the "healthy" partner's support and resources can be solely focused on her needs in pregnancy. Sometimes women in an interracial relationship make their decision based on the ethnicity of their available donor and the preferred ethnicity of their child.

Often one woman desires the experience of pregnancy and birth much more strongly than her partner, but other rationales exist to suggest that her partner should conceive instead. For example, the woman desiring pregnancy may have greater health concerns, take medicine that may cause birth defects, suspect she is infertile, or have inadequate health insurance coverage. She may earn more money than her partner or have fewer maternity leave benefits. Sometimes the woman who is less passionate in her desire to parent wants to give birth as a way of making sure she creates a strong bond with the children. Occasionally, someone who has never desired pregnancy becomes fascinated with it as an option for herself as of result of watching her partner try to conceive.

Communication is key to staying connected through these sometimes volatile discussions. Explore with your partner what exactly is influencing your decision. If you feel you're acquiescing or are ambivalent about your joint decision, be creative in exploring alternatives. We worked with one couple, Janet and Martha, through their decision making about which of them should conceive. They strongly believed that a child needs one stay-at-home parent. The problem was, however, that Janet earned significantly more money than Martha but wanted to be pregnant anyway. After some creative thinking they decided that Janet would become pregnant and take eight weeks of maternity leave after the baby was born. When Janet returned to work, Martha quit her own job and became the stay-at-home mom. Janet used a breast pump at work to provide bottles of breast milk for the baby. They now have two children, both birthed by Janet and both cared for during the week by Martha. Their plan has worked beautifully, but it initially took them a few months to conceptualize such an arrangement.

Single Women Who'd Rather Be Partnered

If you're single and waiting for the right romantic relationship to come along, you may choose to go ahead and parent instead of waiting for the perfect relationship to arrive. Because there's no guarantee that any relationship is "stable enough" to last the many years of parenting, anyone wanting to parent should acknowledge that she may at some point become a single parent. Approaching dating with a burning desire to quickly establish whether the relationship will develop into a long-term, healthy, life-partner and coparent situation can place an unrealistic amount of pressure on both of you. In our practice we've seen many ways in which single women can create viable support options, and we've seen many single parents become coupled during pregnancy or the first few years of parenting. There are many books and support/information groups for single mothers by choice. They may help you reframe your concerns about being a single parent. They also dispel many myths about single motherhood and offer creative ideas about forming various kinds of support networks. See the resource list at the end of Chapter 1.

Sperm Choices

When people ask how you'll get pregnant (and believe us, you'll get a lot of questions), they usually mean "Where will you get sperm?" This decision depends on your original vision of family that Chapter 1 helped you begin to explore. Once you have a sense of the type of family structure that feels right to you, you'll know whether you'd rather have the biological father be an active coparent or just a donor. Part Two of this book will help you thoroughly explore the issues surrounding sperm-donor decisions; it covers the steps of each of these processes in detail and includes exercises to help you articulate exactly what you're seeking. Once you've decided whether you want a coparent or just a donor, we recommend that you plan to take no more than a month to figure out where and how you'll get sperm. One month will afford you a great deal of time to brainstorm a list of possible known donors/coparents, if you think you might want one, and have initial conversations with them. Either you'll find some promising leads, or you'll use the rest of the month to research information from various sperm banks.

If one month seems too short a time, understand that women often find themselves stuck *for years* making decisions about how they'll obtain sperm. Our goal is to help you keep moving forward. Even though sperm-donor decisions are important, they don't need to hold you up interminably. Set your own time frame—one that makes sense to you—and reevaluate as necessary. Keep in mind that making a decision over many months or years doesn't necessarily mean it is better than a decision made more quickly.

Chronic Health Issues

All sorts of health issues can impact a woman's decision to parent. Whether it's chronic back injury, asthma, or a partner's health condition, we recommend a reliable professional appraisal from a health care provider concerning possible risks to pregnancy. Have realistic discussions with him or her about any special support you may require and any financial issues that may arise during pregnancy. Discuss with your health care provider, as well as a midwife or obstetrician, which health goals you want to reach before conceiving and create a reasonable time line for reaching those goals.

Preparing Your Body

Preparing your body for pregnancy has the potential to both optimize your fertility and strengthen your body. Most helpful changes made in regard to nutrition, exercise, or herbal medicine take a good three to six months to fully benefit your body, so now is the perfect time to read Part Three and implement any changes you'd like to make. Many of these changes, such as giving up coffee, can significantly increase your chances of conceiving. Even if you've been inseminating for a number of months already, your body can benefit from any positive changes you make now. If you're still in the planning stages, however, be aware that it's best to make these changes a full three to six months prior to conception.

Many women tell us they wish to achieve a certain body weight before becoming pregnant. We'll speak to this directly in Chapter 9, since we don't feel weight loss is vitally important to fertility or pregnancy; it may, in fact, detrimentally affect fertility. If you decide to try to lose weight before becoming pregnant, give yourself ample time so that you can both lose weight in a healthy way and let your body readjust its metabolism and hormone levels before you inseminate.

Fertility Monitoring

Many women need to complete at least three months of charting their fertility cycles before they feel familiar with the nuances of their cycles. Over these months, they review their charts carefully and plan their optimal time of insemination. If you have irregular cycles, it may take you up to six months to determine the signs that indicate when you should inseminate. If you haven't already sought ways to help balance your menstrual cycle, you may choose to take an additional three months to give any changes or treatments a chance to work fully. The importance of fertility monitoring is discussed in depth in Chapter 11.

Health and Fertility Tests

Most sperm banks require that you complete lab tests for sexually and maternally transmitted infections before you can purchase sperm. But whether or not you're required to, you may wish to have a number of these tests performed. See Chapter 9 for information about these tests and general reproductive and sexual health. Have any tests performed a couple of months before you start to inseminate so that you can seek any treatment you need if your results are abnormal. Remember that some obstetricians and gynecologists are booked for months, so unless you want or need specific infertility tests, you can see any physician, nurse practitioner, physician's assistant, or midwife for health screening tests—not just an ob/gyn. If you have to schedule a visit with your primary care provider or gynecologist, make an appointment as soon as possible.

The Value of Creating a Time Line

A time line for planning when you'll inseminate is useful for a number of reasons. First of all, it will help you notice if you're not moving forward toward your goal. If you set a deadline for a certain step you need to complete, you'll pay attention if you pass the deadline without moving forward and can evaluate both why you're stuck and what to do to move forward. If you don't have the structure that a time line provides, weeks, months, and years may slip by with your making no progress toward your goal.

A time line gives you a manageable perspective on the entire process. You can plan a reasonable length of time for each step on your personal checklist and come up with a realistic date to start inseminating. As you mark the steps off your checklist, you can reassure yourself that you're making progress in the midst of what sometimes feels like a discouragingly long journey.

A time line also gives your mind some peace by predetermining points when you'll step back and reevaluate the process and decide whether you need to change directions. For example, if you know you'll gather information for three months by charting your fertility cycle, you can rest the worried part of your mind, the part that wants to scrutinize the chart daily, sure that you will find some sign of infertility. You can let that part of your mind know that at the end of three months you'll have a comprehensive picture and will then give the interpretation of your chart your full attention. Reevaluation points also help partners make timely and effective decisions when each of you have different approaches to making decisions, especially in terms of pacing. Whether you've been contemplating pregnancy as long as you can remember, or only since age 35, or just since your new partner mentioned she wants to have children, your plan and time line will move you forward systematically.

Remember, your time line shouldn't be a source of stress: You can always extend it or rework it when you reach a reevaluation point or even before. The time line's job is to keep you making conscious choices.

Using Your To-Do List to Create a Time Line

Reviewing the notes you made when reading the previous section about creating a plan will help you devise your time line. For each section, evaluate carefully what your personal vision or goal is. This step isn't necessarily completed quickly. The exercises throughout the book will help you clarify your desires and help you accomplish this step. If you need to, write your thoughts in a journal, talk with friends, or see a therapist or couples counselor as you clarify your vision for each area that requires a decision or action prior to your conceiving. Set aside a specific time at least every two weeks to focus on this part of the process, individually and with a partner, if you have one.

When you clarify your goal, you'll be able to make a list of smaller steps that you need to take to reach that goal. For each smaller step allocate a time length that seems reasonable for the step's completion. In this way you'll create a realistic sense of the overall timeframe needed to complete your pre-insemination goals. Be sure to build in some time for actually creating your time line!

Once you've finished creating the complete task list of everything you want and need to do prior to inseminating, examine your goals and see which you can work on concurrently. For example, you may be able research maternity leave benefits and medical benefits at work while also taking active steps to make your housing situation feel stable enough to raise a child. You may chart your fertility cycle while you work on improving your eating habits or exercise program. Combine and overlap the goals as necessary until you've reached the end of the time line—when you will start inseminating.

When Your Time Line Isn't Working

Choosing to parent isn't a rational decision. It's a choice to enter the unknown, jump off a cliff, commit to a lifelong relationship with someone you've never met (your child!). Choosing to parent is deciding to open your heart wider than you may have ever opened it, with an ecstatic amount of love to experience, and therefore there's a terrifying risk of loss. It's about trust and willingness to grow and change in unforeseen ways. It's a lot of hard work. It's about giving up old identities and activities to make room for new ones. Children challenge us to live our lives with integrity. As you make each decision necessary to begin inseminating, you inch closer to that cliff-edge of parenthood, which may feel so daunting that you hesitate. You may need to address many personal, emotional issues before being able to move steadily toward your goal.

If you feel you're not moving forward because you're just plain stuck, articulate to yourself why you want to have children. (Many women have toddlers before they ever consider putting their desire for children into words.) This isn't your response or justification to society's challenge, but your words of inspiration to yourself. Your reasons for wanting children are deeply personal, and grounding yourself in your original desire can help you move forward.

Although the emotional reality of becoming a parent may be all that is stopping you, practical concerns may also arise. Sometimes you may feel backed into a corner without any options. This may be because you're single but want a partner with whom to parent. It may be because you live in a state that has many legal restrictions about unmarried women parenting, and this scares you. Perhaps you feel you don't have enough financial resources to parent.

Often you actually may have an option but may be reticent to choose it because you feel you'd have to compromise more than you're willing to. Are there creative ways to modify the situation, taking more options into account? Brainstorming all possible options, no matter how crazy they seem, will open you up to new possibilities. Get some outside perspectives by spending time in a lesbian- or single-mom online chat room or even just talking with a friend. More than likely, you'll come up with some creative solutions.

For example, if you really want to use a known donor but your friends have declined, how about asking a relative of your partner, such as a cousin or brother? Are you willing to use the sperm of someone you don't know very well? How about your best friend's circle of good friends? Are any of your original reasons for wanting a known donor modifiable, or are there other ways to satisfy these reasons without using a known donor? Each chapter in this book offers creative solutions to conundrums that may arise in your journey toward pregnancy.

Sometimes women can't move forward, even though multiple options are available. This is often because these decisions can seem so permanent, and have such important consequences, that it's too scary to take the responsibility to make them. Welcome to the world of parenting. Yes, being a parent is an awesome responsibility, but if you allow your already-existing love for your child to guide you, you'll feel strong in your decisions. Trust that you'll always be able to share with your child that the decisions you've made have been made from love.

Differing Opinions in a Partnership

It can be nearly impossible to move forward if you reach an impasse with your partner about a specific decision, which commonly occurs when discussing donor options. If you and your partner are unable to move forward due to a difference in opinion, it's important to figure out whether you actually differ in your preferences or if you simply employ clashing decision-making styles. Sometimes one partner makes decisions much faster than the other. The slower partner may dig in her heels because she feels pressured or wants to research the options more thoroughly, or wants to make it "her own" in some way as an active participant. Other times it's truly a discrepancy in heartfelt desire.

Communication is essential to partnered decision making, as are generosity and an honest awareness of which things you really could compromise on versus which you feel strongly about. Try to have compassion for how each other's past history may be impacting the current decision. What are your emotional stakes in this decision? What are your partner's? Can the needs of both partners be met in ways you haven't considered? Having your concerns acknowledged and validated can go a long way toward reaching a compromise. Relationship dynamics may color your perceptions of your choices and how absolute those choices seem. But by becoming aware of the context within which you're trying to make a decision, and addressing the tensions inherent in the decision at hand, you'll find greater room for compromise.

Ambivalence

If you've made a decision but catch yourself procrastinating about implementing it, perhaps you're ambivalent about the decision. Revisit it. Change your mind if necessary. Renegotiate with your partner. Better now than later.

Pulling It All Together

Use the resources you have available to help you make decisions effectively, whether they are the exercises we suggest, a relationship counselor, a support group, an online chat room, or other parenting books. Determine your decision-making style and tailor it to suit your needs. Communicate as honestly and fully as possible with your partner, if you have one, so that you can make healthy decisions together. Create a personal time line of all your pre-insemination tasks and objectives, and really use the time line as a working tool. Recognize if you haven't moved forward on any decision related to conceiving or parenting, and get help you need to move forward. Finally, trust in your own ability to build a wonderful family and fill it with love.

Chapter 3 Age Considerations

Many women who aren't partnered with men start their conception process in their late 30s to early 40s, and many heterosexually partnered women are also choosing to parent later in life. Many of these prospective mothers are concerned that they may not be fertile simply because they're 35 or older. No matter how fertile or healthy these women might feel, there's a common perception that women who are 35 and older are at high risk for infertility. The medical terminology applied to a woman giving birth after her 35th birthday is that she is of "advanced maternal age." How do you make sense out of the perception that your body's fertility rapidly declines after age 35, and even more so after age 40, if you feel healthy and menstruate regularly?

There *are* increased challenges to conception and increased risks to pregnancy as you grow older. There are also societal prejudices and assumptions about women over 35 that influence medical opinion, despite the myth of its objectivity. Your state of health and fitness can greatly influence your fertility at any age, including your late 30s and early 40s. Many lesbians become ready to parent in their late 30s and early 40s, and they often have questions about the actual risks to conception, pregnancy, and birth that their age may incur.

This chapter will help you explore how aging may create fertility challenges that can affect both your time line and whether you may require initial fertility tests. For ideas on how to optimize and even increase your fertility, be sure to read Part Three.

Egg Changes

Eggs and chromosomes change as a woman ages. Over time this can result in decreased ovulation, ovulation problems, and increased chances of miscarriage and fetal anomalies such as Down's Syndrome. Females are born with all the eggs their body will ever produce. At the start of puberty, ovaries usually contain about 300,000 eggs. Not all of them will be viable, and during each menstrual cycle a number of eggs prepare for ovulation but only one (usually) is released. The unreleased eggs are reabsorbed by the body and thus can't be fertilized. Therefore, women may actually ovulate about 400-500 eggs over the course of a lifetime, but in each cycle up to 1,000 are used that will never be released from the ovaries. By menopause, which occurs at different ages for different women, only a few hundred eggs remain in the body. About 10–15 years before the onset of menopause, the rate at which eggs are used up increases. This rate change is related to a subtle change in the menstrual cycle: Between ages 37 and 38, many women notice that the first half of their menstrual cycle (from menstruation to ovulation) grows shorter by a few days.

Increased difficulty in getting pregnant as women age seems to be related to a decrease in their total number of eggs. In addition, increased difficulty in conceiving—as well as an increased rate of miscarriage—is related to changes in egg health. Among other factors, "egg health" refers to whether or not the egg is able to respond to the hormone message from the brain that tells it to mature and ovulate. Sometimes eggs don't have enough hormone receptors on the outside to recognize hormone messages. Women usually ovulate earliest in life the eggs that have the most receptors, leaving the eggs with fewer receptors for later ovulation. Thus, egg health decreases with age, along with the total number of remaining eggs.

Egg health also refers to the genes inside the egg. The ovaries and eggs of women 35 and older have received more exposure to toxins and radiation than those of younger women. As a result, more of their eggs may contain damaged chromosomes. Also, older eggs more frequently have trouble dividing properly once fertilized.

Because of these factors, fertility rates start to decline after women turn 35, decline more rapidly by their late 30s, and even more so in their early 40s. One scientific study showed age-related rates of conception for women attempting to conceive with frozen donor sperm by intrauterine inseminations (an insemination method that is often used with frozen sperm to increase the chance of pregnancy). For women younger than 35, the rate of pregnancy was 20% per cycle. For women ages 35 to 40, the rate was 12%. For women over 40, the rate was 6%.

Because of these factors, as women grow older they're also more likely to give birth to babies with chromosomal abnormalities and variations, as well as have still births. The risk of having a baby with Down's Syndrome, for example, to a woman age 20 is one in 1,177; to a woman age 35 it's one in 296; and to a woman age 41 it's 1 in 65. Many of these chromosomal abnormalities cause the embryo to stop developing in the first few weeks of life; thus, the early-miscarriage rate for women in their late 30s and early 40s is significantly higher than for women in their 20s and early 30s. By age 35 the early-miscarriage rate is one in four to five pregnancies; by age 40 it's approximately one in two.

Amniocentesis, chorionic villi sampling (CVS), and newer ultrasound technologies are procedures a pregnant woman can undergo to check for certain chromosomal anomalies. Most of these tests have inherent risks, and many women have difficulty deciding whether to have them performed. If you choose genetic testing and learn that your fetus has chromosomal abnormalities, you have the option to terminate your pregnancy anywhere between 12 and 20 weeks.

Initial Hormone Tests

If you're over 37, you may benefit from undergoing initial hormone tests before you begin inseminating. Many women who have undergone complicated infertility tests and treatments regret not having had initial hormonal tests performed when they first became serious about wanting to get pregnant. Had they had information early on indicating that their fertility was declining, they may have made different decisions or sped up their time lines. Still, if you're over 40, fertility specialists agree that hormone test results that show normal values don't necessarily guarantee good ovarian function. The fact that these tests aren't definitive also leads to an opposite truth: Women do conceive with "suboptimal" lab numbers, even occasionally with very "infertile" numbers.

Benefits of Hormone Tests

Numerous benefits accompany initial testing. If your lab values show that you're less fertile than you'd hoped, you can choose to be assertive about creating a comprehensive plan to optimize your fertility, instead of taking your time and trying something new every few months. This may include adopting diet changes, a new exercise plan, a spiritual practice, in-depth emotional work as well as healing modalities such as acupuncture all at the same time. Although Western medicine suggests that egg age and egg health cannot be made "younger" by healthy lifestyle changes, women making these types of changes often do see improvements in their hormone test results. More importantly, their overall fertility often increases, which is much more significant in the long run than a set of lab values that may be inaccurate.

If you have information that suggests your hormone levels aren't optimal, you may be encouraged to start inseminating as soon as possible. Fertility, in fact, can decrease rapidly, often over a period of three to six months. To speed up your time line, you may reprioritize which decisions require lengthy consideration and which can be made more quickly. You may choose to move directly toward receiving medical assistance, whether from intrauterine insemination (IUI), fertility drugs, or assisted reproductive techniques such as in vitro fertilization (IVF). Some women choose to do IVF with an egg donated from a younger woman. (See Chapter 14.)

Some women choose to undergo initial hormone tests before they start to inseminate, because they might choose to adopt or have their partner conceive if their results suggest decreased fertility. If your test results might be significant to you in this way, make sure the person who explains them to you has specific training in fertility and can accurately advise you on your realistic chances of conception. Not every obstetrician-gynecologist or primary caregiver can adequately provide this service.

Choosing to Forgo Hormone Tests

Some women may feel comfortable choosing to forgo initial hormone tests if they have alternative ways of assessing their fertility. You may prioritize your intuition or "body feeling" or other methods of understanding your body, such as Chinese medicine and applied kinesiology, more than you prioritize the significance of medical lab values. Furthermore, you may feel that lab values would label you as subfertile or infertile before your body even gets a chance to try to conceive. You may want to avoid information that casts doubt on your body's ability to conceive or erodes your self-confidence.

If you know you have no interest in using medical technology to help you conceive, and you're working to achieve optimal fertile health, lab values may be irrelevant to you—which is to say, test results may give you new information but won't affect your decision to inseminate.

Basic Types of Tests

Below you'll find descriptions of various hormone tests related to fertility. You may gain a deeper understanding of these tests if you read about hormones and the menstrual cycle in Chapter 11. Additional diagnostic fertility tests and procedures are described in Chapter 14. For general health screening tests you may want to consider before pregnancy, see Chapter 8.

If you aren't experiencing regular menstrual cycles or any noticeable signs of fertility, you may want to undergo these tests regardless of your age. You may also consider them if you've been inseminating for a number of months without achieving pregnancy. In Chapter 14 we'll review what it means to have "premature ovarian failure" or other fertility challenges.

Estradiol, Follicle-stimulating Hormone (FSH), and Progesterone

Two hormone levels that can be checked at the beginning of the cycle, the third day after your menstrual period starts, are those of estradiol and follicle-stimulating hormone (FSH). Estradiol is a form of estrogen made by the ovaries. FSH is produced in the pituitary gland in the brain. It sends the message to the ovary to prepare the eggs and their sets of helper cells, called follicles, to ovulate. If either of these hormone levels is too high, the eggs and ovaries may not respond well to your hormones and/or you may not have many eggs left. Because these tests are sensitive, each laboratory has its own specific range of what is considered normal.

Progesterone, a hormone that helps regulate the second half of your cycle, is tested at seven to 10 days past when you think you may have ovulated, which for many women is about six days before they expect their next period. Your progesterone values can suggest whether or not you've actually ovulated. A high progesterone level indicates that an egg was released and the rest of the follicle has turned into a little progesterone-making gland. A low progesterone level may indicate that an egg was not released. It also may suggest that the follicle didn't get mature enough to turn into a sufficiently effective gland or that your body has an insufficient level of progesterone building blocks. Even if the egg ovulates, a borderline-low progesterone level prevents the uterus from keeping its lining well nourished and well attached. This can cause early first trimester bleeding and/or miscarriage.

Multiple Tests Increase Accuracy

One progesterone blood test drawn during one cycle may not be enough to give you accurate information about whether your progesterone level is high enough to sustain an early pregnancy or whether you'd benefit from supplements. Because progesterone, like other hormones, is released by the body in pulses instead of at a steady rate, your level will swing up and down throughout the day. Whether your level happens to be at a high or low point at the moment your blood is drawn can significantly affect your results. Tests taken from saliva are considered more accurate as hormone levels in saliva don't vary as much as those in the blood, and multiple samples from multiple days are usually checked at once. We'll discuss progesterone further in Chapters 8 and 14.

Luteinizing Hormone (LH), Thyroid, and Prolactin

Luteinizing hormone (LH), produced by the pituitary gland, triggers ovulation. Some women choose to have their LH checked, though levels of this hormone don't usually change drastically until a woman is fully into menopause. Some women also have their thyroid levels tested. The thyroid regulates rate of metabolism and other hormones in the body. More often than you may think, a woman's thyroid level may be somewhat out of balance, which can affect many functions of the body, especially fertility. Western medicine and many other healing practices offer treatments to help balance thyroid hormone levels. Check with your health care provider for available options. Another hormone, prolactin, is a secreted by the brain and is most commonly known for its role in breast milk production. If an abnormally high prolactin level is present in a woman who isn't breastfeeding, her fertility may be inhibited.

Pressure

Many older women are given blanket advice—from family members, friends, coworkers, and doctors—based on their age without any consideration for their unique circumstances. You'll hear frequently that "time is of the essence." Each of us ages, reproductively speaking, at different rates. We tend to inherit our rate of aging from our mother's lineage.

Photo © Cathy Cade

While women's fertility can decrease quickly, you alone know your body and can make the decisions best for you. One of our clients received normal results after having her FSH levels tested by a health care provider, but the following appeared at the bottom of her lab form: "Reassuring results, but advise aggressive management due to age." Don't be rushed past your point of comfort by external pressure to try things, simply because of your age, that you're not ready to try.

For example, many sperm banks recommend that any woman over 35 skip vaginal insemination altogether and move directly to intrauterine insemination (IUI).

This method, discussed more fully in Chapters 11 and 14, involves washing the sperm to separate it from the semen, then placing it directly into the uterus with a sterile plastic tube that is passed through the cervix. You may prefer IUI since it might reduce the number of inseminations for you to get pregnant. On the other hand, it may actually decrease your chances of conception if your timing isn't extremely accurate. If you feel it's important to give at-home, nonmedicalized insemination a try first, go for it! Your intuition is just as valuable a fertility signal as any other. Because of your age, you may modify your decision by planning to try inseminating vaginally for two to three cycles before moving on to IUIs, instead of the six to nine cycles you might give vaginal insemination if you were younger .

Do Everything You Can to Increase Your Fertility

Carefully read Part Three on optimizing your fertility, and start taking any supplements or incorporating the exercise and lifestyle changes you choose now, so that you'll have time to get the most benefit from them. Visualize yourself as fertile. Visualize your uterus and ovaries bathed with beautiful, radiant, fertile light. Trust that you know the most about your body, because you live in it!

Begin Inseminating as Soon as Possible

Based on our experiences working with many women age 38–48, we encourage you to move more quickly, if possible, through the many months to years women often take making decisions about becoming pregnant. Look at which obstacles loom like mountains in front of you and devise an action plan. Necessity is the mother of invention. Be creative in your problem solving so that you can start inseminating as soon as possible. Your fertility can change quite quickly, so time often truly is of the essence. Unfortunately, we've seen a number of women who have trouble conceiving even earlier than age 38. Fertility challenges are on the rise, so use your time wisely.

Make Your Donor Choices Carefully

When you're making your donor choices, be aware that fresh sperm, if your donor has a healthy sperm count, has a much higher success rate than frozen sperm. Because frozen sperm is less fertile than fresh sperm, if you're using it consider doing at least one IUI each month, as mentioned above. If you unsuccessfully inseminate with frozen sperm, consider using fresh sperm, if at all possible. In general, frequently reevaluate your approach to insemination. For more information, see Part Two on donor choices and Chapter 12 on insemination methods.

Work the System

If you want initial hormone tests performed, be pushy, if necessary, with the medical and insurance systems in order to expedite the process. Often, long delays in the insemination process are caused by a woman having to wait weeks to months to see specialists and having endless debates with insurance companies. Be assertive and clear about your time line with care providers and insurance representatives.

Exercise

Now that we've reviewed some information on age considerations, take a moment to check in with your body. Take a deep breath, relax your shoulders, and really feel your body. How is this all of this information affecting you? Does it simply reiterate what you already know? Does it feel discouraging? Thought provoking? Find a way to let the above information filter in to its own place in your mind. Don't put it in the place where you may keep the negative stereotypes you've received about middle-aged and older women.

Often we don't realize how much of our perceptions of ourselves are shaped by our culture. How women's bodies are understood and valued as they age varies greatly from culture to culture. Keep in perspective that this society, which values youthful physique over wisdom from experience and acts as if women's sexuality (closely tied to reproduction) stops by the time they're in their 40s, isn't the norm worldwide. Your interpretation of how your body changes as you age is probably a complicated mixture of personal truth and internalized societal prejudice. The information you receive from others about your fertility contains the same mixture. Keep this in mind as you decide how you will approach conception.

■ ■ ■

While each woman's body is unique, and each woman's approach to the challenge of infertility is unique, some common truths exist: Fertility can decrease rapidly with age, and diagnostic tests are limited in their ability to produce accurate results. These truths are tempered by another truth: Overall health and fitness, as well as specific fertility-boosting practices, can play a significant role in increasing fertility. If you're choosing to parent later in life, it's helpful to establish an assertive action plan best suited to your own needs that enables you to approach the entire insemination process efficiently and reevaluate your methods in a timely manner.

Part Two
Sperm Options

Introduction

Before you begin the insemination process, it's important to read each of the following chapters on sperm choices: Chapter 4: "Coparenting," Chapter 5: "Known Donors," and Chapter 6: "Unknown Donors and Sperm Banks." Decisions about how and where you'll acquire sperm carry lifelong consequences. Reading these three chapters will help you make sure you're thoroughly informed of your options, and completing the exercises in each chapter will help you clarify your values, assumptions, and expectations. You may find making decisions about where and how you'll obtain sperm to be challenging. We recommend that you set a goal of making your final choices within three months so that you aren't indefinitely stuck at this decision point. If you find that it's taking you longer, consult Chapter 2: "Making Decisions."

Remember, initially you can gather information about multiple options at the same time, while you explore emotionally which one seems most right for you. As you obtain information from sperm banks, you can also interview potential donors. Saving as much time as possible in the decision-making process becomes increasingly important as you grow older, since you'll want to start inseminating, if you can, before your fertility begins to decline.

In our experience, lesbian, bisexual, and single women often start with a particular plan for their sperm source, then find for a variety of reasons that it changes over time. Your plan may change before you start inseminating or even a number of months after you've begun trying to conceive. Reading all three chapters in this section will familiarize you with the diversity of possibilities if decide you need to change your path.

Chapter 4 Coparenting

Coparenting provides many wonderful, creative parenting opportunities as well as options for innovative family structures. Coparenting, however, almost always takes more work, communication, and lifelong commitment than most people initially expect. A growing number of lesbian and bisexual women are choosing to have and raise biological children outside of the model of the traditional spousal two-parent family. This is a particularly appealing option for single parents and for women who aren't interested in bearing full-time parenting responsibilities. In this chapter we discuss a number of coparenting options, focusing specifically on the biological father as coparent. Compared with that of other coparents, the biological father's role is unique because he is automatically granted certain custody rights other coparents rarely have. We also explain the differences between a coparent dad and a known sperm donor. We look at various types of coparenting arrangements and their challenges and benefits. Finally, we offer tips for negotiating coparenting contracts and clarifying expectations, and present a number of anecdotes that exemplify the best and the worst scenarios.

What Is a Coparent?

A coparent is what you and your family members define it to be. It may be difficult to find family role models with coparenting relationships similar to your ideal ones unless you live in a large, diverse queer community with many parents and children. You may find some useful coparenting role models in families with heterosexual parents in which divorces have occurred and stepparents are present, extended relatives are key family members, or best friend "aunties" or uncles play important roles. These parents, however, rarely start out intending to have the family structure they end up with. So, depending on where you live, you may find yourself in uncharted waters if you're interested in a coparenting or group-family situation.

The term *coparent* often refers to someone who takes responsibility for a child's care and well-being but isn't a primary parent. Occasionally the term refers to someone who does equally share responsibility with other parents but isn't romantically involved with the woman who gave birth to the child. A coparent may be a stepparent, an ex-spouse, a housemate, or a friend. A coparent may or may not be biologically related to the child. If the biological and nonbiological moms are lovers, living together, and sharing equal responsibility for the child, they often refer to themselves simply as parents instead of designating the nonbiological mom as the coparent. Occasionally both will call themselves coparents. Some nonbiological moms do refer to themselves solely as coparents when they want to identify themselves specifically as the nonbirth parent and feel hampered by not having any other positive title to choose from in our culture.

Often when lesbian, bisexual, and single women refer to a male coparent, they specifically mean the biological father who isn't romantically involved with the biological mother. Sometimes they include the biological father's partner under the title of coparent as well as the biological mother's lover, if a gay male couple and a gay female couple are all sharing parenting responsibilities. Some people use *coparent* as a verb, as in "The children have four parents; we all coparent the children." Others use the terms *parent* and *coparent* as nouns: A parent is an adult with primary responsibility for the child, while a coparent has a secondary responsibility.

When we consider that housing arrangements, time, finances, and labor divisions vary from family to family, we begin to understand how the imprecision of the term *coparent* can lead to confusion and lack of clarity about who plays what role. The lack of a rigid definition, however, can provide wonderful opportunities to create a unique family structure suited precisely to the needs of your family members—i.e, a coparent can be whatever you define it to be.

Types of Coparenting Arrangements

Two-Couple Families

Two people have more resources than one to put toward raising a child; three or four have even more. For example, Elena and Martha parent with Raul. Elena stays home full-time while the other two work. When their jobs and career goals change, Elena and Raul work half-time and perform child care half-time, while Martha continues to work full-time. Elena and Martha live together; Raul lives in the same apartment building. Their child lives with Elena and Martha. They all share a portion of living expenses informally to allow their work and child-care arrangements to be flexible.

Coparenting does not always mean sharing expenses. Gema and Karen are raising older children from Karen's previous marriage. Gema decides she'd like to get pregnant and give birth. Her partner is encouraging but doesn't feel she can fully commit herself to sharing the responsibility of a baby when she has two kids already. She suggests that they find some other people for extra support in raising the child. They know they want to get sperm from someone they know personally, and they want the baby to have a relationship with his or her father. So they ask Bruce and Toby, a couple they met in a lesbian/gay coparenting discussion group, if they would be interested in coparenting with them. Bruce, who's very excited about parenting, offers his sperm, and Toby (who feels a little less committed) is supportive of the arrangement but will wait to see how his relationship with the child evolves. The two men live nearby, offer some financial participation, and help out tremendously in the early infancy of baby Isaac so that the older children can keep receiving quality attention from Karen and Gema. Over time the men develop a special relationship with the older children, though their primary relationship in the family is with Isaac. They see him once or twice a week on an informal basis.

Single Parents

Maryam, a single woman, has committed parenting participation from someone other than a lover. Her friend Dion primarily spends time with their child at night and on weekends. He has more job flexibility than Maryam if one of them needs to take time off work when their child is sick. Dion shares a close emotional bond with their child, and Maryam enjoys the parenting relationship and mutual support she and Dion share.

Kaya, a single woman, lives with two men in a duplex. One is Manuel, her best friend from college; the other is his lover, James. Manuel and James intend to be the primary parents for their soon-to-be-born baby. Kaya wants to return to work soon after giving birth, and the two dads plan to take care of their child during the day. Manuel is a student; James telecommutes two days a week. The fathers have arranged their schedules so that one of them will be home between 8 A.M. and 6 P.M. daily. All three parents have decided to equally share the costs directly associated with the child. The truth about sharing financial responsibility for a child is that the earning potential of a man on average still far exceeds that of a woman, and adding the income of one or two men to a one- or two-woman family can be of substantial benefit.

Group Households

In group families, a number of people may live together, each bearing a different amount of responsibility for the child. For example, Noelle and Jackie live in a house with their child Jonah and with three other housemates. They all identify themselves as a family. One of the housemates has a regular weekly committed "special time" with the child, while the others have more casual connections. The housemates all help out with the child as needed, although the two primary parents are fully financially responsible for the child and make all important decisions in the child's life, such as those regarding discipline style, bedtime, education, and health care.

In a different situation, two couples, each primarily parenting their own kids, move into a house together and form a social/support unit for each other, each couple acting as coparents to the other couple's kids. For example, they share the responsibility of driving their kids to extracurricular activities, and they share meal preparation and shopping duties. Sometimes they take vacations together, but they split up to visit grandparents. These relationships may be similar to those of close godparents or *comadres/compadres*.

Coparenting With Men

Queer women choose to coparent specifically with men for many reasons. Lesbian or bisexual women who feel strongly about their children having fathers, not just uncles or donors or male friends, can arrange father-relationship opportunities for their children without being heterosexually partnered. Some single women, both gay and straight, have had a solid stable relationship with a male best friend for longer than any lover they've had. They realize their best choice right now for a parenting partner isn't a lover. Male coparents need not necessarily be biologically related to the child, but they often are.

The differences between a coparent and a known donor vary from family to family, and this is where the flexibility of coparenting can be a weakness. Often the expected level of participation in making parenting decisions differs between the parties involved. A woman or women may be willing to have their known donor develop a close relationship with their child over time, but if they choose the biological father to be a coparent, they're specifically asking him to make a parental commitment from the start. In so doing, they state their willingness to not only share the child's daily life with him, but also possibly share in making decisions about how to raise the child. The challenge lies in the fact that what is entailed in the commitment to shared parenting needs to be spelled out clearly, often before everyone involved knows much about parenting. A coparenting relationship requires the structure of clearly defined roles and expectations as well as the fluidity necessary to accommodate change. The more people involved, the more difficult it can be to negotiate change successfully.

Who Makes the Parenting Decisions?

Some women are willing to share decision making equally with their coparents, while others want to retain the right to be the "bottom line" in decisions about schooling, health care, discipline, diet, bedtime, weaning, and social activities. Some moms with coparents decide that the biological mom (and her partner, if she has one) will be the primary decision maker(s) until the child turns 7, at which point the mom(s) and coparent(s) will share ultimate decision-making authority and the child will be old enough to provide some input. In some coparenting situations, everyone is comfortable with the idea that house rules and parenting styles may vary between parents, knowing that, within reason, children have a capacity to understand that different adults interact with them differently and each household may employ a somewhat unique set of rules. Too much variation in parenting styles, or in fundamental parenting philosophy, however, can be very challenging for a child, and therefore warrants thorough discussion.

For example, Claire is 7 and lives primarily with her moms Kelly and Annette, her older sister, and two other housemates in a large house. She spends Thursday night, Sunday afternoon, and Tuesday evening at her dad Robert's apartment. Robert and Claire spend most of their time together one-on-one and have a set of routine activities they enjoy, including eating out, watching videos, listening to music, and playing computer games. At her main house Claire is around more people and noise, and participates in multiple activities, including crafts and hiking. At each house, she has a somewhat different diet, including how much sugar and junk food she is allowed, although she sticks to a vegetarian diet all the time. At each house Claire has similar household responsibilities and is disciplined in a similar manner, and all parents have similar expectations regarding her manners and behavior. Some of the topics all parents have recently discussed as a team—although Kelly and Anne have the final say—are their approaches to spirituality, discussions about sexuality, ideas for helping Claire resolve conflicts with school classmates, and when Claire might be old enough to stay home alone. Kelly and Anne have made primary decisions recently about Claire's health care and extracurricular activities.

Exercise

Examine the following topics and consider the opinions you have about them in regard to childraising. Which values do you feel so strongly about that anyone you would coparent with would need to share them?

- health care
- religion/spirituality
- diet
- expenses
- household responsibilities
- discipline style
- day care/preschool/education
- urban, suburban, rural living
- housing arrangement
- playtime activities: videos, music, TV, movies, etc.

Now think of any lesbian/gay/bisexual families you know who have coparenting arrangements and glance back at the examples of family structure you have just read. In relationship to household structure, division of income and child expenses, time spent with the child, and naming of relationships, which examples do you like or find insightful? Which sound completely distasteful to you? For each topic (housing arrangement, expenses, etc.) finish this sentence: "My ideal would be..." Then finish the sentence "I would be willing to consider _____ if..." Finally, write a working definition for yourself that fits your values: "A coparent is..."

Choosing a Coparent

One of the main challenges of entering into coparenting is that a woman usually doesn't know a coparent as well as she would know a life partner, nor does she have as much experience with him or her (or perhaps with men in general) in making important decisions about intimate topics. It's essential to realize that no matter how smooth or rocky the relationship is, coparenting is a lifelong connection and commitment. Coparenting is a complex relationship that requires trust, mutual respect, some level of shared values, and the ability to creatively work through the unexpected as a team.

Prior to parenting it's often difficult to realize that a shared parenting relationship is an intimate relationship. This is one of the most important points to consider when evaluating whether coparenting is right for you. This intimate relationship is unique in that it often occurs between people who haven't chosen to be intimate in other ways. Thus, coparents need to communicate frequently. Whether or not they live together, they're affected by events in each other's personal lives and are affected by each other's idiosyncrasies—communication style, decision-making style, punctuality, etc.—just as if they were life partners.

Many women choose to coparent with a good friend and wouldn't consider parenting with people they don't know well. Still, more and more women specifically looking for men to be biological fathers or coparents meet these men in support groups or online groups devoted to arranging such relationships. The problems we've seen arise in coparenting relationships are exponentially more likely to occur in a situation in which the adults involved don't have a lot of shared history from which to draw.

Often coparent dads start out as known donors who discover they'd like more involvement in the child's life. The switch from known donor to coparent usually happens after the child is born, and often occurs when the donor grows to love the child and the mother(s) feel closer to the donor. Or the donor may later be unable to conceive children due to HIV infection or a health problem that limits his fertility. Having your donor suddenly want to be a coparent once you're pregnant or once the child is born can be stressful for all involved, in part because you don't have the sense of relaxed time line that you would while negotiating before conception.

Coparent Negotiations

Think carefully about the initial points of negotiation and discuss these points clearly with your partner, if you have one, before moving on to negotiations with a potential coparent. Without this preparatory work, many women find themselves quickly acquiescing to an agenda they may not feel comfortable with. Sometimes this is due to feeling pressured in the moment, not wanting to say no to a friend, or feeling a tremendous urge to get pregnant and to get your donor/coparent to commit so that you can move forward. If a couple is seeking a coparent, it's crucial that they're in agreement about their desires and their limits so that they don't feel undermined or betrayed by each other when talking to potential coparents. Read over the next sections carefully and then take time to clarify your visions individually and as a team if you're partnered.

Initial Topics of Discussion

Health Issues and Logistics

If you're seeking a male coparent who will be the biological father, the same health issues and conception logistics that apply to known donors apply to coparents. In the next chapter on known donors, you'll find detailed information on safer sex, sexually transmitted infections, and lab tests for infections as well as information on sperm counts and semen analysis. Often it's easier for women who are just asking a man to donate sperm to request lab tests and a sperm count from him than it is for them to ask the same of a coparent. When you're interested in having a particular man help you raise a child, discussing your desire for health screening can sometimes go by the wayside, which in part stems from the fact that there's so much other information to discuss. Many women are so thrilled that they have found a suitable coparent that they wish to avoid the bad news of his having a low sperm count or other health problems. Often women don't want to offend a man by asking for a sperm count before they discuss other key topics, as he may feel objectified.

The Value of Getting a Sperm Count and Other Tests Early On

Because his health may affect your health and the health of your baby and partner, we recommend that you overcome any hesitations you may have and ask your potential coparent to get the health tests for sexually transmitted infections recommended in Chapter 5 before you proceed in your negotiations. A borderline-low sperm count may be increased through changes in diet, vitamins, or Chinese medicine (see Chapter 8). Having a semen analysis performed early on will give the man a few months to seek treatment if necessary and see if it works while you continue negotiations. A low sperm count may also lead you to consider different methods of insemination that concentrate the sperm—such as IUI—right from the start. Likewise, finding out that someone is completely infertile early on will allow him the time to find a diagnosis and possible treatment, or will save all of you the emotional heartache of building a very close relationship on a potential that doesn't exist. If you discover the donor is infertile, but you're still wed to the idea of coparenting with him, you'll need to make other choices about where to obtain sperm. This will take time if you've been considering him your only suitable option for a biological father for your baby.

Living Arrangements

Many coparents don't live in the same house but share a duplex or live in the same neighborhood. Some people live far away from each other, but this is rare and is usually the result of a job-based move. Where the child lives should be a detailed point of initial negotiations. Not all coparenting relationships include the desire for the child to spend any nights away from her or his primary house, especially in the child's early years. If you desire this option, read ahead carefully.

Many parents don't realize that a baby's needs are different than those of an older child. People who have created a clear image in their minds of parenting an elementary-school-age child need to trust that that image may manifest itself eventually but will not look anything like the day-to-day life of raising an infant or toddler. This misconception often causes many tensions and insecurities during the first year(s) of shared parenting. With a realistic view of how a baby's needs evolve, you can incorporate flexible arrangements into your parenting agreements.

If the woman who gave birth is breastfeeding, she'll find it difficult for the child to spend the night away from her until the child is eating quite a bit of solid food, which begins usually at 8 to 14 months of age. (Although a baby may start eating solid food at 5 to 6 months, breastfeeding frequency won't immediately decrease.) Nursing is a very intimate and important bond. In our practice we've seen women before or during pregnancy commit to wean the baby at 6 months, so that the child could start spending the night regularly at the dad's house. Once these women actually started parenting and felt the strength of mothering instincts, they were miserable being under the pressure of a rigid timetable. In fact, any promises about nursing versus bottle-feeding that come with dates attached are a set-up for hard feelings, whether or not they relate to sleepover arrangements. Therefore, we strongly recommend that you make no specific commitments about breastfeeding time lines.

If your ultimate goal is to have actively involved coparents who live in a different house, it's crucial to include the above information about breastfeeding needs, when discussing how the first year will work. Using "half-time," "equal-time," or "50/50" language to conceptualize the living and time-sharing arrangements of the first few years is unrealistic. If the baby nurses every hour to three hours in the beginning, your coparents may be spending all their time with the baby at your house. Is it feasible for them to see the baby four times a week or more, for several hours each time, in your living room? Have you ever spent that much intimate time with your potential coparent(s)? If not, you'd better go camping together for a week and see what happens.

Finally, some parents are fine leaving their infant with a grandparent, aunt, coparent, or best friend for an occasional night. Others won't consider having their child sleep away from them until he or she is 3 or 4 years old. Even if your potential coparents don't expect the infant to spend the night regularly at their house, they may have many fantasies of special sleepover parties occurring later that may or may not come to pass on the time line they expect. It's not too soon to discuss this in your pre-pregnancy negotiations. On the contrary, this kind of discussion of expectations is essential.

As they grow older, some children adapt well to living in two households, while others find it disruptive. If you'd like your child to live in more than one household, it will be difficult to plan in advance at what age your child will be ready for this arrangement, if at all. Some parents don't want their child to spend equal amounts of time at each household, or they feel it would be unfeasible, so they plan instead on their child spending one weekend a month at the second house or having impromptu sleepovers and participating in regular daytime visits and outings. Other families find that an equally divided schedule will work fine at some point. How much participation the child will have in choosing for him or herself as s/he grows older is an important question to consider in your living-arrangement discussions.

Exercise

When your child's desires differ from your plan, conflict can quickly arise if you haven't foreseen such potential challenges. Imagine your daughter living with you, and your partner if you have one, and spending regular time at her father's house. Write down your immediate responses to the following questions: How would you respond if your daughter at age 4 says she wants to spend one night a week at her dad's house? What if she wants to spend two to three nights a week there? How would you respond if she asks at age 10? How do you want her dad to respond to your 4-year-old if he hears about this from her first? How do you want him to respond if she is 10? How will you feel if he tells her you all have already agreed that such an arrangement will never be an option? Or what if he tells you it's unfair not to let the child have a voice in her own living situation now that she is older? What if he tells the child the idea delights him but that you'll have to agree, putting you in the "bad guy" position if you say no?

If the two of you are mothers legally sharing custody rights with your child's biological father, your response to the above situation may differ because of your legal circumstances. It's important to talk out scenarios like this with your coparent(s) early on. If you wait until the situation arises, having assumed that it won't, you may be surprised at how complicated your emotions and communications can quickly become. You may feel threatened when you realize that if an irresolvable situation ends up in court, you won't necessarily be awarded full custody of your child. If the court has never pronounced an official custody arrangement for your family, the father may feel threatened as well, since he knows he has to trust you, as you control his access to the child (unless he takes you to court to fight for it). If both of you feel threatened in regard to your child, your animal instincts will surface. "Cornered mother bear" isn't the most successful negotiating position for amiable resolutions. Again, have in-depth discussions early.

Building Lasting
Coparent Relationships

The time you put into your negotiations with potential coparents prior to pregnancy is invaluable. Don't let your "baby lust" alone govern your choices of coparents; take the time to explore together whether you're truly a good match. We've found that coparent relationships that last more than just a few years are the ones that have followed these guidelines:

- Agree that each individual will seek counseling about the kind of family each wants to create.
- All couples involved need to have clear lines of communication and solid, healthy relationships with each other.
- Agree that all involved coparents will attend family counseling sessions every six weeks for the duration of your child's life—starting at preconception.
- Agree to stay out of court if conflicts arise.
- Take the time to draw up thorough, personalized contracts.
- Agree to uphold the intentions that are laid out in your contracts.
- Discuss in-depth your opinions on religion and spirituality, medical and health approaches, education, values, and other important issues.
- Make provisions for possible career changes and/or relocation.
- Be clear in your contracts about mutual expectations about finances, decision making, and time commitments with the child.
- Clarify not only to yourselves, but also to lawyers, therapists, extended family members, and friends what your agreements and intentions are for your family. This structure will help to hold you all accountable in times of tension.

Vacations

Another variation on the theme of time and housing is vacation planning. You may think it's ridiculous to discuss these kinds of hypothetical situations in your initial conversations, but many times we've seen this topic bring up heated conversations that underscore the real differences between donors and coparents.

Exercise

Imagine the following scenarios and write down your answers to the questions that follow:

1. Your coparents tell you they want to bring your son home to visit one of their families of origin. Would you want to be invited? Would you feel obliged to go? Would you agree that they will bring the child alone? Does this depend on the age of your child?

2. You want to travel internationally with your daughter for a month. Would the coparents think a month away from them is too long in the child's first year of life? What about when your daughter is 5?

3. You decide you want to live abroad for a year. Would the coparents have the option to veto your decision? Would they come with you?

Often women are quite far into the negotiation process before they realize the assumption is that they're committing to live in the same town as the coparent(s) for the next 18 years, no matter what happens with your careers or personal lives. Once again, this is an opportunity to clarify whether all of you will be primary parents or if your coparent(s) will be auxiliary parents. This can impact who ultimately gets to make such decisions.

Issues With Families of Origin

Coparenting almost always includes negotiating holiday plans. When your child is in school, the one- or two-week winter holiday may not afford him or her enough time to see all the grandparents. You'll have to decide how to handle this. Perhaps you'll all visit the relatives together. If you don't, you'll need to decide if your relatives will see your daughter only with you, or with you and your partner, or with her other coparents as well. If, for example, your extended family never sees your child with her dads, they may have a difficult time acknowledging your child's relationship with them. By the time all the relatives get visited, you may not have time to take your own family vacation. Through working out specific examples like this, you and your potential coparents can begin to understand the level of communication necessary to make your relationships work and use these topics as practice exercises to get the feel of one another's expectations, and communication and conflict-resolution styles.

Finances

We've witnessed many creative financial arrangements between coparents. Some families decide that all parents will contribute a percentage of their income to the child's expenses, based on much each makes individually. Others pay a monthly amount each, which may or may not vary with the income of the parent. Some split the costs of parenting among those adults who are working, exempting the person/s doing the primary child care. Some families make financial arrangements that reflect the amount of time each parent has with the child or how parental decision-making power is distributed. It's a good idea to discuss how arrangements might change if someone gets a large pay raise, gets laid off, or goes on disability. Financial discussions are often charged and can lead to conflict, which often arises from a difference in opinion about the child's needs. A common conflict occurs in regard to specific expenditures: One person thinks private school is worth $12,000 a year, while the other parent can't or won't pay, feeling it's an unnecessary expense.

Negotiation Dynamics

In your discussions with a potential donor, be honest about exactly why you want a coparent; then you may ask for the same level of honesty in return. Good negotiating builds trust and betters communication skills, which will help you resolve problems together more smoothly later on. You'll probably want to discuss what everyone's family life was like growing up, whom each of you hold as your parental role models, and why. Discuss how you imagine the details of a regular day in your child's life and what might happen in the event of everyday surprises. For instance, what would happen if your child needed to stay home sick from school when you all have busy schedules?

If you're having deep and detailed conversations before deciding to parent together, you'll almost certainly experience initial misunderstandings, feel threatened, or doubt each other's intentions. You can realistically expect these feelings to arise during such important conversations, but you can also use these tense moments to deepen your communication if you openly acknowledge the tension and work through it. Often you both may subconsciously skirt around possible points of contention for months, because ultimately no one wants to find a point that is nonnegotiable. When people are wed to the idea of parenting together, possibly believing it's their only option for creating a family, the stakes can feel very high.

Stay Connected to Your Truth

Women often think men have the essential ingredient: sperm. Men who want to parent but aren't partnered with a female would argue that a uterus is harder to come by. It's much easier to get sperm from a sperm bank than to find a surrogate mother. We mention this because we see women negotiate from very disempowered positions unnecessarily. In our practice, we've seen that women have a tendency to want to be very fair and to not take advantage of someone. This tendency causes them to avoid starting a conversation with a discussion of their own desires. When you're creating your family, however, your desires are central. It's crucial for you to lay out for your potential coparent(s) what your ideal vision is, as well as which parts of it you can compromise on or negotiate. If you can directly and clearly communicate your desired family structure and the framework of your relationships, your conversations will be much more efficient and fruitful. Your potential coparents will then have a specific image to work with when asking themselves, *Can I imagine this being my future?* If s/he says no, you can reevaluate your limits and see whether you might be willing to compromise, or you can thank this person for considering the arrangement, and move on.

Stick to Your Vision

When negotiating with coparents, women often don't bring up all the issues they initially had planned to. Too often women find themselves telling a potential coparent they can have as little or as much participation in parenting as they want. Most women have preferences, as well as limits, about how much participation they desire from a coparent dad, especially if they've done some preliminary thinking before starting negotiations. Presenting a man with an option to create a family and giving him carte blanche to decide its structure can often confuse and pressure him. He probably hasn't been thinking about parenting as long as you have. If he has, he's probably already prepared himself to compromise a great deal and will feel reassured when you articulate your desires and limits.

Thoroughly discussing all the variables will help each of you develop an accurate vocabulary for understanding what you each feel is your ideal vision of family and parenting. Often it's helpful to negotiate in the presence of another person, so that you'll have a third party involved. Be aware, however, of the bias this third party may bring to the conversation (no one is completely objective), in terms of how well this person knows each of you or whether they've had personal experience with the topic at hand. Also, remember, this is your life: If you find you've offered too much right away, you're not stuck. Simply have another conversation and clarify what you feel. This will allow you to create the family you want and will also set the stage for honesty and for dealing with the emotional and circumstantial changes inherent in raising a child.

Partner Dynamics and Biological Fathers

When a lesbian couple negotiates parenting with a man, the nonbiological mom-to-be commonly feels more threatened by the role of the biological dad than the birth mom does. This difference can certainly affect negotiation dynamics. The nonbiological mother's insecurity can be heightened if the woman conceiving is better acquainted with the man. If the nonbiological mother is more interested in the man having a known donor role instead of a "father" role, her insecurity can also increase. The mom who won't conceive often places less importance on the child needing a biological father. She may feel that two parents are enough, regardless of gender, and that she can adequately fulfill the role of second parent. If a man is involved, she may feel she has no place in the family.

If you have a partner, clearly discuss any feelings of threat either of you may harbor about the role of the biological father and/or male coparents. Sometimes it will take extensive conversations for both of you to get to the root of these emotions. When you can name the cause specifically, you'll be able to actively address it. If one woman doesn't know the man as well, arrange ways for her to spend time with him, perhaps even without her partner present, so that they can develop their own relationship and communication style. Keep in mind that it will be harder for many people to recognize the nonbiological mom as a primary parent if a man is involved in any way, especially if he has the title of "Dad."

To assure a sense of safety for the nonbiological mom, it may be helpful to choose a donor whom she already knows well. This may be especially important if you live in an area where you won't be able to secure parental rights for both moms. If the donor/father retains his legal parenting status, you and your partner need to be sure that he will honor your intentions as a family. If the man in question is closer to the biological mom-to-be, this may be too large of a leap of faith for the nonbiological mom to make.

Sometimes, in negotiating, even though they may be in firm agreement about what they want, partners will fall into the roles of "good cop/bad cop" when they present their needs to a potential coparent: One is firm about clearly stating and enforcing boundaries with the potential coparent(s), while the other compromises and smoothes over emotions. Unfortunately, the nonbiological mom often falls into the "bad cop" role, which, if she has already been feeling extraneous, can further alienate her. Within the partnership, agree on boundaries and limits as well as which specifics you feel you might be willing to compromise on. Choose who will present during each part of the conversation each time. To keep the power dynamic more equal, consciously take turns expressing the topics that are the most difficult to bring up.

Courting a Coparent

The process of negotiation can feel a lot like courtship. Occasionally, it may actually bring up the romantic feelings common with exciting and new relationships. In a couple, both women may not equally feel this "romantic" aspect. One may feel "swept away" while the other remains pragmatic. Sometimes sexual attraction springs up between a mom and a male or female coparent, even if the mom is exclusively lesbian. Boy, does this surprise people! We've even seen women end up in counseling, concerned that they're really heterosexual. The conception/coparenting relationship is intimate, and creating new life is profoundly cosmic. This intimacy can move naturally into sexual energy and doesn't necessarily signify a change in sexual orientation or the need to act on these feelings. Sometimes one woman feels she must hide the depth of these feelings from her partner; her partner, however, is usually quite aware of the situation. If these issues arise, discuss your feelings honestly in order to reduce the emotional charge that secret feelings often harbor.

Contracts and Legal Issues

A contract benefits a coparenting family in a number of ways. Some think of it as a bureaucratic task; others approach it with dread, fearing it will cause conflict. We encourage you to regard a parenting contract as a powerful tool. Approaching it in this spirit, most parents find the process of creating the contract deeply rewarding. The security of having a parenting contract is invaluable.

Many people believe a parenting contract isn't necessary because they share a high level of trust and communication. In reality, what we've seen is that people who go through the process of writing a contract—clarifying on paper their intentions about roles, responsibilities, values, and conflict resolution—feel even greater trust and a higher level of communication when they finish. Developing a contract can provide you with guidance through important initial conversations so that crucial pieces aren't overlooked. Furthermore, if and when a time arises that a coparenting group or couple don't communicate as well as hoped, a contract will clearly state beyond the ambiguities of memory what the original intention of the family was. The contract serves as an essential tool for reminding everyone to act with the utmost integrity, especially if it's not written in "legalese" but in a language that conveys your heartfelt intentions when you agreed to parent together.

Planning for Disagreement

At some point you'll likely reach an impasse in making a parenting decision. This may happen prior to pregnancy or when your child is much older. Perhaps you differ in your opinion on vegetarianism, your comfort with Western medicine versus "alternative" health care, or whether the child will spend a month of their summer with a specific grandparent. What will you do when conflict arises? Having a well-articulated plan of action will help put all of your minds at ease. An agreement to see a family counselor is a good example. In your parenting contract it's wise to work out all the details, such as who will choose the counselor, who will pay, and whether all need to agree that counseling is necessary or if one party can demand it. A number of families we've worked with see a therapist as a team every six weeks to keep channels of communication open, to maintain healthy relationships, and to prevent the need for crisis intervention.

Legal Meaning

Legally speaking, if you find yourself in court in a custody dispute, your contract won't be binding. In a court of law, a notarized contract serves only as a document stating your original intentions. Some women want to have a coparenting relationship with their child's biological father without giving him legal custody. In the state of California, for example, a biological father has a claim to paternity even if he isn't listed on the birth certificate, even if he signed a "sperm donor only" contract, and even if the mother was inseminated by a physician. All the biological father needs to do is prove that he has a unique relationship with the child that is recognized by the child or the community, based on his paternity status. He has even more of a claim if you had intercourse with him to conceive.

Many states do not legally recognize lesbian mothers as parents if they didn't give birth to the child. Therefore, these women can't complete a second-parent adoption. Nonetheless, they can still request that the biological father sever his paternity rights. Some women choose a male coparent with whom they feel comfortable listing on the birth certificate and acknowledging legally his paternity. The nonbirth mom may still feel that her relationship with her child is very vulnerable. Legally speaking, it is. If the biological father has a partner who's an active coparent (in our experiences, usually a man), his relationship with the child is also not legally recognized.

The current legal system holds all of your written and verbal family arrangements secondary to the will of the court, if you end up there. The court doesn't make decisions based on its interpretation of your original intentions but on what it deems to be in the best interest of the child. Few legal precedents have been set by coparenting families arguing in court.

If a dispute occurs and you all agree to resolve it through binding arbitration or mediation, a notarized contract *will* be a powerful tool for you. One of the most useful aspects a coparenting contract can contain is specific language that spells out a process for conflict resolution, including an agreement by all parties to partake in family counseling first, followed by mediation or binding arbitration if necessary, to avoid staying out of a usually homophobic court system.

The best source of current legal information on this topic is the National Center for Lesbian Rights. (See the resource list at the end of Chapter 1. Sample contracts can be found at the end of this chapter.)

Contract Content

Besides containing a detailed plan for conflict resolution, your contract may include a communication plan, specifying how and why you'll keep these channels open. The contract should specify the details you've worked out in the areas we mentioned earlier: finances, decision making, household and living arrangements, and special areas of importance. It may also include some history about how you all came together to parent and why you specifically chose one another. It could also list the reasons why each of you want to parent, what the concept of "family" means to you, and what commitment each of you is making to your child now and in the future. Write the contract in the language you could imagine reading to an older child as a beautiful tribute to the love you brought to creating family; this will keep you writing your own truth, not what you imagine a legal document should sound like.

Dealing With Change

After you set up a coparenting relationship, it will eventually change (no matter how you expect it to turn out) because the rest of life continues in its dynamic way while you parent. People who aren't yet parents have a difficult time understanding both the permanency of the relationship and the inevitable flux the relationship will undergo. You must, however, prepare yourselves for the unexpected. If you aren't someone who can adapt well to unexpected change, you'll want to either develop these skills or seriously consider not entering into a coparenting situation, since when you parent with other people, changes are bound to arise.

Issues for Single Women

Many people make an apparently solid agreement about parenting roles that is then challenged by unforeseen change. We've seen single women choose to coparent with a man or two men in order to share child-rearing responsibilities. In some cases the women were very close to the men; in others they were not. If the women later become partnered, everyone has to do a lot of work to sort out the new relationships. The new lover can feel like she's a third wheel in an intimate preexisting family dynamic, which can spur a lot of jealousy and insecurity if she develops a close relationship with the child. The father may feel resentful or that he has been "used." He may feel that he and the birth mother went through all sorts of negotiations to determine whether they could parent together well, while a new woman is allowed access to a parenting role solely based on the mother's recent attraction to her. The birth mother may feel under great pressure if she becomes the mediator between the new partner and the male coparent.

Example

Beth wanted to parent and felt pressured to get pregnant right away, since she was in her early 40s. Although single, she wanted to share financial and parenting responsibilities with someone. She met Alan at a meeting of gay men and lesbians interested in parenting together, and they started to talk every two weeks to two months over dinner. It took a year for them to feel they were a good match. From the onset of the process, she met with us often to clarify her desires and concerns, and to receive suggestions about how to approach meetings with him. Once Beth and Alan started talking in earnest, she brought him in to see us for a joint consultation so that they could benefit from facilitated discussions. In our private sessions, we reviewed with Beth what her heart desired versus what her mind told her was appropriate, fair, or polite to ask for. She did a lot of personal work to realize that she was creating her family and coparenting relationship from the bottom up; therefore, she could negotiate from her highest vision without apology. She needed to remember that she didn't have to protect Alan in her negotiations, that he, as an adult, could take care of communicating his own needs to her, and that he was responsible for not agreeing to arrangements that didn't feel fair to him.

One of their main points of discussion concerned finances, especially since his income was higher than hers. He wanted them to buy a duplex together so they could live next door to each other, but she couldn't afford to buy a house; at the time, she was renting a small studio. In divorce situations, the person who has less childcare responsibility usually contributes more financial support. But in coparenting relationships, people often feel that whoever spends more time with the child should hold more financial responsibility. In Beth and Alan's situation, Alan had the money and wanted to contribute substantially to the child's expenses, but Beth didn't want to feel dependent upon him. She wondered whether financial dependence would result in her feeling a debt toward Alan, and she feared it might lead to an unequal power dynamic in their parenting. She wanted to be the primary parent but was concerned that he would feel he could buy decision-making power. She didn't want to feel disenfranchised in her parenting.

In her early meetings with us, Beth said she felt it would only be fair to give Alan 50% of the decision-making capacity. In her heart, however, she felt strongly that she needed to retain authority as the primary parent, especially when the child was young. We encouraged her to state honestly in her communication with Alan what she wanted. He could agree or disagree. If he disagreed, she could decide to negotiate further, or not. It was difficult for her to conceptualize that wanting more than "half" wasn't "wrong." When she expressed her desires, she found that Alan agreed that, for the child's early years especially, she would be the primary parent.

They had explicit conversations about Alan's sexual practices with his new lover, who was younger and not ready to be a primary parent. Alan's lover was HIV-positive, and for Beth to feel safe inseminating with Alan's sperm, she needed him to agree to practice safer sex within her definitions. When Alan's lover felt left out of this new evolving primary relationship, he would pressure Alan to have sex that was less safe, in effect to demonstrate that he was more important than Beth. Alan discussed this situation frankly with Beth and committed to a plan of how he would handle it, including being honest with Beth if, in the moment, he did have sex that was less safe than the standard to which he had agreed.

One of the most beautiful things we saw come out of their negotiations was a written agreement that discussed not only the nature of the relationship they would share, but also the nature of love and why they were choosing to bring a child into the world.

Beth became pregnant after two months of inseminations, and at four months of pregnancy became involved with a new lover, Dora, who wanted to participate in raising the child. Dora resented Beth's previous commitment to a man, who would be an ongoing, intimate part of Beth and Dora's family life. Alan felt some resentment that he had to go through such extensive negotiating with Beth but that Dora was allowed to move right in and become actively involved in the baby's life solely because of her romantic connection to Beth. Beth felt exhausted at times trying to keep peace and harmony between all the members of their parenting team. She appreciated Alan's taking care of the child and giving financial support, and she acknowledged that the situation is more complicated and time-consuming than she'd ever imagined.

New Relationships

If a coparent becomes partnered, the mother(s) may feel uncomfortable with the coparent's partner taking on a close role with the child when the mother barely knows this person. This is, in effect, a stepparent situation with all the opportunities and difficulties of a blended family. If two women who share parenting with a coparent break up, the child now potentially has three households. This can result in the child having many stepparents if both women partner with new people. Not all possible scenarios can be worked out in advance, but in general the point is that coparenting situations have the potential for many complicated relationships.

In conclusion, no matter how clear you think your vision is, ask honest questions of yourselves and your potential coparents. More discussion is far better than less. Use your contract as a means to achieve even deeper discussion. Examine how solidly you trust your own communication skills as well as your ability to be flexible and to compromise. You'll need to rely on all of these skills if you choose to coparent. We also remind you that coparenting with anyone means a lifelong commitment to each other as well as the child. Two truths exist about coparenting: The struggles are real, and with enough creativity the opportunities are broad.

Sample Coparenting Contracts

Parenting Agreement for Two Biological and Two Nonbiological Parents

1. The purpose of this agreement is threefold. First, it protects the interests of the child(ren) in our family by expressing our understanding of the parents' rights and responsibilities to our child(ren) and their agreement to provide for their upbringing and support in the most responsible and cooperative manner possible. Additionally, we believe that child(ren) should have free and open access to those people whom the child(ren) identifies as her/his parents. These bonds should only be suspended or severed if a parent proves her/himself to be unfit or abusive. Second, this agreement states that _____ and _____ are to be the biological parents of the first child(ren) in our family and that they will have full and equal legal custody under the laws of the State of_____. OR [Second, to recognize that _____ and _____ will be the biological parents but that the two mothers, _____ and _____ intend to be the legal parents.] Third, this agreement states that our child(ren), regardless of law, will have four people whom they will identify as parents and who will function as parents with all rights and responsibilities. The nonbiological parents are _____'s domestic/life partner, _____ , and _____'s domestic/life partner, _____ . Hereafter, the aforementioned adults will be jointly referred to as the Parents.

2. We fully realize that our power to make this agreement may be limited by state law. There are legal questions raised by the issues involved in this agreement that have not been settled by statutes or prior court decisions. With this knowledge, and in a spirit of cooperation and mutual respect, we wish to enter into this agreement.

3. _____ and _____ intend to become biological parents together, in that _____ will provide his semen to _____ for the purpose of alternative insemination. "Child(ren)" in the agreement applies

to any child or children born as a result of said alternative insemination.

4. Our purpose and our hope is to do our best to see that our child(ren) maintains a close and loving relationship with each of us, regardless of external demands that might affect our relationships with each other. Our intent is to create an extended family for our child(ren) and for ourselves based on the principles that ideally guide all families: love, mutual respect, responsibility, cooperation, emotional support, and clear communication. We are committed to creating a loving, safe, and secure environment for our child(ren).

5. Although _____ and _____ are not partners and their respective partners, _____ and _____, will not be biological parents to our child(ren), and although we are using alternative insemination, we intend to be equal parents to our child(ren). Legal and physical custody shall be joint. This means that all major decisions regarding physical location and any other major decisions, such as those relating to the child(ren)'s support, health, education, spiritual education, etc., shall be made jointly by the Parents, and that our child(ren) shall be involved in the decision making to an extent consistent with his/her/their age(s) at the time.

6. We intend to remain in _____ (geographic area) until the child(ren) has finished high school unless jointly agreed upon by the Parents. We agree that it is preferable for us to live in close proximity. If, for professional and/or personal reasons, this becomes difficult or impossible, we agree that the parent(s) who remains in _____ will have custody of the child during the nine-month school year. The parent/s leaving _____ (geographic area) will have custody during major school breaks and summer vacations. We will discuss any necessary changes with the aim of minimizing negative effects on our child(ren) and our family.

7. We acknowledge and agree that the biological father, _____, will be named on the birth certificate of any child(ren) born from the alternative insemination procedure. OR [We acknowledge and agree that the second-parent adoption process will allow the two parents named on the birth

certificate to be the two mothers, _____ and
_____.]

8. We acknowledge and agree that the child(ren)'s names will be agreed upon by mutual consent of the Parents.

9. We acknowledge and agree that the child(ren) will be given a sense of their cultural heritages. We agree to respect our differences with regard to our religious and cultural heritages.

10. We acknowledge that we may maintain two separate households. If we do, it is our intent that all Parents will have substantial and continual contact with the child(ren). If we maintain two separate households, we will divide the child(ren)'s time approximately _____between the two households. We understand, however, that physical custody may vary over time depending on the best interests of the child(ren). The child(ren) shall primarily reside with the mothers, _____ , during the first _____ months/years of the child(ren)'s life. After this time, s/he (they) shall reside with the fathers, _____ , a minimum of _____ (for example: three days per week and every other weekend). We agree to alternate by holiday and by year the following days: (birthdays, Rosh Hashanah, Yom Kippur, Halloween, Thanksgiving, Hanukah, Christmas Eve, Christmas Day, President's Day, Passover, Easter, Memorial Day, Independence Day, Labor Day, etc.).

11. (If necessary) For tax purposes the legal parents, _____ and _____ , will alternate years for claiming "Head of Household" and the child as dependent and using the child care credit, unless otherwise agreed upon by the Parents. _____ will have even-numbered years and _____ will have odd-numbered years. Earned income credit can be claimed by the legal parents _____ or _____ when applicable.

12. We acknowledge and agree that all four parents will provide support to the child(ren) to the extent that we can, depending on our income. We shall pay routine costs for food, shelter, and clothing while physically caring for our child(ren).

13. The Parents will include the child(ren) in a health and dental insurance plan through one of our workplaces or through a

private plan. The Parents shall contribute to health care costs, including health and dental insurance premiums, for prenatal, childbirth, day care, and educational expenses as follows:

a) When incomes are approximately equal (+/- 10%), each shall contribute an equal amount.

b) When incomes are unequal we will contribute amounts proportional to our respective incomes. We acknowledge that physically caring for the child has monetary value since care not voluntarily provided would have to be purchased on the open market.

c) Any expenses related to the items mentioned above are subject to mutual agreement before implementation.

14. If the biological mother, _____ , is unable to work for a period of time due to pregnancy, or during the first six months after the child(ren)'s birth, and thereby suffers a decrease in her income, the other parents shall bear a larger share of the child support and related expenses with the exact amount based on the mother's monthly expenses. This amount will not exceed $_____ per month.

15. The Parents each will separately have authority to authorize consent for medical, surgical, or dental examination or treatment of their child(ren) to any person(s) in whose care the child(ren) is/are temporarily placed. The legal (biological) parents, _____ and _____, will seek to have legal medical power of attorney drawn up so that the nonbiological parents, _____ and _____, will be able to act with appropriate speed in case of an emergency and if neither of the legal (biological) parents is available.

16. In consideration of the ongoing support of the minor child(ren), both the Parents will hold life insurance policies in the amount of $_____, designating each other as beneficiary in trust for the child(ren).

17. Except as set forth in this agreement, the Parents waive rights to receiving child support. We are fully informed of the right to court-ordered child support and are not acting under coercion. In addition, none of us is receiving welfare aid nor expects to in the future. We believe the financial needs of our child(ren) will be adequately met by this agreement and have made this agreement in the child(ren)'s best interests.

18. In the event of the death or permanent mental impairment of one of the legal parents, this document nominates for partial or full guardianship the surviving domestic partner of the deceased or disabled parent.

19. The Parents each agree to write a will designating the child(ren) to receive a share of their estate.

20. If any dispute or problem arises between the Parents regarding some aspect of this contract in caring for the child(ren), we agree to seek counseling and/or professional help to resolve those problems. The child(ren) shall be involved in this process to the maximum amount consistent with their age at the time. In the event a resolution cannot be reached by the above, a more formal mediation procedure will be followed.

a) Mediation: We will engage in three sessions of mediation in good faith in an attempt to resolve our disputes. How the cost of the mediation is divided will be decided during the course of the mediation.

b) Binding arbitration: We agree that, should the above mediation be unsuccessful, we shall submit to binding arbitration. We understand that, by agreeing to binding arbitration, the decision of the arbitrator will be final and we will not have the right to have the decision reviewed in a court of law. Binding arbitration shall proceed accordingly:

i. The request for arbitration may be made by any parent and shall made be in writing and delivered to the other parents;

ii. Pending the outcome of arbitration, there shall be no change in the language of this agreement;

iii. The arbitration panel that will resolve any disputes regarding this agreement shall consist of five persons: one person chosen by each parent and one person chosen by the other four panel members. By mutual agreement this number may be reduced to three;

iv. Within 14 days following the written arbitration request, the arbitrators shall be chosen;

v. Within 14 days following the selection of all members of the arbitration panel, the panel will hear the dispute between parties;

vi. Within 7 days subsequent to the hearing, the arbitration panel will make a decision and communicate it in writing to each party.

vii. The Parents agree that the arbitrator(s) will decide who pays the costs of the arbitration.

viii. The Parents agree to request that the arbitration panel to consider the best interests of the child(ren)—if the dispute involves child(ren)—as paramount, outweighing the interests of any Parent;

ix. If both Parents agree to submit their dispute to an existing gay and/or lesbian arbitration panel, the above process may be forsaken.

21. We acknowledge and agree that we signed this agreement voluntarily and freely of our own choice and not under duress of any kind. We further acknowledge that we each have been advised to secure the advice and counsel of an attorney of our own choosing, and that we each understand the meaning and significance of each provision of this agreement.

22. This agreement contains our entire understanding. There are no promises, understandings, agreements, or representations between us other than those expressly stated in this agreement.

In a spirit of cooperation and mutual respect, it is our clear and strong intention to raise loving, caring child(ren) simply and harmoniously.

The parties have executed this agreement on this _____ day of _____.

Signatures:

_____
Biological Mother

_____
Nonbiological Mother

_____

Biological Father

_____

Nonbiological Father

_____

Witness

Sample Parenting Agreement Between Mother and Father
Who Are Both Biological Parents

_____ (mother) and _____ (father), desiring individually and cooperatively to bring forth and love a child within the context of a loving and diverse community and according to the values they hold in relation to spiritual, cultural, and political matters, hereby enter into the following agreement. It is the mother and father's intention to share in the physical, emotional, and financial support of the child. The process that led to this agreement has been a considered and conscious one.

A. Child's Residence

1. We intend for the child to have a strong emotional bond with both parents. The child shall reside with the mother and father as stated below, with the goal of fostering a strong relationship with both parents. The mother and father both acknowledge that each has a strong commitment to the child being reared in with the help of other adults, and furthermore, both parents intend to foster and support these extended community relationships with the child.

2. General principles:

a. Residence: The child shall reside with the father 2/7 time and the mother 5/7 time, beginning no later than age 2, except that the time for beginning this arrangement is subject to the mother's ultimate decision-making authority as to when the child is ready for such an arrangement. The mother and father agree that the father's 2/7 time shall generally mean at least two time periods a week of approximately 24 hours each. If the child is not residing with the father 2/7 time by age 2, and if the mother and father disagree about when the 2/7 time with the father should occur, the disagreement shall be resolved by the procedure for conflict resolution specified under section F.2.a of this agreement.

b. Flexibility and cooperation: Both parents will make their best effort to coordinate with and accommodate and coordinate with each other's schedules. Both parents agree that it may be necessary to be flexible with the physical custody schedule and arrangements to accommodate the child's needs, special events, family emergencies, holidays, and vacations. Both parents agree to discuss the celebration of the child's birthday, parents' birthdays, religious and other holidays, and vacations in a timely manner.

3. Prior to age 2: During the first month of his or her life, the child shall live with the mother, and the father may visit the baby daily at the mother's home at a mutually acceptable time. Recognizing that the mother will be making a major adjustment during that time period, the father agrees to be flexible and sensitive to the needs of the mother and the baby as to the timing and length of his visits. During the rest of the nursing period, which could last until age 2, both parents agree that it would be preferable that the father have the child at his home as soon as it is deemed healthy for the child and at times when it will not interfere with the child's nursing schedule.

B. Cooperation in Decision Making

1. Birth to age 7: Both parents agree that during the first 7 years of the child's life, all decisions regarding the child are subject to the mother's final decision-making authority, except as specified in section A.2.a above regarding the child's 2/7 time residence with the father by age 2, and section C.2 below (regarding relocation). Except in the event of a medical emergency, both parents agree to cooperate in making decisions about topics including, but not limited to, the child's health care, child care, and education. To achieve this cooperation, both parents agree to consult with each other and treat each other with respect. In the event of disagreement, the mother has the obligation to hear the father's views and to consider them in making a final decision.

2. After age 7: Both parents will make decisions regarding health care, child care, and education by consensus. If a decision cannot be reached, both parents will utilize their procedures for resolving conflict set forth in section F below.

3. Consistency in child-rearing practices: Both parents agree that their child-rearing practices and everyday routines will be consistent with each other and will be discussed on an ongoing basis. These practices include, but are not limited to, diet, bedtime, television, and setting appropriate limits on the child's behavior.

4. Religion: Both parents acknowledge the fundamental importance of Judaism in their lives and wish to impart to their child
the ethical, cultural, and spiritual values of Judaism. They are
also committed to including other traditions in their cultural
celebrations. They each intend to teach their child to understand and respect all religions and cultures.

C. Proximity of Parents' Households

1. Goal of physical proximity: Both parents agree that it
would be best if they are able to reside near each other in order
to easily transfer the child between households and to facilitate their face-to-face contact and communication. Both parents
shall make their best effort to reside no farther apart than approximately one hour by car.

2. Relocation: If either parent intends to move from the city
of San Francisco, both parents shall meet as far in advance of
the move as possible and attempt to arrange a plan for the
child's residence that maintains the agreed-upon time-sharing to
the maximum feasible extent. The goal will remain a time-sharing arrangement comparable to 2/7 and 5/7, and every effort will
be made by both parents to achieve it. In the event that time
cannot be shared as previously set forth and a mutually agree-
able plan cannot be arranged, the mother and father will utilize their procedures for conflict resolution set forth in Section F. below.

D. Financial Matters

1. Day-to-day expenses: The mother and father shall be individually responsible for food, clothing, toys, entertainment,
and other day-to-day expenses incurred while the child is living at their respective residences. Both parents acknowledge
that the greater day-to-day expenses will be incurred by the
mother, as the child will reside with her 5/7 of the time. Both
parents will make their best effort to create and maintain eq-
uitable environments for the child at their respective homes,
including but not limited to the child's belongings, clothing,
toys, and other play equipment.

2. Specific large costs: The father will pay 67% and the
mother will pay 33% of the uninsured costs for prenatal care and
birth care, child care, education, medical care (including insurance premiums and out-of-pocket expenses), dental care, and

extracurricular activities (camp, lessons, etc.) until the child completes his or her undergraduate studies or reaches age 25, whichever is sooner. Both parents agree to notify each other promptly of significant changes in their income that might affect their ability to comply with the 2:1 ratio. In the event of such a change, both parents agree to meet and discuss whether to alter the ratio. Out-of-pocket medical costs will include, but are not limited to, noncovered alternative health care, dental, orthodontics, deductibles, and copayments.

3. Medical insurance: The child will have continuous medical insurance from birth until he or she has completed undergraduate studies or reached age 25, whichever is sooner. The child will be covered by whichever parent's medical insurance offers the most comprehensive and least costly coverage for the child. Coverage may be provided for the child under both parents' medical insurance if such coverage is complimentary.

4. Life insurance: Both parents agree to provide funds for the care of the child in the event that one or both of them should die. The father will name the child as sole beneficiary for an existing life insurance policy in the amount of $_____, and agrees to maintain that coverage in effect, or obtain equivalent life insurance coverage to be effective until the child reaches age 25. The mother will not purchase life insurance but instead will name the child in her will as heir, to wit: (1) all her devisable assets remaining after payment of taxes and other valid claims against her estate, if the value of such remaining devisable assets is less than $_____ or (2) a portion of her devisable assets remaining after payment of taxes and valid claims against her estate at least equivalent to $_____, if the value of such remaining devisable assets is greater than $_____.

5. Income tax benefits: Both parents will split income tax benefits related to child care expenses according to the actual financial contributions of each parent. Other tax deductions and credits will be taken by the parent who will accrue the largest financial benefit.

6. Disability insurance: The father will continue to maintain in effect a policy of disability insurance, or equivalent disability insurance coverage, which is in effect at the time he

signs this agreement. Upon the birth of the child, the mother will purchase and maintain in effect disability insurance for herself.

7. Higher education: Both parents agree that it is their intention that the child receive a college education. Each parent agrees to contribute to the cost of this education. A college fund will be established with gifts and may be maintained by regular monthly or annual contributions by each parent. Both parents will confer annually to determine the amount of their contributions.

8. Mother's lost income: The father will pay the mother for 50% of her lost income due to her inability to work during pregnancy and after the birth of the child. It is the mother's intention to resume her normal work schedule gradually during the first year, as her physical and emotional health and the needs of the baby permit. The father's obligation under this paragraph will be limited in duration to one year and in amount to $10,000. The father shall pay up to $5,000 of this amount in monthly installments to the mother during the first six months of the period in which she is unable to work, and up to $5,000 of this amount in monthly installments to her during the second six months of the period in which she is unable to work. The father's payments to the mother under this paragraph shall be due on the first of each month.

E. Death and Disability

Prior to the birth of the child, both parents promise to make a written and properly signed, witnessed, and notarized will that sets forth guardianship and other arrangements for the child in the event of their deaths.

At this time, neither the mother or father is in a committed long-term relationship with a life partner. Both of them want to make such a relationship in the future. When such relationships occur, the partner and the child may form a significant attachment. Recognizing that these attachments may be very important, both parents agree that they will meet periodically and review the statements of arrangements in this agreement for the disposition of care and custody of the child if either parent should die before the child reaches the age of majority. It is the intent of both parents that if either of them has a long-term life partner who develops a significant relationship with the child prior to the parent's death, that the surviving partner should be assured a significant continuing role in the child's life. Both parents further agree that they are committed to honoring the child's established relationships with persons other than themselves, and that this commitment extends beyond the lifetime of either parent, if either parent should die before the child reaches the age of majority.

F. Conflict Resolution

1. General principles: The mother and father intend to resolve all conflicts that might arise between them without resort to courts.

2. Procedure for resolving conflicts:

a. Meeting. If a conflict arises in which both parents cannot reach a consensus, upon the request of either the mother or the father, they together will convene a discussion group consisting of one friend of the mother's choosing, one friend of the father's choosing, and a third person both parents agree to include.

b. Counseling and/or Mediation. If the meeting described in the previous paragraph does not resolve the conflict, and the issue is outside the scope of the mother's final decision-making authority, both parents agree that they shall meet with a mutually acceptable professional counselor and/or mediator. The cost of the session or sessions with the mediator shall be shared equally.

c. Binding Mediation. If the dispute is not resolved by the means stated in paragraphs a and b above, both parents agree that they shall submit the dispute to binding mediation by a mutually acceptable mediator. The cost of the session or sessions with the mediator shall be shared equally.

d. Binding Arbitration. If a dispute involving the child or this agreement cannot be resolved by discussion, counseling mediation, both parents acknowledge that each of them has the option to seek to resolve the dispute by obtaining the agreement of the other person to binding arbitration. This paragraph shall not be construed to impose any obligation on either parent to submit to such arbitration.

G. Review and Amendment of This Agreement

Proposed Changes. If either parent would like to consider a clarification of, or change to, the terms of this agreement, both parents shall meet together and attempt to reach agreement on any such proposed change.

Amendment. The agreement may only be amended by mutual written consent between both parents.

H. Miscellaneous Provisions

1. Multiple originals. This agreement shall be signed in four counterparts, each of which is an original of this agreement. The parents will retain one original each; the other two originals will each be held by a person known to both parents.

2. Governing law. This agreement is made in the state of _____. It is the parents' intent that all questions regarding the interpretation, performance, validity, and legal effect of this agreement shall be determined by the laws of the state of _____, regardless of the actual location or residence of either parent now or at any later time.

3. Effectiveness. This agreement shall remain in effect until voided in writing by both parents or until the child reaches the age at which all terms of this agreement no longer apply or control.

4. Severability. If any clause of this agreement is determined to be unenforceable, those clauses shall be severable, while the other provisions of this agreement shall remain in effect.

Each of us has read this agreement. Each of us understands and agrees to all of its terms.

_____   _____
mother   date

_____   _____
father   date

Chapter 5 Known Donors

A known donor is someone you know who donates sperm to you to help you become a parent. There are numerous reasons for choosing a known donor. In this chapter we will cover the advantages and drawbacks of working with a known donor and also examine the logistics of working with a known donor.

Why Women Choose Known Donors

Donor-Child Relationship and Guaranteed Access to Donor Information for Your Child

Many women feel daunted by the decisions parenting requires them to make before they even give birth to their children. One of the first decisions you may struggle with is how much information about and contact with the donor you think should be available to your child while he or she grows up and later as an adult. You may feel strongly that it wouldn't be ethical to make a choice about sperm donation that limits in any way a child's ability to have information or a relationship with his or her donor. You may choose a known donor because you aren't sure whether you might regret your child having limited or no access to his or her biological father and you don't want to preclude that option in the future. If you have strong feelings about your child's right to know his or her donor, it's important for you to acknowledge and explore these feelings.

Some women want their child to have personal contact with the donor, although they don't want the donor to fulfill the role of father. Perhaps they plan for the donor to have a special relationship with the child: "Uncle" or "Super Uncle" are common terms women use to describe this role. They don't define their donor as a coparent, though, since he will not have parental responsibilities. They would, however, like the donor to be involved in the child's life—not as a father but as an extended family member.

One sperm bank (Rainbow Flag Health Services in Oakland, Calif.) offers what it calls "known donor" options by giving donor contact information to the mother when the child turns 3 months old. Women work with this sperm bank specifically because they do wish to meet the donor and have the child know the donor as he or she grows. If the parents don't contact the donor within one year after the child's birth, the donor receives their contact information. This is a practical option for some women who prioritize their child's ability to know the donor. It's important to point out that the women will not know the donor's identity at the time of insemination, and there's no guarantee that they will like the donor when they meet him.

You may have heard of other sperm banks that offer known-donor options. These few sperm banks allow the child to contact the donor when he or she becomes an adult, but not before. We'll discuss this concept here briefly, although we cover sperm banks in depth in the next chapter. Sperm banks used to be places built intrinsically around the secrecy and shame that heterosexual married couples were assumed to feel about having fertility problems. Parents received very little, if any information about a donor, no future contact with the donor was available, and almost always the parents were advised never to tell the child that she or he was conceived with donor sperm. Thanks in part to the open-adoption movement and in part to some lesbian-friendly, feminist-oriented sperm bank directors (see the resource list at the end of Chapter 6), a number of sperm banks have changed their policies and are more forthcoming with information about each donor. Nonetheless, many sperm banks continue to only give a one-line description for donors. When you work with a sperm bank that doesn't offer known donors, no matter how much information you receive, you'll never meet the donor after choosing him.

The few sperm banks that do release a donor's name and contact information—when the child becomes an adult and requests it—call these donors "identity-release" or "yes" donors, although many women call them "known donors." There are a few sperm banks that don't have this policy but agree that if the facility is still in existence when the child turns 18, they will attempt to contact the donor and ask if he is willing to have them pass on his name to the now-adult child. It is important to remember that the identity of the donor in these circumstances will not be known to you at the time of insemination, nor will it be known before your child turns 18.

Adoption Concerns

Women often choose a known donor when adopted people in their lives (perhaps even themselves) have had painful experiences with adoption and not knowing their biological parent/s. Wanting to prevent a child from feeling "half-adopted" and needing to seek the other origin of her/his biology can lead these women to choose a known donor. Most lesbians who choose to use sperm banks do so with a spirit of openness rather than secrecy. They explain to their children from an early age about the nature of their family and conception. They explain that their children's conception was carefully planned and incredibly desired, and that the man who donated sperm gave a gift so that their family could come into existence just as it has. In this way they work to prevent the children from developing the feelings of shame, emptiness, and inadequacy that are common for people who have been adopted.

Some children who are conceived with anonymous donor sperm never seek out their biological origins, while others will feel a great lack if they can't contact the donor or learn his identity. Many children go through variations on both themes, depending on what developmental stage they're in and how much understanding they receive from friends and community about their family story. There's no way to predict your child's feelings on these issues, although you can decide how you'd like to address their emotions and concerns. Therefore, make sure you feel comfortable with your decision so that you can share it with your child from a place of clarity and love.

Ability to Assess the Donor's Character

Many women feel it's imperative to meet a donor to determine whether he is a "good person." Many of our clients have told us that, at the very least, they want to ensure that their baby will receive half of his or her genetic material from someone they feel has "good energy" or "the right vibe," is "a person with integrity" and "someone who feels like a good connection," or is "not an ax murderer." This desire brings up fundamental questions of nature versus nurture. Which traits are genetic? What are the results of childhood family dynamics and environment? Can your loving support as a parent counterbalance inherited tendencies in personality and character from the sperm donor? Obviously, there are no universally known answers to these questions; we must each find our own answers. For some women for whom this assessment is important, the detailed sperm bank questionnaire an anonymous donor fills out seems sufficient data to decipher the man's character. Most sperm banks offer sample questionnaires that are available online. Some women feel that asking the staff at the sperm bank for their intuitive sense about each donor is adequate information. Other women, however, feel that meeting the donor is imperative, and thus, they decide to go with a known donor instead of an anonymous one.

Inexpensive and Available

Using a known donor's sperm is usually the most cost-effective way to get pregnant, since it's usually much less expensive than buying sperm from a sperm bank. Most women don't pay their known donor more than a token amount, if anything at all. Any costs incurred will probably arise from the following: travel, health-screening and sperm-count tests, as wells as the freezing of sperm. (For details, see the section on freezing donor sperm later in this chapter.) Since using a known donor is usually inexpensive, women who choose this option can perform many more inseminations each month and are able to cover a wide window of fertility, if their donor's schedule allows it.

Sperm from a known donor is also more readily available if you live in a state or country where you can't access sperm through the medical system unless you're heterosexually married. In these situations—unless you're willing to travel to a lesbian-friendly sperm bank and see a lesbian-friendly practitioner (see Chapter 6 for details)—your access to sperm is limited to personal arrangements and home inseminations: known donors or coparents.

Fear of Homophobia

Depending on the homophobia a woman expects to experience, she may feel very private about her conception situation and would rather not have any record of the choices she makes in the creation of her family, out of fear of discrimination or threat to her parenting autonomy by the state. It's hard to know whether our fear that our children may be taken from us at any time due to our sexual orientation is paranoia or common sense, especially since the political tide can so easily shift. Because internalized and external homophobia coexist, differentiating between the two can often be difficult. Therefore, some women simply feel more secure knowing there's no documentation linking them to a sperm bank.

Some people attach a stigma to a woman using a sperm bank. Being able to avoid the judgments and homophobia from such people—be they friends, family, or coworkers—often drives many women to choose known-donor sperm.

Gay and Bisexual Donors

Some women feel strongly that they would like to have a gay or bisexual donor for their child. They're proud of their sexual orientation and feel more comfortable with the idea of obtaining sperm from a gay man than that of a straight man. Many queer people believe that we are "wired" differently—and prefer our own kind of wiring! Almost all sperm banks do not allow gay or bisexual men to donate sperm; to be fully licensed a sperm bank must follow rules, just like blood banks and organ banks, that prohibit men who have sex with other men from donating. This is to reduce the possibility of the sperm bank carrying HIV-infected semen. (Rainbow Flag Health Services in Oakland, Calif., is the only sperm bank that currently sells sperm from gay and bisexual donors, and the owner does so by forfeiting some of the licensure available.) Thus, women who want to use the sperm of a gay or bisexual donor usually must work with a known donor.

Increased Chance of Conception With Fresh Sperm Compared to Frozen

There are many key benefits to using fresh sperm instead of frozen. For one, fresh semen from a known donor's ejaculate almost always contains significantly more—and longer-living—sperm than a vial of frozen sperm. If you're using fresh sperm, you'll often have a much larger amount of semen with which to inseminate than what you'd get in a vial of frozen sperm. Frozen sperm is stored in quantities of 0.5 or 1.0 cc, a portion of which is buffer solution. The volume of semen in one ejaculation received from a known donor is usually 2–5 cc. Additionally, freezing often lowers the sperm count per cc of semen as well, sometimes drastically. On average about 50% of sperm don't survive the freeze/thaw process. Fresh sperm live longer (2-3 days) than frozen sperm (24 hours), allowing you to cover a longer stretch of fertile days with fewer inseminations. Thus, women often achieve pregnancy more quickly when inseminating with fresh sperm. Some women reentertain the known-donor option after inseminating unsuccessfully with frozen sperm for a number of cycles, simply because of fresh sperm's higher rate of success per cycle.

Challenges of Using a Known Donor

A number of serious factors must be considered when deciding to work with a known donor. The most significant of these are the health and legal risks associated with using fresh sperm from someone you know. The rest of the concerns we've encountered are less frightening but can nonetheless significantly affect the life of you and your child.

Health Risks

When conceiving with fresh sperm, you can never know for sure whether you're exposing yourself to the risk of contracting a sexually transmitted disease. No matter how much pre-insemination risk assessment you've done with your donor, you may have forgotten to ask something, or he may not have told you the entire truth, or he may think he is monogamous when his partner actually has sex with others. There's always the chance when using fresh sperm that the donor has acquired an infection too recently to show up on lab tests or that he will contract a disease in the future and thereby put you—and your baby—at risk. This potential health risk is one of the primary reasons lesbians choose not to use known donors. Later in this chapter you can read about recommended tests and questions to help decrease your chances of contracting an infection if you choose to work with a known donor.

Despite all the detailed information we'll provide, we need to say that frozen sperm that has gone through the quarantine process has statistically the lowest chance of transmitting an infectious disease to you or your fetus. The quarantine process involves retesting a donor for infectious diseases six months after his sperm is first frozen. If all of his test results come back negative at the six-month mark, his sperm is released.

Legal Risk

The other primary reason lesbians choose not to use known donors is the potential legal risk. Until you've formally terminated a donor's parental rights and secured those of your partner if you have one, your donor may claim these rights. Until he has formally terminated his rights, he is a legal parent to your child. This means your donor could gain custody rights. Although the legal procedures of both severing paternity rights and formalizing second-parent adoption are supposed to ensure that a donor will not be able to gain custody, laws and the attitudes of judges vary from state to state and county to county.

Additionally, the parents of a donor may sue for custody as the child's grandparents. Unfortunately, in some parts of the country, antigay attitudes are so strong that a lesbian or bisexual woman can lose custody simply because of her sexual orientation. Although the donor contract and/or other legal documents you may draw up prior to insemination will assist you, there's no guarantee when conceiving with sperm from a known donor that you'll retain sole custody of your child.

The longer you know someone prior to choosing him as a donor, the more thorough and explicit the conversations you have with him regarding each of your roles and intentions, and the more documentation you have clearly stating your mutual intentions, the less room there will be for confusion in the future. Even when you know a donor well, there's often no way to predict the life changes that may influence your donor to want to be a full participatory and/or legally recognized parent. Terminal illness, religious conversion, injuries or disability, or other life changes can affect a donor's change in attitude toward parenting.

We've included a sample contract at the end of this chapter for use with known donors. For your agreement to suit your specific situation, however, you and your donor should visit a lawyer who's familiar with nontraditional families and can help you draw up a contract together. For such referrals contact the National Center for Lesbian Rights. (See the resource list at the end of Chapter 1.)

Other Issues to Consider

By asking a friend, coworker, or associate to donate sperm, you're inviting change in your relationship with that person, which may be for the better or worse. Unfortunately, we've heard a number of stories from women who wished they'd never asked the intimate questions necessary when working with a known donor. These women discovered information about their potential donors' characters that drastically affected their friendships with them. Often the discovery was accidental, while sometimes the donor did the great service of disclosing the information directly. Many of these men disclosed disturbing information about their sexual proclivities, pedophiliac behavior, and participation in sexual assault. These are but a few of the stories we've heard directly.

Additionally, after the child is born, there's no guarantee that a donor won't change his mind about the role he will play. For example, you have a mutual understanding that the donor will participate in the child's life during holidays, barbecues, or even more often, but he gets a job in France. Or perhaps he has said he has no interest in children, until later, when he is diagnosed with a terminal disease, he faces his mortality and wants to become an active parent to your child. It's essential to realize that change happens and to plan for it whenever possible.

In our experience, unfortunately, a number of donors change their minds about donating or disappear just before starting the insemination process. Although many women console themselves that their donor's disappearance is a sign that he wasn't right for them, this can often cause a tremendous amount of wasted time, energy, and money.

Logistics

Another challenge women frequently encounter is that of coordinating logistics. Often women choose donors who live far away. The geographic distance gives them the benefit of parenting security but also introduces travel costs and timing challenges or the costs and limitations of freezing the donor's sperm. Sometimes, too, even a local donor may be just too busy to adapt to your schedule or have to travel frequently. These are significant issues to focus on before moving ahead too quickly.

It's helpful to sit down with your calendars and plot out what this form of commitment to each other might look like. When planning, remember that your time of ovulation can at best be narrowed down to a few days of the month and even that may not be a sufficient window. Many women are devastated if they're unable to inseminate one month because of scheduling conflicts. It may be necessary to rule out an otherwise viable donor simply due to his schedule.

What Do You Want From a Known Donor?

Once you've decided to try to find a known donor, it's essential to clarify exactly why you're choosing this option. If you're partnered, you need to make sure both of you are communicating clearly with each other about this decision. Being able to articulate your feelings will help you remain clear when you negotiate with a potential donor. We recommend you do this internal exploration and external verbalization before you even make a list of potential donors.

Exercise

Imagine your ideal vision of your donor, leaving the picture of his face blank, without a name. Don't censor yourself here; you may learn some interesting things from your subconscious. Perhaps picture the donor meeting your child or playing with your child, or the conversation you'll have with your child about his or her conception. Be aware of the feelings in your body. Do you feel warm with love at some of the images? Does your throat or stomach tighten in response to other images? Create a vision that allows your body to relax and calms your breathing.

Your ideal vision may not be fully achievable, but you need to start with it and then slowly sort out which aspects you may be willing to compromise on and which are nonnegotiable. Start these discussions internally and then be sure to include your partner, if you have one. You may unconsciously assume the two of you have the same vision, only to find out much later that you do not.

Take a moment now to review Chapter 4 on coparents, if you need to. Initially, many women are unclear about the differences between a donor and a coparent. Others are quite clear but find, when trying to communicate their vision, they use labels and language that each of us may define differently such as: "donor," "dad," "uncle," "coparent," and "biological father." Try to be precise with your language—with yourself and your partner—providing examples to illustrate exactly what you mean. Define your terms out loud. Read through the negotiations section later in this chapter and decide what your "bottom lines" are for each category. Practice stating these out loud as well.

Some women first need to discuss what they want from a donor with someone they trust in order to clarify their needs and desires. If this is the case for you, use a good friend, a therapist, or an "advisory committee" of family or friends—anyone who can actively listen and provide feedback but won't try to impose their agenda upon you. (Don't use your potential donor in this capacity.) Again, clarifying what you want prior to negotiating will dramatically increase your chances of establishing the relationship you desire from the start.

How to Find a Donor

Women use a variety of approaches to ascertain who would make a good donor. Some feel they can intuit a man's character early in a relationship and feel comfortable proceeding even though they both don't know each other well. Others feel they need to have known the man for a long time prior to considering him a potential donor, since he will be in their lives from that point on. Some feel comfortable simply trusting character recommendations from close friends or coworkers. Some women even intuit that a donor may be a "good connection" if they can imagine being sexual with him.

You may find a potential donor anywhere in your life: coworkers, current friends, old friends from school or work, relatives of your partner (such as a brother or cousin), nonbiological relatives, etc. A trusted friend may introduce you to his or her circle of relatives, friends, or colleagues. We've known more than one woman who pulled out her Rolodex and called everyone in it, asking whether they'd consider being a donor or if they knew anyone who might be interested. Sometimes women place personal ads in gay and lesbian magazines and newspapers. Sometimes men who would like to be known donors or coparents also place ads. There are also prospective lesbian/bisexual/gay parenting support groups where you meet men and women wanting to create families. Many gay men are looking for coparent or special uncle relationships, but occasionally a man is interested in just being a donor.

Make a list of any men you know whom you could imagine being your donor. Try to make this list as freely as possible to start with. Get creative or even silly, and try to add people you might have forgotten from earlier in your life. As soon as you start weeding out some of them, you'll be surprised by how many you cross off, so think big. Sometimes women aren't completely clear on the desires and limits they have for donors until they go through the exercise of attaching real peoples' names and faces to the donor images created in the previous exercise. Flip through a few of the men on your list, putting them into the donor role like slides in a slide show. Do you have a visceral body response that gives you more information than you've had so far? Sometimes at this point women realize they actually want an **unknown** donor. Sometimes they come to such a realization even later, after they've approached or interviewed a few men.

If you're partnered, you should each make your own list. You might each agree to have veto power upon review of the other's list, no questions asked. If you read through each other's lists and reject everyone, you may need to reexamine your criteria. Are they impossible to meet? On the other hand, you may trust all the reasons you said no, so try to get even more creative and make a new list of possible donors. Check in with yourself at this point to make sure that you aren't saying no out of fear of having a child. You may find, with yourself or a partner, that discussing your reasons for eliminating potential donors will help you further clarify your desires.

Unequal Power Dynamics

Unequal power dynamics may exist between you, a partner, and the potential donor. We recommend that you take the time to explore whether these dynamics are actually reenacting an unhealthy pattern for you. Make sure you approach this life-changing decision from the most centered and honest place within you.

Exercise: Write down the names of your potential donors. Then write in a free association style about the power dynamics that may exist between you and each donor. Next, write about past relationships that mirror these dynamics. What was the quality of these relationships? Do you feel centered when you're in this role? Is it a place of safety? A place of insecurity? A place that makes you feel better than or worse than your donor? Is it a typical relationship you've had with other men in your life? Now include your partner, if you have one, in this picture. Does this produce any additional power dynamics? Although not all relationships with unequal power dynamics are bad, it's important to enter these types of relationships with care. Some examples follow.

Your Boss

We've seen a number of women start negotiating with their boss or their boss's husband. Either because things fell through, boundaries got crossed, or relationships became too intimate, most of these women ended up leaving their jobs because of the ensuing discomfort.

Relatives

Sometimes women ask their partner's brothers, stepbrothers, in-laws, or cousins to be donors. You may trust relatives more than you do other people in your life. Blood relatives of your partner specifically may be appealing because your child would share genes with both of you. This can be especially important for interracial couples.

Before jumping ahead, consider how your extended families may view the relationships. Sometimes this type of arrangement may unintentionally undermine the ability of your partner and you to view the baby as belonging to both of you. Think through the following questions: Will this seem like incest to you or your families? Will you tell your friends and coworkers or will it remain a family secret? Will your child feel comfortable with the dual role of his or her uncle/donor?

Usually, women don't choose a donor from their family's previous generation, as many cultures have an incest taboo about intergenerational conceptions. Even if the potential donor isn't genetically related to the birth mother—for instance, he may be her or her partner's stepfather—the situation may create feelings of shame for the child or parents.

Discussions and Negotiations With a Potential Donor

The First Conversation

Every initial conversation with a potential donor is unique, with no universal formal structure. Women may first ask a man by calling him, writing him a letter, or asking in person. If you and the donor live near each other, it's probably best to meet in person. It's normal to feel nervous, vulnerable, and awkward. In our culture there's no established model for this kind of request. Keep in mind, however, that there's nothing wrong or embarrassing about asking someone to be a donor. If you act self-confident, you'll set a good tone for the conversation. Many women start by telling the donor they're planning to have children, then ask him if he'd consider donating his sperm to help them. This is the best place to start. If he immediately responds favorably, you could then have an initial conversation discussing why in particular you're asking him, what you envision as his involvement after the baby is born, and what might be the logistics of the process (he may have misperceptions and be shy to ask). Most men, however, need time to consider the prospect before discussing any details.

You aren't obliged to discuss with him who else you've asked, whether he is first or fifth on the list, or why you aren't asking other, perhaps more obvious, people. Do set a tone of candor and direct communication for him to follow. If he needs time to think about it, arrange a time to check in, perhaps in two weeks, so he'll know you want him to seriously consider the proposition. Let him know you can meet again to discuss the details you'll both need to know to decide mutually whether this will work.

Don't expect this first meeting to necessarily be long. It'll probably be most comfortable for both of you if you don't invite him over for a nice dinner and ask him over appetizers to be your donor. Not only may he feel awkward if his answer is clearly no, but you may find yourself stuck with hosting the rest of the meal, when you actually need the privacy to feel disappointed or even rejected. Also, occasionally a man may think your request is some type of sexual proposition and feel very uncomfortable. Plan a way to provide a comfortable end to the meeting for both of you. If you're partnered, remember to include her in this process. If she can't be present at the initial conversation, at least include her in your donor planning. We find that it's common for one woman in a couple to ask a man to be a donor without first consulting with her partner. Sometimes the woman who's planning to conceive will start interviewing people informally without even thinking about involving her partner. This is usually innocently done but can easily hurt the partner's feelings.

Remember, in general, that the nonbiological partner may be concerned about not feeling involved enough. She may also feel that her parental role won't be securely recognized by the other mom, the child, or society in general. This is especially true when using a known donor, since it can resemble a heterosexual connection. Both of you need to be communicative with each other from the very start; you'll both appreciate it later. When you speak with a potential donor, plan ahead that neither you nor your partner will agree to anything in the moment but will confer privately after the meeting. Either of you can put the other on the spot if you speak enthusiastically on behalf of both of you when your partner might actually disagree. Once your potential donor agrees, you're ready to initiate more in-depth negotiations.

Asking for a Sperm Count

As forward as it may seem, we advise you to ask your donor to undergo a sperm count before you go enter into in-depth negotiations. This is a practical first step. If his sperm count is low, he can get an exam to try to discover the cause and begin a program of herbal or vitamin supplements, nutritional changes, or Chinese medicine to improve his fertility. This type of program often needs to be undertaken for a few months to be the most beneficial. If you discover his sperm count is completely not viable, then you'll have saved everyone a tremendous amount of emotional energy and time.

Clarity of Vision

You're trying to negotiate what's possibly going to be one of the most important decisions you'll make in your lifetime. Don't let this overwhelm you; many women choose known donors. Once more, however, we'll remind you that if you haven't fully articulated your desires for yourself, you may find yourself acquiescing to things you normally wouldn't. Clarify your vision before you ask, "What role would you like to have?" You may hear him answer, "Well, I'd like to see the child one night a week, or one weekend a month from the time he or she is six months old." You may hear yourself responding on the spot, "OK, I think I could work with that" before you honestly know whether you can or even want to. Often a woman will feel very strongly about choosing a known donor, but after realizing she has few potential donors in her life, she feels desperate to "make it work." Sometimes women start negotiations from an unexamined place of internalized sexism: *Whatever you want is more important than what I want. As long as I can get the sperm, I'm willing to do whatever it takes. I need to be fair. I need to be grateful.* We often fall into two traps: agreeing to things we don't want and refraining from stating what we do want. We even go so far as to offer things we'd rather not give, before he has even requested anything. It's common to feel indebted to our donors and to want to please them, but don't second-guess your donor at your own expense.

Clear Communication

Entering into this level of dialogue with someone can bring up many emotions. In fact, many women report experiencing the same exhilarating and nervous feelings that arise when they begin to date someone. This is a very powerful thing you're considering doing with each other. In our practice, we've noticed that many lesbians don't have much experience talking with men about intimate issues. It isn't uncommon to have these types of discussions at a very adolescent level. If you feel this may be the case for you, consider bringing a friend or having a third party facilitate these conversations.

When negotiating with a potential donor, stop and reflect back to each other frequently to make sure you're understanding each other: "What I hear you saying is…" Some people find themselves involved in negotiations for years; this isn't necessary. If you're dragging out the process, get some help from a therapist or friend. Either find a new donor or understand why you're holding up the process. If your potential donor is the one taking months to decide whether or not to donate, this should be a red flag. (Months of discussion about a coparenting relationship, on the other hand, can be reasonable.) Reexamine how direct you're being with him. Does he have a specific understanding of your needs and wants, and when you'd like to start trying? Early on in your discussions, ask your potential donor to bring his partner if he has one, so that you can discuss together how the commitment he makes to you will affect his intimate relationship(s). If your donor's partner isn't equally committed to the process, his or her resentments about impositions on their schedules and sex life may create substantial tension in their relationship. It's helpful to meet the partner and get a direct sense of how s/he feels about this joint project, so that your donor doesn't surprise you by bowing out later in deference to his primary relationship.

Partner Issues

Many partnered women fall into certain roles when working through initial conversations with a potential donor. Perhaps one woman knows the donor better. Perhaps the other feels a little more wary. Perhaps because she doesn't know the donor as well, she'll have an easier time asking the tough questions. Perhaps one woman is a softer negotiator, more prone to acquiesce or compromise in the moment. The other may find herself needing to draw all the boundaries, having to say what they both really mean.

If two women haven't known a potential donor for an equal length of time, this inequality might benefit or hinder them in terms of how comfortable they each feel. A nonbiological mother may feel especially left out if the birth mother is very close to the donor. It's important to try to resolve this rather than ignore it. The nonbiological mother can share her feelings with her partner and arrange to spend more time with the potential donor on her own to feel more comfortable with the arrangement. If the choice of donor, however, continues to make her feel left out even prior to the start of insemination, it may be best to seek out a more suitable donor.

Issues for Single Women

It's important to present a clear message to potential donors. Tempting as it may be, a single-mom-to-be should not use her donor as her primary confidante. If you aren't sure what you want from a donor, use a friend or therapist to help you clarify your desires before going further.

Since the donor is the only other person involved in making the baby when you're single, this relationship can often seem like a heterosexual relationship, which may be confusing to you and others. In fact, single women are more likely to put the donor's name on the birth certificate under "father" than partnered women are. It's common to slip into more of a coparenting relationship with a donor than you might have otherwise. This often becomes painfully apparent when a woman later meets a lover—and at that point it's often difficult to change things.

Romantic Feelings for the Donor

Just as with coparents, discussed in Chapter 4, we've seen some women develop romantic feelings for their donors. In fact, it isn't unusual for negotiations with known donors to feel like a courtship. Sometimes a single woman, or either woman in a partnership, will feel like she is falling in love with the donor, which can be a rather awkward surprise. The emotions may not contain any sexual component—just more of a cosmic, romantic "ah, I want to make a baby with you" theme. These feelings can bring up jealousy or cause some women to question their sexual orientation. Sometimes a woman's partner recognizes the energy before she herself does. If you've never been romantically involved with men, or if the connection you're feeling isn't explicitly sexual, it may be a while before you can name the dynamic. Usually, these feelings subside when the baby is born.

In part because of this courtship quality, you may procrastinate about approaching your most promising potential donors because the potential of rejection is so great that perhaps you don't want to even ask.

If you feel your negotiations are emotionally charged, take a look at any negotiations and decision-making situations you've found yourself in in the past. Were they breakups, divorces, past pregnancies, business-partner decisions? Were you and other(s) involved on an equal footing? What was your role? This may help you gain deeper clarity and reduce the emotional charge of your negotiations.

Contracts

We encourage people to draw up contracts as a process of clarification. Documenting all agreements is a good exercise and provides greater legal safety. We find that the document is more meaningful if it's written in language that is legally clear yet heartfelt. This way it will be accessible if you ever want to share the contract with your child. Take note that most of your personal papers will be discovered by your children at some point, so make sure your contract reflects your truest intentions in conceiving your child so that it doesn't serve to undermine your child's self-esteem.

This contract can include a statement of intention on the donor's part to sever paternity rights. The contract needs to state in no uncertain terms what each person's role will be and who will be considered the child's parent/s. Create the contract in such a way that, as the child grows and can verbalize her/his desires, you'll have room for renegotiating any of the decisions to meet your actual circumstances.

Establish guidelines in the contract for addressing conflict between the parties. What will the process be? Will you meet with a therapist or a mediator? Who will pay for these services? Do all parties have to agree to seek outside help or can one party initiate the conflict-resolution process? How will you choose the third party?

These guidelines are the most important part of the contract. Everything else can change over time, but if you have problems, it's essential to have established mechanisms to keep you out of court. Change is fundamental to parenting; therefore, the points in the contract are only your intentions. When change occurs, established agreements about how to work through them will be monumentally helpful. (See the end of the chapter for sample contracts.)

Change Happens

As we started to discuss above, no matter how clear you feel you've been prior to insemination, the nature of your relationship with the donor may change because the child changes it, you change it, or the donor changes it. It's precisely this human element of the unknown that makes using the sperm of a known donor very different from using frozen sperm. With a sperm bank, your relationship to the sperm donor isn't going to change before your child turns 18 (unless you use the sperm bank that releases information when the baby turns 3 months of age). With known donors there's always the chance of change. Perhaps it will be for the better; perhaps it will be a struggle. Part of the nature of parenting is that you often won't know for sure what you really want until you actually are a parent. Before the birth of your child, try not to lock yourself into commitments with the donor that can be tricky to get out of later.

When a Donor Backs Out

If a donor backs out during the process, you'll probably feel rejected, abandoned, or overwhelmed at having to start the process all over. Sometimes these feelings arise because the donor isn't very direct in communicating; he stops returning phone calls or showing up for meetings. Sometimes he gets cold feet at the last minute. This type of loss is often hard to find support for and can feel like being left at the altar. Unfortunately, as mentioned earlier, this is fairly common.

If this happens, don't let it devastate you. It's much better for him to back out now than change his mind in the future over key issues such as custody. Try to take this in stride and use it as an opportunity to reevaluate your options and move forth with either new known-donor possibilities or with a sperm bank.

Specific Topics to Discuss With Your Donor

Will Your Donor Be Out?

As you'll recall, many women choose a known donor so that their child will have options about meeting and knowing him. Don't assume that the donor has the same understanding. He may want to remain anonymous, except to you, of course. Bring up this topic with him before you tell close friends about your negotiations with him, especially if you and your donor share some of the same professional and social circles.

Does your donor have strict guidelines about who may know his role in your baby's conception? Do you have strict guidelines about to whom your donor may disclose the information? Does your donor understand the importance of your guidelines and will he respect them? Do you plan to disclose the donor's identity to your child? If so, bear in mind that as soon as your child is old enough to talk, you'll lose control over who knows and who doesn't.

What does your donor plan to tell his biological family? Will your child be viewing these people as grandparents? Do his family members pose any legal threat to the security of your family? It isn't uncommon to rule out a donor because his family is homophobic. In fact, it's a very important consideration when selecting a donor.

Language

Take the time to decide what you'd like to call the donor, what you'd like the child to call him, and how you'd like the donor to refer to himself. What will the title be for the nature of this relationship? For example, will it be "our donor Greg"? "Uncle Greg"? "Greg"? "Dad"? This is important to discuss. You and your donor may have a discrepancy in terminology. Even if your understanding of the role is similar, the language you each naturally choose to use may be unintentionally different.

You need to know that the donor will support your choice of terminology and will use the same language both in public and directly with the child. Many donors innocently refer to themselves as fathers when the women would never consider "father" to be the appropriate term.

Even if you have a donor agreement stating that he won't share custody, it won't always hold up in court. According to the National Center for Lesbian rights, it's vital to know that if your donor took you to court and could demonstrate that he has a unique role in your *child's* life based on donor status, or that the words "dad" or "father" have been used by people to name his relationship to the child, this testimony may take precedence over any agreements you've made.

Amount of Time in Your Child's Daily Life

How much time would you like this man to have in your life? You need to answer this before you ask yourself how much you would like him in your child's life. Will the child occasionally sleep over at his house? Will the donor see the child once a month? Once a week? On birthdays or holidays? What's important to you? Will your child get to decide when he or she will see him? If you or the donor moves away, how often will the child see the donor? Who decides? Who will pay the travel costs?

Logistics: The Nitty-Gritty

Time Commitment

Prior to inseminating, you should clarify with the donor how many months he will commit to helping you. If your donor is providing fresh sperm, ask if he'll commit to one year. Six months often feels very rushed; it could very well take less than that, but don't limit your options prematurely. You'll want to be clear about whether the specified time period includes months in which you won't inseminate.

If you're freezing sperm for safety reasons or because your donor lives far away, decide on the minimum number of vials you'd like to freeze. Depending on his volume of ejaculate, he may be able to produce one to five vials per ejaculate. Most sperm banks recommend that a donor on average make three to five visits to deposit sperm there. Would you like to have a second child from this donor's sperm? If so, consider freezing enough now for both children. Men can make a deposit every 48 hours, provided they don't ejaculate at any other time outside of their sperm bank visit.

Availability

It's essential that your donor have a clear picture of what will be expected of him on a monthly basis. Make sure he is aware that you can give him a best guess at the start of the cycle but that you often won't know exactly when your most fertile time is until one to two days before or even the day of insemination. How flexible is his daily schedule? Is he willing to rearrange his day with little or no notice? Does he travel often on business? Will he try to arrange to be in town every month during your fertile days? If he will be flying to your location, a flexible schedule is key. Is he available if you need him to inseminate at 10 P.M. or 6 A.M.? How easy is he to reach? Will he return calls promptly? How much advance notice might you receive if he won't be available? Once you start inseminating, you might find it emotionally difficult to skip a cycle. Discuss this with him from the get-go.

Abstinence and Your Donor's Sex Life

You'll need to ask your donor not to ejaculate for 48 hours before he donates for you. If he has ejaculated more recently, his sperm count may be significantly lower. Asking a donor to make this commitment may greatly affect his sex life, and thus it's important to discuss in your initial conversations. Your donor's sexual partner may feel jealousy or resentment when you request this, which is common. Sometimes the partner may pressure the donor to have sex when he's supposed to be abstaining, to prove his loyalty to the romantic relationship. Eventually, the pressure may become too great, and your donor may feel he can no longer donate for you.

Expenses

It's customary for the woman/women to cover any donor expenses. You may incur transportation costs to get to the donor or bring the donor to you. You'll often incur medical costs if you ask the donor to undergo health screenings. If your donor is depositing sperm in a sperm bank, you'll have a sizable up-front cost to have the donor receive the necessary medical screenings and to freeze and store the sperm. If you store the sperm longer than one year, you'll be charged an annual storage fee as well. You can be creative, however, with some of these costs. If you want the donor to undergo initial medical tests, his health insurance may cover a portion of the costs if his primary-care doctor orders the tests. If he doesn't have insurance, he may be able to get a number of the tests for low or no cost at a community health clinic or Planned Parenthood. Sometimes a financial exchange helps the strength of a legal contract. Some women pay their known donors a token amount, or pay them with something other than money, such as food or gifts. Often this exchange helps women feel that they're not indebted to their donor—and vice versa.

Health History

You have the opportunity to find out very specific information about your donor's personal and family health history, if you ask. Women who are involved romantically with men rarely would reject a relationship with a partner because of concern over an inheritable disease. You, however, may choose to make such decisions about a potential donor for your health and that of your child.

For example, you may feel it's important that the donor not have a family history of asthma because you yourself have a family history of asthma, allergies, or eczema. Or the mental health of his family members may be important if chronic depression runs in your family. You may have an understanding of disease that emphasizes environment and lifestyle over genetic predisposition. It's up to you to choose how specific to be when you ask questions, and how relevant the answers are to your decision.

At the end of this chapter is a comprehensive list of medical questions. Adapt it for your own use; you may ask your donor verbally or have him answer the questions in writing. Or you may simplify and ask him whether he or anyone in his immediate family (parents or siblings) has had any illness that may be hereditary. Perhaps you'll only ask about the specific illnesses that concern you. An alternative to doing this detective work for yourself is to ask him to get a physical exam from his health care provider—and fill out a medical history questionnaire at the office—and give you a copy of the records.

Drugs and Alcohol

It's important to inquire about your potential donor's drug, alcohol, and cigarette intake. Marijuana use can significantly decrease men's sperm count and/or motility. Stimulants and alcohol can also decrease fertility. Alcohol, cocaine, and other recreational drugs have recently been shown to affect not only sperm count, but also the health of each individual sperm. Cigarette smoking is detrimental to sperm health, especially if a man has a borderline semen analysis. Some information also suggests that caffeine, a stimulant, can negatively affect male fertility. Other information suggests that some caffeine intake can increase the motility (swimming movement) of sperm. For a discussion on ways to increase men's fertility, read Chapter 8 on fertility inhibitors and enhancers.

A man's drug and alcohol use can be particularly relevant in relationship to safer sex. Many people practice safer sex until they have a few drinks. When unsafe sex occurs under the influence of drugs or alcohol, a man may have no memory of it. This is an important issue to discuss with all potential donors. Make sure that your donor agrees to inform you if he has had unsafe or risky sex.

Sexual Health History

For the sake of your own health as well as that of your sexual partner(s) and your unborn baby, when inseminating it's important to minimize your risk of contracting an infection. This risk, in fact, is what deters most women from using fresh sperm. Your health risks, however, can be significantly decreased if you know which questions to ask your potential donor. Therefore, we want to give you detailed information to prepare you so that you can approach this sometimes touchy subject with your donor.

Many women have inadequate safer-sex discussions with their donors not because of a lack of information on the subject but because of their own discomfort with the intimacy of the topic. If you don't feel comfortable discussing sex practices and sexually transmitted diseases, you can ask a health professional to do this type of screening for you. Perhaps you could see a health professional with your donor. Likewise, for extra safety you may want to consider freezing and quarantining his sperm.

If you think you'd like to ask the donor about his safer-sex practices yourself, or just be better informed, please read on. The amount of information we provide is not to overwhelm you, but to make sure you don't have any gaps in your understanding that may jeopardize the health of you or your unborn child. Again, the key to a positive experience with a known donor is taking the time to communicate carefully.

Specific Infections

Gonorrhea and Chlamydia

Some sexually transmitted (and insemination-transmitted) infections are curable, like gonorrhea and chlamydia. Gonorrhea and chlamydia can be completely asymptomatic in men, meaning they don't cause any noticeable discomfort or sign of infection. These infections are easily treatable with a single course of antibiotics. Because of the serious side effects these infections could have on you or your baby, ask your donor to get a current culture (see recommended health screening tests at the end of this chapter). Although treatable, gonorrhea and chlamydia in women can inhibit conception, inflict permanent infertility (by blocking the tubes with scar tissue), prompt preterm labor during pregnancy, and cause serious eye and lung infections in newborn babies.

HIV, Syphilis, and Hepatitis

A number of other sexually and insemination-transmitted infections are more difficult or impossible to treat. HIV is probably what first comes to mind, but syphilis and various types of hepatitis also fall into this category. HIV is a virus that can destroy the body's immune system. Syphilis is a bacteria that can inflict major organ damage throughout the body. Hepatitis B and C are viral infections that can cause severe liver problems. All of the above infections frequently do not cause noticeable initial symptoms when a person is first infected.

Hepatitis and syphilis will show up in a blood test up to three months after infection. The commonly used ELISA blood test for HIV has become so accurate that, on average, antibodies show up within one month after infection but sometimes take up to six months to appear. Therefore, to ensure your own safety and the safety of your baby, your donor must scrupulously practice safer sex 100% of the time following his health tests until you're pregnant. Ideally, you should get him to commit to practicing safer sex until your pregnancy is well established, so that if you miscarry, you may still continue to use him as a donor.

If a woman becomes infected with any of these diseases, she can transmit them to her baby in utero, possibly causing chronic health problems for the child, or even death. You'll want to ask your potential donor to get screened for HIV and other sexually transmitted diseases. You'll also need to have a detailed discussion with him about sex practices so that you can agree on your definition of safer sex.

Monogamy

If your donor is monogamous (he and his partner only have sex with each other), and he and his partner have both clearly tested negative for HIV and other infections, they have no risk of contracting these diseases, except from the nonsexual ways that infection is transmitted. You should be aware that people have varying definitions of monogamy. Some define monogamy as having sex only within their primary relationship. Others define it as limited and specified kinds of sex outside of a primary relationship. And still others define monogamy as having sex within a primary relationship, but also having group sex with their partner present.

Some people may be sexually exclusive within their relationship but haven't been tested for STDs prior to the beginning of that relationship. Some may have been tested initially but not long enough after leaving their previous partner for the test to be fully accurate. If your donor has been in any of these situations, he should be tested again. **Remember, your donor may be monogamous, but his partner may not be, and your donor may not know this.**

If your donor's partner isn't monogamous, your risk of infection—and your child's risk—substantially increases, unless he or she always practices safer sex with other partners.

Safer-Sex Practices

HIV and all other sexually transmitted diseases (STDs) are transmitted by infected blood (including menstrual blood), semen, vaginal secretions, or other body fluids entering the bloodstream of another person. This infected fluid may enter the bloodstream via blood transfusion, needles shared for drug injection or tattooing, or some S/M practices. It may also enter the bloodstream through tiny invisible openings in the mucus membranes of the mouth, rectum, or vagina. These openings may be sores or irritations from other types of infections, abrasions in the vagina or rectum from incurred through inadequate lubrication, or openings in the mouth from recent flossing, brushing, or gum disease.

Penetrative penile intercourse, whether vaginal or anal, is unsafe if a latex condom isn't used, whether or not ejaculation occurs. The risk of infection is higher for the receptive partner. Oral sex without a latex barrier has been found to be a source of transmission of HIV, although it occurs *much* less frequently than with intercourse. Before a man ejaculates, he secretes a little bit of pre-ejaculatory fluid, also called pre-come, which may also be a source of infection. If a man puts another man's penis in his mouth, there are a variety of ways in which it could be more or less safe. The least safe is if someone ejaculates in his mouth. He may reduce his risk, but not eliminate it, if he doesn't let his partner ejaculate but still puts the head of the penis in his mouth, because he will still be exposed to pre-ejaculatory fluid. Not putting his mouth on the head of his partner's penis reduces his risk even further. Protection can be provided by using an unlubricated latex condom.

Men wanting to be "safe" when having oral sex with women need to use a dental dam or plastic food wrap so their mouths don't come in contact with vaginal secretions and/or menstrual blood. Oral-anal contact is also considered a less-than-safe sexual practice, most notably for the partner using his mouth. Those wishing to partake in this activity may also use dental dams or plastic wrap. In addition, body fluids may be exchanged if shared sex toys are not washed between use.

Condoms

There are a few things to make sure your donor knows about condoms: Lambskin condoms aren't effective barriers against viruses; latex condoms are. Latex condoms can only be used with water-based lubricants, as oils will dissolve the latex. Some people are allergic to the latex in condoms. If so, more recently invented polyurethane condoms can be used. They're more expensive, but they have another benefit in that they can be used with oil. Condoms lubricated with spermicide are slightly more effective in preventing HIV infection and can also be used, except by those who experience reactions to the spermicide.

Condoms may occasionally break if they're old, have been left in the heat or the sun, are poorly made, or have been put on too tightly with no room at the tip for the ejaculate. Sometimes a condom breaks or leaks without either partner being aware of it.

Talking About Sex Practices

It's often challenging for lesbians to question men in detail about their sex lives. Usually, our donors are fairly well known to us, and we may have difficulty being as explicit as possible. You may feel you're invading their privacy. You may also feel that this type of discussion adds yet another level of intimacy to a relationship that would feel more comfortable remaining less intimate. Having a conversation about sex may also seem inherently sexual. Or you may be invested deeply in working with this donor and don't want to discover information that may jeopardize your decision. Finally, you may fear appearing ignorant about gay or straight men's sexual practices.

Many women are able to have the following conversation: "So, do you practice safer sex?" "Yes, I do." "OK, all the time?" "Yeah." Often that is the extent of their discussion. To be thorough, though, read through the above section on safer sex again, thinking about how you might phrase specific questions to find out what you need to know. You might ask the following:

• What does safer sex means to you?
• What is your definition of "monogamous"?
• Do you have oral sex with other men, and if you do, do you use a condom?
• Do you put your mouth on the head of his penis? Do you do that before he ejaculates? When he ejaculates?
• Do you ever drink or do drugs when you have sex? Do you ever have sex when you're intoxicated? Can you be certain you adhere to the same safety standards at those times?

It may help to bring a copy of this book to your donor (and his partner) and read it together. You can photocopy this section and give it to him, and he can read it at home before discussing it with you. It might be easier for him if he reads that this conversation is difficult or awkward for many women (and men too!).

The definition of safer sex differs from person to person. In the gay male community, for example, for years a debate has raged about the risk of unprotected oral sex. Some people feel it's a negligible risk. You can find information from your local health department, the San Francisco AIDS Foundation, and national AIDS hotlines. Your focus in these discussions, however, should be what makes you (and your partner) feel safe and whether your donor can agree to these restrictions, whatever they may be.

Once you both have established exactly what kind of sexual practices your donor can engage in, you need to discuss with him his commitment to tell you if something changes. If you've been through all the testing and negotiating and have started inseminating, he may feel an immense pressure not to admit that he's done something that doesn't adhere to your guidelines. You need to let him know that you trust him to tell you immediately.

If you aren't comfortable with his answers to these vitally important questions about sexual practices, you may want to consider looking for another donor. If you're set on working with a specific donor, but decide after your sex discussion that you feel unsure of his risk of contracting a sexually transmitted infection, consider freezing and quarantining his sperm.

Freezing Donor Sperm

Advantages

If you bring your donor into a sperm bank to have his sperm frozen, it's very much like getting other sperm from the sperm bank except that your donor's sperm is only released to you. In sperm bank lingo he is then called a "directed donor." Women choose to ask their donor to have his sperm frozen for many reasons. They may have concerns about his health; he may not live in their area; he may be planning to have a vasectomy; or they may want to have a second child with his sperm.

Reduced Chance of Infection

You may choose to freeze and quarantine your donor's sperm if you're unsure whether he is HIV-negative. If his sperm freezes well, he can donate a number of vials over a few weeks and have them stored. For his sperm to be released, he'll need to test negative for all the tests for sexually transmitted infections the particular sperm bank requires at the time of donation, and again in six months. If all tests come back negative after six months, his sperm has an almost 100% likelihood of being HIV-negative at the time it was frozen. From that six-month point on, you may use any of that frozen sperm. If you run out before you become pregnant, you'll need to repeat the process.

Geography

Some women choose to freeze sperm because they don't live near their donor. He could donate at a sperm bank near him and have the sperm transferred to a bank near you, or you could order his frozen sperm monthly by mail if you don't live near a sperm bank. He may also travel to your area and freeze a number of vials. Frozen sperm can be brought home in a liquid nitrogen tank where it will remain frozen for up to one week. You can use the sperm whenever you're ready to thaw it.

At the time of this writing, there's a new method for preparing fresh sperm that allows it to be mailed overnight unfrozen without it losing its viability. The technique requires that you inseminate by intrauterine insemination (described in Chapter 12). You may consider this method if your donor's sperm doesn't survive freezing or to avoid the other disadvantages of freezing described below. This is an exciting new option!

Disadvantages

Lower Sperm Count and Effectiveness

Unfortunately, freezing may lower sperm count and/or motility so substantially that it's not a useful option for your particular donor. Doing a semen analysis and freeze-thaw test (described below) is advised immediately upon choosing a long-distance donor so that you may find out how well his sperm survives freezing.

Whenever possible, we recommend using fresh sperm because of its increased effectiveness. You may, however, have a found the perfect donor and feel he warrants this kind of creative problem solving.

Costs

Freezing sperm is expensive. Typical costs include:
- $200 for the first consultation (includes the semen analysis and freeze-thaw test)
- $100 for each donor deposit
- $75 storage fee per year per ejaculate after the first year
- $25 retrieval fee for each vial
- $300-$800 for screening tests and health exam if the sperm bank only accepts tests that they themselves perform on the donor (instead of his private physician's) or if you're paying out of pocket for tests not covered by the donor's health insurance

If you have a long-distance donor, however, freezing sperm may in the long run be less expensive or stressful than paying travel expenses for multiple months of insemination.

Tissue Bank Laws, the FDA, and Gay/Bisexual Donors

State and federal regulations are continually changing about whether gay and bisexual men can be directed donors (and anonymous donors, for that matter) regardless of their HIV status. In the past years, policy changes have occasionally affected a woman's ability to obtain her directed donors' sperm if he was open about being gay or bisexual when he donated. Call your sperm bank to inquire specifically about its policy and any federal changes on the horizon that may affect that policy. If the sperm bank's policy changes, you may not be able access your donor's sperm when you're ready to use it; therefore, inquire about the policy in advance—and periodically.

Medical Testing for the Donor

Semen Analysis

Whether you will request donor health tests is always a personal decision. We recommend, however, that you get a semen analysis (sperm count) for any potential donor as soon as he agrees that he is open to being a donor and that you'll be having further talks. If he doesn't have a high or functional sperm count, you'll want to know immediately, so that you both can come up with a plan. You may know instantly that you'll want to choose another donor, or you may be committed to this donor and want to wait and see if his sperm count can be raised. Your donor would probably want a physical exam for his own information and peace of mind. We know of donors who learned they had testicular cancer when they underwent an exam after an abnormal semen analysis. Furthermore, some men find their infertility is caused by a dilated blood vessel in the testes called a varicocele, which often can be surgically repaired. If Western medicine gives no answers, studies have confirmed the efficacy of acupuncture and other non-Western approaches to improve fertility in many subfertile men. For more information read Chapter 8 on fertility inhibitors and enhancers.

A semen analysis usually costs $60-$100 and can be performed by a sperm bank or in a private physician's lab. At a sperm bank, your donor will probably be given a small container and shown to a private room. If he's working with a private lab or physician, he'll be given a small container and lid, he'll ejaculate at home, and then he'll drop the sample off at the lab within 20-30 minutes of ejaculation. Prior to a semen analysis, he should abstain from ejaculating for at least 48 hours but not more than a week.

Accuracy of the Semen Analysis

Sperm quality can fluctuate greatly from day to day and is also influenced by stress, sleep, drugs, and eating habits. Therefore, if your donor receives abnormal test results, he should have the test repeated so that his fertility can be more accurately assessed. Although a semen analysis is a good starting place to assess a donor's fertility, it isn't the be-all and end-all of fertility tests. If your donor's sperm count is normal and you don't conceive after a number of inseminations, don't assume that

112

you've ruled out all the problems with his sperm with one analysis. Some studies suggest that a sperm count isn't a very accurate predictor of the sperm's fertilizing capacity, beyond identifying obviously abnormal sperm samples, because numerous men with "normal" sperm counts have other infertility challenges. Other tests, such as those that assess how the sperm swim through fertile mucus or whether the sperm can fertilize a hamster egg in a petri dish, often can more accurately tell you whether the donor is infertile or subfertile.

What Exactly Does It Tell Me?

Normal semen contains sperm, hormones, sugars, salts, and secretions. During the semen analysis, a semen sample is examined, shortly after ejaculation, under a microscope and then hourly for up to three hours. Sometimes the semen is incubated at human body temperature for 24 hours and then the sperm is counted again.

A number of factors are evaluated in the semen analysis, not just the number of sperm. The most important is motility (movement), followed by count and morphology (size and shape). We'll describe these factors below, but don't expect to read the following descriptions and then be able to easily interpret your donor's semen analysis. If the results are questionable to you, or clearly low, seek further expertise. If your donor has the analysis performed at a sperm bank, they should explain the results to both of you. Some will even invite him into the lab to look through the microscope and see what they're measuring. If his private doctor orders the test, she or he may be able to do some basic interpretation, although male infertility will probably be not the doctor's specialty. In Western medicine, male and female infertility specialists are called reproductive endocrinologists.

• **Volume:** 1-5 cc is average. A cc is the same as a milliliter (abbreviated ml). The number of cc's in the ejaculate multiplied by the number of motile (moving) sperm per cc, will give the total number of motile sperm for that fresh donation. For example, if an average volume of ejaculate for one man is 3 cc's and his average count is 70 million motile sperm per cc, then an average ejaculate will contain 210 million motile sperm total. Volume can vary quite a bit depending on the man's mood, whether he has ejaculated within the past 24–48 hours, and often whether he ejaculates alone or with the help of a sex partner.

• **pH:** Level should be similar to that of fertile cervical mucus, slightly alkaline; 7-8 is normal.

• **Viscosity:** Semen liquefies after ejaculation, which makes it easier for the sperm to swim. At 15-30 minutes, desired viscosity is plus 4 on a scale of 1-4.

• **Motility:** Normal motility (movement) is 50% or greater with good forward movement within 2 hours of ejaculation.

• **Sperm count:** This is the actual number of sperm (motile and nonmotile) per cc of semen. Currently, 20-160 million/cc is normal. Sperm banks usually guarantee a minimum of 20 million motile sperm in each vial for vaginal insemination, and about 25 million motile sperm in each vial washed for intrauterine insemination. A donor's fresh (not frozen) complete ejaculate, however, will ideally have considerably more than this because you get an entire ejaculate (not just .5-1cc) and none of the sperm are lost during freezing.

• **Morphology:** This describes the shape of the sperm; for example: two tails, no tail, two heads, wrong-size head, or tail not as long as normal. There's a lot of variation in how sperm are classified as normal or abnormal and what percentage of sperm can be abnormally shaped before fertility is affected. Because of this, different labs doing different kinds of morphology assessment may give you different amounts and kinds of information.

You may be surprised at how many sperm, on average, are abnormally shaped. It's helpful to understand that the body's approach to sperm production focuses on quantity more than quality. Millions upon millions of sperm are produced constantly by the male body. Most of these sperm that are misshaped do not move as effectively through the fertile mucus into the uterus, and therefore are naturally filtered out during intercourse or vaginal insemination. If too many of the sperm are abnormally shaped, the number of normal, functional sperm may be significantly low even if the overall sperm count is high. Furthermore, if many of the sperm are even slightly abnormally shaped, a high percentage of them may not be able to complete the various steps they need to perform in the fallopian tube near the egg in order to fertilize it. Therefore, some information about the shape of the sperm can indicate other aspects of its fertile potential that cannot be observed just by looking through a microscope.

In terms of morphology, the World Health Organization classifies a "normal" semen sample as one with less than 30% of its sperm abnormally shaped. A different type of classification that counts even slight differences in shape and size as abnormal is called a strict Kruger assessment. Some men have few sperm that are *very* abnormally shaped but many that are just *slightly* abnormal. These may not be counted as abnormal on a "regular" semen analysis that only defines abnormal as very misshaped or sized. Slight abnormalities, however, may actually be significant factors in the ability of sperm to fertilize an egg. Therefore, a semen analysis that includes a strict Kruger assessment can give you more detailed information. Sperm banks often define normal semen as that which contains up to 40% abnormally shaped sperm.

• **White blood cells (WBCs):** These are part of the body's immune system. More than 10 per high-powered microscope field (hpf) could indicate an infection of the reproductive tract. This should be treated prior to insemination.

• **Freezing viability (when applicable):** A semen analysis is repeated after sperm have been frozen for 48 hours and then thawed. Remember, even men whose sperm freezes well can expect to lose 50% of their live sperm through freezing and thawing, which means that starting with a high sperm count is important. Most men have adequate fresh sperm counts in their semen samples but lose more than 50% of this sperm during the freezing process. In fact, one sperm bank tells men that, on average, only one man out of six has sperm that will freezes well, and another sperm bank turns away 80-90% of donor applicants, primarily because their sperm won't freeze well enough. In other words, most men won't be giving you an optimally fertile sample if their sperm will be frozen.

Other Tests

The following is a comprehensive list of the medical tests required of men who donate sperm at sperm banks. You may choose to ask your donor to have some or all of these, depending on your budget, his insurance, and his sexual or health history. Most tests come back from the lab with the normal healthy results printed next to your donor's results for reference. Go ahead and ask for a copy of the lab work if you wish. We provide brief descriptions here for your information; however, the health practitioner who orders the tests should explain the results to you or your donor. Speak up if you don't completely understand.

• **HIV-1 and HIV-2:** HIV 1 is more prevalent in the U.S. HIV 2 is a different strain of the virus and is much more common in Africa. If a donor is tested at an "anonymous" testing center, he will probably only be tested for HIV 1. The "regular" blood test isn't a test for the actual virus, but a test for the antibody that one's immune system makes after it has been infected. One never has the HIV antibody without being infected. The time between infection and seroconversion (when the antibody being tested for will actually show up in the blood) is usually two weeks to three months, although it can take up to 6 months. The test very rarely shows negative when someone is actually infected. If the test comes back positive, it's retested twice, once with a more specific and expensive test, before results are released. Thus, a positive HIV result is confirmed by three tests.

There are a few other more expensive tests that check for parts of the virus itself. These will produce positive results sooner after infection than the antibody test. If you're ready to inseminate very soon and your donor has had a recent risk of exposure to the virus, you or your donor may discuss these types of tests with a physician. Some donors who have HIV-positive partners do such a test, called a PCR, before each insemination to make sure they haven't recently become infected.

• **RPR (also known as VDRL, STS, or serologic test for syphilis):** This blood test is for syphilis, a sexually transmitted bacteria that can be treated with penicillin.

• **Hepatitis B surface antigen and antibody, core antibodies:** This is a blood test for the sexually and blood-transmitted virus that causes Hepatitis B, an infection of the liver that can cause serious liver damage. Someone who has been vaccinated against Hepatitis B will show positive surface antibodies.

• **Hepatitis C Antibody:** If a person tests positive for hepatitis C antibodies, they're considered to be infected with hepatitis C. An entirely different virus than hepatitis B, hepatitis C is transmittable sexually and especially through blood exposure (sharing any kind of needles, for example). After many years, hepatitis C can cause severe damage to the liver. Current statistics show that 5% of pregnant women infected with hepatitis C transmit it to their infants in the uterus.

• **Cytomegalovirus (CMV), IGG, and IGM:** CMV is a virus that many of us have been exposed to at some point in our lives. It usually will only make you sick if your immune system isn't working well. Once exposed, you'll test positive for IGG antibodies for the rest of your life, meaning that your immune system has a memory of the infection. Active infection will give you a positive test result for IGM antibodies in the bloodstream. Getting an active CMV infection while pregnant can cause birth defects such as central nervous system damage, brain damage, and hearing loss.

• **Chlamydia and Genital Culture:** This is the test for chlamydia and gonorrhea, bacterial infections that can be treated with a short course of antibiotics.

• **Urinalysis, Complete Blood Count (CBC), and Chem Panel (Blood Chemistry):** These are tests with many components that assess someone's overall health. Most laboratories print out a range of normal values next to the results of the tests, so that you can fairly easily see when a result is abnormal. Interpretation of what that information means requires help from a health care practitioner.

Some of the inheritable diseases that can be tested are: Tay-Sachs, cystic fibrosis, and abnormal hemoglobins such as those that cause sickle-cell anemia and thalassemia.

When Will You Know You're Ready to Start Inseminating?

You may start to inseminate as soon as any important health test results come back, or you may all know months in advance that you're ready, just waiting for the month to arrive that you plan to start inseminating. You'll know that you're either stuck at an impasse or don't actually want to use this donor if the month that you were going to begin inseminating comes and goes without insemination. Likewise, when you've worked out all of logistics but cannot bring yourself to call the donor, you'll know some hidden feelings may need to be examined.

You have the right to decide at any time that you don't want this man to be your donor. This is your family you're creating, and if at any time you don't feel fully at ease, you need to speak up. If you're partnered and both of you have different senses of comfort with the donor, you both need to have some careful, honest, specific—and possibly uncomfortable—conversations. Not feeling safe about the sperm you put in your body, or your lover's body, for whatever reason, isn't conducive to conception. Be sensitive to the fact that your donor has feelings too, and through this process he has undoubtedly grown emotionally invested. Be kind, considerate, and prompt in letting him know that you no longer wish to use him as your donor, if that is your decision.

You also have the right to declare that you're ready whenever you feel so, regardless of the cautious advice you may get from others. Listen to their advice, decide if it merits some attention, then moved forward. You're the one(s) who are making a baby. The initiative to jump off that cliff into parenthood can only be taken by you. Trust your intuition. Go forward. You may have spent six months or four years planning with your donor; you may have spent two weeks or two days. When you're ready to start inseminating, it's time to read Part Four: "Conception."

Resources

Books
Challenging Conceptions, Lisa Saffron, Cassell, 1994
Having Your Baby by Donor Insemination, Elizabeth Noble, Houghton Mifflin, 1998
Helping the Stork: The Choices and Challenges of Donor Insemination, Carol Frost Vercollone, Heidi Moss, and Robert Moss, Hungry Minds, 1997

Organizations
National Center for Lesbian Rights (offers legal lesbian family support nationwide)
870 Market St., #570
San Francisco, CA 94102
(415) 392-6257
www.nclrights.com

OverNite Male™ Program (sends fresh semen donations via Federal Express)
University of Illinois at Chicago Andrology Laboratory
Call the andrology coordinator at (312) 996-7713
or visit www.uic.edu/com/mcsr/androlab/welcome.htm

Prospective Queer Parents (support group with contacts for lesbian women and gay men wanting to create family together)
E-mail: Pqp@gayspermbank.com or contact Leland Traiman at (510) 854-2358.

Known-Donor Health Screening Questions

Your donor's answers to these questions will provide you with a wealth of information about his health. You'll probably need assistance from a health care provider to interpret how some of these questions may affect the health of you or your future child. If your donor is planning to undergo a physical exam, which we recommend, ask him to bring this completed form with him so that his health care provider can review it; it's probably more specifically fertility-related than the list of questions his care provider would normally ask. During the exam, his health care provider will also do something called a "Review of Systems," which includes many questions about current symptoms your donor may have that he might otherwise forget to mention. We haven't included basic questions of this nature here.

Environmental Exposure

- In your work are you exposed to any health hazards such as asbestos, radiation, toxic chemicals, etc.?
- Have you been exposed to any of these in any of your hobbies or pastimes?
- Have you been exposed to any toxic agents in the military or anywhere else?

Sexual Activity

- Do you have sex with men, women, or both?
- Please mark the activities you engage in sexually, even if not frequently. Note how often you use condoms or plastic protectors: always, mostly, sometimes, never.

1) put someone's penis in your rectum
2) put someone's penis in your mouth
3) put your penis in someone's rectum
4) put your penis in someone's mouth
5) put your penis in someone's vagina
6) put your mouth on someone's rectum
7) put your mouth on someone's vagina
8) only engage in mutual masturbation

- Have you recently had an HIV test? If so, how long ago and what were the results?
- Do you have a regular partner?
- Do you have sex with people other than your partner?
- Does your partner have sex with people other than you?
- Has your partner had an HIV test? When was the most recent? Was it negative or positive?

• How many people have you had sex with in the past year?

• If you have used condoms, have any broken in the past year?

• In the past year have you experienced a change in the type or safety of your sexual activities on occasions when you have drunk alcohol, used drugs, or partied?

Drug and Alcohol Use

• How often do you drink alcohol:

____ not at all

____ once a week or less

____ 2-3 times a week

____ daily or almost daily

• Which of these applies to your alcohol consumption:

____ When I drink it's usually one or two.

____ When I drink it's usually three or more.

____ When I drink I never get drunk.

____ When I drink I rarely have gotten drunk.

____ When I drink I occasionally get drunk.

____ When I drink I usually get drunk.

____ I get drunk most weekends.

• Do you smoke cigarettes? If so, how many per day?

• Are you exposed to secondhand smoke at work, home, with friends, or when you're out socially?

• Do you smoke marijuana? If so, how often?

• Do you use other recreational drugs? If so, which ones and how often?

• Are you in recovery from alcohol or substance abuse? If yes, from which substances and how long have you been clean and sober?

Medical History

• Has a woman conceived with your sperm in the past? If so, how many times? How many children have you helped conceive?

• Are you adopted?

• Do you have access to the medical history of both of your biological parents?

• If no, which do you not have access to?

• Do you have any inherited disorder, such as hemophilia or sickle-cell anemia?

• Do you carry a gene for any inherited disorder, such as anemias caused by thalassemia, sickle-cell anemia, or Tay-Sachs disease? Cystic fibrosis?

• Have you ever had a serious illness or accident? If so, explain.

• Have you ever had surgery?
• Have you ever been hospitalized for anything other than surgery?
• Have you ever had a blood transfusion? If so, when and where?
• Do you currently take any medications? If so, for what?
• Check and describe if you've had any of the following diseases or conditions:

___ allergies
___ anemia
___ arthritis
___ asthma
___ blood diseases
___ cancer
___ coronary artery disease
___ depression
___ diabetes
___ dyslexia
___ epilepsy
___ gallbladder problems
___ glaucoma
___ heart attack
___ heart malformation
___ high cholesterol
___ hypertension
___ liver disease
___ migraine headaches
___ polycystic renal disease
___ nervous or mental disorders
___ phlebitis/blood clots
___ respiratory illness
___ shingles
___ spina bifida
___ stroke
___ thyroid disease
___ tuberculosis
___ ulcers

Sexually Transmitted Infections:
___ chlamydia
___ genital herpes

____ genital warts

____ gonorrhea

____ syphilis

____ other sexually transmitted infections

Family History

- Do twins or multiple births run in your family?
- Does any member of your family have a serious birth defect?
- Are there known genetic diseases in your family?
- Did your mother take the drug DES when she was pregnant with you?
- Did any of your siblings die in infancy or childhood?
- Do you or any member of your family have any diseases or conditions that you haven't already mentioned in the questionnaire?
- Have any of your blood relatives had any of the following problems? (include your parents, your children, your siblings, grandparents, first cousins, aunts and uncles)

____ alcoholism/drug addiction

____ any medical problem with a possible genetic cause

____ blindness

____ colon cancer

____ congenital anomalies (birth defects)

____ congenital heart disease

____ congenital hip dysplasia

____ convulsive disorders

____ deafness

____ diabetes before age 50 controlled by diet

____ diabetes before age 50 not controlled by diet (type 1 or 2)

____ heart disease before age 50

____ intestinal cancer

____ manic depression/bipolar disorder

____ mental retardation

____ muscular dystrophy

____ neural tube anomalies (anencephaly, hydrocephaly, spina bifida)

____ neurological disorders

____ polycystic renal disease

____ schizophrenia

____ severe high blood pressure before age 50

____ thyroid disorders

• List the age of your relatives, or if they have died, the age they were when they died and the cause of death:

mother's mother _____

mother's father _____

father's mother _____

father's father _____

mother _____

father _____

brothers _____

sisters _____

children _____

Sample Known-Donor Contract

This is one version of many boilerplate contracts women have used with known donors. We encourage people to make their contract personal by using their own names instead of "donor" and "recipient." Include the recipient's partner if she is also taking on the role of parent, and include a paragraph by the donor and the recipients about what is motivating them to make this agreement. Our suggestions here are based on how a child or young adult may feel in the future when reading the agreement that preceded their conception. This document should be written out of love and conscientious choice—not just to prevent a possible legal dispute.

This agreement is made this _____ day of _____ by and between _____, hereafter referred to as the DONOR, and _____, hereafter referred to as the RECIPIENT, who may also be referred to herein as "parties."

Now, therefore, in consideration of the promises of each other, the DONOR and RECIPIENT agree as follows:

1. Each clause of this AGREEMENT is separate and divisible from others, and if a court should refuse to enforce one or more clauses of this AGREEMENT, the others are still valid in full force.

2. The DONOR has agreed to provide his semen to the RECIPIENT for the purpose of insemination. (Add the following clauses if applicable.) [The parties have further agreed that the DONOR's semen may be frozen at the time of donation and may be used by the RECIPIENT at a subsequent time.] [However, the frozen semen remains the property of the DONOR and its use for the insemination my be stopped at any time the DONOR deems appropriate.]

3. In exchange for the DONOR's services, the RECIPIENT agrees to pay the sum of \$____ dollars or _____ in lieu of cash to the DONOR each and every time he makes a semen donation.

4. (The marital status of each party. One example given.)
Each party is single and has never been married.

5. (Statement about how long the DONOR agrees to donate and that the RECIPIENT is inseminating.)
Each party acknowledges and agrees that during the calendar

year/s _____, the RECIPIENT is attempting to become pregnant by insemination and that such inseminations will continue until conception occurs.

6. Each party acknowledges and agrees that the DONOR is providing his semen for the purpose of said inseminations, and does so with the clear understanding that he will not demand, request, or compel any guardianship, custody, or visitation rights with any child(ren) resulting from the insemination procedure. Further, the DONOR acknowledges that he fully understands that he will have no parental rights whatsoever with said child(ren).

7. Each party acknowledges and agrees that the RECIPIENT, through this AGREEMENT, has relinquished any and all rights that she might otherwise have to hold the DONOR legally, financially, or emotionally responsible for any child(ren) that result from the inseminations. The RECIPIENT may legally share her sole parenting responsibility with a partner of her choice, if the partner adopts the child. The DONOR need not be consulted, nor is his approval required for the adoption (if this is legally the case). OR the DONOR will not interfere in any decisions the RECIPIENT makes to have another person, male or female, adopt and coparent the child (ren). OR the RECIPIENT acknowledges that she and _____ share full parenting responsibility of the child(ren) of said known-donor insemination.

8. Each party acknowledges and agrees that the sole authority to name any child(ren) resulting from the insemination shall rest with the RECIPIENT.

9. Each party acknowledges that the DONOR shall not be named as the father on the birth certificate of any child(ren) born from the insemination.

10. *(if applicable)* Each party acknowledges and agrees that the use of a licensed physician to receive the semen donations as well as the execution of this agreement, were specifically chosen to avoid any finding that the DONOR is the legal father of the child(ren) pursuant to _____ (name and section number of state statute, if applicable). Consistent with that purpose, each party has executed this AGREEMENT with the purpose of clarifying his or her intent to re-

lease and relinquish any and all rights she or he may have to bring suit to establish the paternity of any child(ren) conceived through insemination.

11. Each party covenants and agrees that, in light of the expectations of each party as stated above, the RECIPIENT shall have absolute authority and power to appoint a guardian for her child(ren), and that the RECIPIENT and such guardian may act with sole discretion as to all legal, financial, medical, and emotional needs of any said child(ren) without any involvement with or demands of authority from the DONOR.

12. (*if desired*) Each party covenants and agrees that neither of them will identify the DONOR as the parent of the child(ren), nor will either of them reveal the identity of the DONOR to any of their respective relatives or to any individual without the express written consent of the other party. OR Each party agrees that the DONOR will not be referred to by himself or by the RECIPIENT as "Father" or "Dad" to friends and family, as he has relinquished paternity rights.

13. Each party acknowledges and agrees that the relinquishment of all rights, as stated above, is final and irrevocable. The DONOR further understands that his waivers shall prohibit action on his part for custody, guardianship, or visitation in any future situation, including the event of the RECIPIENT's disability or death.

14. Each party acknowledges and agrees that any future contact the DONOR may have with any child(ren) that result from the insemination in no way alters the effect of this agreement. Any such contact will be at the discretion of the RECIPIENT and will be consistent with the intent of both parties to sever all parental rights and responsibilities of the DONOR. All parties do also acknowledge that in the best interest of the child, if the child at any time requests to meet or form a friendship with the DONOR, it is the intention of the DONOR to be receptive to such contact. All agree that any friendship formed between the DONOR and the child(ren) does not construe a parental relationship with any of its concomitant rights or responsibilities.

15. (*if desired*) The DONOR agrees to keep the RECIPIENT

updated with current address and other contact information so that the child(ren) can make contact in the future.

(Other points to add as appropriate: anything else you negotiate specifically about health practices, safer-sex practices, how he'll be available to you during the month to donate, how he'll communicate if he needs to change your arrangement, etc. You can be as specific as you want; whether or not the points of your contract are enforceable in court, they are important to include for all of your mutual understanding and memory.)

16. Each party covenants and agrees that any dispute pertaining to the AGREEMENT that arises between them shall be subject to the following process:

(Outline the process in detail, whether it will be with a family counselor or a mediator or through binding arbitration. Binding arbitration may be listed as the process to be used if all others fail. Specify how a counselor or arbitration team will be chosen, who will pay, and what the time line will be for the process.)

17. Each party acknowledges and understands that there may be legal questions raised by the issues involved in this AGREEMENT which have not been settled by statute or prior court decision. Notwithstanding the knowledge that certain clauses stated herein may not be enforced by a court of law, the parties choose to enter into this AGREEMENT as binding.

18. Each party acknowledges and agrees that she or he signed this AGREEMENT voluntarily and freely, of his or her own choice, without any duress of any kind whatsoever. It is further acknowledged that each party has been advised to secure the advice and consent of an attorney of his or her own choosing, and that each party understands the meaning and significance of each provision of the AGREEMENT.

19. Each party acknowledges and agrees that any changes made in the terms and conditions of this AGREEMENT shall be made in writing and signed by both parties.

20. This AGREEMENT contains the entire understanding of the parties. There are no promises, understandings, agreements, or representations between the parties other than those expressly stated in this AGREEMENT. In witness whereof the parties hereunto have executed this AGREEMENT, consisting of ___ typewritten

pages, in the City of _____, County of _____,
State of _____, on the date and the year first written
above.

DONOR _____

RECIPIENT _____

Chapter 6 Unknown Donors and Sperm Banks

The proliferation of sperm banks friendly to lesbian, bisexual, and single women in the last two decades has introduced new possibilities and decisions into the realm of conception options. Lesbians started their own sperm banks for several important reasons. Unmarried women, both now and in the past in many states and nations, have often had limited access to sperm bank services and infertility treatments. When the first overtly lesbian-friendly sperm bank opened in 1982, the AIDS epidemic was just beginning. Lesbians were seeing their male friends getting sick and dying from a disease whose modes of transmission were not yet well understood. Lesbians wanted to be able to choose sperm that had been quarantined and retested. They also wanted easier access to sperm from anonymous donors, which would eliminate the risk of being sued for custody by the biological father. Up until that point, many lesbians relied on go-betweens to choose and screen a donor, arrange the sperm exchange, and maintain each party's anonymity. Some women still choose to use a go-between.

Purchasing sperm from a sperm bank has become a common choice for many women. Despite the benefits sperm banks offer, finding one's way through a medicalized, profit-driven business often feels confounding. Working with a sperm bank requires that women entertain the philosophical and spiritual questions raised by choosing to conceive in a fashion that precludes a child's access to information regarding the identity of his or her biological father. In this chapter, we focus mainly on sperm banks as the primary option for women seeking anonymous donors, although we also address working with a go-between and choosing to partake in anonymous sex.

Sperm Banks

This section covers in detail the benefits and drawbacks of sperm banks, how sperm banks work, and tips and tricks for optimizing your relationship with them.

Sperm Bank Benefits

Sperm banks may offer you the best chance of finding healthy sperm that is free of transmittable infection. There is, however, no system that can completely guarantee your safety, but the exhaustive method of testing, quarantining, retesting, and releasing is the standard today. Any donor option that doesn't involve freezing and retesting the sperm must rely upon the donor's word that he practices safer sex, either by monogamy or through safer-sex practices. Tests taken by a donor giving fresh sperm will reveal if he has not been infected up until recently, but will not necessarily show infections contracted in the past few weeks to few months (depending on the type of virus or bacteria).

Using sperm from a bank ensures that you won't have to worry about the threat of a custody dispute from the donor or any of his family members. Of all available options, many women feel most secure obtaining sperm from an anonymous donor. Some don't want to have to interact directly with any men when choosing how they would like to conceive their child. This donor option certainly removes the need for interacting with donors. Interactions must occur, however, with all sorts of other people, including health care practitioners, the sperm bank receptionist, and the sperm bank health educator.

A number of women wish to select sperm from a sperm bank because they may select a donor based on many details of his identity: ethnic background, height, weight, education, religion, aspects of his medical history, etc. In addition, sperm banks won't change their minds like known donors can, and you can count on their regular business hours for scheduling. Still, if you need to pick up sperm from the bank, you may be inconvenienced by their hours. Having sperm shipped to your home or doctor's office may be easier, although you'll incur cost and have to send the liquid nitrogen tank back as well as create a system for where and when the tank will be delivered.

Ethical Considerations of Using Sperm Banks

Women who choose to work with a sperm bank often need to make some kind of peace with the idea that neither they nor their child will have access to the donor, even if they're very happy about the other advantages the sperm bank offers. In fact, many women who are pleased about not having to interact and negotiate with a man about the sperm still feel a sense of fear or loss about making a permanent decision to give up access to their donor's identity. This is an important issue to work through, so that you don't hold some subconscious grudge each time you inseminate. This issue is especially important to work through before you try to explain to your child how and why you made the choices you did about his or her conception. Making peace with your decision will allow you to convey pride in your choices regarding his or her creation.

Continuing the discussion from earlier in this book, you may feel secure in your belief that "family" is who loves and cares for you, not who you're biologically related to. You may believe that your openness to your child's questions, and your confidence about your answers, will help your child feel secure with the choices you've made. Or you may have mixed feelings about not being able to give your child either information about or access to the donor, if he or she should ask, and you may be concerned that your child will feel "half-adopted."

Many women find that their attitudes toward anonymous sperm donors are influenced by their conversations with friends who have been adopted. Some adults who were adopted as children feel adamant about reserving a child's right to access information about their biological parents, while others feel their adoption has lead to their belief that love, not biology, is what makes a family. Many feel it's important to distinguish between the experience of someone whose biological parents gave them up for adoption and the experience of someone raised by people who actively chose to create him or her assisted by a donor who also consciously chose to contribute to the child's creation.

All these ethical questions are very personal and intimate, with no clear right or wrong answers. Making a final decision about using a known or unknown donor is, in fact, where the majority of women reach an impasse in moving toward their goal of getting pregnant; they feel incapable of making such a big and permanent decision about someone else's life. Feeling secure in your decision requires trusting your own beliefs and values as well as your thoroughness of researching what you need to know to make an informed decision and your good intentions to make the best choice for your future child and family. Making this decision takes self-love and confidence. If you're partnered, it also requires clear communication and respect for each other's points of view. If you feel paralyzed about making a decision about where to obtain sperm, review Chapter 2: "Making Decisions."

As we've mentioned, several sperm banks offer "identity-release" programs that provide your child access to donor contact information when he or she turns 18. These programs allow women to choose to use sperm banks while alleviating some of their concerns about not having a known donor. For more information, see the resource list at the end of this chapter.

Sperm Bank Drawbacks

Frozen sperm is less fertile than fresh sperm for a number of reasons. First, the freezing process somewhat reduces the sperm's capacity to fertilize an egg, in part from the solution added to the semen to help it freeze better. Also, instead of living in the cervix for two to three days post insemination, sperm that has been frozen usually only lives 24 hours due to changes caused by the freezing process. Furthermore, the amount of sperm purchased in a vial is only one portion of the ejaculate, and a number of the sperm die during the freeze-thaw process. Thus, both the total number of sperm and their longevity are reduced.

Because of these limitations, women using frozen sperm must chart their cycle carefully to take advantage of optimum timing for their inseminations each month. Many women choose intrauterine insemination (IUI) instead of vaginal insemination, in hopes that it will increase the efficacy of each insemination.

Finally, women need to be aware that it often just takes more cycles to conceive with frozen sperm. On average, the probability by having intercourse is 20% per cycle. By vaginal insemination with frozen sperm, the probability is 4-10% per cycle. By intrauterine insemination with frozen sperm, the probability is 8-18% per cycle. Very little data exists for the probability of vaginal insemination with fresh sperm, but it's probably equal to or slightly lower than that for intercourse.

If a woman lives in an area where doctors refuse to provide fertility services to unmarried women, or are limited in their ability to do so, she may not be able to find a provider who can help her perform an intrauterine insemination.

Additionally, if women wish to inseminate with more than two vials per cycle, they may be frustrated by inflexible sperm bank policies that allow the release of only two vials per woman per cycle, or by the costs of buying three to four vials of sperm per cycle.

The high cost of buying sperm at a sperm bank can be prohibitive. It's also difficult to budget for an expense that could be incurred for one month or 12. Many women charge all of the expenses on their credit cards, wondering how they'll start to pay off the bill when they're in mid pregnancy, while simultaneously saving for maternity leave and the expenses of their newborn child.

Almost all sperm banks choose to receive tissue-bank certification as a marker of quality control. Tissue-bank certification requires sperm banks to follow the same rules as those of blood banks, denying men who have had any sexual contact with other men in the last seven years the opportunity to donate, regardless of their sexual-practice history or their disease-screening results. Many gay women would prefer to use sperm from gay men. But unless gay men lie when filling out their sperm-bank questionnaires, they cannot donate. One sperm bank on the West Coast, Rainbow Flag Health Services, offers donors who are gay or bisexual. Their contact information is listed at the end of this chapter in the resource section.

Sometimes women have trouble trusting a business, and the strangers who work there, to do such important screening and maintain the high level of integrity necessary in regard to sperm quality. Some women choose to be inseminated at their doctor's office instead of at home, just so they can see the sperm under the microscope to verify that it's actually moving. Others buy an inexpensive microscope at a toy store or use a fertility lens for this same purpose at home.

Often sperm donors are in their early 20s. As they get older, donors may discover things about their health history that would be significant for you to know. In extreme situations, sperm banks try to contact women who have received the donor's sperm and update them; this can only happen, however, if the donor contacts the bank about a change is his health. This is a valid concern for anyone working with a young donor, whether known or unknown. If the donor is known to you, however, you may feel assured that you'd be contacted by him in such an event.

How Do Women Choose a Donor?

Choosing a sperm bank donor is different from choosing a known donor. A sperm bank can offer a more in-depth interrogation about personal and family medical health history than social convention easily allows. Sperm banks offer a wider range of options in terms of donor race and other inheritable characteristics than many women have available in their communities of potential known donors.

Most women find the concept of choosing a donor based on height, weight, ethnicity, skin tone, age, eye color, hobbies, or level of education to be somewhat surreal or even uncomfortable. Women wonder how to make a decision based on these characteristics and what that says about themselves and their values. Lesbians conceiving with sperm from a known donor often pick a man with whom they have a solid relationship of trust, without a primary regard for his physical characteristics. It's uniquely through a sperm bank catalog that a whole new method of selecting genetic makeup occurs.

Matching Your Partner's Characteristics

Sometimes women choose a donor based on their desire to match his characteristics to their partner's in terms of skin tone, hair color and texture, etc. This often comes from a desire to create a likeness that will publicly symbolize family, since many will perceive the child as being of the same or similar ethnic background as the nonbirth mother. Many lesbian couples share a common desire with heterosexual couples that their child look similar enough to either mother that a biological connection might be assumed. In this way lesbians often hope to lessen how often they need to answer questions about family structure and biology as mothers of adopted children or interracial children often must: "Are you her *real* mother?" This reduces the amount of basic education queer women and their children have to do with strangers in casual situations.

Single Women's Freedom

In many ways single women aren't as bound by these concerns. Many single women choose a donor who looks similar to them, on paper at least, although the baby will share half of his or her genetic makeup, and therefore some physical characteristics, with his or her mother, no matter what the donor looks like.

Donor's Interests and Passions

Some women choose a donor based not on physical characteristics but on other qualities, such as physical or intellectual capabilities or temperament. This kind of information, which is usually available on the donor form, may describe years and type of formal education, self-reported hobbies and crafts, and interest in sports. Women may extrapolate from this to form a picture of the donor in regard to his innate capacities. Or they may perceive instead that education and abilities are as much mitigated by circumstance, opportunity, and culture as by inheritable capacity. You may have numerous realizations about the assumptions you make along these lines, especially if you see your assumptions reflected back to you or contrasted by your partner's choices or your friends' opinions about your donor list.

Identifying Positive Attributes

Some women feel that a substantial shortcoming in the anonymous donor choice is not being able to get a sense of the donor's personality in terms of inner qualities such as generosity, compassion, kindness, patience, or any other trait that feels important. Many women feel that at least some aspect of these traits is a matter of inherited potential, not environmental upbringing. They pore over their donor forms trying to gather a sense of these qualities from his volunteer or political activities or even his handwriting style. Some women put a lot of trust in their own intuitive sense or that of the workers at the sperm bank.

Examine How You're Selecting a Donor

Take a careful look at your ideas about what exactly influences people to be who they are fundamentally so that you can be clear about how you're making your choices. If you and your partner are at odds with how you're going about the process, understanding your own and each other's preferences and beliefs will help you both to communicate more effectively and less defensively. Choosing a donor will usually not be a casual decision where compromise is easy.

It's a common and natural progression for your criteria for choosing a donor to change over time. Personal characteristics often become less important than sperm count and motility if you've inseminated a number of times without conceiving.

That doesn't mean that your earlier choices were awry or that you care less now about who the donor is. Your priorities are merely shifting to focus more directly on your primary goal: getting pregnant!

How Do Sperm Banks Work?

Sperm banks are businesses. There's only one nonprofit sperm bank in the U.S. (The Sperm Bank of California); nonetheless, it too is a business. Sperm banks sell sperm to women wishing to conceive. They recruit donors, screen them, freeze and store sperm and release it to you or your doctor for a fee.

Where Do Sperm Banks Find Donors?

Often donors are solicited through advertising at local universities or medical schools. Usually, sperm banks are located in large urban areas where young, healthy men are specifically recruited. Many sperm banks also rely on their donors' word-of-mouth referrals to other men.

Why Do Men Donate?

Men donate sperm for a variety of reasons. You may be able to read their answers to this question and many others on their history form. Many donors are in their early 20s, and their answers reflect their worldview. There are a few common reasons for donating sperm. Many donate for money as well as for humanitarian reasons. Often donors have family members or friends who have struggled with infertility, and they're familiar with these families' deep desires for children, and how other sperm or egg donors have helped them conceive. Sometimes donors feel they will never start their own family but would like to know that their genes/offspring are out there in the world. This gives them a certain feeling of immortality. Still other donors are acquainted with women who have chosen to conceive without a male partner, and feel they'd like to help more women have this option.

How Much Are Donors Paid?

Some programs don't compensate their donors, but most pay $40–$50 per donation, provided that the donation meets the bank's sperm-quality criteria. This usually requires that the potential donor refrain from ejaculating for two to three days prior to each donation. To be enrolled in a donation program, a potential donor must fill out extensive history forms and undergo many medical tests. They must also be retested periodically. Often donors must complete this process before they start in order to be reimbursed for their time and effort. Thus, a man cannot simply walk in off the street to donate for quick income. Becoming a sperm donor for a bank becomes a fairly daunting commitment for many. In this way it is self-screening.

How Is a Donor's Medical History Taken?

A health worker takes the donor's medical history in private conversation with him and by reviewing the form he fills out, which is often very detailed. He is asked to give a thorough description of his family's medical history for three generations. The history usually also includes questions about physical features, athletic and intellectual capacities, hobbies, languages spoken, personality traits, personal preferences, why he has chosen to donate, etc. Many sperm banks have sample donor questionnaires available online.

How Are Donors Screened?

First, a donor must provide a semen sample. If the sample meets the sperm bank's criteria, it's frozen for 48 hours to one week. It's then thawed and reexamined under a microscope to see how the post-thaw sample compares to the unfrozen sample. Often men have a high sperm count, but for some reason their sperm don't survive the freeze-thaw process in very high numbers. If the sperm do survive, a donor undergoes a physical exam performed by a health care practitioner as well as extensive blood and urine tests.

What Does "Quarantine" Mean?

The donor's semen is frozen for at least six months. After six months, the donor is retested. If he tests negative for infection at the end of six months, the sperm he donated earlier is presumed to be safe to release. This quarantine process is used because some infections, notably HIV, may take some time to show up on a blood test after they're contracted. This means that if a donor became infected with HIV just prior to inseminating, his semen may be HIV infected but the HIV antibodies haven't yet appeared on a test. The vast majority of people who contract HIV or other diseases such as hepatitis will show the disease in their blood within six months. Nevertheless, no test is 100% accurate.

What Counts as "Quality Sperm"?

Sperm banks vary in their parameters for accepting donor sperm. Usually sperm banks guarantee 20-30 million motile (moving) sperm per sample. However, the higher the motility, the better the sample. Remember, sperm banks ship all over the country, so it's worthwhile to comparison-shop; you don't have to use your local sperm bank. Many sperm banks offer samples from donors in the 40–70 million range, so get the best samples available.

How Are My Parenting Rights Legally Protected?

Your donor will never have access to your identity. If you choose an identity-release donor, your child will be given his name upon request when he or she reaches age 18. Even if you were to discover who your donor is, state laws require that a man sever his paternity rights when he donates sperm anonymously to a medical facility and must sign a written contract of formal consent to do so. He would not be able to sue for custody; you would not be able to sue for child support.

Identity-Release Donors

As stated above, identity-release donors have given permission to a sperm bank to release identifying information about themselves to the child when the child turns 18. Only a few sperm banks offer ID-release or "yes donors," also sometimes called "known donors," although they won't be known at the time of your choosing them or for the next 18 years. At that time there's no guarantee that the donor will still be living.

Some sperm banks, under consumer pressure to offer comparable benefits, have policies that when the child turns 18 he or she can request that the sperm bank attempt to contact the donor and ask permission at that time for his identity to be released. There's no guarantee of how hard the sperm bank will work to find the donor or how the donor will respond. Four to 20 pregnancies may result from one donor's sperm, depending on the sperm bank's policy. A donor might need to plan in advance how he wants to respond to numerous young adults calling him up within a year or two of each other.

The California sperm bank that took the risk to spearhead this new trend in sperm banking did so in recognition of the growing movement two decades ago to give adopted people more access to information about their biological parents. Children from the very first ID-release sperm donors turned 18 in 2001.

How Sperm Bank Bureaucracy Works

When you first contact a sperm bank, they'll usually set up an orientation meeting for you if you're local. You'll need to fill out some paperwork, usually pay a fee for the orientation or to set up your account, and talk to a health educator who will not only explain the process, but also give you some basic information about charting your cycle.

You'll be given brief one-line biographical sketches of the available donors. Most sperm banks offer you copies of additional lengthy questionnaires for a $15–$50 fee. After reviewing the donor profiles, you let them know your top donor choices and when you want to start inseminating.

Some sperm banks encourage or permit you to purchase a number of vials of sperm in advance from a preferred donor. In this way, you can be assured that his sperm will be available for you when you need it. Otherwise, his sperm may run out temporarily before more is released from quarantine, or permanently if he stops donating or if he has reached the maximum number of pregnancies allowed from one donor. In this case you either wait or choose a different donor for those months. Sperm banks that don't let you purchase a large number of vials in advance usually allow each person to purchase just two vials per month.

Doctor Sign-Off

Before the sperm is released to you, you'll need a form signed by a health care provider. Some sperm banks insist that the form be signed by a physician rather than a nurse practitioner or midwife. Some forms only need to state that you're in "good health," while others require that your health care provider perform certain tests such as a Pap smear or tests for HIV, syphilis, gonorrhea, and chlamydia.

Pick-Up and Timing

At the beginning of the cycle during which you wish to inseminate, you'll phone the sperm bank to let them know when you may be inseminating, which donor you want, and whether you'd like one vial or two, washed for intrauterine insemination or unwashed for vaginal insemination. If they're sold out of your preferred donor, you may be put on a waiting list for the next month. You may have to use the sperm of your second or third or even fourth favorite donor. Then, as soon as you know exactly when you'll need the sperm, ideally at least one to two days in advance, you'll call the sperm bank to arrange either to pick it up or have it shipped to you or your doctor.

If you're going to pick up your vials and use them within the next 24–48 hours, you can get them in a small cooler with pieces of dry ice inside. If you need the vials shipped to you, they will arrive in a liquid nitrogen tank where they will stay cold for four to seven days. If you're unsure when exactly you're going to ovulate or need to pick up your sperm early because you'll be bringing it with you out of town, or simply want to have it early for peace of mind, ask if your sperm bank has a liquid nitrogen tank that you can borrow or rent.

Tips and Tricks

The following section offers suggestions that may help you obtain the highest-quality sperm samples with the fewest number of unpleasant surprises. Each sperm bank has its own personnel, policies, and attitudes. You may choose a sperm bank based on proximity, cost, donor selection, or how safe or helpful they feel. As a client you should also be treated with utmost respect, regardless of your sexual orientation, partner status, race, age, class, ability, choosiness about your donor, irregularity of menstrual cycle, or emotions about the entire process. By all means, change sperm banks if you're frustrated with the quality of service you're receiving and have already tried other methods of addressing your concerns.

Limor Inbar-Hansen, Indelible Images

Connect With a Friendly Staff Member

Befriend the receptionist, health educator, shipping manager, or whoever seems to have the lowdown on what's actually going on. It's very common to be told conflicting stories by different staff members about the availability of a certain donor or about shipping and storing policies. It will quickly become apparent who actually has decision-making power about each aspect of the business. If someone guarantees the availability of a specific donor or agrees to an unusual policy, write down their name and the date of your conversation. They are representing the bank when they make an agreement with you, and the bank should honor that agreement, whether or not the staff person was in the position to make such a promise. Don't be afraid to ask for the manager or director. He or she may have more flexibility to accommodate your needs than the bank's other employees. Usually, you'll get good service and be treated fairly. At some point, however, you'll probably become frustrated or confused about their policies or the information or service you're receiving. When this happens, speak up for yourself.

Be Assertive

Although sperm banks may take a long time or need to receive a number of complaints before they change an unpopular policy, the bottom line is that sperm banks sell a product to consumers. Because they value their reputation and customers, they're usually responsive (to a certain degree) to consumer input. Therefore, it ultimately behooves you and the greater community to give them direct feedback, when you can, in regard to both the positives and the negatives. Not all women feel comfortable doing this, especially when they're reliant upon the sperm bank's services. If you feel uncomfortable giving feedback during the insemination process, please consider offering feedback once you're well into pregnancy and no longer need to rely upon the bank.

Often women feel private or shy about interacting with a sperm bank when dealing with such an intimate topic as conception. This shyness can leave them feeling less empowered to negotiate for themselves than they otherwise might. If any issues of internalized homophobia arise for you, you may find it even harder to be assertive. Nonetheless, try your best to be direct and straightforward about your needs, acquiring help from a partner or friend to advocate for you if necessary.

Buy the Best Sample Available

When you order the sperm, request sperm that has been donated the most recently. See if you can obtain the samples from your selected donor that have the highest motility or concentration. One of our clients was having a tearful conversation with a sperm bank worker about the trouble she was having conceiving. The worker offered her special "high-motility" sperm, which had never been mentioned to her previously. Whether or not sperm is categorized this way and available to physicians only, or to anyone who knows to ask for it, is completely unknown. The sperm bank had let this client know she could specifically request this high-motility sperm. Nonetheless, the story is a reminder that the sperm bank does a semen analysis on each sample that is donated to ensure that it's adequate. This information is kept available, and can be looked up by a worker, if they're willing, when they release your monthly samples.

If you're going to inseminate more than once each cycle, ask for all the vials you'll use in one cycle to come from the same ejaculate if possible or from dates close together. These may be the most biochemically compatible with one another as they will have been in the donor's body at the same time. Because you usually inseminate over a period of time where the sperm from each insemination comes in contact with one another, it's best to use samples from the same donations. This is because the chemical makeup of each ejaculate varies; some studies indicate that this may be significant.

Choose a Donor With a Strong Track Record

When you choose a donor, you'll undoubtedly have many of your own personal criteria for making the decision. One that may be useful is to ask how many pregnancies to date have resulted from a variety of your top donor choices, since it's best to work with a donor whose sperm has resulted in successful pregnancies. Many variables can affect this number, including one donor being more often selected than another for a variety of reasons. If one favorite of yours, however, has only been on their catalog nine months and resulted in four pregnancies, and the other donor has been available for two years with no pregnancies, you'll probably want to factor this into your decision.

If you set your heart on a donor whose sperm has resulted in nine pregnancies to date at a sperm bank with a 10-pregnancy limit, you may be setting yourself up for disappointment if he reaches his limit before you achieve pregnancy. The reality of sperm banks is that demand often exceeds supply. Donors of certain ethnicities are often hard to find. ID-release donors are in high demand at sperm banks that offer these programs. You may be amazed at how long you spend choosing your initial donor, and how often your top choice isn't available.

If you don't get pregnant after three to six cycles with your donor, move on to a new one. Your "chemistry" may just not be compatible.

Anonymous Fresh Sperm Through a Medical Office

Rarely, women may find an infertility practice that maintains a pool of screened anonymous donors who can be contacted via pager to give fresh donations. Although these donors have been medically screened, no test guarantees that they haven't very recently contracted an infection. Sperm banks that offer fresh sperm must rely on donors' statements about their safe-sex practices. Usually in these situations there isn't a huge selection available, and the information you receive about the donor may be substantially less than you'd get at a sperm bank that offers frozen sperm. Scheduling donations and inseminations is up to the schedule of the office and the donor, and is therefore fairly inflexible. Although you may be undergoing a straightforward vaginal insemination, for legal reasons you must perform the insemination in the clinic without the option to take it home and do it privately.

The women we've worked with who have been willing to take these potential risks are those who have inseminated multiple times unsuccessfully with frozen sperm from a sperm bank. All of these women did conceive within the first two cycles of using fresh sperm, and none has had regrets. Because of the medical liability of sexually transmitted infection, however, as well as the hassle of finding donors who will remain available, many practices have stopped offering these services.

Anonymous Donor With a Go-Between

Before sperm banks were accessible to lesbians, many women chose to make private arrangements with a go-between in order to obtain anonymous sperm. The go-between was usually a friend, a friend of a friend, a community yenta, or a midwife who would screen the donor to some extent and maintain confidentiality by picking up and dropping off the donated semen. A smaller number of women still prefer this arrangement to any other sperm-donor choice, although along with its benefits, it does have some drawbacks.

Benefits

Your go-between may be able to find a man who will donate sperm to you for free. This in and of itself is appealing or essential to many women. If you really want an unknown donor but can't afford to use a sperm bank, you might consider using a go-between. If you want anonymous sperm and need it to be fresh in order to increase your chances of conception, you may also consider this option because so few clinic programs offer anonymous fresh sperm.

You may be intrigued by the go-between option if you're philosophically opposed to working with the legal and medical systems or getting their permission to conceive your baby. Likewise, you may prefer anonymity but not like the idea of using frozen sperm. As with other anonymous-donor situations, you wouldn't have the opportunity to get a sense of this person. You may know your go-between well enough, however, that her character assessment is more credible to you than that of a sperm bank.

When your go-between negotiates terms of donation with your donor, she may have some flexibility in negotiating that you won't have with a sperm bank. For example, you might arrange that if you or your child ever wanted to meet the donor, your go-between could find the donor and ask him if he is willing to be contacted. Your go-between could let him know from the start that when your child reaches puberty or becomes a teenager, she or he would probably want to meet him. You could make any arrangement, potentially, that you all agree to before your donor gives you sperm.

Drawbacks

One drawback concerns confidentiality. You need to be able to trust your go-between to maintain the anonymity of the donor from everyone she knows for the child's whole life, or until the year on which you all agree. Many people feel itchy holding a secret like that. If you crossed social paths with your donor—which could

happen if you live in the same area—could either of you figure out the other's identity, either intentionally or unintentionally? If he decided he wanted to figure out who
your family is, could he? Probably, depending on how determined he is. If he discovers your identity, he becomes a known donor. He would become a known donor without your having had the legal opportunities to draw up a contract that you may have if
you use a planned known donor. In this way, you may be signing on for the eventual
potential risks of a known donor without the benefit of planning and negotiating.

The second area of concern for many women considering using an anonymous
donor with a go-between involves potential health risks. You could have your go-between ask the donor about his medical history. He or she could have him fill out an in-
depth medical questionnaire like the one provided at the end of Chapter 5. You'd need
to trust your go-between's ability to interpret the donor's medical history and repeat it
to you accurately. You could then find a medical person to ask about it if you had questions. You couldn't directly see the donor's test results or a note from his health care
provider attesting to his good health or family medical history, unless he gave a copy to
your go-between that had his identifying information removed. You'd have to rely on
your go-between to ask the detailed questions and give the detailed information sometimes necessary to reach an agreement on safer sex that feels secure to you. You'd have
to trust the donor to uphold these agreements without having met him in person.

You may find scheduling fresh sperm donations between yourself, your partner
if you have one, your donor, and your go-between to be very difficult, depending on
your work and vacation schedules.

Anonymous Sex

Some women become frustrated with their known-donor prospects or with
the financial realities of using a sperm bank. The thought often crosses someone's
mind to pick up a man at a bar and have casual or anonymous sex as the easiest
way to conceive. Casual or anonymous sex does, however, pose substantial health
risks. Still, despite these risks, people do have casual unsafe sex all the time in our
culture. Often women who imagine this scenario are sure they'll conceive the
first time they have unprotected intercourse with a man. More often than not,
however, they don't conceive on the first try. The more times a woman has sex in
this situation, the more she exposes herself to the risk of contracting a sexually
transmitted infection.

Picking someone up may not be as anonymous as you'd like it to be. How many
times have you been surprised by how small the world is? Unless you travel to a dis-
tant city to find a sex partner for conception, you may live in fear that he'll show up
on your doorstep one day. Legally, you wouldn't have any redress against a custody

suit from him because 1) he wouldn't have formally consented to be a donor instead of a parent; and 2) conception by intercourse undermines even those arrangements where this agreement is made.

Sexual intercourse as a conception method is discussed further in Chapter 12. If you're considering this option, first examine if you feel any ethical obligation to the man involved. It's also important to make sure that you feel comfortable with the idea of having sex with a man. You don't want to feel ambivalent later about the circumstances of your baby's conception.

Finally, imagine this situation down the road and ask yourself just as you would with other possible sperm options: What story will you tell your offspring and others?

Anonymous Donor Considerations

Using sperm from an anonymous donor requires thoughtful consideration of your feelings about the permanence of the anonymity and how it may impact your child. Any deep reservations you have in this department usually arise as ambivalence or procrastination about choosing a donor or actually beginning to inseminate. If you feel comfortable with the anonymity, there are many strong benefits to using sperm banks as your donor source.

Using a go-between or having anonymous sex each have benefits as well as substantial health risks that should be considered carefully. No matter what you choose as your most perfect donor option, you'll be interfacing and negotiating with someone, be it the known donor, the sperm bank staff, a doctor performing the inseminations, or a go-between.

Keep in mind that the emotional work of clarifying why you feel right with your choices is work towards the creation of your child. This will allow you to be assertive and clear in creating the arrangements that make you feel safe and comfortable with the above people. It will also provide you with the clarity and confidence you need to tell your child the beautiful story of how you chose to create her or him, and how he or she came to be in the world.

Resources

Sperm Banks
New England Cryogenic Center
665 Beacon St., Suite 302
Boston, MA 02215
(617) 262-3311 or (800) 991-4999
www.necryogenic.com

Pacific Reproductive Services
444 DeHaro, Suite 222
San Francisco, CA 94107
(415) 487-2288
www.hellobaby.com

Rainbow Flag Health Services
543 30th St.
Oakland, CA 94609
(510) 763-7737
www.gayspermbank.com

The Sperm Bank of California (Reproductive Technologies, Inc.)
2115 Milvia St., 2nd Floor
Berkeley, CA 94704
(510) 841-1858
www.thespermbankofca.org

Xytex
1100 Emmett St.
Augusta, GA 30904
(706) 733-0130
www.xytex.com

Part Three
Optimizing Your Health and Fertility

Chapter 7 Nourishing Yourself With Food

Nourishing yourself means taking care of and loving yourself through eating. Nourishment means more than just getting sufficient calories or maintaining a healthy diet; it's feeding the soul through feeding the body. Nourishing yourself means taking what you need from the world and bringing it into your body in a gentle, joyful, compassionate way. It's the process of creating a loving home in your body for yourself and your baby. If you're the partner of a woman about to be pregnant, feeding your partner in a healthy way shows your love, your participation, and your commitment to this journey; it nourishes both of you and your relationship.

Because conception is about physically manifesting your love for another life, preparation for conception includes practicing how to embody love. Nourishing your body with food is one of the most direct and powerful ways you can manifest love in the physical body.

Making healthy lifestyle changes always feels best and lasts longest when you make them from a place of self-love instead of self-criticism. Making healthy and sustainable changes in your diet requires you to understand what food and nourishment represent to you. It's worthwhile to take time with us now, through this holistic approach, to examine your relationship to food. Healthy eating will significantly increase your fertility, ease your early pregnancy discomforts, and decrease your risk of miscarriage and birth defects.

In this chapter we will help you explore what food means to you on an an emotional level, a relationship level, a community level, a cultural level, and a physical level. This chapter covers the following topics: your relationship to food, healthy eating habits, specific nutritional suggestions for preconception, and nutritional advice for both pregnant and postpartum women. We encourage you not to skip this chapter even if you have long explored nutrition.

Understanding Your Relationship to Food

Food isn't just about eating; it's symbolic, emotional, intimate, and complex. Your relationship to food directly influences what, where, and when you eat. Understanding your history with food will allow you to be more conscious in your food choices.

Exercise

Food is often a very personal topic for women. Many women are most comfortable beginning their exploration privately. Sit quietly and think about any of the following questions. You may wish to write about your thoughts and feelings in a journal, or do any form of artwork if writing is too linear a form for you. At some point you may want to discuss these questions with someone else or even in a small group.

- What does food mean to you now?
- What has it meant to you at different times in your life?
- Is food a source of pleasure for you?
- Do you feel loved or nurtured when you're fed?
- Do you enjoy feeding others?
- Are you realize when you're hungry?
- Do you feed yourself when you notice your hunger?
- Does eating when you're hungry make you feel guilty or out of control?
- As a child were you fed when you were hungry?
- What were you told about food?
- How do you experience just watching someone eat?
- What does eating make you feel like physically?

In our culture women receive many messages about food and their bodies. From billboards to magazine ads, women are bombarded daily with images of what they're supposed to look like. Take some time to reflect on the barrage of images and expectations you receive from mainstream culture and other ethnic, religious, or family cultures that influence you. Examine messages from television, books, billboards, movies, and the people in your life. What messages have you received about body size and food and being female?

Naming the historical messages we've internalized and the current messages influencing us helps to dispel their power and allows us to make active choices about food. Which of your messages have been positive and which have been negative? Which would you like to keep? Which would you like your child to receive from his or her family or environment? Which messages about his or her body and food would you like your child to receive directly from you? How might you communicate messages both verbally and nonverbally to a young child who's developing his or her sense of self? When you imagine this scenario, notice if your child's gender influences your message or the way you communicate it. Does it need to?

By acknowledging our attitudes about our bodies and food, we can actively choose which attitudes to impart to the next generation, our children.

Establishing Healthy Eating Habits

Why Now?

The desire to have a baby is an excellent incentive to make any diet changes you've previously been interested in and a strong incentive to educate yourself about your body's specific nutritional needs during preconception and pregnancy. Remember, when you're actively trying to conceive, the second half of every menstrual cycle is potentially the first trimester of pregnancy. Pregnancy brings a feeling of urgency to making changes for the health of your baby. Prior to conception, you can make changes at a pace that works for you. Improving eating habits is much easier before the mood swings, hormone changes, and morning sickness of pregnancy set in. In fact, healthy eating habits help decrease those first trimester discomforts. Even before pregnancy, healthy eating will help stabilize the emotional roller coaster that the insemination process inevitably brings. If you're still some months away from starting to inseminate, even better. Some diet suggestions for increasing fertility take three months to produce the maximum benefit.

Compassion Under the Microscope

During the preconception period and pregnancy, you'll focus much attention on your relationship to food. This self-scrutiny, as well as the scrutiny of others, can feel uncomfortable. Your focus, as well as that of your obstetrician or midwife, your partner, well-meaning friends, and the general public is shining not only on your diet, but also on your health habits and body functions. Please have self-compassion. The purpose of our suggestions is to optimize your chances of getting pregnant, sustaining the pregnancy, and feeling good while pregnant. It's not to make you feel bad about the choices you've made up until now or to feel bad if you continue to make choices that aren't as healthy as they could be.

Maternal guilt is prevalent in our culture, and you may suffer from it before you've conceived, especially when the topic of food arises. Guilt, however, does not make anyone parent better. The best parenting choices come from a place of self-love. If you make beneficial changes in your life for your child that you wouldn't normally make for yourself, that's fine. Your deeper motivation comes from a place of love, so use it if it helps. In parenting we must strive to do the best we can and keep loving ourselves as we grow.

If you're partnered, make sure your partner understands that her role is to support you at this time. Scrutinizing and/or criticizing your eating habits is not supportive. Her actions as a "food cop" will only alienate you, not nurture you. Discuss with your partner as specifically as possible what might make you feel supported. For example, you might tell her: "Please help me prepare some healthy lunches and snacks, instead of calculating my sugar intake."

Slow Changes Are Lasting Changes

Creating healthy eating habits is a slow, evolving process. The amount of time it takes varies from person to person. There's no right way to eat that is appropriate for everyone; we each conduct our own personal experiments. Some people make dramatic changes overnight and then adjust emotionally to those changes over time. Others integrate small changes one step at a time.

We strongly recommend approaching change gradually and gently, in a way that makes sense to you. If you make too many changes at once, you may not be able to sustain them. A fanaticism similar to that of eating disorders usually accompanies dramatic diet overhauls. Our goal is to help you create long-term healthy habits, not offer a magic "fertility diet."

Rapid changes aren't necessarily healthy. Slow change avoids unwanted metabolic shifts and the potential toxic release into the bloodstream that can occur when you make dramatic changes in your diet.

Feelings You May Discover When Making Diet Changes

As you make changes you may be surprised by some of the sensations in your body. Many women feel more alive and awake than ever, and their newfound energy inspires them to keep refining their diets. If the process of diet change leads a woman to feel more embodied, she might be rewarded by feeling like she's found a long-lost friend. For other women, change stirs up painful memories of them trying to control their lives through food. Sometimes the changes feel forced. Making diet changes from a place of guilt or pressure can quickly lead to resentment. Make sure you're ready for the changes you're choosing to make.

Diet Changes and Past Trauma

If your diet changes lead to weight loss, you may experience what many health practitioners call a "healing crisis." Diet changes that release painful memories and emotions stored in our bodies can cause temporary exhaustion, overwhelming emotion, or general malaise. Although challenging at the time, the long-term outcome will be positive. If this happens to you, have self-compassion and allow yourself time to address these feelings as they arise and then let them go. You're letting go of old, unresolved feelings. Everything you release at this time makes more room in the present for a baby, both physically and emotionally.

Diet changes and attention to nourishment may also release feelings about sex and sexuality. It's important to realize that your abuse history may be surfacing alongside any uncomfortable or traumatic memories about food. The connection between sexual history, food, and pregnancy is complex and individual. Pregnancy is a time of tremendous change; body size and self-image are changing at a rate that is often faster than you can integrate. Pregnancy includes hormonal waves and cycles that can mimic times in your life when you may have felt out of control, such as adolescence. For many women, adolescence was a time of insecurity about body, image, sexuality, and food. Even if you think you've reached resolution with difficult aspects of your past, note that some of these feelings may come up again with a new twist.

If preconception and pregnancy are stressful times for you (and they may well be), coping mechanisms adapted long ago to any type of past trauma or abuse may arise. With advance warning, however, you can take greater measures to secure support for yourself during these times of change. One of the benefits of having time to prepare for pregnancy is the potential to do some of the emotional work of pregnancy beforehand at your own pace, before increased hormone swings occur.

Eating Disorders

Many women have had or still have eating issues, whether they identify them as "disorders" or not. These unhealthy relationships to food are one example of the coping mechanisms just mentioned. Old habits may arise quite silently and surprise you. For example, your self-image might go askew and cause self-deprecating patterns to arise. Unable to see an accurate reflection of yourself and your body, you may stop eating or start binging. Again, use this time as a way to identify and practice strategies for avoiding falling into compulsive eating behaviors. This type of preparation will be immensely helpful for both pregnancy and parenting. The emotional charge of food's role in your life may be lessened if you make sure you have sufficient other nonfood-oriented ways of being nurtured and receiving love.

Eating Regularly

Let's start with an exercise to explore how frequently you feed yourself. Later we'll refer back to this exercise to examine the specific nutritional components of the food you eat.

Exercise

Take out a piece of paper to do a "24-hour diet recall." Start the page with what time you woke up yesterday. Next, write what time you first ate. Describe what you ate and about how much. Continue through your memory of yesterday, writing down anything you ingested, the time, and the amount. Include water, tea, coffee, soda, alcohol, cigarettes, drugs, medicines, herbs, vitamins, and supplements. This exercise is private, so be accurate in your recording. If you experience resistance to this exercise, examine why that may be. Now glance at your page and notice how many hours passed between the times you ate anything that had solid nutritional value.

The exercise you've just done will give you something to start with as you work your way through this chapter. For a more accurate analysis, pick three consecutive days and repeat the exercise. Include a workday and a non-workday to get a more complete look at your diet. Know in advance that you probably won't find any one day that you feel precisely typifies how you eat. For now, just note the frequency with which you eat. Then put the pages away until we get farther into the chapter.

Signs of Hunger and Low Blood Sugar

Many people in our culture, especially women, aren't aware of their body's hunger signals. One study shows that women frequently don't recognize hunger signals, misinterpreting them at first as a need to urinate. They recognize hunger as a body-function signal but aren't initially aware of which one. Hypoglycemia (low blood sugar) is the step beyond hunger and gives its own signals. It occurs when you haven't eaten enough food for your body's needs. Signs of hypoglycemia include: irritability, light-headedness, panic, exhaustion, nausea, mood swings, headache, and extreme emotions such as rage, dizziness, and the inability to think clearly.

All of these signs of hunger/hypoglycemia are more apparent during pregnancy. Pregnant women often have to learn new ways of recognizing hunger, because the familiar grumbling or empty feeling in the stomach is often absent. Only in retrospect do many women realize they've experienced the symptoms of low blood sugar all their lives; since these signs perhaps weren't quite so extreme, however, they ignored them, suppressed them, or chose not to respond to them. Frequently, women don't recognize these symptoms as signs of hunger at all.

By the time hunger has advanced to hypoglycemia, the other common sign that appears is sugar craving. Your body at this point is seeking a quick fix to raise its blood sugar rapidly. Refined sugar is actually not healthy to eat in this situation, as it causes a fast high blood sugar, which then quickly cycles to another low blood sugar level. A food with some sugar, such as fruit or a small glass of fruit juice, eaten with a protein-rich food such as cheese, nuts, or meat, will quickly raise blood sugar and then stabilize it. If you often experience hypoglycemia away from home, carry nutritional bars high in protein and carbohydrates with you as they'll quickly raise and sustain your blood-sugar level. Check the labels on these items, though, since many nutritional bars contain large amounts of refined sugar, including high fructose corn syrup. A healthy nutritional bar should contain at least 9 grams of protein with no more than 13–17 grams of sugar. If your blood sugar is low and you eat a high-sugar-content bar, it will alleviate your symptoms temporarily, then set the "high/low" blood-sugar cycle in motion.

In the following pages we'll discuss frequent eating, which is by far the most important thing you can do to avoid low blood sugar. Reducing your overall refined sugar intake, especially that which is consumed on an empty stomach, is also key to avoiding the "high/low" blood-sugar cycle.

When trying to conceive and while pregnant, it's best to maintain a steady blood-sugar level so that your body doesn't experience blood-sugar extremes. Maintaining a balanced metabolism is also important. Consistency helps maintain balanced hormone levels. If the body is stressed from going without food or experiencing extreme blood-sugar swings, it becomes reluctant to embrace pregnancy as being healthy for the body—that is, if a body is focused on self-preservation, it's more likely to reject a pregnancy. Also, babies in the uterus can be severely stressed by blood-sugar swings in the mother's body. In fact, extremes in blood-sugar levels can affect their organ development.

Learning to avoid low blood sugar during preconception will benefit you significantly in early pregnancy. Look at the list of signs of hypoglycemia again. How many of these are what our culture views as symptoms of a "normal" pregnancy? Hormone changes play a role in these discomforts and are unavoidable, but low blood sugar, the main culprit, is avoidable. You don't have to feel sick for 12 weeks!

Throughout pregnancy a baby needs to have a constant supply of food available in the bloodstream. A woman's metabolism and body chemistry change during pregnancy to make nutrients constantly available to the baby. If you're eating infrequently, your body will be low in certain nutrients that are important for both your growing baby's development and for your health. Because babies have a desire to grow in a healthy way, they will take what they need from your body. If you aren't regularly refilling your body, it may become depleted. Your baby may be born healthy and appropriately sized, but if your body is depleted, it's much more likely that you'll feel exhausted in the postpartum period. If your body is depleted, it's at higher risk for bleeding heavily, not healing a birth tear well, having an insufficient milk supply, and contracting breast or uterine infections. Over the long term you may lose a significant amount of bone density, since your bones may dissolve into your bloodstream during pregnancy or nursing to make calcium available for the baby if it isn't available from your diet.

How Often Should I Eat?

Every four hours you should eat food with nutritional value. You don't have to eat a lot, but you should eat something. Pull out your "Three-Day Food Log" from the last exercise. How many meals do you eat each day? Do you go for long stretches of time without eating or with eating foods of limited nutritional value? Are you not sure what counts as nutritious? Many women who theoretically understand the necessity of eating regularly still find increasing their food intake to be challenging. Unfortunately, for many women, eating has become optional. In the following sections, we offer tips for incorporating more frequent healthy eating into your life. Think through the questions we ask along the way and you'll come up with your own creative solutions to any areas you'd like to improve.

Bring Food With You

Frequently, women go out in the world without bringing along food and/or stopping to eat. Many women leave the house without having eaten breakfast and come back eight or more hours later not having eaten at all. During the day, some women subsist only on coffee and "munchies."

To avoid going longer than four hours without food, you'll need to bring food and drink with you wherever go. Some women have access to food nearby, whether at a vending machine, a fast-food drive-thru, or a restaurant. When women are at work or outside the house, however, they often don't have access to *nutritious* food. If you don't eat often, start with steps that seem manageable—steps that will enable you to eat something of value, even if you only take two bites every four hours. To integrate changes that are truly viable, however, you'll have to get really practical.

What to Bring When You Leave the House

Planning is the key to eating well. Consider what time your last meal or snack will be before you leave your house and how many four-hour periods will pass until you eat next at home. How many meals or snacks is that? Now, how will you carry your food with you? Are you only willing to bring a purse? Are you willing to bring a lunch bag? A cooler? Will you bring food only if it fits in your backpack or doesn't take up room in your briefcase? Do you have a water bottle? A thermos? Answer honestly so that you can realistically plan what types of and how much food you'll bring. Do you have a refrigerator at work? A microwave? Hot water?

Now that you've considered your limitations, let's think about what kind of foods are nutritious, starting with snacks. Many people have a piece of fruit for a snack. Fruit will give you vitamins and perhaps some fiber, as well as some fruit sugar. Fruit is digested fairly quickly, isn't particularly substantial, and gives you very little—

if any—protein. If you enjoy fruit, could you supplement it with a cup of yogurt? How about a handful of peanuts, almonds, or sunflower seeds? Supplementing what you already enjoy and are accustomed to is always better than trying to change what you eat completely.

If your in-between-meal food is fruit juice, you might consider exchanging some of it for whole fruit and other foods. The natural sugar in fruit juice is very rapidly absorbed by the body. Furthermore, many fruit juices have added sugars. Drinking fruit juice when you need a quick pick-me-up after lunch or breakfast will give you immediate energy. Unfortunately, as we mentioned, the body's response to easily absorbed sugar is a yucky-feeling sugar low soon after. The same process occurs with refined sugars in soda and candy bars, although these contain none of the beneficial vitamins in fruit juice. Substituting a smoothie—made with yogurt or protein powder—for fruit juice keeps the same liquid fruit element in your body while adding protein and staying power.

Look at the following suggested snacks and see which ones you could add to your diet, taking into account your cooking and carrying restrictions. Then think about the preparation time a snack may require. Would preparing your food the night before be easier or more likely than in the morning? Consider bringing a small serving of the previous night's leftovers for a snack if it isn't already going to be your lunch.

Healthy Snack Suggestions
- 1/2 cup precooked canned kidney beans or garbanzo beans, seasoned at home
- 1/3 cup hummus with raw carrots or broccoli, pita bread, or crackers
- 1/3 cup tuna salad with whole wheat crackers
- 1/4 cup almonds with a piece of fruit
- tortilla chips and bean dip
- peanut butter and jelly sandwich
- 1/2 cup trail mix, including any of the following: raisins, banana chips, walnuts, almonds, dried coconut, cashews, dried apricots, sunflower seeds (make your own trail mix or purchase from bulk bins at the grocery store)
- 1 cup yogurt
- 1 cup cottage cheese with fruit
- small container of leftovers: stir-fry, lasagna, soup, etc.
- chopped raw vegetables with salad dressing for dipping: celery, bell pepper, zucchini, broccoli, carrots
- cheese and crackers

Meal Planning and Cooking in Advance

Many people rarely cook, especially those who live in large cities, have hectic schedules, or live and work near restaurants. These people either eat out, order in, or defrost and microwave prepared meals for lunch and dinner. At breakfast they may only grab a piece of fruit or a bagel. While eating something is better than not eating, the benefits of cooking are numerous. Home-cooked food is usually fresher and healthier than you'd find elsewhere, with fewer preservatives and saturated fats. Do you enjoy cooking? Are you willing to cook? If so, how often and when? Could you plan meals for the week and cook them on the weekend? Could you freeze meals in one- to two-serving portions so they can be thawed easily? A pot of soup, beans, or a casserole not only serves as a lunch option, but also a fast nutritious dinner, ready when you get home. When you cook dinner, make enough so that you'll have leftovers for the next day. When you clear the table, pack the leftovers directly into lunch containers so that your food will be ready to go in the morning. You may want to keep some prepared healthy food stocked in your kitchen that you can fix it quickly if you get in late or if your blood sugar drops. Many cookbooks provide quick, easy-to-follow, healthy recipes.

Shop With a Plan

Of course, if you plan to cook, prepare, or bring food with you, you'll need to shop. Having a list helps to avoid impulse buying, thereby saving you money. Planning what to buy at the store so that your kitchen is full of foods you enjoy takes some practice and effort. For some women the hardest part of making diet changes is the planning required. This is sometimes challenging, because it means acknowledging that you consider feeding yourself to be a priority. Many women find that creating a computer-generated list of all the foods they need on hand in their kitchen helps them organize and simplify their kitchen and shopping needs. That way, when you run out of something you can just check a box next to the item and have a ready-made list at the end of the week.

Divide Labor Between Partners

If you live with a partner, examine and evaluate how your household food tasks are divided. Who does the shopping? Who does the cooking? Is the division of labor fair? Or is it by default and full of tension? Is there no cooking or shopping at all? Can your partner help with or take over food preparation and planning?

Single Women and Eating Alone

Women who are becoming single mothers can feel isolated when given a list of nutritional recommendations. They may miss the practical help as well as the enthusiasm a partner can provide. Some women find eating by themselves or cooking for themselves a lonely activity. Therefore, many solo eaters don't eat meals at home. Does cooking for one person seem like too much work for you? If you're single, do you have a friend to cook with one night a week for company? Can you swap half of what you made for half of what s/he made to add variety to your menu? It's helpful to get a few good cookbooks designed for single people since the recipes in most cookbooks are for multiple servings. It can be disheartening to follow a recipe, especially when you're just learning how to cook, and find that you're going to be eating the same soup for seven days! Finding the inspiration to cook is well worth the results.

Community Support

It's wonderful to bring your community into the experience of your growing family. One particular way to ask for help is to let friends know if it's difficult for you to get up the energy to cook when you're in certain phases of your menstrual cycle, such as going through the depression of starting your period or the chaos of timing your insemination. It's really nice to be fed; it feels nurturing and supportive.

What Do I Need to Budget for Food?

When you focus on the food you eat, your eating habits will change. This doesn't need to inflate your food bill. The cost of food usually increases just before and during pregnancy because women begin eating higher-quality food, and they inevitably eat more.

It's worthwhile to put extra discretionary money toward food. Luckily, some of your new eating habits will actually lower your food costs. You can make healthy meals inexpensively at home, more cheaply certainly than eating out or buying fast food. Cooking can be less expensive when you buy in bulk or from farmers markets. Decreasing coffee and fast-food consumption will also save you money. If the only way you can get food into yourself is to purchase it already prepared, then an increase in food costs is fairly unavoidable but worth it.

Some people with extra money who don't cook get homemade meals delivered or hire someone to cook for them. Others buy healthy prepared food that only requires heating it up. Work within your means and needs. Quick eating often costs more since it isn't planned ahead of time. Forethought truly saves. Remember, healthier eating makes your body feel better.

Specific Healthy Eating Suggestions

It's important to strive for realistic improvements in your eating habits. Read the following sections and look for suggestions that resonate with you, ideas that sound good to you.

Water

Most Americans are perpetually dehydrated. How many glasses of fluid do you drink during one day? How many glasses of water specifically? We encourage women—both pre-pregnant and pregnant—to drink at least eight 8-ounce glasses a day. Carry water with you. If you use a container that you can refill, you can keep track of how much you drink during the day. There are even some bottles with straps that can make carrying water with you wherever you go less cumbersome.

Water helps both kidney and liver function. When you're pregnant your body is the filtration system for your developing baby; thus, it becomes even more essential to drink enough to support your body. There's a difference between water and other beverages such as soda, fruit juice, coffee, tea, or milk. Water serves a unique purpose in our bodies that other beverages do not.

High-quality water is vital for health. The wide array of chemical contaminants in public water contributes to miscarriages, developmental abnormalities, and degenerative diseases, among other health problems. Regulations for bottled water are notoriously weak. Because hot water releases contaminants into the air where we breathe them directly into our bloodstream, people absorb five to 100 times more chemicals from the water they bathe in than from the water they drink. A good filter for drinking and cooking water, and a shower filter for bathing water, will help protect you and your baby from contaminants.

Stimulants

One of the most direct ways to increase your fertility is to remove all stimulant intake. This includes caffeine, cigarettes, sugar, and any other stimulants. We will discuss addiction to adrenaline and stress later on. Giving up stimulants is often the hardest change for people to make in their lifestyle.

Stimulants serve many purposes, including acting as appetite suppressants. Stimulants allow us to function at a level we wouldn't usually be able to maintain without the assistance of artificial energy. Many people have ingested stimulants on a daily basis since their teenage years or even earlier, and thus stimulants have become an integral part of their lives. In addition, stimulants such as coffee are central to many social interactions.

Stimulant cessation may prove to be a major lifestyle change for you. Please transition gently, with compassion for yourself during the inevitable withdrawal period. Know that stimulant withdrawal is often accompanied by headaches or severe mood swings that can last for a number of days. Many people find that homeopathic remedies and acupuncture ease this transition. Also, don't forget to increase your water intake during this time.

Caffeine

Giving up caffeine may dramatically increase your fertility. Studies have been shown that caffeine can cut both female and male fertility by up to 50%. Caffeine intake can also significantly increase your chance of miscarriage. Caffeine consumption depletes the vitamins and minerals in your body by interfering with absorption; it reduces iron absorption by up to 50%. So if you're using a known sperm donor, be sure to ask him to give up caffeine or reduce his intake as well. Just removing caffeine from both of your diets may significantly decrease the amount of time it will take for you to conceive. Giving up caffeine now means you won't have to go through withdrawal headaches during pregnancy.

Caffeine comes in many forms; chocolate, soda, and coffee are the most popular. Black tea has less caffeine than coffee, green tea even less. Unless you're buying water-filtered decaffeinated coffee, decaf coffee beans have been soaked in acetone, the primary chemical in nail-polish remover, as part of the decaffeination process. Green tea has beneficial herbal properties, including powerful antioxidants, especially if steeped less than three minutes; thus, switching from coffee to tea may be better for you than switching from coffee to decaf. Green tea and black tea are available in decaffeinated forms, though many people replace caffeinated tea with herbal teas.

Take some time to examine what purpose caffeine has served in your life. For some it's a social ritual. For others it feels like it feeds the soul. For still others it's a reward they look forward to in the day. Unless you determine what role it plays in your life and substitute something for it, you'll more than likely feel an emptiness and a sense of deprivation when it's gone. If you like the treat of coffee, try some of the more exotic herbal teas, and add half-and-half, rice milk, honey, or lemon.

Many people don't realize that when they stop drinking coffee they're going to feel exhausted by mid afternoon. Some form of revitalization is necessary. To boost your energy, you can substitute healthy, nutritious protein-rich food. If you take a five-minute break to go for a walk, you'll raise your energy level by increasing your blood circulation. Some women take lunch walks with a coworker or get regular massages; others take Tai Chi classes. These suggestions also substitute an activity for the ritual break and socialization that coffee drinking usually involves.

It's often hard on a partnership if one partner gives up caffeine and the other doesn't. It's always a good idea for family members to engage in healthy patterns together; it makes change seem possible and lasting change more likely. For some, giving up caffeine is too large a step, and that's their personal decision. If you aren't able or willing to give it up completely, at least reduce your intake. Your goal is to reduce caffeine consistently, not just during the second half of each month you inseminate.

Sugar

One of our most important recommendations—and something that may be a daunting prospect—is to eliminate refined sugar from your diet. Sugar is an appetite suppressant and immediately raises blood-sugar levels after ingestion. In response to higher blood-sugar levels your body secretes a lot of insulin. As soon as the insulin starts to work your blood swings toward a sugar low. A sugar low makes you feel tired, sluggish, and emotional. Often this causes you to eat more sugar and thus continue the yo-yo cycle of high/low blood sugar. If you reread the section on low blood sugar earlier in the chapter, you'll see that overlooking your body's signals of hunger for nutritious food will cause a sugar craving. If you regularly eat protein-rich foods, you'll probably reduce the frequency of your sugar cravings. Sugar needs to play a supporting role in your diet, not a leading role.

It's essential to monitor and reduce not only refined sugars, but also "natural" sugars. Dried fruit and fruit juices contain high amounts of quickly absorbed sugar. Eating whole grains, fresh fruits, fresh vegetables, and healthy meats while eliminating sugars helps to stabilize your blood-sugar and insulin levels. For more information on regulating your blood sugar, read *The Zone* by Barry Sears. Remember, it's much easier to weather the mood swings of conception by keeping as many aspects of your life and physical being as consistent and stable as possible.

Regional Foods

Amazingly enough, the food on your table has, on average, traveled 3,000 miles to get there. This dramatically redefines the concept of "fresh" food. When food travels such distances from field to table it loses many of its vital nutrients along the way. Focus on eating what is in season and what is regional to where you live. This theory comes from macrobiotic eating, which is founded on the belief that the foods that grow in our environment at different times of the year are the foods that are appropriate to our bodies, as they too move through each of the yearly cycles and seasons.

Consider shopping at your local farmers market or seeing if any of your local farms has a delivery service. The fresher your foods, the healthier your foods. They also taste remarkably better.

Organic Foods

Organic foods are grown without the use of synthetic pesticides, hormones, antibiotics, or other additives. Organic foods are obviously much better for your body, but often only people with chronic or terminal illnesses or "health nuts" strive to eat organic foods. Think about growing your baby on organic foods and continuing to feed your baby organic foods through your breast milk and as your child grows. The vast majority of pesticides in use today haven't been approved for human consumption; in fact, they haven't been tested on humans at all prior to use. Environmental toxins are also on the rise. Eating as organically as possible is one way to support your body to be as strong and healthy as possible.

Many fruits and vegetables are now genetically engineered. The long-term effects of eating these foods are unknown. Organic foods are usually not genetically engineered. For more information on genetically engineered food, see the resource list at the end of the chapter.

Organic foods are often hard to find and are usually only available in health food stores and farmers markets. As people continue to ask supermarkets to carry them, however, accessibility to organic foods will increase. Organic foods can be expensive. If you need to prioritize which organic foods you can afford, the order we recommend is: meat, dairy, eggs, fruits, vegetables, grains. Toxins are more concentrated in foods that are higher up on the food chain. Meats that come from animals that have been given antibiotics and growth hormones are less healthy choices for our bodies. Ingesting such medications and hormones on a regular basis can have long-term effects, such as suppressing our own hormonal and immune systems. In addition, recent studies have suggested that the ingestion of growth hormones found in meat and dairy products may contribute to the onset of early puberty in children.

Organic milk, cheese, and butter may cost twice what conventional dairy products cost, but they don't contain the pesticides that cattle have eaten and then concentrated in their bodies. In fact, various carcinogens (cancer-causing agents) such as dioxin are concentrated in fat cells. Thus, they're concentrated in a cow's milk and when ingested by us they become concentrated in the fatty tissues of our breasts, and subsequently in our breast milk. These toxins may become quite concentrated in the small bodies of breast-fed babies. Besides being pesticide free, organic dairy products are free from growth hormones such as Bovine Growth Hormone and antibiotics, which are pumped into nonorganically raised cattle. Ingesting synthetic hormones can throw your own hormones out of balance, which may affect your ability to conceive. In addition, organic meat and dairy products usually come from farms or facilities in which animals are treated humanely.

Eggs from chickens that are organically fed are significantly higher in quality than their counterparts. We still know very little about the long-term effects of pesticides, hormones, and antibiotics on the human body. Meat and dairy production is big corporate business, with large lobbies and media campaigns that often make information difficult to access. Many fruits have been sprayed with pesticides up to 12 times before you eat them. If you choose not to buy organic foods, or they aren't available to you, washing your fruits and vegetables to remove as much external pesticide residue as possible is important. "Fit" is an organic cleanser for fruits and vegetables. If you can't find it, you can use soapy water and a thorough rinse.

In fish products, mercury from industrial waste has become a significant concern to women who are pregnant, as methylmercury can cross the placenta and slow nerve and brain growth. The FDA has recently advised pregnant and nursing mothers and young children to avoid eating shark, mackerel, swordfish, or tilefish, and to limit their consumption of all other fish to 12 ounces or less a week. The EPA warns against eating no more than one meal a week of freshwater sport fish caught in local waters. Environmental groups contend that these recommendations aren't nearly stringent enough, and to this list they add tuna steak, sea bass, Gulf of Mexico oysters, marlin, halibut, pike, walleye, white croaker, and largemouth bass. Because fish offers important nutrients and protein to the diet, environmental groups suggest that pregnant women eat farmed trout and catfish, fish sticks, Pacific salmon, flounder (in the summer), Mid-Atlantic blue crab, and haddock.

Vegetables

We are going to sound like your mother here, because we are mothers: Eat lots and lots of vegetables. Take the rainbow approach: Eat as many colors of vegetables and fruit as you can. This is a simple way to ensure that you'll get the entire variety of trace minerals and vitamins you need. Eat something green and leafy daily: dark leafy lettuces, spinach, kale, collard greens, mustard or dandelion greens, tatsoi, broccoli, or chard.

Fresh vegetables contain many more vitamins and minerals than frozen, and frozen vegetables and fruits have more retained vitamins and minerals than canned. This is particularly true for vegetables you buy that have been grown locally, since vegetables that are shipped from far away lose vitamins as they sit in boxes and on shelves. Overcooking can quickly reduce the content of some vitamins and minerals, such as folic acid, in vegetables. The brighter the green of the vegetable, the healthier. Vegetables do not need to be cooked until they are olive drab. In addition, steamed vegetables retain more vitamins than those that have been boiled or fried.

Whole Foods and Complete Digestion

Good digestion is key to fully absorbing the nutrients you've worked so hard to get into your body. Hormone levels are affected by poor digestion. Much of the basis of our hormones comes from plant hormones and hormone-building blocks. If our food isn't well digested, we won't get what we need from it. Whole foods are whole grains that haven't had all the fiber (and protein) removed, such as whole wheat and brown rice. Whole foods are also whole fruits and vegetables with their skins and peels and pulps instead of fruit juices. They aid in digestion and also reduce your risk of colon cancer.

Flax Seed

Flax seed is a phenomenal plant seed with many important properties: It fights cancers, increases progesterone, and reduces allergies. Another primary benefit of flax seed is how it aids digestion of food, especially protein, in the stomach itself, before it reaches the intestine. Flax seed is inexpensive and can be found organically in the bulk section of health food stores. Two tablespoons of ground flax seed equal one tablespoon of flax seed oil and contain the fiber that the oil doesn't. Taken daily, it not only provides hormone building blocks, but also helps our bodies better absorb the hormone-building blocks of other plants we've eaten. It also has the pleasant side effects of bowel regularity and increased vitality of skin, hair, and nails. We recommend that all women add ground flax seed to their diet.

Vitamins

Although we recommend that you start taking a food-based prenatal vitamin three months prior to conception, we do not recommend that you try to receive all of your nutrients through vitamins or supplements. Vitamins and especially minerals are often hard to absorb effectively in pill form. Your primary source of vitamins, ideally, should be fruits and vegetables, with supplements as a back-up to fill in the gaps.

Some megadose vitamins don't contain the correct balance of vitamins and minerals, and therefore can inhibit the absorption of other vitamins. For example, large doses of calcium should be balanced with magnesium and vitamin D. Vitamin A should be balanced with vitamin E. In high doses, some vitamins can be toxic and tax the liver and kidneys. When you're inseminating or pregnant, it's best not to ingest more than 8,000 IU of vitamin A, 4,000 IU of vitamin D, or 1,000 mg of vitamin C on a daily basis.

Prenatal vitamins contain much more iron than regular multivitamins, much more than needed if you aren't pregnant. Therefore, hold off on taking prenatal vitamins until two to three months before you start inseminating. If you don't conceive after a number of months, take a break from prenatal vitamins and switch to a regular multivitamin and a folic acid supplement so that your total folic acid dose equals 800-1,000 mcgs. Some women experience negative reactions to the iron contained in prenatal vitamins, including diarrhea, constipation, or stomach pains. If this is the case for you, see the following section on iron for alternative sources and try a regular multivitamin plus a folic acid supplement instead of prenatal vitamins.

Iron

Iron is at the center of each red blood cell in our body. Its job is to carry oxygen to organs and tissue. Low iron is the main cause of anemia. Signs of anemia include exhaustion, dizziness, shortness of breath, and coldness. Your blood volume increases by 50% during pregnancy, so it's important to begin pregnancy with a high hemoglobin/iron level. Because iron supplements are often difficult to absorb and cause negative side effects, eating iron rich foods is a good place to start if you aren't significantly iron-deficient. If you're low in iron (which you can tell from a simple blood test) you'll need to eat a higher level of iron daily for two months to replenish your body's reserves. Foods rich in iron include eggs, beef, pumpkin seeds, prunes, beets, lentils, tofu, molasses, dried apricots, and seaweed. Cooking food in cast-iron skillets increases its iron content. Don't take iron supplements at the same time you eat calcium-rich foods, as they'll bind to each other and not be absorbed by the body. Luckily, if you're anemic, your body will absorb iron more easily from food than if you have an adequate iron level. Nonetheless, iron is one of the more difficult minerals for our body to absorb from food sources. Often anemic people find it helpful take a food-based liquid iron supplement or make herbal teas rich in iron as well as increase their intake of iron-rich foods. The iron content of many common foods is listed on pages 180–181 of this book.

Folic Acid (Folate)

Many women who do not eat a lot of fresh leafy greens do not get enough folic acid. Low folic acid during the first few weeks of pregnancy correlates with increased rates of neural tube defects—spinal and nervous system problems in the developing fetus. 800-1,000 mcgs a day is the standard recommended dose during pregnancy, and that's what you'll usually find in prenatal vitamins. Regular multivitamins often contain 400 mcgs of folic acid.

There are many natural ways to get folic acid: dark leafy greens, dried peas and beans, whole grains, whole-grain breads and cereals, citrus fruits, bananas, and tomatoes. If you have a diet rich in fresh whole foods, you may well be getting enough folic acid.

Vitamin C

In addition to helping the body to absorb iron, vitamin C helps in tissue repair. It also assists in the formation of healthy gums, teeth, and bones for the baby. Foods high in vitamin C include broccoli, blueberries, asparagus, citrus fruits, red pepper and chilies, strawberries, and cauliflower. Eating one serving of vitamin C-rich food daily is recommended during pregnancy. This equals one cup of broccoli, two small oranges, or one cup of strawberries.

Protein

Proteins are the building blocks for our cells, so proteins are crucial. Sufficient protein also helps to balance blood sugar. Sources of protein include animal products, dairy products, nuts and seeds, soy products, and beans. If you eat a diet of fresh foods and vegetables, you're likely to get sufficient protein. We've noticed, however, that many people's diets overemphasize carbohydrates. This is especially true with vegetarians. Try increasing your proteins and decreasing your carbohydrates and notice if your body feels more alive. Protein-rich smoothies are easy to make at home in a blender. Try yogurt or milk, fresh fruit or juice, and "silky" tofu. Add protein powder, chlorella or spirulina for a big boost. But remember, moderation is the key to a healthy diet. If you aren't pregnant yet, be careful not to overindulge in proteins, since some studies indicate that excess protein consumption can hinder the body's ability to absorb calcium. See our chart on page 181 for the protein content of a variety of foods and recommendations on how many grams of protein per day you should eat.

Calcium

Calcium is essential to creating a strong skeletal system and good muscle function. High-calcium foods include sesame seeds and tahini, sunflower seeds, almonds, dairy products, turnip/radish/mustard/beet greens, kidney beans, tofu, miso paste, and sea weeds. Many seafoods are high in calcium, especially sardines or anchovies that one eats with the bone included. If you cook soup, putting an egg (still in its shell) in your soup stock with a tablespoon of vinegar will dissolve the calcium out of the shell and into the water. You can then fish out the egg after 20 minutes and eat it hard-boiled.

Many sea vegetables (seaweeds) are high in calcium, iron, and protein. Look for them in any store that carries Asian food. Nori is the sea vegetable dried in sheets that is used for sushi. Other sea vegetables are kombu, wakame, arame, dulse, and hijiki. Some have a mild flavor, like nori or kombu, and others such as hijiki have a stronger flavor. Kombu can be added to grains, beans, or soup stocks. If added to beans in a strip (which can be removed after cooking, as you would do with a bay leaf), it will reduce the flatulence and indigestion often caused by beans. Most seaweeds can be found in powder form or ground at home into powders and sprinkled on foods as a condiment; this is especially tasty if mixed half and half with sesame seeds. This Japanese mixture, called gomasio, is incredibly rich in minerals, has a salty flavor from the seaweed, and can be used in place of table salt. See the calcium chart on page 182 for the calcium content of a variety of foods.

Vitamin A

Beta carotene is vitamin A's precursor, and it promotes healthy skin, eyesight, and bone growth. Vitamin A is found in most orange vegetables and fruits, including carrots, squash, sweet potatoes, apricots, melons, and chili peppers. As mentioned earlier, vitamin A should not be taken in supplement form in doses exceeding 8,000 IU per day. The vitamin A content in food alone, however, is not high enough to cause physical problems, even if you drink carrot juice daily. During pregnancy, one serving of Vitamin A-rich foods daily is recommended: two small carrots, one quarter melon, or three apricots.

Lactose Intolerance

Most adults experience some form of lactose intolerance, meaning that they don't digest dairy proteins well, which can lead to stomach pains, flatulence, and bloating, and sometimes food allergy symptoms such as asthma or eczema. Ethnic groups with higher rates of lactose intolerance have generally developed dairy-free or dairy-light cuisines. Unfortunately, mainstream American cuisine is dairy-rich. Calcium is found in many sources other than milk, cheese, and ice cream.

As sufficient intake of calcium is crucial during pregnancy, lactose-intolerant women who haven't yet focused on calcium in their diets should look at our calcium-rich food list and make sure they include nondairy sources in their diets. Indeed, no one should rely solely on dairy for their calcium intake, as dairy products are one of the leading food allergens and contain high levels of pesticides, hormones, and cholesterol. There is evidence that the number of people suffering from some level of food allergy or lactose intolerance, both of which effectively limit the absorption of calcium, is actually quite high, suggesting further that all should work to include a variety of nondairy calcium sources during preconception and especially during pregnancy and lactation.

Vegans and Vegetarians

Vegans (those who eat no animal products) need to make sure they have a regular source of vitamin B-12, which is found in animal products or synthesized by microorganisms. Brewer's yeast is an excellent source of B-12, and you can add it to your diet by sprinkling it on casseroles, toast, popcorn, cooked vegetables, and soups. Another source of vitamin B-12 is fermented food, such as tempeh, miso paste, and high-quality tamari soy sauce. Other sources of vitamin B-12 include: fortified cereals, fortified soymilk, fortified soy products, and vitamin B-12 supplements. Vitamin supplements are available that do not contain animal products. If you eat organic vegetables, you'll receive some B-12 from the microorganisms living on the plants. Pesticide-sprayed vegetables are not a source of B-12.

Women who eat no meat need to be more aware of eating iron- and protein-rich foods. Unfortunately, a number of women who are vegan or vegetarian eat diets high in starch and sugar but consume relatively few fresh vegetables. Vegetarians who eat many vegetables and whole foods should have little trouble meeting the caloric, protein, vitamin, and mineral requirements of conception and pregnancy. Many prenatal care providers are insufficiently trained in nutritional counseling to be able to accurately advise vegetarian women about meatless pregnancy diets. Contrary to popular belief, with adequate knowledge and planning, vegetarian and vegan diets can be very healthy for pregnancy. For helpful tips you can share with worried health care providers and family members consult *Macrobiotic Pregnancy and Care of the Newborn* by Michio and Aveline Kushi and *The Vegetarian Mother and Baby Book* by Rose Elliot.

Cravings and Comfort Foods

People often crave certain foods when they're under stress, and therefore you may crave some foods preconceptionally. As your stress level increases, it's common to crave the comfort foods you ate as a child. In our nutritional counseling work with immigrant women and their daughters, we've found that as people change from their traditional diets to mainstream American diets, the nutritional quality of their diets decreases drastically. For some women, craving childhood foods can signal a return to a more balanced diet. For others, these cravings may not be particularly healthy— packaged macaroni and cheese or instant mashed potatoes, for example. If this is the case for you, know that a food craving often signals a hidden emotional craving that needs to be nurtured.

Food represents love and nurturing, and frequently what we really are looking for is to be touched, held, hugged or to cry and be able to feel young and vulnerable. Don't feel guilty about any of your cravings, no matter how unhealthy they may appear. Just gently explore the possible underlying emotional need, and see if there's another way to meet some of it.

Sometimes during pregnancy, women crave nonfood items such as starch, clay, freezer frost, or ice. This phenomenon is called pica and can signal a mineral imbalance—especially a deficiency in iron. Talk to your prenatal provider if you experience this.

Weight Gain and Loss

Often women want to diet immediately prior to pregnancy. Some women are told by their health care providers that losing weight will increase their fertility. Preconception is not the time to diet. Times of great metabolic shifts do not create optimal circumstances for your body to get pregnant and your risk of miscarriage is higher in these instances. Being as stable and consistent as you can is important. If you're going to diet, maintain your final weight goal for at least three months before you start to inseminate. This will stabilize your metabolism. Also, understand that the building blocks for hormones are stored in our body's fat. Without sufficient fat, hormone levels for both conception and pregnancy are difficult to maintain. You need to weigh enough to feed your baby from your body both during pregnancy and breastfeeding. Therefore, if you're underweight, gaining even 10 pounds may increase your fertility.

How Much Weight Gain Is Healthy During Pregnancy?

The pattern of weight gain during pregnancy is different for each woman. Often women gain very little weight during the first 12 weeks of pregnancy, then, on average, they gain a pound a week. Sometimes, though, the reverse is true, and most weight is gained during the first trimester. There's no right or wrong pattern; each woman's body is unique.

Over the course of pregnancy, a weight gain of 30–50 pounds is healthy and normal. If you're gaining weight extremely slowly or not at all, you'll need to eat more. Try food that is somewhat higher in fat and lower in bulk than what you normally consume. For instance, could you substitute whole milk for skim? Or how about adding some cheddar cheese and avocado to your eggs in the morning? Could you eat french fries occasionally instead of a baked potato? Remember, moderation is key, so don't think you can gain weight in a healthy way by snacking on candy bars and soda throughout the day. A little extra fat in your diet, however, will help provide a home for the important hormones that are stored in your body's fat.

If you feel like you're gaining too much weight too quickly, replace sweet or high-fat foods with healthier alternatives such as grains, legumes, fruits, and vegetables. You could also substitute low-fat nonmeat protein sources such as beans, tofu, and soy products for beef, pork, and fatty fish. If you already eat well, try to exercise more. Of course, discuss your goals with a health care provider before beginning any exercise regimen during pregnancy. Some exercises, especially those that work the abdominal muscles, may look easy and harmless but can, in fact, interfere with fetal development.

Tips for Relieving Morning Sickness

- Eat small meals every two to three hours throughout the day
- Nibble some dry saltines or graham crackers before arising
- Incorporate many high-carbohydrate foods into your diet: dry toast, bananas, potatoes, whole-grain cereal, rice
- Try sweet juices in the morning
- Avoid coming into contact with strong smells
- Avoid eating fatty and spicy foods.
- Abstain from alcohol, tobacco, and caffeine
- Drink peppermint or ginger tea

Ultimately, your body will let you know when and how much you should eat during pregnancy. If you eat healthy foods throughout the day and exercise moderately, your hunger signals will let you know when and how much you should consume. Remember, weight gain varies from woman to woman, body to body. Don't criticize yourself or believe you're "abnormal" if you feel you're gaining too little or too much weight before or during pregnancy.

Exercise

When women start to eat more they often increase the amount they exercise in order to balance calorie input and output. Beginning a rigorous exercise program or drastically increasing your exercise routine can change your metabolism significantly. As with dieting, metabolic shifts may be beneficial in the long run, but they don't facilitate fertility in the short term. Please see the section on exercise in Chapter 9.

Relationships and Partner Issues

We've talked about the role of nutrition in increasing fertility and stabilizing your body. Unfortunately, the incredible potential for positive change can sometimes backfire. Feelings of guilt, shame, and blame—self-blame and blaming your partner for not eating well—can easily arise. During times of stress it's common to slip into less healthy relationship patterns. For food changes to feel truly nourishing, your relationship has to feel nourished as well.

It's often helpful to reflect on the roles each of you play in your relationship: Does one of you play the nurturing role? Is it an equally divided role? Or does one of you express nurturing through food and the other express nurturing in another way? The roles you've established in your relationship aren't necessarily consciously chosen, comfortable, or healthy. Sometimes the extra burden of changing your eating habits can bring up hidden resentment in your relationship.

Offering to share the extra focus and time required to make healthier eating choices, especially at the beginning, can feel very supportive. Making food and diet changes is a sensitive area in which respect for each other is key. Discussing how you both can support the new choices you'll be making about food can make all the difference. In your partnership are you both committed to making these changes? Will both of you give up your morning coffee ritual or nightly glasses of wine? Will you both change your eating schedules? Or will just one of you make these changes? Look at the potential impact these changes may have on your social and personal lives, and your life together. This can be a joint growth process. We've seen many couples use healthy diet changes to strengthen their relationship. It's one way of making a joint commitment toward the baby that the whole family will benefit from.

Food and Extended Conception Periods

If it takes more than a few cycles for you to get pregnant, you may start to resent the diet changes you've made. Often women only intend to temporarily eliminate their consumption of caffeine, alcohol, or sugar. As this period lengthens, any changes you've made can trigger resentment, the need to be in complete control of your food intake, and monthly binging. These are not mutually exclusive. They can come up all together or change from day to day, cycle to cycle.

Every month many women try to "perfect" their diets (and for that matter their whole beings) under the assumption that if they merely eat better they'll become pregnant. Then they work to control their eating even more. Rather than making healthy choices, many women become fanatics. The emotional undercurrent of stress and self-blame is incredibly defeating. All the pleasure is taken out of eating.

Attempting to control anything tends to greatly increase stress. It makes sense, however, that we have a natural tendency to try control anything we can during a time of feeling out of control. Don't be hard on yourself and fall into the trap of trying to control how much you're trying to control. If you find yourself in this place, slow down and honor yourself. You're doing the best you can. Let the love, nurturing, and self-compassion flow in.

The resentment women often feel toward their bodies when they don't get pregnant overflows into the changes they've made in their diets and/or toward their partners or others who encouraged, pushed, or suggested these "ineffective" changes in the first place.

There is a potential at some point to want to stop all fertility-related changes in your life if they haven't "worked." With this usually comes a desire to binge on all of the "forbidden" foods and substances. It's fine to do whatever you need to do. Just be kind to yourself afterward. This is part of why you should incorporate slow changes that establish long-term, lifelong patterns. If you've made slow changes, it won't feel like you're sliding down a mountain when you do slip. This is also one reason why, if you're partnered, it's beneficial to make these changes together.

Nutrition During Pregnancy

The information we've presented so far about eating healthy is applicable to both the preconception and pregnancy periods. During pregnancy, some of the nutritional tips we covered are extra important. We'll remind you that avoiding low blood sugar will not only decrease the discomforts of pregnancy, but will also provide a more stable and healthy environment for your baby to grow. Avoiding caffeine, artificial preservatives and sweeteners, and pesticides is most advisable during pregnancy as well as during breastfeeding. A number of diet changes may help with other specific complaints of pregnancy, from vaginal yeast infections to bleeding gums. The books in our resource list give specific information on many of these remedies.

Protein, Iron, and Calcium

During pregnancy, a variety of vitamins and nutrients are essential to healthy growth. To this end, our recommendations about eating as many different colors and types of vegetables and fruits are essential to making sure your body has all the key ingredients. Three main nutrients used in great quantity in pregnancy deserve special attention and review: protein, iron, and calcium.

Protein

Protein is the main component of our tissue (besides water). It's essential to all aspects of fetal growth, including brain development. During pregnancy, regular protein intake will help you avoid the awful feeling of low blood sugar. More importantly, we've seen toxemia problems in the third trimester of pregnancy resolved with an increase in protein intake. Toxemia, also called preeclampsia, is a pregnancy-related condition involving swelling and high blood pressure that can put both mother and fetus at serious risk. Eating foods that support the kidneys and liver will decrease your risk of toxemia. Protein is, in our opinion, the most crucial nutrient during pregnancy.

Iron

When a woman is pregnant she has to produce enough blood for her baby's circulatory system and then increase her own blood volume by eight to 10 cups. Iron is stored in deep reserves in the body as well as the bloodstream. Eating iron-rich foods throughout pregnancy helps ensure that a woman finishes her pregnancy without having depleted these reserves and becoming anemic. Anemia during pregnancy not only makes a woman feel exhausted, but also increases her chances of heavy bleeding after the baby's birth, and decreases her tissue's ability to heal well. Anemia also decreases the amount of oxygen the baby receives through the blood. Since the average American diet doesn't contain adequate iron for pregnancy, pregnant women need to make a conscious effort to increase their consumption of iron-rich foods as well as take iron supplements. The U.S. recommended daily allowance (RDA) of iron for nonpregnant women is 18 mg per day. For pregnant women the RDA is 30-60 mg per day. Many women figure they can make up this 12-42 mg difference by taking prenatal vitamins that contain iron. As we've described, however, iron in most prenatal vitamins is poorly absorbed by the body; therefore, not all of the iron in the vitamins is used. We suggest taking a food-based prenatal vitamin or a natural iron supplement such as Floradix, which is absorbed more easily and causes significantly fewer side effects.

Calcium

Remember, inadequate calcium intake during pregnancy dramatically increases the risk of osteoporosis later in life, because the baby will take calcium from the mother's bones. Because calcium is a key mineral used in muscle movement, leg cramps during pregnancy can be eased by increasing your calcium intake.

Calorie Intake

The main difference between a healthy preconception diet and a pregnancy diet is that you'll eat more during pregnancy. The field of obstetrics constantly revises its official opinion on how many calories pregnant women should consume. Not too long ago women's caloric intake was severely restricted during pregnancy to the great detriment of women and their babies. Dominant culture's prejudices against large-bodied women affect medical research in terms of what questions are asked and how data is interpreted in studies about obesity and pregnancy. A lot of the information available, in our opinion, is fear-based and not very useful, since it doesn't take into consideration the great diversity of women's body types and metabolisms. See the resource list at the end of this chapter for helpful books on food and pregnancy.

A good place to start is to eliminate as many processed high-fat foods as possible from your diet, minimize your sugar intake, and then learn to eat when you notice you're hungry. In pregnancy you'll probably be eating somewhere between every hour and five small meals a day, as compared to eating two to three larger meals a day. Review our section on low blood sugar to understand how signs of hunger during pregnancy may feel different than what you're used to.

During pregnancy, to avoid insomnia caused by low blood sugar, place snacks by your bed that can be consumed easily in the middle of the night and that do not require any further preparation. Many women who wake up 2 A.M. without feeling hungry will go right back to sleep when they eat something such as a banana, cheese and crackers, or a premade peanut butter or tuna fish sandwich. Eating right when you wake up in the morning and then, throughout the day, regularly nibbling snacks of almonds, dried apricots, trail mix, yogurt, etc. will help prevent the vicious cycle of morning sickness. Some women can get by on six small meals throughout the day. Others need to eat one or two bites of something every 20–30 minutes to prevent nausea.

Postpartum and Breastfeeding

During the immediate postpartum period, women need to eat as well and as much as during pregnancy in order to establish a good milk supply and heal torn tissue. Extra iron intake is also important if heavy bleeding occurred during the birth of the baby. Drinking extra water helps avoid constipation and keeps the urine diluted, both of which are important for comfort if a birth tear or episiotomy is healing. New mothers should drink a large glass of water every time they nurse as well as with each meal, to ensure that they're well hydrated.

Women need to be fed during their first few weeks postpartum in order to feel loved and nurtured. Making breast milk and nursing a newborn are acts of incredible giving. New mothers will feel emotionally and physically replenished if friends and

family nourish them with food and drink. Low blood sugar along with sleep deprivation and hormone changes can make motherhood feel overwhelming. During postpartum, mothers need to have food and drink by their bedside throughout the day and night. The emotional vulnerability of early postpartum can often be alleviated by providing a nursing mom with nourishing food on a regular basis.

Arranging to drop off cooked meals during the first two weeks after birth is the most essential support friends and family can provide a new mother. Even if a partner can be home from work to cook, she herself has just become a new mother and should focus her attention on bonding with the baby, getting enough sleep, and helping the biological mother with tasks such as bathing the baby and changing diapers.

A Nursing Mother's Diet

Some infants are sensitive to certain foods that are absorbed into breast milk in the first five to 10 weeks postpartum. These may include spicy foods; cruciferous vegetables such as broccoli, cauliflower, and cabbage; beans, garlic, or onions; caffeine; and chocolate. These foods often upset the newly developed digestive system. Less often, a baby may be sensitive to wheat or dairy products during the entire breastfeeding period. These reactions fall more into the category of food allergies. This will be apparent if the baby continues to show signs of discomfort past the first few weeks and seems frustrated or cranky while nursing as well. These babies are often called "colicky," when more frequently than not they're suffering from an allergy to dairy, wheat, or caffeine. Sensitive babies often react with gas pains within an hour or two of nursing. Passing this information on to whomever is organizing the food brigade will help avoid unnecessary challenging evenings with a cranky, crying baby.

Conclusion

We want food to be nurturing and loving for you, and we want to remind you to approach the topic slowly and thoughtfully. Gradual changes are the strongest. Try not to chastise yourself if you're not yet ready to give up your cherished coffee; we're merely offering suggestions. For now, implement the ones that feel right. Don't try to do a complete overhaul. Baby steps are the right-size steps. Eventually, your healthy eating habits will be lifelong. You've got plenty of time.

It's validating to respect the impact that making food and diet changes has on our bodies and psyches. Do take the time to write in a journal and share with your friends and lovers what comes up, both initially and along the way. If necessary, consider joining or starting a support group of women who examine the role food plays in their lives. Any choices you make toward greater health will improve the quality of your life and your pregnancy. Good luck!

Sample Pregnancy Diets

Jennifer's Normal Diet

6 A.M.: woke up

7 A.M.: one cup of half regular/half decaf coffee

10 A.M.: one cup of fruit-flavored yogurt and a plain doughnut

12:30 P.M.: turkey and cheese sandwich, small bag of cookies, Pepsi

7 P.M.: medium plate of pasta with jarred tomato sauce, small lettuce salad with tomato, glass of milk

8 P.M.: popcorn with salt and butter, glass of water

9 P.M.: bowl of vanilla ice cream with chocolate sauce

Suggestions: We'll focus mainly on making substitutions for sugar and caffeine, increasing protein intake, and decreasing the length of periods without food. Also, we recommend increasing water intake to 8-12 cups a day, especially since Jennifer is losing water through the diuretic effect of caffeine consumption.

Jennifer is probably trying to reduce her caffeine intake. She may want to make sure her decaf coffee is water-filtered or switch to black or green tea. She should switch to a caffeine-free coffee-like drink such as Inka or Roastaroma tea, and she should substitute a caffeine-free nonsugar lunch beverage for the Pepsi. In the afternoon, eating food high in protein will probably give her an energy boost right around the time she's really wishing she had the sugar and caffeine in a Pepsi to keep her alert.

Adding a piece of toast with nut butter, a hard-boiled egg, or another source of protein at 7 A.M. will help her body by giving it some protein after a night of going without food. It will probably also decrease any mid-morning sugar cravings she might have. She could add protein to her dinner by adding tofu, ground beef, or vegetable protein to her spaghetti sauce. Protein can be added to salads by using sunflower seeds, almonds, or shredded cheese.

Besides adding more protein to decrease her sugar cravings, Jennifer could substitute fruit for some of her refined sugar snacks (cookies, doughnuts, ice cream, etc.). Fruit will add vitamins, especially important since caffeine depletes them. Adding a variety of orange and green vegetables to her pasta sauce or her salad and bringing a bag of vegetables to work, such as baby carrots and celery, to eat with her sandwich will significantly increase the vitamins, minerals, and fiber she gets. In today's diet she had three servings of dairy products, providing calcium but almost no iron and very few other vitamins and minerals. Jennifer will receive some extra minerals and good fiber if she uses whole-grain bread in her sandwich and eats whole-grain pasta for dinner.

Jennifer's Changed Diet

6 A.M.: woke up

7 A.M.: one cup decaf green tea, two pieces whole wheat toast with almond butter, glass of water

10 A.M.: one cup plain unsweetened yogurt with fresh melon and banana, glass of water

12:30 P.M.: turkey and cheese sandwich; small bag of trail mix with nuts, raisins, and chocolate; orange juice; one cup carrots and broccoli in bite-size pieces with ranch dip; glass of water

3:30 P.M.: peanut butter and crackers, large nectarine, glass of water

7 P.M.: medium plate of whole-grain pasta; jarred tomato sauce with ground beef, carrots, onion, bell pepper, celery added; small mixed-greens salad with tomato, alfalfa sprouts, and toasted sunflower seeds; glass of milk

8 P.M.: celery sticks, popcorn with salt and butter, glass of water

9 P.M.: bowl of strawberries and blueberries, glass of water

Corrinne's Normal Diet

Breakfast: bowl of cornflakes with milk

Snack: peanut butter sandwich, apple juice, corn chips

Lunch: fast-food hamburger and fries, caffeine-free soda

Dinner: roast beef, mashed potatoes, green beans, water

Throughout the day: two liters of water

Suggestions: It seems like Corrinne packed a lunch then ate it for her mid-morning snack, so she had to resort to eating fast food for lunch. One bowl of cold cereal with milk is a breakfast that many people subsist on, but in reality it isn't much food. Supplementing whole-grain cereal with fruit will add some vitamins and minerals. Even better, Corrinne could try a bowl of hot cereal such as oatmeal and add any of the following: walnuts, almonds, dried apricots or figs, molasses, flax seed, or wheat germ. All these toppings add iron, protein, and/or calcium. Corrinne could pack herself a snack as well as a lunch, in case she needs it at 10 or at 3, so that she can have nutritious foods available throughout the day.

From mid morning on she consumed plenty of protein, eating meat twice and peanut butter once. If she has no choice but fast food for lunch, we would suggest that she drink milk or orange juice instead of soda, and most fast-food restaurants offer some type of salad now. Adding more vegetables will aid her diet substantially, especially dark leafy greens and an orange or yellow vegetable.

Corrinne's Changed Diet

Breakfast: bowl of instant unsweetened oatmeal with dried figs, minced apple, walnuts, one tablespoon wheat germ, one tablespoon honey, and milk

Snack: peanut butter sandwich, apple juice, corn chips

Lunch: fast-food restaurant chicken strip lunch salad, glass of milk

Snack: whole wheat crackers and cheese

Dinner: roast beef, mashed potatoes, green beans, water, pumpkin squash

Throughout the day: two liters of water

Marisol's Diet

Early morning: eight-ounce smoothie of banana, tahini (sesame seed paste), yogurt, and soy milk

Mid morning: peanut butter on one piece of whole-wheat toast, big glass of water

Mid day: one cup leftover greens, rice, and tofu; one orange; more water

Afternoon: three baby carrots and a quarter cup of humus dip, peppermint tea with honey

Supper: half-cup of casserole made with corn, kidney beans, and corn bread; small salad with mixed greens, avocado, red bell pepper, and sprouts; iced tea; more water later

Evening: soy milk

Suggestions: Marisol has eaten regularly throughout the day, with quite a colorful variety of fresh fruits and vegetables. It seems she has time to cook one well-planned meal a day and makes enough to last for lunch the next day. Our main recommendation for her regards her food portions. Overall, she needs to increase her caloric intake. Hopefully, she could increase her portion sizes without feeling overly full at the end of each meal or snack. She may have some weight-gain concerns she needs to discuss with someone. Challenge: Can you find five nonmeat sources of protein in her diet?

Amounts of Iron, Protein, and Calcium in Common Foods

Iron

The recommended daily allowance of iron for nonpregnant/nonlactating women is 18 milligrams per day. The recommended daily allowance for pregnant or lactating women is 30-60 milligrams per day (see iron sections on pages 166 and 173-174 for tips on absorption).

Food	Amount	Milligrams of Iron
Almonds	1/2 cup	3.3
Apricots, dried	5	1.65
Bagel, enriched	3 oz.	3.2
Blackstrap molasses	2 tbsp.	7
Broccoli, cooked	1 cup	1.1
Chicken (light meat)	4 oz.	92
Collard greens	1 cup	1.2
Currants	1/2 cup	8
Eggs	2	2
Figs, dried	5 medium	2
Floradix Liquid Supplement	4 tsp.	15
Garbanzos, cooked	1 cup	7
Ground beef	4 oz.	1.96
Lentils, cooked	1 cup	6.6
Liver	4 oz.	7.7
Kidney beans, cooked	1 cup	5.2
Oysters	6	5.6
Peaches, dried	5	5.28
Pears, dried	5	3.7
Pinto beans, cooked	1 cup	405
Pistachios	1/2 cup	4.3
Pumpkin/squash	1 cup	1.5
Prune juice	1 cup	3.0
Quinoa, cooked	1 cup	6.3
Raisins	1/2 cup	2.2
Seaweed (dulse)	100 gms	6.3

Seaweed (hijiki)	100 gms	29
Seaweed (kombu)	100 gms	10
Seaweed (nori)	100 gms	12
Soybeans, cooked	1 cup	8.8
Spinach, cooked	1 cup	2.9
Tahini	2 tbsp.	2.6
Tuna	7 oz.	3.03
Veggie burger, commercial	1 patty	1.1-4.5

Protein

The recommended daily allowance of protein for nonpregnant/nonlactating women is 44 grams per day. Our recommended daily allowance for pregnant or lactating women is 60-100 grams per day.

Food	Amount	Milligrams of Iron
Almond butter	2 tbsp.	5
Almonds	1/2 cup	12
Beef	7 oz.	43
Brown rice, cooked	1 cup	5
Chicken	7 oz.	58
Eggs	2	16
Garbanzos, cooked	1 cup	15
Lentils	1 cup	18
Milk	1 cup	8
Peanut butter	2 tbsp.	8
Peas, cooked	1/2 cup	9
Pinto beans, cooked	1 cup	14
Potato	1 medium	4
Quinoa, cooked	1 cup	11
Spinach, cooked	1 cup	6
Soy milk	1 cup	6
Spaghetti, cooked	1 cup	7
Soybeans, cooked	1 cup	29
Tahini	2 oz.	6
Tempeh	1 cup	38
Tofu, firm	4 oz.	8-15

Tuna	7 oz.	53
Veggie burger, Commercial	1 patty	5-24
Veggie dog	1 link	8-26
Yogurt	1 cup	12

Calcium

The recommended daily allowance of calcium for nonpregnant/nonlactating women is 800 mg per day. The recommended daily allowance for pregnant or lactating women is 1200 mg per day.

Food	Amount	Milligrams of Iron
Almonds	1/2 cup	200
Blackstrap molasses	1 tbsp.	137
Brazil nuts	1/2 cup	134
Broccoli	1/2 cup	89
Cheddar cheese	1oz.	213
Cheese pizza	1 slice	107
Collard greens	1 cup	350
Cottage cheese	1/2 cup	115
Corn tortilla	1 (6-inch diameter)	60
Egg	2	54
Green beans	1/2 cup	31
Ice cream	1/2 cup	288
Kale, cooked	1 cup	206
Kidney beans, canned	1 cup	74
Macaroni and cheese	1 cup	362
Melon	half	27
Milk	1 cup	288
Okra	8 pods	78
Orange	1 medium	54
Oysters	1/3 cup	113
Peas	1/2 cup	18
Rhubarb, cooked	1/2 cup	184
Rice Milk (fortified)	1 cup	300
Salmon	3 oz.	271
Sardines	3 oz.	372

Spinach, cooked	1 cup	258
Soy milk (fortified)	1 cup	300
Sweet potato	1 medium	47
Whole wheat bread	1 slice	25
White beans, cooked	1 cup	170
Yogurt	1 cup	294

Resources

Books

Macrobiotic Pregnancy and Care of the Newborn, Michio and Aveline Kushi, Japan
    Publications, 1983

Nutrition for a Healthy Pregnancy, Elizabeth Somer, Henry Holt, 1995

The Pregnancy Cookbook, Hope Ricciotti, WW Norton and Co., 1996

The Vegetarian Mother and Baby Book, Rose Elliot, Pantheon, 1997

The Vegetarian Pregnancy, Sharon Yntema, McBooks Press, 1994

The Zone, Barry Sears with Bill Lawren, HarperCollins, 1995

Web Sites

The Shopper's Guide to Genetically Modified Foods
www.greenpeace.org.uk/Products/GM/backg2.htm

The Vegan Diet During Pregnancy and Lactation
www.vrg.org/nutrition/veganpregnancy.htm

Chapter 8 Fertility Inhibitors and Enhancers

Our bodies interact with our physical environment in thousands of invisible yet profound ways. How the environment influences our hormonal balance specifically is, to a great extent, still shrouded in mystery. Increases in technology and industrialization have introduced new chemicals into the environment at a rate that exceeds our ability to track the long-term negative consequences to our bodies. Nevertheless, you have at your fingertips many simple ways to lower your exposure to toxins and chemicals that may inhibit your fertility. Many ancient and recent healing philosophies offer insight into optimizing fertility health, and easy-to-obtain supplements and herbs can have a far-reaching impact on regulating an irregular menstrual cycle.

This chapter covers which chemicals, medicines, and products to avoid both during preconception and in pregnancy, and provides specific suggestions for enhancing your fertility. Male fertility inhibitors and enhancers are detailed at the end of the chapter, and you should review this section if you plan on using a known donor. Exercise, sleep, and stress, which all greatly influence fertility, will be discussed in the next chapter. Good nutrition, which is essential to optimizing fertility, was reviewed in depth in Chapter 7. These three chapters together present a comprehensive picture for making the most of your body's innate resources to conceive and grow a healthy baby.

Fertility Inhibitors

Environmental Toxins

Because of the difficulties inherent in assessing one's true risk to toxin exposure, we encourage you to take seriously what information is available and to err on the side of caution when exposing yourself (and possibly your baby) to toxins during preconception, pregnancy, and breastfeeding. Ultimately you must make your own choices about what level of risk you're comfortable exposing yourself to. Often, avoiding certain environmental toxins is out of anyone's individual control. You may react to this by not making any changes, as the changes you can make may seem insignificant compared to what you can't change. Our belief, however, is that any reduction of your toxin exposure is significant, and there are all sorts of creative yet simple ways to reduce your exposure to all sorts of fertility-inhibiting toxins.

Toxins abound in work and home environments, outdoors and indoors. People may be exposed to toxins through specific hobbies and activities they enjoy. Toxins are found in food, water, air, and soil. Our environment is full of numerous pollutants and toxins that can inhibit both male and female fertility. Unfortunately, the information available to the public on toxins and reproductive health is inadequate. Some chemicals cause little damage if exposure is minimal, yet many have a cumulative effect whereby years of low exposure can concentrate them in the body to a significant and potentially harmful level. The effects of many chemicals are not immediately apparent, and obtaining unbiased information about the possible toxic reproductive effects of chemicals is often difficult, since researchers and scientists are often heavily pressured from various industries to underreport problems. In addition, it's difficult to sort out exactly which chemical out of thousands may be linked to a birth defect over the course of a pregnancy. In their first few weeks of development, fetuses are much more susceptible to low doses of chemicals than grown adults. Little is known about the toxicity of chemicals to developing fetuses, and even less is known about how chemical exposure affects fertility.

Detoxifying

Detoxifying is the process of releasing toxins stored in the body, especially those in the intestines, colon, and liver. If you wish to begin a detoxification program, you'll need to do it at least three months before you'd like to start inseminating. Once you are (or may be) pregnant, it's best to use remedies that support and nourish your liver, intestines, and kidneys instead of trying to detoxify them. The detoxifying process moves toxins from the deeper recesses of the body into the bloodstream and intestines on their way out of the body. As these toxins move into the bloodstream, they can cross the placenta and come in contact with your baby if you're pregnant.

Acupuncturists and homeopaths offer sound treatments for helping to stimulate the body to clear itself of a number of chemicals, including heavy metals. Detoxification methods include the use of herbal and homeopathic remedies, acupuncture, enemas, juicing, fasting, and diet changes. Detoxifying your body is best attempted under the guidance of a trained professional.

Reducing Toxins at Home

Housecleaning

Using nontoxic cleaning products is a significant and simple change you can make to reduce your daily interactions with toxic chemicals. Many common cleaning products are quite toxic, not only to you but also to children and pets. Chlorine combines with organic compounds to cause a variety of negative effects on fertility. Chlorine is found in chlorine bleach, bleached menstrual products, chlorinated water, and water contaminated by pesticide runoff. We recommend that you do not use chlorine bleach. Use gloves when cleaning, and open windows for good ventilation. If you're starting to inseminate, have a housemate or partner trade household responsibilities so that you won't be exposed directly to toxic cleaning products. Environmentally safe cleaning products are available in health food stores and online.

House Repairs

When making repairs and improvements around the house, keep in mind that many toxic chemicals are found in paint, caulk, solvents, glues, and finishes, and should therefore be avoided. If someone is using these products in a space you plan to be in, at the very least open a window so that the area is well ventilated before you enter it. Ideally, depending on the toxicity of the product being used, you should thoroughly ventilate the area for one to two days before reentry. Whenever you use paint products, be sure to follow the safety guidelines of your public health department or paint store to avoid exposure to old lead-based paint. Nontoxic paints are available at many hardware and home improvement stores.

Dry Cleaning

Dry-cleaning chemicals are particularly toxic. Environmentally friendly dry-cleaning businesses, however, are beginning to appear. If you can't find one, at least throw out the dry-cleaning bag after you pick up your clothes from the cleaner and air your clothes out outside, if possible, before putting them in the closet. Don't leave your dry cleaning sitting in a hot car. The off-gassing of the chemicals in an enclosed space increases the intensity of your exposure to them.

Gardening

While gardening, you'll want to minimize or eliminate your use of chemical fertilizers and pesticides. Use organic fertilizers and employ natural methods to control garden pests. Wash store-bought fruit and vegetables—whether they're organically or conventionally grown—with soap and water. Many resources exist to help you find alternatives. For helpful tips, visit www.backyardorganicgardening.com or www.greengardener.co.uk or see the resource list at the end of this chapter for books on organic gardening.

Menstrual Products

The variety of menstrual products available to women is greater than ever, but many women are unaware of both the products available and their value over brand-name pads and tampons. Most tampons contain absorbency enhancers that may include polyester, rayon, or asbestos, as well as metals linked to infertility, such as boron. Synthetic fibers in conventional tampons can cause vaginal inflammation and irritation. The rayon in many tampons depletes natural magnesium from the vaginal tissue, leaving it more susceptible to infection from bacteria such as *Staphylococcus aureus*, which is linked to toxic shock syndrome. To obtain their characteristic white color, tampons are bleached with chlorine, which gives off a by-product called dioxin. Dioxin builds up in the body over time and has been linked to reproductive cancer and birth defects.

Perfumes and fragrances in deodorant tampons can upset the naturally healthy microbial balance of the vagina and cause irritation and allergic reaction. Super-absorbent tampons absorb not only blood, but also vaginal fluids that help cleanse and balance the vagina's natural bacteria. If the natural bacteria aren't cleansed and in proper balance, vaginal infection can occur. Since infection increases the amount of white blood cells in the vagina, large numbers of white blood cells will attack sperm, recognizing them as "foreign." Thus, infection makes the vagina less "sperm-friendly" and can reduce your chances of conception.

If you choose to use tampons we suggest that you use eco-friendly tampon brands that have no fragrances and are unbleached. Use the lowest absorbency possible, and change tampons frequently. Don't sleep all night without changing your tampon. Instead, consider using pads at night. If you're using disposable pads, use fragrance-free unbleached pads, available at health food stores or online.

Consider using washable cloth pads, a menstrual sponge (a natural sea sponge you can rinse out and reuse like a tampon), or a menstrual cup such as the Keeper (which is reusable) or Instead (which is disposable). See the resource list at the end of this chapter for information on where to buy these products.

Douching

The vagina has a unique immune system composed of healthy bacteria that keeps its pH very acidic so that other bacteria (such as those in the rectum) have trouble growing. The vagina naturally self-cleanses with an outward flow of vaginal secretions and cervical fluid. Douching is unhealthy for the natural balance of bacteria in the vagina, since it washes out healthy bacteria. If a douche is store-bought and contains perfumes, deodorants, or dyes, it can chemically irritate the vaginal tissue, causing an inflammation that is not conducive to conception. Finally, douching can be dangerous during pregnancy, as it may push fluid up through the cervix and into the bloodstream, interrupting pregnancy and potentially causing harm to the mother and baby.

Other Personal Products

During pregnancy, avoid using nonorganic hair dyes and hair bleach as well as chemicals used for permanents. Be aware that the fumes from most nail polish and nail polish removers are toxic and very readily absorbed when you breathe them. Non-toxic nail polishes are available at health food stores and some fashion boutiques. If possible, paint your nails outdoors. If you get pedicures and manicures, make sure the room is well ventilated. Avoid using pHisoHex or any other antiseptic skin cleanser containing hexachlorophene, which is considered toxic for pregnancy.

Arts and Crafts

Think carefully about any crafts or other projects in which you partake regularly and whether you need to modify them. Many reproductively toxic chemicals are found in solvents, glues, paints and varnishes, dyes, and detergents. Also, many crafts require chemicals that contain toxic metals such as lead, mercury, and boron. Consider using alternative products during preconception and pregnancy, reduce the frequency of your projects, or reduce your exposure by wearing protective clothing and ventilating your workspace.

Cigarette Smoke

During pregnancy, smoking increases the likelihood of low-birth-weight babies, preterm labor, still birth, and miscarriage. The toxic chemicals in cigarettes target the lung cells so that babies born to smoking moms may have precancerous changes in their lung tissue at birth, even though no cigarette smoke has directly entered their lungs. The nicotine to which a baby is exposed in the uterus permanently changes the biochemistry and nerve patterns of his or her brain. This appears to be related to the higher rates of criminal activity, drug addiction, and attention-deficit disorders of children born to smokers. Also, on average, children whose mothers smoked while pregnant demonstrate lower IQ scores.

Smoking while trying to conceive can negatively affect how the cilia (tiny fibers) work in the fallopian tubes to move the egg, and then the embryo, toward the uterus. The chemicals inhaled in cigarette smoke also leach from the body many vitamins and nutrients—especially vitamin C—that are important for optimal fertility.

If you smoke, start decreasing how much you smoke several months before you start trying to conceive. This is important if you use smoking as a response to stress, since trying to conceive can be quite stressful, and you'll want to have enough time to implement healthier ways of dealing with stress before you feel challenged by the emotional roller coaster of inseminating. Also, as you cut back and eventually quit, take a daily multivitamin that contains vitamin C, the B's, and E to help replace the vitamins you've lost from cigarette use. Eliminate as much as possible any exposure you may have to secondhand smoke from family and friends as well as at social events or in the workplace.

Smoking requires deep, slow breathing, so be sure to focus on continuing to breathe deeply and slowly a few times a day after you quit. Although you may not realize it, in this way smoking is similar to a relaxation exercise. Smokers also have an excuse to go outside during the workday. When you quit smoking, coworkers might not understand that you should be entitled to that time and fresh air also. Smoking is also often a social connecting point, so when you quit you need to find alternative connecting points. Know that quitting smoking can feel like a big loss—just from the point of socializing. Whatever perk smoking brings, you need a substitution.

Having a cigarette or smoking a joint often relates to communication patterns. If a conversation gets too intense, you may be used to leaving to go smoke as a way of ending the conversation. It's important to recognize if you use smoking in this way. Because you no longer have an easy excuse to leave the room when you need a break, you might find yourself feeling trapped or angry and not knowing why.

Ask for the support you need during the preconception period, just as you would if you were pregnant. We understand that quitting smoking often takes a number of tries and a lot of support, whether through smoking-cessation programs, friends, or family. Consult your local public health department or the American Lung Association for resources. Herbal and homeopathic smoking-cessation remedies are also available in most health food stores.

Over-the-Counter Medicines and Herbal Remedies to Avoid

Many medicines are best avoided in pregnancy, especially in early pregnancy. A few days after conception, blood flow has not yet been exchanged between embryo and mother. By six to 10 days after conception, however, the embryo has implanted itself in the wall of the uterus, and the exchange of blood has started. At this point the embryo is most susceptible to exposure to drugs or toxins, up through about eight weeks from the mother's last menstrual period. Once you begin inseminating, you're spending each second half of your cycle in the possible pregnancy zone, so it's a good idea to take a careful look at the medications you take.

In general, during pregnancy it's best to avoid aspirin and ibuprofen (Advil or

Motrin); acetaminophen (Tylenol) is preferred by obstetricians, although it taxes the liver. Before conception, in the first half of the menstrual cycle, it's also best to avoid these medicines, as they inhibit prostaglandin production, which in turn can inhibit ovulation. (Prostaglandins are natural chemicals essential to the working of the muscle in the ovary to release the egg.)

Avoid antihistamines and decongestants, including Sudafed, Ma-huang, Ephedra, and Osha root, as they can dry up mucus, including fertile mucus, which you need to conceive. Avoid cold and flu formulas, most of which contain antihistamines and decongestants. Herbally, echinacea is safe during pregnancy, but goldenseal root should be avoided. Avoid most laxatives, including senna, aloe, castor oil, turkey rhubarb, buckthorn, and cascara sagrada.

It's also best not to take over-the-counter diuretics (products that make you urinate more) nor herbal diuretics such as buchu, horsetail, and juniper berries. Avoid motion-sickness or antinausea drugs (Bendectin) as well. Do not ingest large amounts of herbs containing steroid-like ingredients, including agave, ginseng, licorice, hops, and sage, which can suppress your fertility hormones. For these same reasons, in the first trimester avoid eating copious amounts of basil or parsley.

When you see a physician or other health practitioner, let him or her know if you're going to start inseminating soon, or are already, as some medicines have a long half-life, meaning they stay in the body for a number of hours or days before being fully metabolized. Some vaccinations should be avoided for up to three months before conception in order to prevent infection-related birth defects in the first trimester. If in doubt, ask your health care provider.

Alcohol

In moderation, alcohol ingested before pregnancy shouldn't have harmful effects, although regular nightly or binge drinking before pregnancy can impair absorption of many vitamins necessary for reproductive health. If regular drinking is a part of your lifestyle, decide to eliminate it at least a few months before conceiving. It's best to figure out how you can modify your lifestyle in a thoughtful way—in which you can substitute other pleasurable activities or healthy coping skills—than to feel rushed to adapt because you find yourself pregnant sooner than expected. During pregnancy it's important to avoid all alcohol consumption.

Electromagnetic Fields and Radiation

Electromagnetic fields (EMFs) are present wherever electricity flows. Much controversy has surrounded the potential risks of living under power lines and near transistors, but strong evidence shows a link between increased EMF exposure and cancer. Studies also show increased miscarriage rates in pregnant women who use electric blankets. To enhance fertility and avoid miscarriage in early pregnancy, we recommend avoiding electric heating pads and electric blankets. If you have an electric blanket that you love, turn it on to heat up your bed before you get in, then turn it off. If you regularly use a heating pad, try using a hot water bottle instead or fill up a tube sock with rice and microwave it for two minutes until warm.

Microwaves

Many microwave ovens leak as they get older. If you have one, have it checked for radiation leaks. And, of course, don't stand in front of a microwave oven when it's on.

Computers and the Workspace

Try to arrange computers in work and home life so that you don't face the back of a terminal. More modern video display terminals expose people to lower levels of magnetic fields than terminals used in the '70s and early '80s. Epidemiological studies don't show a significant increase in miscarriage rates in the last 10 years in women who use computers. Nonetheless, for many reasons related both to repetitive stress injury and to the difficulties of accurately assessing factors that contribute to miscarriage risk, be mindful of the number of hours you spend in front of a computer. Also make sure you're positioned ergonomically, to protect your wrists and back, which are more susceptible to injury during pregnancy. To assess the ergonomics of your workspace, visit www.globaltotaloffice.com/canada2001/ergonomic_checklist.htm.

Chemicals in the Workplace

The Occupational Safety and Health Administration (OSHA) requires all workplaces to provide information on any unsafe chemical to which a worker may be exposed. This includes chemicals that are unsafe during pregnancy. Employers are also legally required to follow standard safety procedures to minimize risk to workers. You're probably aware, however, if you and your coworkers feel pressured not to take the time to comply with safety standards or if you don't have adequate protection available on the job. Unfortunately, the for-profit motivation of employers doesn't always prioritize worker health.

If you choose not to tell your management that you're trying to conceive, and you work in an area in which you're regularly exposed to chemicals, it may be difficult for you to get the extra protection you need. Minimizing your chemical exposure is not only crucial during pregnancy, but also for the months preceding pregnancy. We understand that being out about both being lesbian or bisexual and trying to conceive can feel like a threat to your job security at a time when you need it the most. Think carefully about what your best solutions may be, whether it's transferring temporarily to different tasks or being more careful about toxic exposure in your work routine.

Fertility Enhancement

Many diverse healing practices offer a variety of approaches to optimizing fertility. In fact, we have seen many instances in which alternative medicine has helped to dramatically increase a woman's fertility. Practitioners of alternative healing practices are often found in the yellow pages, especially in large urban areas. Information about non-Western healing practices is also available online and in books. The descriptions that follow give a simple introduction to the philosophy of each healing approach, which may sound odd or difficult to understand if your conceptualization of how the body works has been limited to a medical perspective. Exploring alternative healing modalities for their potential benefits to your fertility is worthwhile for a few reasons: 1) Non-Western practices offer alternatives to Western medical treatments that often have fewer risks or side effects; 2) Non-Western practices can work in conjunction with Western medicine to increase its effectiveness and ameliorate its side effects; 3) Non-Western practices can increase overall fertility, health, and comfort even if you don't suspect that you have a fertility "problem" requiring treatment. After our descriptions, we'll focus more specifically on what various herbs have to offer.

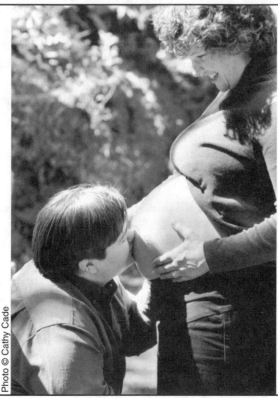

Photo © Cathy Cade

Homeopathy

Homeopathy is a healing practice that has been used in Europe and the United States for decades. Homeopathy, simply, is based on the premise that "like cures like," as compared to Western medicine's allopathic approach of curing by providing an opposite to the symptom. Since the body tries to maintain a state of balance, imbalances can make people susceptible to illness or decreased functioning of the body's systems. Very minute doses of a substance that actually produces the symptom you wish to cure are given in the form of vinegar-based tinctures or pellets that dissolve under the tongue. These doses are so small that if an inaccurate remedy is chosen, no side effects will occur. When the appropriate remedy is chosen, homeopathy can rebalance the body in a powerful way that optimizes fertility.

Acupuncture

Acupuncture is one pillar of traditional Chinese medicine, a complete system of healing almost 3,000 years old that includes Chinese herbal medicine, specific exercise and nutritional recommendations, and traditional massage such as Chi Nei Tsung. Acupuncturists insert very fine sterile needles into points on the body that lie on any of a number of meridians, or energy pathways, in order to rebalance and increase the flow of *qi*, which translates loosely as "vital energy" or "life force." Traditional Chinese medicine, like many non-Western healing practices, focuses on improving the natural balance of the body and its systems, thereby improving its functioning and immunity, more than it focuses on providing a treatment specific to one infection or disease. At Maia, we've seen very tangible results in women who receive weekly acupuncture treatments: 1) many begin to ovulate again; 2) endometriosis often subsides; 3) hormones often return to optimum levels; 4) and many women have copious amounts of fertile mucus, whereas the month before none was to be found!

Ayurveda

Ayurveda is the 5,000-year-old Indian framework of healing practices that includes yoga, herbal medicine, specific diet recommendations, meditation, massage, and stress-reduction techniques. Ayurveda recognizes that each person is born with a specific natural body-mind type, or constitution, that determines, among other things, her type of metabolism. Employing the various practices within ayurveda, one seeks to optimize her health by taking care of her body in ways that are best suited to her constitutional type or *dosha*. When radiant health is created and sustained, fertility always increases.

Chiropractic Treatment

Chiropractic is much more than care for backaches. Chiropractic views the nervous system as the primary regulator of the body's other functions. Nerve patterns, and therefore other body processes, can become imbalanced by lack of align[...] skull, spine, and pelvis, causing pain, illness, and less-than-optimal body[...] Adjustments made manually can realign the bones, nerves, and support tissues, thereby rebalancing the body, which may greatly enhance fertility.

Herbal Support

Herbs can encourage pregnancy by nourishing and toning the uterus, nourishing the entire body, relaxing the nervous system, and balancing the hormonal system, in part by providing a wonderful source of easily absorbed trace minerals and vitamins. When considering using any herbal supplement, it's important to understand how they work, for whom they work, and when to use them. Fertility herbs need three months or more to reach their full effect. Taken on a daily basis, the herbs we suggest will increase your overall health. The herbs we suggest are safe to use in tandem with fertility medications.

The following herbs can be safely taken by women at any time in life. Because they're nourishing and toning herbs, they can be safely ingested as a tea on a daily basis. Since they have an overall ability to enhance the functioning of the female reproductive system, these herbs—taken together or alone—can be used during preconception and through pregnancy. We recommend that every woman drink a tea made of these herbs on a daily basis. It's an inexpensive, relatively effort-free means of fine-tuning your hormones and inner balance.

• **Red clover** is known for its ability to balance hormones. It's a rich source of calcium, magnesium, and trace minerals and supports various hormone-producing glands. Red clover also relaxes the nervous system.

• **Nettle leaf** strengthens and nourishes the uterus and body. It also tones the blood, especially by providing large amounts of readily absorbed iron and vitamin C.

• **Red raspberry leaf** nourishes the uterine muscle and endometrial lining of the uterus, as well as the other reproductive organs. Because of its effect on the uterus, one cup a day of raspberry leaf tea throughout pregnancy has been shown to decrease the likelihood of a long labor or cesarean delivery.

• **Alfalfa, oat straw, and mint teas** are very high in calcium and can be combined with the above herbs to make a tasty and effective blend.

How to Make Herbal Teas

Always try to purchase or harvest organic herbs. Put a small handful of each herb in a one-quart glass jar, then fill it with boiling water and cover with a lid or saucer. Let it steep for a minimum of 4 hours; overnight is preferable. Strain the leaves out and store the tea in the refrigerator, where it will stay fresh for three to four days. Drink one to two cups a day. Some women buy herbs that come prepackaged in tea bags. If only steeped for a few minutes, however, tea made this way is less potent and probably less fresh.

These herbs can also be taken in tincture form, one to two droppers daily. This is more expensive and considered less effective than drinking a well-steeped tea.

Progesterone Precursors

Progesterone is necessary to hold the uterine lining both to conceive and to sustain a pregnancy. Progesterone precursor supplementation is helpful for women with histories of miscarriage as well as those with short luteal phases. You can determine whether your luteal phase (the time between ovulation and menstruation) is short by monitoring your basal body temperature. See Chapter 11 for more information. If your temperature stays high for fewer than 12 days, you could benefit from progesterone precursor supplementation. You may, however, have to wait up to three months to see the full effect of progesterone-increasing remedies. You may find your menstrual cycle length increasing, your overall sense of warmth in your body increasing, and your sex drive increasing as your body begins to produce more progesterone.

One herbal tincture that encourages progesterone production, if taken daily between ovulation and menstruation, is Vitex, also known as Chaste Berry Tree. Another means of naturally increasing your progesterone is to use a liquid supplement, produced by Biomatrix, that is placed under the tongue. The absorption rate for sublingual progesterone is 98% within the first two to three minutes. After that, saliva dilutes it. One drop of tincture is equivalent to 1.2 mg of transdermal progesterone (a medically prescribed vaginal suppository). Their effectiveness rate for absorption is equivalent. Vaginal suppositories, however, require a longer amount of time for absorption.

If you conceive during a cycle in which you've been using a progesterone supplement, continue to use the supplement throughout the first trimester of pregnancy until the placenta is ready to take over progesterone production from the ovary.

Increasing Male Fertility

In the last 50 years, male fertility rates have dropped significantly worldwide. Statistics show that the average sperm count is decreasing by 1.5% every year in the United States, and 3% per year in Australia and Europe, more than likely as a result of environmental toxins. Many men have suboptimal fertility without experiencing any symptoms or having a medical history that suggests it. We recommend having your donor undergo a semen analysis early on, precisely because low fertility is so common for men. If your donor's semen analysis results are not optimal, the test can be repeated for greater accuracy. Also, a more highly detailed analysis called a Kruger strict morphology, as well as a sperm penetration assay, may help more fully explore the quality of his sperm. These tests are reviewed in depth in Chapter 5.

If you're considering working with a donor with fertility problems, think over this choice carefully before starting to inseminate. Unfortunately, Western medicine has very little to offer men in terms of fertility treatments, except to manipulate sperm and egg either through intrauterine insemination (IUI) or by combining the sperm with an egg in the laboratory and transferring the resulting embryo directly into the uterus (in vitro fertilization or IVF).

Non-Western healing practices, however, have a lot to offer men who want to increase their fertility, especially acupuncture and traditional Chinese medicine. In addition to seeking alternatives in health care, some common-sense lifestyle changes and a specific focus on good nutrition can cause significant increases in fertility of sperm.

The information provided earlier in the chapter about environmental toxins found at home and in the workplace is crucial to men's healthy fertility. Toxins can not only lessen a man's sperm count to the point of infertility, but may also alter sperm so that the egg is fertilized but grows in an unhealthy way, leading either to miscarriage or birth defects. The public has become aware of this through the media's coverage of birth defects of children of veterans of both the Vietnam War and the Persian Gulf War.

Getting regular and sufficient sleep and keeping levels of stress to a minimum are important for men's hormone levels to stay constant, just as with women. See Chapter 8 for a more detailed discussion of this.

Sperm Temperature

The testicles hang in the scrotal sac outside the body to keep the developing sperm cooler than body temperature. Regularly overheating the sperm at any time during the 67 or so days they take to develop can negatively affect sperm count and function. To avoid overheating their testicles, potential donors should not wear tight underwear, pants, or exercise shorts and should avoid spending long periods of time in Jacuzzis, hot baths, showers, or saunas.

Caffeine, Alcohol, and Drugs

Studies show a direct link between marijuana use and lowered sperm count and a significant increase in malformed sperm. Caffeine and other stimulants such as sugar or amphetamines can also detrimentally affect sperm quality and count. Caffeine concentration is highest in coffee but is also abundant in cola drinks, black teas, and even chocolate, depending on how much is consumed.

Alcohol use can decrease both the health and count of sperm. Ideally, your donor should not consume more than one alcoholic drink per day. The use of cocaine and other recreational drugs can directly damage sperm.

Cigarettes

Cigarette smoke, as well as secondhand or environmental smoke, seems to have a devastating effect on sperm count and quality if a man is already borderline infertile. If he has a good sperm count to start with, his sperm will not be affected quite as significantly by exposure to cigarette smoke. Studies have shown, however, that if both the biological mother and father smoke, or if just the biological father smokes, the chance of miscarriage may increase by as much as 64%.

Prescription Medicine

Some medicines can temporarily decrease sperm count and motility and should not be taken within two and a half months of sperm donation. These include some antifungal and antidiarrheal medications as well as the antibiotics erythromycin and nitrofurantoin.

Ejaculation

Frequent ejaculation (at least once a week) stimulates the testicles to keep up a higher level of sperm production than that of men who don't ejaculate often. Asking your donor not to ejaculate for 24–72 hours before donating for your inseminations will increase his sperm count, but asking him to refrain for longer than that will not improve results. A man with a less than optimal sperm count should wait 48 to 72 hours between ejaculations to let his sperm count rise, but a man with a healthy sperm count should be able to replenish his supply within 24 hours after he ejaculates.

Vitamins and Nutrients

Common sense suggests that fresh, nutritious foods; adequate calories; and a well-balanced diet positively influence sperm quality and number. In fact, many micronutrients and minerals are essential for the glands in the testicles to be able to constantly produce so many millions of sperm cells. Further, the incredibly active motion of sperm constantly swimming requires a high amount of the micronutrients that allow liberation of cellular energy. Finally, the entire sperm-growth process is mitigated by a variety of male hormones, including testosterone, luteinizing hormone (LH), and follicle stimulating hormone (FSH). These hormones require building blocks from the diet, just as they do in women.

Vitamin C has been demonstrated to radically improve sperm count, motility, and morphology (shape). In two studies the dose given was 1,000 mg per day, although one nutritionist specializing in infertility recommends taking 1,500 mg twice daily. Zinc is essential for testosterone synthesis in the testes. Mild cases of zinc deficiency have been linked to lower sperm counts. Thirty to 50 mg zinc picolinate is the recommended supplemental dosage.

A lack of B vitamins can affect the pituitary gland in the brain, where LH and FSH are made to stimulate sperm production in the testes. Two thousand mcg of vitamin B12, 800 mcg of folic acid in a multi–B vitamin containing B1, B2, and B6 can decrease sperm malformation and increase sperm production. Four hundred IU of vitamin E daily and 200 mcg selenium daily are also helpful (although not more than 300 mcg of selenium should be consumed in one day). Almost half the male body's supply of selenium is located in the testicles and seminal ducts. The sperm cells contain significant amounts of selenium and zinc, which are lost upon ejaculation. Finally, some nutritionists recommend taking 1,500 mg of the amino acid arginine (a protein building block) twice daily to raise sperm counts. Men with herpes should not take this supplement, as it can trigger an outbreak.

Clean Drinking Water

Water contaminated by pesticide runoff contains organochlorine compounds thought to be mistaken by the body for estrogen compounds, and therefore decreases sperm counts. Drinking water also may contain hormones from a variety of sources in our environment, including hormones used to grow large cattle or keep cows lactating for dairy production, or the hormones that women excrete in their urine after taking birth control pills or menopausal hormone-replacement therapies. We strongly encourage men to use a high-quality water filter. Filtered water is preferable to bottled water, as bottled water varies greatly in terms of how well it's been filtrated and the minerals it contains from its source; furthermore, water sitting in plastic containers may become contaminated by chemicals leaching from the plastic.

Organic Foods

To further reduce pesticide and hormone exposure, men should increase their intake of organically grown foods. High levels of pesticides, hormones, and antibiotics can be found in nonorganic meat and dairy products and should be avoided whenever possible. In addition, exposure to unnecessary chemicals can be avoided by limiting intake of processed foods, including those with artificial dyes, sweeteners, and preservatives.

Take Charge of Your Fertility

We wish to leave you with the awareness that you have great influence over the state of your fertility. While a number of environmental toxins are decidedly detrimental to fertility, many creative options exist for avoiding and reducing your overall exposure to toxins. Beyond this, you have a world of diverse resources open to you to explore how to increase your fertility beyond its current state. Whether your focus is physical, emotional, spiritual, or a combination of all three, you'll find many ways to optimize your hormone balance and the functioning of your uterus, ovaries, cervix, fallopian tubes, brain, and other aspects of your body that are essential to conception and pregnancy. Optimizing your fertility is up to you and is within your power. We encourage all women planning to get pregnant to employ as many of the suggestions in this chapter as possible for an easier conception and a healthier baby.

Resources

Books

Burpee—The Complete Vegetable & Herb Grower: A Guide to Growing Your Garden Organically, Karan Davis Cutler, Hungry Minds, Inc., 1997

Slug Bread and Beheaded Thistles: Amusing and Useful Techniques for Nontoxic Housecleaning and Gardening, Ellen Sandbeck, Broadway Books, 2000

Ecological and Healthy Alternative Menstrual Products

Glad Rags Cotton Menstrual Pads
P.O. Box 12648
Portland, OR 97212
(800) 299-4523
www.gladrags.com

Green Marketplace (sells nontoxic tampons and menstrual pads made by Seventh Generation and offers other nontoxic household and body care items)
(888) 59-EARTH
www.greenmarketplace.com

Nontoxic Cleaning Products

Environmentally Responsible Cleaning Solutions (sells nontoxic, biodegradable, cruelty-free products)

(866) 541-6909
www.espesp.com

Simple Green (sells nontoxic, biodegradable, environmentally safer cleaning products for household, industrial, and institutional applications)
(800) 228-0709
www.simplegreen.com

Sun and Earth Environmental Cleaning Products (sells safe, all-natural, effective cleaning products that are competitively priced)
(800) 596-SAFE
www.sunandearth.com

Chapter 9 Choosing a Fertile Lifestyle

A fertile lifestyle promotes balanced hormones, regular menstrual cycles, monthly ovulation, and a healthy uterus. It also optimizes health before conception occurs, which increases healthy development of the baby during pregnancy and decreases chances of miscarriage, birth defects, and pregnancy complications. The first part of this chapter discusses how to check on aspects of your overall health, including sexual and reproductive health, before you conceive. The middle part focuses on exercise, sleep, and reducing stress. Although many people realize there's a connection between nutrition and fertility (covered in Chapter 7), many don't realize that these three other lifestyle factors are also essential to optimal fertility. As we explore each of them in this chapter, you'll notice the common thread is consistency. Maintaining equilibrium in your body will keep your reproductive hormones in equilibrium—probably the most important aspect of optimizing fertility. At the end of the chapter we'll discuss choices about taking antidepressants and antianxiety medicines during preconception and pregnancy.

What You'll Want to Know About Your Health
Before You Conceive

It's a good idea to get a general physical exam before trying to conceive, whether by a medical doctor or any other primary health care provider. Many of the standard tests a woman receives in early pregnancy as part of prenatal care are actually more informative before pregnancy, when you have more options to treat any abnormal results. In this chapter, we'll describe the more common of these tests, which any health care provider—not just an obstetrician—can do. See the safer-sex section in this chapter for more information about the tests for sexually transmitted infections listed in the following section.

• **Pap smear:** Contrary to popular belief, a Pap smear does not test for "everything vaginal." It's a specific test that examines a sample of the cells on and in your cervix to make sure they're growing in a healthy way. It's a screening test, therefore, for cervical cancer. It isn't incredibly accurate, but it's the best we have. Some women have heard that lesbians don't need to get Pap smears. This is untrue. Although most cancerous cervical changes are related to infection by a sexually transmitted virus called HPV, not all are; some have an unknown cause. Furthermore, HPV can be transmitted years before it causes symptoms, lying dormant the entire time. Therefore, a person may have been infected through sex that wasn't recent. Also, no one has proven that HPV (the same virus that causes genital warts) cannot be transmitted between women. It makes no sense to think that lesbians are immune. Finally, some women who identify as lesbians occasionally have sex with men and don't take this into consideration when deciding whether they need an HPV screening test. If you get a Pap smear and learn that your cervical cells are very abnormal or cancerous, it's best to seek treatment before pregnancy, as the hormones of pregnancy can cause the abnormalities to worsen rapidly if untreated. Once pregnant, you won't want anyone performing any procedure or treatment on your cervix that could disrupt pregnancy.

• **CBC:** This stands for "complete blood count" and looks at qualities of the cells in your blood. It will tell you if you're anemic or have an abnormal type of hemoglobin such as sickle cell and provides other information about your general health.

• **RPR, Hep B surface antigen, HIV:** These test for syphilis, hepatitis B, and HIV accordingly. All can be tested for from one tube of blood, and all are sexually transmitted diseases (spread by shared needles as well) that are transmittable to a fetus during pregnancy.

• **Rubella:** Also known as German measles, this virus makes people sick for a couple days and is rarely specifically diagnosed. Many of us are immune from exposure as a child or from having been vaccinated. If you aren't immune, however, and become infected in the first trimester, you'll have a significant risk of giving birth to a baby with serious birth defects. If you find out you aren't immune, you may choose to get vaccinated before pregnancy. You shouldn't conceive for three months after getting the shot.

• **ABO and Rh factor:** This test can be performed using the same tube of blood as with the last four and will tell you your blood type. If you're Rh-negative and have many donors to choose from, you may choose one who's also Rh-negative, although you don't have to. Your health care provider will explain the results in more detail.

• **Chlamydia/gonorrhea screen:** This is not a blood test. It's done with a swab sample from the cervix, just like a Pap smear, and screens for these two sexually transmitted infections.

• **Tests for genetic diseases**: Hemoglobin electrophoresis checks for abnormal hemoglobins such as sickle cell or thalassemia. A variety of abnormal hemoglobins appear in people of many different ancestries, least frequently in people of Northern European descent. Cystic fibrosis occurs most often in those of Northern European descent, and Tay-Sachs Disease is associated primarily with people of Jewish or French-Canadian ancestry. A physician or genetic counselor can describe these tests in detail.

• **Ureaplasma/mycoplasma:** This swab test checks for specific kinds of bacteria that occasionally live in men and women, can be sexually transmitted, and are not accompanied by symptoms. Some studies suggest a connection between infection with any of these and a higher chance of early miscarriage. Treatment is a one-week course of oral antibiotics. Unless you always have protected sex with your partner, she'll also have to undergo treatment.

Bring this list of tests to your health care provider, and you can decide together which ones you may want to have done before pregnancy. A general exam will reveal other health problems these tests don't necessarily cover that might affect your health or your baby's health during pregnancy. Some sperm banks require you to take some or all of the above tests before you purchase sperm. We encourage you to make a thoughtful, informed decision about whether to choose any of the above tests before you start inseminating.

Safer Sex Is for Dykes Too!

If you're pregnant or trying to become pregnant, practicing safer sex is crucial, whether this means being monogamous or reducing how much bodily fluid you share with your partner(s). Sexually transmitted diseases (STDs)—also called sexually transmitted infections or STIs—can have devastating effects on your fertility and your unborn baby's health.

Many women don't know that STDs can be passed from woman to woman through blood (including menstrual blood), breast milk, vaginal secretions, feces, and open wounds (including small cuts on your hands, canker sores, and bleeding gums). STDs are spread most easily through mucus membranes. This means that you can contract an STD through your vagina, anus, or mouth. You don't need to come into contact with semen or have vaginal or anal sex in order to put yourself at risk of contracting an STI. Sharing bodily fluids and sex toys can put both sexual partners at risk.

Effects of STDs on Childbearing

• **Gonorrhea**, which can be contracted vaginally or orally, can cause pelvic inflammatory disease (PID). PID leaves an estimated 30% of women infertile. Pregnant women with untreated gonorrhea can pass it to their babies, who may develop gonococcal conjunctivitis and go blind.

• **Chlamydia**, which can be contracted through the eyes as well as vaginally and anally, can lead to PID, infertility, ectopic pregnancy and urinary tract infection (UTI). Even a low-level infection can cause inflammation in the tubes and block conception. Pregnant women with untreated chlamydia are at risk for uterine infection, miscarriage, premature labor, and postpartum infection. Their newborns may develop conjunctivitis and pneumonia. Chlamydia, which is easily treated, often doesn't cause noticeable symptoms.

• **Herpes**, which can be contracted through broken skin, the eyes, and vaginal, anal, or oral contact, can lead to miscarriage or premature delivery. The newborn may suffer blindness, brain damage, or death.

• **Syphilis**, which can be contracted through broken skin, and vaginal, anal, or oral contact, can be passed from the pregnant mother to her unborn child. The child may become diseased, deformed, or even die.

• **Genital warts**, which can be contracted through vaginal or oral contact, can make the vagina less elastic and delivery of the baby difficult.

• **HIV**, which can be contracted through broken skin, breast milk, and anal, vaginal, or oral contact, is a potentially fatal disease. It can be passed to the baby during pregnancy, birth, or breastfeeding.

Monogamy Is a Very Effective Safer-Sex Technique

If you're partnered, have an honest discussion about monogamy with your partner when you start inseminating or find out you're pregnant. Topics to cover include:

• Does monogamy mean the same thing to both of you? Create a working definition for your relationship.

• Will you agree to tell each other if you break your agreement?

• How do you think drug and alcohol use might affect your remaining monogamous? What agreement can you reach about drug and alcohol use?

Safer Sex Begins Before Sex

• **Get a physical exam so that you know your own state of health.** Ask your health care provider to test you specifically for STDs, not just give you a Pap smear. Unfortunately, your health care practitioner may not have any understanding of woman-to-woman transmission of STDs. Remember that some STDs don't always cause pain or discharge, but can still be harmful to your uterus and fallopian tubes.

• **Request that your partner(s) do the same.** Ask your your partner and donor to test for STDs with urine and blood tests. Some infections, such as chlamydia, may cause no symptoms in men or women, but can still be quite harmful to fertility.

• **Evaluate your lifestyle.** Learn more about risky practices and consider safer ones.

• **Talk honestly with your partner about:** employing safer-sex practices, evaluating your risk factors based on your sexual histories, getting tested for STDs, and making safer-sex practices feel more natural and fun.

• **Be careful when using drugs or alcohol,** as these may impede your judgment about the importance of practicing safer sex.

Safer-Sex Suggestions

• **Be creative.** Expand your sexual practices to include less risky activities such as massage, rubbing, mutual masturbation, breast play, role-playing, talking dirty, dressing up, phone sex, bondage, and non-skin-breaking S/M.

• **Know that even kissing can be risky** if one partner has open blisters, cold sores, oral herpes, deep cuts, or scratches in her mouth (even from brushing or flossing).

• **Keep plastic wrap handy.** It forms a nice barrier between mouth and vagina or anus. Other barriers include: dental dam (Good Vibrations sells garters to hold them in place. See the resource list at the end of the chapter for more information.), a latex or polyurethane condom cut into a rectangle and laid flat, or a latex or polyurethane glove cut into a rectangle with the fingers cut off. Some women leave the thumb on and use it to stick their tongue into. You can also save the cut-off fingers to use for manual stimulation of the clitoris or anus. Try lube on the receiver's end for greater sensation, and honey or jam on the giver's side for a tasty treat. Be sure to use extra care if your partner is menstruating or has a vaginal infection.

• **Use gloves or finger cots for vaginal and anal fisting or finger play.** Make sure to put on clean gloves/cots before switching from vaginal to anal play or vice versa. Some women wear two gloves and simply remove one when they change locations. Fisting should never be performed on a pregnant woman, as it can cause miscarriage.

• **Always store latex in a cool, dry place.** Never reuse it. Avoid using it after the expiration date or more than five years after the manufacture date.

• **Each partner should have her own sex toys.** Dildos (everything from cucumbers to strap-ons) shouldn't be shared unless a new condom is used for each partner. Condoms should also be replaced whenever the dildo moves from vagina to anus and back. Dildos and toys should be well cleaned with bleach solution (one part bleach to 10 parts soapy water).

• **HIV can be passed through breast milk.** If your partner is lactating, use a barrier, such as plastic wrap or a dental dam, between your mouth and her nipples.

• **Water sports (sexual activities involving urine) are relatively safe on unbroken**

skin, but avoid getting urine in the eyes, nose, or mouth. Water sports involving enemas or douches can be made safer by using disposable nozzles, individual bags, latex gloves, and lots of lube. Carefully dispose of all expelled liquids.

• **S/M or rough sex is safer when no blood is involved.** Partners should have their own whips and toys.

• **Dispose of used latex/plastic carefully.** Turn gloves inside out, stuff other used barriers inside, tie gloves closed, and place inside a plastic garbage bag. Keep the garbage bag out of reach of children and animals before the trash is collected.

Safer Sex With Men

• **Always use a condom for vaginal intercourse.** You can use a male or female condom made of latex or polyurethane (but *not* lambskin). Always use water-based lubes, as oil-based ones such as Vaseline, butter, or oil damage the condom. Put a drop of lube inside the condom before it goes on to increase sensation for the man. Put some lube on the outside of the condom or in the vagina to help keep your vagina from getting too dry and to help prevent the condom from breaking. Be sure the man pinches the tip of the condom before putting it on so that air doesn't get trapped inside and cause it to break. Use a new condom every time you have sex.

• **Always use a condom for anal intercourse** (see above for condom tips). Remember that anal tissue is fragile and tears easily. Use lots of lube to help prevent the condom and tissues from tearing.

• **Oral sex on a man is risky, even if he doesn't ejaculate in your mouth.** Use an unlubricated condom (they even make ones that taste good). Use a little lube inside the condom, and use a new condom every time you have oral sex.

• **A word on spermicide:** Some people think safer sex is made even safer by using lubricants containing spermicide (nonoxynol-9, for example). For people who aren't irritated by spermicide, this is probably a good option, since nonoxynol-9 can kill the HIV virus. Spermicides, however, often irritate the tissue of the vagina and anus, which may actually increase one's risk of contracting HIV. You should make a decision for yourself based on your own sensitivity to spermicide.

Specific Ways to Increase Fertility

Now we'll discuss three topics that are key to optimizing your fertility: exercise, sleep, and stress reduction.

Physical Exercise

Many women in today's industrialized world lead more sedentary lives than those of their ancestors. What to their ancestors was movement necessary for the work and play of daily life is compartmentalized in the modern world into activities called exercise. Some women do a substantial amount of exercise in daily work: in fields, on construction sites, at restaurants, or in factories. Many women, however, have sedentary jobs and don't have much time or energy for exercise at the end of the workday. Those that do exercise may do so in a binge form: heavy frequent exercise for a short period, followed by little or no exercise—much like the pattern of American dieting.

We want to reframe the idea of the "chore" of exercise into the enjoyment of an active lifestyle. We'll discuss how exercise can promote fertility, how much exercise is too much (or too little), and some of the common myths that surround exercise, body weight, and pregnancy.

Fertility and Pregnancy Benefits

Moderate and regular exercise optimizes fertility and benefits the body in many ways. The deep breathing performed during exercise increases lung capacity, keeping body tissues well oxygenated. Regular aerobic exercise strengthens the heart, allowing it to beat more slowly, which increases its longevity. Regular exercise helps keep the blood pressure in a safe range, which supports the kidneys. It also balances the metabolism, which in turn balances hormone levels. Regular exercise keeps your body flexible and strengthens the back and the abdomen, which significantly increases comfort in pregnancy. Aerobic exercise increases stamina, crucial during labor and new parenting.

Moderation

There can be too much of a good thing when it comes to exercise and fertility. When women exercise very heavily, especially while restricting their calorie intake, their body-fat percentage can drop so low that the body has nowhere to synthesize and store its hormones, so it stops menstruating. This issue may appear to be more about body fat and weight, but to reduce body fat to the level of amenorrhea (when a woman has no menstrual period) usually requires substantial exercise as well, unless the woman is truly starving herself.

Studies have shown that a low percentage of body fat can detrimentally influence fertility, even if regular ovulation occurs. In these cases, gaining just five to 10 pounds can significantly increase a woman's fertility.

Starting a heavy exercise program as you begin to inseminate can change your body's metabolism and thyroid levels, which in turn will affect your fertility hormones. If increasing your daily exercise is important to you and you decide not to postpone starting to inseminate for a few months until your exercise regimen is stable, then make sure you start lightly and increase your exercise level in small steps. Be aware that you may need to increase your caloric intake as you increase your exercise so that your body doesn't go into diet or starvation mode.

Once you begin inseminating, for half of each month you may possibly be in early pregnancy. After inseminating, take your pulse occasionally to monitor how fast your heart is beating during exercise. During pregnancy, your heart should beat no more than 140 beats per minute. You can get a good workout while achieving this pulse rate by exercising at a medium level for a longer duration compared to exercising at a more difficult level for a shorter duration. Monitoring your heart rate will also keep your core body temperature from getting too hot, which is especially important in early pregnancy. Moderately priced heart-rate monitors are now available at most sporting goods stores and range in price from $25-$230.

Fear of Exercise

You may have heard some inseminating women express concern about exercising in the second half of each cycle, from ovulation to period/pregnancy. They often fear they'll "shake the embryo loose" and cause an early miscarriage. They end up exercising regularly for two weeks, then stopping completely for two weeks, which confuses the body. For the first six to 10 days after conception, the embryo hasn't yet implanted in the lining of the uterus; it's still migrating down from the top of the fallopian tube. Once it implants, it embeds into the thick endometrium, which eventually grows into the placenta. We advise women to avoid particularly bouncy or strenuous exercise at this time but to continue exercising in other ways to provide the body with consistency. Likewise, light to moderate exercise throughout pregnancy is always best. Avoid any intense exercise regimen, even if your body is accustomed to it, as it's just too much for the body during pregnancy. Also, do not swim for 24 hours after inseminating, as the chlorine in pools may hinder the sperm's viability. See the resource list at the end of this chapter for books and videos on exercise during pregnancy.

Myths of Thinness

Obstetric approaches to weight gain and pregnancy are constantly changing. Our mothers—if they went to obstetricians in the United States for prenatal care— were advised to gain little weight during pregnancy in order to retain their feminine figures. Often they were given prescriptions of amphetamines to suppress their appetite or told to smoke during pregnancy for the same effect. Obviously, women at that time weren't given the healthiest advice about weight gain and pregnancy. You may still hear this advice from older relatives. Obstetrics now still takes the approach that there is an "ideal" weight gain for pregnancy, although the "ideal" is somewhat higher than it used to be. Obstetricians also commonly have had a limited amount of training in nutritional counseling, so you may hear a lot of bias and little valuable information from both doctors and friends as you plan for pregnancy.

If you feel you're "overweight" you wouldn't be alone if you wanted to lose a certain number of pounds before you gain it back during pregnancy. But trying to lose weight by dieting just before conception can be challenging to your fertility, as the body can move into a starvation mode. In fact, dieting can actually impair fertility. Eating healthy foods without limiting your intake and exercising regularly will keep your body balanced as you try to conceive.

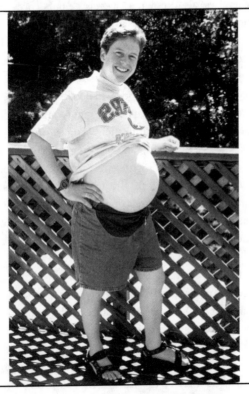

If you haven't lost any weight before conceiving, don't panic. Larger women who eat healthy foods when hungry during pregnancy often gain less weight than skinnier pregnant women. In our practice we've noticed that the most slender women often gain the most weight, as the body needs to have a minimum amount of fat to store hormones to support pregnancy and the milk production of breastfeeding. Postpartum exercise will slowly use up the fat you've acquired throughout pregnancy in a way that doesn't throw your body out of balance.

Some women are told that being skinny increases their fertility. This is more about American fatphobia rather than sound medical knowledge. A woman needs a certain amount of fat to sustain the hormone levels necessary for ovulation.

Usually, if a woman is slender, gaining a few pounds will improve her fertility.

For larger women, weight loss can help the body recognize hormones and fine-tune the hormonal balance. Thus, if you weigh 200 or more pounds and are having trouble conceiving, an increase in exercise and a diet rich in protein and low in carbohydrates may facilitate conception.

Pelvic Floor Exercises (Kegels)

Pelvic floor exercises, also known as Kegels or pubococcygeal (PCG) exercises, increase circulation and strengthen tone in the horizontal sheet of muscles that supports the organs in the pelvis, such as the bladder and uterus. These muscles form a figure 8 around the openings of the vagina and the rectum. Pelvic floor exercises also increase your awareness and ability to relax these muscles, which benefits childbirth. Good muscle tone in this part of your body will benefit you the rest of your life. These exercises are what women do to prevent incontinence after childbirth and to prevent their uterus or bladder from sagging into their vaginas (prolapsing) later in life.

These exercises involve tightening and releasing the muscles around the vagina—the ones you'd tighten to stop urinating midstream. You can tighten and relax the muscles rapidly in succession, and you can also tighten the muscles slowly, focusing on pulling up high into the pelvis then relaxing slowly softening and opening (but not pushing down). Many women start slowly, working up to 20–30 long Kegels lasting to a count of eight each day.

Back and Abdominal Exercises

For four-legged animals, the weight of pregnancy is dispersed throughout all their abdominal muscles. Our upright posture as humans, however, places extra pressure on the pelvic floor and extra strain on the lower back and lower abdomen during pregnancy. Any back-strengthening exercises you can do before pregnancy will serve you in good stead. Your abdominal muscles are stronger than your back muscles and can help do a lot of the work if they're strong enough. As pregnancy progresses, your abdominal muscles will stretch more and more over the outside of the uterus, until they become less effective in supporting your back and abdominal organs than before pregnancy. How your abdominal muscles help your back during pregnancy depends on how strong they are to begin with. Start now by doing yoga or by finding abdominal exercises that have been designed so that they don't strain your back.

Sleep

Sleep serves the body in many ways. The time your body spends sleeping is an essential restorative period when damaged cells are repaired. Your immune system needs plenty of sleep to do its work cellularly to prevent infection. Lying down at night relaxes the muscles that are used all day to hold the body and head upright. It takes a lot of work to hold our bodies erect for so many hours, whether we're sitting or standing. On average, the human head weighs 25 pounds. Think of the amount of rest your slender neck muscles need by nighttime. Adequate sleep is key in the body's recuperation process. Finally, sleep is when the psyche gets some unfettered time to come out and play. Dreamtime plays a crucial, if not well understood, role in emotional and cognitive functioning.

The body's circadian rhythms—the body's daily clock—can be thrown off by irregular or insufficient sleep. Many hormone levels in the body have a 24-hour pattern that differentiates between night and day. Getting regular nightly sleep helps keep hormone levels balanced.

There are different types of sleep, each with a different type of brain-wave pattern. Each type is essential for a specific bodily function. You need a good balance of all types of sleep for your body to complete its nighttime healing and reenergizing functions. Different types of sleep occur in a cycle of set sleep patterns. If the body is interrupted before it gets through a whole sleep cycle, which is three to four hours, it can't complete all aspects of its functioning.

When women chart their basal body temperature, they often immediately see how interruptions and changes in their sleep pattern affect their temperature, making it higher or less predictable. Sleep plays many roles in balancing and maintaining the body, many of which are yet to be discovered. You might be someone who feels rotten if your sleep is interrupted, or you may have adapted to getting very little sleep. In either case, sleep deprivation causes your body to draw on other resources to maintain itself. The goal of a fertile lifestyle is to optimize the state of your body's health, not just give it the minimum it needs to keep functioning. Regular, plentiful sleep is an essential element of a fertile lifestyle.

Sleep and the Work Week

In general, Americans are sleeping less and less—and suffering for it. Sleeping five to six hours nightly is the norm for many people, and with sufficient stimulants this may be possible but isn't healthy. Sleep isn't optional. Many people routinely work more than 40 hours a week and don't have or make time for adequate rest.

If it seems impossible to find a way to cut back on your work hours, ask yourself what your ideal work vision will be while you're raising children. Children need you to stay home and take care of them when they're too sick to go to school or child care. Children require daily routines in regard to waking up and going to bed that promote their sense of security, family, and home. Missing your children's bedtimes by frequently working late can be very disruptive to them. As you imagine making room for your baby in your life, consider how your work life will affect you and your child. Setting new limits at work may take some creative problem solving and can be stressful. Consider changing your work life now, if you need to, before you're riding the emotional roller coaster of insemination. Prioritize sleep as a non-negotiable need when you think of work and other commitments and how they'll fit into a 24-hour day.

Jean Weisinger

Insomnia

Insomnia is an epidemic in the United States. Here are some tips for ensuring you get a good night's sleep:

- Try not to do a lot of "wake time" activities in bed, such as reading, schoolwork, laundry folding, etc. Save your bed for sleeping.
- Don't stay in bed if you're wide awake in the middle of the night. Go somewhere you associate with being awake. Save your bed for sleeping.
- Take a hot bath or shower before going to sleep. As your core body temperature cools off, your body naturally responds by becoming tired.
- Try eating something with tryptophan, an amino acid that promotes sleep, such as turkey or milk.

- Exercise regularly to promote regular deep sleep.
- Avoid products containing caffeine, including chocolate and cocoa, especially after lunch and anytime later. Caffeine has a half-life of six hours, meaning that six hours after you ingest it, half of it is still active in your bloodstream.
- After dinner, avoid ingesting other stimulants such as nicotine and sugar.
- Drink a mild, relaxing herbal tea such as chamomile before going to bed.
- Try taking a homeopathic formula such as calms forte.
- Don't keep bright lights on late in the evening (including staring at a computer monitor), as it triggers the body to wake up.
- Write free-form for a few minutes before bed each night to let go of anything that might have made you feel stressed or upset during the day.
- Create a calm bedtime ritual that you start 30 minutes before bed—just as you would do for children, that trains your body to prepare for sleep.

Ovulation and Sleep

Studies show that the amount of light you sleep in can affect your ovulation. Before electric lights came along, the amount of light emanating from fires and candles at night was minimal. Since the light of the full moon is significantly brighter than when the moon is new, women often menstruated when the moon was full, apparently triggered by the changing cycle of nighttime light. (Women also didn't use all the deodorant products we use now, and most didn't bathe as frequently as we do; thus, women's cycles were also in sync with each other through more exposure to each other's pheromones.) Current studies demonstrate that sleeping in light one night out of many dark nights can trigger ovulation. Women who sleep in darker rooms have more regular cycles. Do you use a nightlight or does light come into your bedroom from the hallway? Does light stream in through your bedroom window from streetlights or lighted signs? If so, try to minimize the light you're exposed to at night. Some women choose to sleep in complete darkness, using heavy curtains to block out any extraneous light.

Stress

Stress has a tremendous affect on fertility and is so common in everyday life that many people barely notice it. We'll explore the evolutionary purpose of stress, how people use stress unconsciously, ways to reduce stress, and how stress affects fertility.

The "stress response" actually evolved as a reaction to imminent danger, called fight-or-flight. Fight-or-flight refers to the way the body physically changes almost instantaneously when experiencing what it perceives as a threat. Many biochemical and hormone shifts occur, the greatest being the immediate release of adrenaline directly into the bloodstream. These hormones and other biochemicals cause the blood pressure, pulse, sense of smell, vision, and pattern of blood flow in the body all to switch to "survival mode." This survival mode causes the brain to focus sharply on the threat and not notice much else in the surrounding environment. Fight-or-flight allows the body to release the most energy and strength in the moment possible, to either fight back or flee from the threat. The fight-or-flight response is not under our conscious control; it is, however, powerful and very useful in specific situations. It takes a lot of the body's resources to respond in this way, and it is not meant to be a sustainable state of being but a temporary response to a dangerous situation.

Stress is the "emotional state" you feel when you're having some level of fight-or-flight response to something in your environment. These stressors—situations or people causing stress—can be momentary, such as a near miss on the freeway or a boss raising her voice at you. Stressors can be long-term, such as poverty, racism, or an abusive relationship. Often stressors are things you feel you have little control over; you feel you can only respond and react but not necessarily change your stressors.

Sometimes positive events in your life can be stressful too, since they involve a great deal of change or expectations, or you don't feel in control. In fact, three of the most stressful events, on average, in adult lives are getting married, buying a house, and having a baby—all of which are usually considered joyful occasions.

Stress as a Tool

Most people perceive stress as a negative influence, and yet many adapt to it and even use it subconsciously as a life tool. Because of the stimulation of the adrenaline involved in stress, if you pay attention you may find that you use stress as a motivational tool to complete a task you know you need to get done. If you don't feel stressed about it, you might not have the energy required to do it. The stress response, like many other body responses, can be learned and patterned so that certain things trigger it. As it is recognized and accepted as a common physical state, people can actually fine-tune their control of the level of stress they permit themselves to feel about certain things.

Examine How Stress Serves You

When you make a plan to reduce the amount of stress in your life, you need to recognize how you use stress as a tool and what you'll substitute in its place. This might include examining the framework of your life in general. You may feel that the number of commitments you have requires you to use a low level of stress throughout the day just to get you out of bed and through your schedule. If this is the case, you may realize that your normal mode is stress and that brief moments of relaxation are the exception. This, unfortunately, is the case for many people.

Quick stress-reduction techniques can substantially calm and relax you, but if stress is the cornerstone of your emotional/physical state, you ultimately need to reframe how you organize your life in terms of scheduling, work, productivity, and play. Reducing your stress will help you to prepare for motherhood.

Using Stress to Numb Feelings

Stress in and of itself, although it is a mind-set and feels like a specific emotion, is not a true emotion. It's not one of our innate feelings. It's a learned response to a biochemical state. Stress numbs people from feelings of fear, anger, sadness, and even happiness. If you use stress this way, even subconsciously, you may have many self- protective reasons for doing so. Feeling great sadness, fear, or anger isn't something most people are raised to do in a healthy way and isn't usually comfortable. Any emotion felt very strongly can seem "out of control," which often doesn't feel safe. Avoiding the depths of these emotions is often about avoiding feeling vulnerable.

Benefits of Yoga

Yoga is one of the oldest systems of mental and physical enhancement practiced in the world today. Yoga is based on the principle of mind/body unity. If the mind is chronically agitated, the health of the body will be compromised. Thus, the practices of yoga can help restore mental and physical health and radiance. Research shows that if practiced regularly, yoga can prevent and manage stress-related chronic health problems. It's also helpful in optimizing fertility and counterbalancing infertility.

One aspect of yoga that distinguishes it from other exercises and sports is the attention it gives the endocrine and nervous systems of the body. These systems are toned and regulated through the physical postures of yoga, thus aiding the regulation of all hormones, including the reproductive hormones. Yoga also tones and firms the body's muscles and aids in proper digestion and regular elimination.

Yoga is highly recommended for all women preparing to conceive. Once pregnancy is well established, yoga postures can be adapted for pregnancy. Although books and videos on yoga postures are widely available, it's best to begin and augment any personal practice under the guidance of a trained yoga instructor, then supplement your program at home with videos or books. (See the resource list at the end of this chapter for more information.)

Acknowledging the depths of your feelings about a situation can sometimes give you the impetus you need to change the situation. You may be in uncomfortable or untenable situations in terms of love relationships or work commitments but not be ready or even know how to change these situations. If you aren't going to change a negative situation, it's easier and safer not to feel the emotions brought on by the situation. Even feeling great happiness is difficult for many people, as irrational as this seems. Sometimes feeling really happy brings up fears from the subconscious: *I don't deserve to be this happy* or *If I let myself be this happy, I'll feel even worse when the happiness goes away.* Stress is a non-emotion that masquerades as a feeling, dampening the effect of the real feelings you may be experiencing. A commitment to reducing stress often means a commitment to *feeling more.*

How Stress Affects Fertility

The chemicals used in the body while under stress affect reproductive hormones in a variety of ways, many of which are yet undiscovered. The immediate hormonal response to stress is the production of adrenaline. If the body is in an ongoing or long-term stress state, it uses up a great deal of cortisol. When the body starts to run out of cortisol, it takes progesterone and turns it into cortisol. Hormones are very interchangeable in this way. Testosterone and other androgens, for example, are turned into estrogen in the ovaries in the first half of the menstrual cycle. A deficiency of one set of hormones often causes depletion of others through the body's ability to reform hormone molecules. The body regards stress as a greater priority than fertility, in terms of allocating hormone resources. This makes sense if we think of it in terms of evolution: You wouldn't want to compromise your safety by putting your energy into pregnancy in the midst of a dangerous situation. Long-term stress can cause subtle long-term imbalances in fertility hormones. If a woman is stressed enough during one menstrual cycle, her stress can be powerful enough to stop her body from ovulating altogether for that month.

Stress is also hard on fetuses, since the changes that adrenaline causes in heart rate and other physiological functions are significantly more difficult for a growing baby to withstand than for an adult body. Also, the biochemicals that affect brain function set up many of the basic patterns of how the brain works while a baby is still in the uterus. As it develops, a baby will adapt to excessive chemicals to which it is exposed. When born, however, its body will feel imbalanced if it isn't exposed to this same level of chemicals. The same is true for sugar and drugs the mother may ingest while pregnant. The placenta isn't an effective barrier for any of these. Children exposed to excessive levels of certain chemicals or drugs may seek out similar brain-chemical states from their environments as they grow older, which puts them at higher risk for attention-deficit problems, substance use, or thrill-seeking behaviors.

How to Notice When You're Stressed

Do a body check-in as described in Chapter 2: Do you feel tension in your jaw, neck, or shoulders? How does your stomach feel? Is your digestion disturbed? Does your breath fill your lungs deeply or stop at the top of your chest? Are your shoulders hunched? Are your arms crossed tightly in front of you? Is your heart beating quickly? Often people don't fully realize their stress level until they sit quietly for a moment and focus on their bodies, away from distractions. If you do a check-in like this throughout the day for a few days in a row, you'll start to get a realistic feel for how much stress you experience in everyday life.

Stress-Management Techniques

The process of insemination is inherently stressful. The longer it takes you to get pregnant, the more stressful the experience. Thus, in order to take care of yourself, you'll need to incorporate stress-management techniques into your daily life. Relieving stress can be as simple as taking five deep breaths and as complicated as finding a new job. We'll discuss the quick, simple ways here. Keep in mind that utilizing a variety of approaches will be the most effective.

• **Breathing:** Put your hand on your chest and take a breath so that your chest rises and pushes your hand out. Now put your hand on your abdomen and bring your breath down lower so that your belly pushes your hand out. This second type of breathing is called abdominal breathing. It triggers your nervous system to relax your body and create a physical state that is the opposite of the stress state. Try breathing abdominally, keeping your hand on your belly if you need to, five times in a row. Do you feel different? You can do deep breathing anywhere whenever you feel stress.

• **Muscle relaxation:** Lie on your back and take a couple of deep breaths. Starting at the top of your head, contract all the muscles in your face, shoulders, neck, chest, arms, pelvis, legs, and feet. Scrunch up everything as tightly as possible and hold it as you count slowly to five. Then let everything fully relax, and see how soft and loose you can make all the different parts of your body. You can modify this exercise if you need to, just including your hands, shoulders, and face.

• **Unstructured time for yourself:** Find a little time every day (this may be just five minutes, although ideally a half-hour or more) when you won't be interrupted by people, the phone, or anything else. If you only have a few minutes, you might just choose to sit quietly and take some deep breaths. If you have more time, choose something that is just for enjoyment with no expectation of the outcome.

For example, don't choose to do a project that involves finishing and cleaning up; choose a bath instead. Really pamper yourself and give yourself permission to experience whatever thoughts come into your head. Don't judge or analyze them; let them slip on by like a movie you can watch without interacting. You may notice some feelings arising. This time for yourself has no "shoulds" attached, and you don't need to have structure or goals for it. This free time is essential for letting your mind unwind. Sometimes you'll find that your mind really needs more than five minutes to relax, so when you can, schedule an hour or more just for being, not *doing*.

• **Exercise:** As we mentioned in this chapter, physical exercise is a wonderful way to mentally and physically reduce stress. Movement is the means by which the body works adrenaline out of its system and gets out of the fight-or-flight response. It also helps to put the mind into a different state; many people report that regular exercise helps to "clear their head" and allows them to feel calmer.

• **Therapy:** Seeing a therapist or counselor can help you recognize patterns in your life that are stressful. It can also help you to develop tools to cope with stress more effectively.

• Other effective stress relievers include meditation, yoga, martial arts, and sex.

Prescription Medicine During Preconception and Pregnancy

Antidepressants and Antianxiety Medication

Many women who struggle with anxiety or depression regularly take Paxil, Prozac, Zoloft, Wellbutrin, or other medications to help them feel chemically balanced. Some women continue to take this medicine throughout pregnancy and breastfeeding, while others feel strongly about getting off these medicines before conception occurs.

Whether or not to continue taking your medication is a personal decision that should be made carefully, based on an assessment of the strength of your support system and coping mechanisms, your past history with depression or anxiety, whatever information you obtain about the safety of your medication, your personal philosophies, and input from your therapist/psychiatrist as well as your partner.

Medicine Safety

Prescription medicine, for ethical reasons, cannot be tested on pregnant women. Information about the safety of medicines on fetal development is obtained through animal testing and data on pregnancy outcomes once the drug has been approved for use. Drugs are classified into five categories describing risk for pregnancy. Most drugs like Paxil and Prozac are classified as Category B, which means that animal studies on mice and rats have shown no fetal development problems but that no studies have been performed on humans. But because human bodies don't always behave like those of mice, these drugs should only be used if their potential benefit clearly outweighs their potential risk.

Making a decision about these drugs can be difficult because we don't know the actual risks involved. Most of these drugs are very new in the United States, so data hasn't been gathered for more than a few years. A few of these medicines have been used in England and Europe for a longer period of time and thus have a longer track record. If you decide to continue taking your medicine, know that the least risky drug to take while pregnant may not be the same as the least risky drug to take while breastfeeding. Some women in their late second trimester taper off one type of medication and begin another for this reason.

Coping Skills

If you suffer from anxiety or depression, you had coping skills before you took this medicine, and you may have learned new skills or refined others since then. In fact, some people find their medicine so effective that they no longer need to focus on their other coping skills. If this is your case, it might take some careful thinking as well as asking your therapist, partner, family, or close friends to reflect back to you practices that they've noticed seemed to support a healthy mental state for you. They may also be able to remind you which practices seem specifically detrimental to your well-being.

For many people, regular exercise, regular sleep, and stress management are often essential to avoid anxiety, depression, or obsessive/compulsive behavior without them having to take medicine. For many, a sense of balance is more easily maintained when they avoid caffeine, alcohol, excess sugar, and other drugs. Eating regularly to avoid low blood sugar will help maintain mental constancy. Supplementing a healthy diet with a B-vitamin complex can also help avoid depressive feelings brought on by vitamin-depleting stress.

Some people have refined techniques such as affirmations, visualization, meditation, yoga, or nondepressive thinking that they can put into daily practice with great success. All of your coping skills will be useful in dealing with the stresses of conception, pregnancy, and birth, whether or not you take medication as well. An assessment of your coping skills will help you decide whether you have adequate alternatives to taking medicine to maintain your mental health.

Support Team

Assess the strength of your support team if you're considering getting off your medication. Include your key support team members in your decisions on the topic, and enlist their help throughout your baby-making process, whether or not you stop taking your medicine. If you haven't gone through a rough time recently, the people in your life may not realize that your mental health will need to be a primary focus for you if you stop taking antidepressants or antianxiety drugs.

Your support team may include your partner, good friends, family members, a body worker/acupuncturist/other health care provider, your therapist or psychiatrist (or other MD who prescribes your medicine), or a fertility specialist/ob-gyn/midwife. Your team may also include your boss, church or spiritual group, 12-step community, or other support group members. Ask the important people in your life for their commitment to help you through this process. Unfortunately, because of the misinformation and prejudice that surrounds mental illness, you may have chosen self-protectively to be quite private about any medicine you take or special needs you have. Revisit your choices now to see who might be an ally if you discussed your situation with them. Ultimately, trust your judgment if you don't feel safe sharing this information with someone.

Fertility Drugs and Psychotropic Drugs

If you're taking fertility drugs, make sure that both your psychiatrist/therapist/prescribing MD and your ob-gyn/infertility specialist know you're taking or have recently taken antidepressants or antianxiety drugs. Let them know you need to discuss specifically and accurately the emotional side effects that your fertility drugs may have in store for you. You need a fully informed team. Don't taper off your antidepressant/antianxiety medicine right when you start taking fertility drugs such as Clomid or injectables, if at all possible, since the physical and emotional changes may be too difficult to handle all at once.

Getting Off Antidepressant/Antianxiety Medicine

Many women want to wait until the last minute to stop taking their medicines. We advise a slow process of tapering off, after informing your partner and/or support team, one to three months before the beginning of your first insemination cycle. This time line will let you more fully adjust to getting off your medicine before you experience the emotional ups and downs of the insemination process. Many psychotropic medicines have a long half-life, taking three to six weeks to fully leave your body. We recommend you prioritize your alternative coping skills before you stop taking your medicine so that as few changes as possible will be happening concurrently. Take a few months to make this transition thoughtfully and gently; your mental stability is worth your patience, and your body needs time to restabilize before trying to achieve pregnancy.

Monitoring Your Mental Health

Because the insemination process has its own innate cycle of excitement and depression, you may confuse these feelings with signs of depression or anxiety. Hormonal changes that you notice from early pregnancy, fertility drugs, or regular PMS may also confuse you in this way. Talking to a health care provider who has experience with both fertility issues and mental health issues can help you (and your partner) gain perspective on the possible causes of the changes in your mental state. If you start to feel depressed or feel your mental state is "out of control," evaluate whether you're using your other coping skills and your support system to the best of your ability.

You may need to make significant decisions, such as cutting back on your workweek or increasing your therapy sessions, to reduce your stress sufficiently to protect your mental health throughout conception and pregnancy. Often these choices incur financial costs. Your mental health is worth it, however, and is crucial to your ability to bond with the baby you're creating. Allow yourself to shamelessly make your mental health needs a priority for both you and your baby-to-be.

How each woman taking antidepressants or antianxiety medicine approaches pregnancy is uniquely defined by her own circumstances; nevertheless, prioritizing exercise, sleep, and stress management, as well a having a reliable support team will offer immeasurable benefits for weathering the highs and lows of insemination and pregnancy. This is the case whether you choose to stop, continue, or restart taking your medications.

Indeed, any woman focusing on these three areas of healthy living can experience a powerful enhancement of her fertility. Any incremental change you make has potential effects not only on your fertility, but also your pregnancy health, fetal development, and general physical and emotional well-being. Include your family members and friends as much as possible in any habits you choose to start or reinforce for a lifetime of health.

Resources

Books

Birgitta Gallo's Expecting Fitness, Birgitta Gallo, Renaissance Books, 2000

The Complete Book of Yoga and Meditation for Pregnancy, Theresa Jamieson, Sally Milner Pub., 2000

Drugs in Pregnancy and Lactation: A Reference Guide to Fetal and Neonatal Risk, Roger K. Freeman et al, Lippincott, 1998

Meditations for Your Pregnancy, Sheila Lavery, and Pippa Duncan, 1999

Pregnancy Fitness, the editors of *Fitness* magazine with Ginny Graves, Three Rivers Press, 1999

Step-by-Step Yoga for Pregnancy, Wendy Teasdill, McGrawHill-NTC, 2000

Water Fitness During Your Pregnancy, Jane Katz, Human Kinetics, 1994

Yoga for Pregnancy, Rosalind Widdowson, Creative Publishing International, 2001

Organizations

Yoga for Pregnancy and Fitness
(offers classes in the Boston area)
(617) 970-5320
www.mom.to/baby/pregnancy

Safer-Sex Products

Good Vibrations
1210 Valencia St.
San Francisco, CA 94110
(800) BUY-VIBE
www.goodvibes.com

Videos

Jane Fonda's Pregnancy, Birth, and Recovery Workout, VHS, Warnervision, 1993

Kathy Smith's Pregnancy Workout, VHS, Sony, 1989

The Method: Baby and Mom Prenatal Yoga, VHS Parade Video, 1998

Yoga Zone: Postures for Pregnancy, VHS, Alan Finger/Koch Vision, 1997

Well Sexy Women: A Lesbian Woman's Guide to Safer Sex, VHS, The Unconscious Collective, 1993

Web Sites

Safersex.org (Web site produced by the Safer Sex Institute)

Yogabasics.com
www.yogabasics.com

YogaFinder Online (listings of yoga classes and instructors by state and county)
www.yogafinder.com

Part Four
Conception

Chapter 10 Emotional Preparation: Welcoming the Baby

The process of making, growing, and parenting a baby is transformative. Just as your child will change your life when s/he arrives, the mere intention of expanding your family changes your life as well. You may be well on the pathway already and aware of how you've grown and changed so far. Perhaps you're at the beginning of the process and are just starting to imagine what your life as a parent may be like.

Acknowledging change is crucial to surviving and flourishing from it. A good metaphor to use is the idea of making space in your life for the baby, which includes making space for the changes that come with a baby. Most people imagine making room for a baby physically in their home, but we also mean making room in your heart, your relationships, and your day-to-day schedule, even during the preconception phase. How might you do this?

Intentionally set and affirm your priorities regularly, with both yourself and your partner, if you have one. Discuss not only what kind of parent you would like to be and why you'll make a good parent, but also specifically how you'd like your conception to be. Make sure your conception vision aligns with your values and worldview.

Regularly setting and reevaluating your intentions helps you affirm the place inside yourself that so dearly knows you want to be a parent. It keeps your desire for a child vital and vibrant, as a positive part of your life. Encouraging and strengthening your vision of family helps ease all parts of the decision-making process and keeps your relationship healthy. The practice of naming and embracing your desires allows you to build a strong base upon which to center yourself, and will allow you to weather any difficult and unexpected challenges that arise.

Many women make room in their home for their baby-to-be by setting up a special area where they place items that remind them of the desired baby. These can be photos, baby toys, poems, nature items, etc. This can be a physical place to center yourself and remind yourself of your love—for it's always love that draws us to make children.

Some people already have a fertility altar in their home, or a place where they pray or meditate. Sometimes it feels natural to combine your existing place with your baby altar. For others, having a special place set aside in their home is a new concept. You can use a bedside table or an area on your dresser or mantel. Simply collect what seems right and what reminds you of the baby you want to have. This place can be an area where you connect with the strength of your love and desire by visualization or communication with the baby-to-be, or it may simply serve as a visual reminder of your desire to parent.

We know one couple who kept a menorah at their baby altar, and every night before going to bed they lit a candle and said a prayer about the baby. They continued this ritual from the preconception period through pregnancy. They felt it not only allowed them to feel connected with their intentions and the baby, but it gave them a time and place to connect with each other.

It's helpful to set up some sort of visual prompt or ritual from the beginning. This altar or special area will be especially meaningful if it takes longer than expected for you to conceive. Established rituals can help carry you through as time marches on.

Things to Work on Internally Prior to Insemination

There are a number of topics that are helpful to examine in your life prior to insemination. Not all of these pertain to everyone. Although we feel that finding peace in these areas is significant to increasing fertility, you may be unfamiliar with or wary of the idea that your mind and body have a reciprocal relationship. Regardless of your views on this topic, an awareness of your feelings about the following topics is at the very least interesting and may well help you gain insightful information about yourself.

If you've already been inseminating for a while with no success, examine the following issues and see if you feel any tension about them. The premise is that this tension is constricted energy, held in your body, that could otherwise be freed to encourage pregnancy. This is not a blaming approach. It comes from us to you in alignment with the theme of the book: Approach everything with self-love. Use only what you find useful.

Whether you've started inseminating or have yet to begin, you'll find it's beneficial to engage in self-reflective activities such as keeping a journal, receiving bodywork, getting in touch with your body through yoga or chi gung, or going to therapy or couples counseling. Only you know which of the following issues may concern you. In the following sections we describe a number that arise time and again for many women.

Your Relationship to Sperm

In the history of humanity to date, a woman must put sperm into her body in order to conceive. Sperm is available in various forms—straight from a penis through sexual intercourse or deposited into a receptacle such as a jar; frozen in a solution; or centrifuged, washed, or otherwise separated from semen. Regardless of its form, it is sperm. A drop of semen contains millions of sperm. It's amazing. It's alive. It potentially contains the perfect component to help you start making your baby. Sperm, so microscopic, has a cosmic component: It will ultimately bring your baby to you.

Limor Inbar-Hansen, Indelible Images

Despite its amazing qualities, lesbian and bisexual women have a variety of responses to the idea of interacting with it. Some of these responses are similar to the responses some women have toward men in general. Many women are uncomfortable just thinking about sperm, let alone touching it. Often sperm reminds us of anger we may have that we, as women, are dependent on something outside ourselves and our love relationships to make babies from. Also, sperm has a particular smell that some women say revolts them. Many women are surprised by their reactions to sperm, since either they've never come in contact with sperm before, or it's been so long since they have that they've forgotten its unique odor. Most experience a visceral response to sperm, either positive or negative.

Some women can feel its aliveness. This can feel wonderful and powerful or "creepy-crawly." Some resent feeling as though there's another presence in the room with them; others feel that presence as the baby. Some women adamantly experience sperm as bad. Others experience it as sacred. Many women try to disconnect the concept of sperm from the concept of men.

We encourage you to examine your feelings about sperm. Try to come to peace with the concept of sperm prior to insemination so that any charged feelings about it won't negatively affect your insemination experience. Make with it so that you can welcome it into your body rather than reject the very substance that will allow you to realize your dreams.

Both the woman who will be putting the sperm into her body, and her partner if she has one, should work to discharge any negative feelings they may have about sperm. We've worked with a number of women who've chosen clinic inseminations based solely on the fact that their partner wouldn't have to come in contact with sperm. We've also worked with women whose partners find sperm so offensive that they will only touch their partner with gloves and can't imagine being sexual with her for days after she's been inseminated. This kind of response from your partner can feel humiliating and invalidating. Conception is usually a time when you not only need great support but also want to feel connected as a couple. It's a time to feel that you're in this process together.

We've heard multiple stories of women discharging any negative hold sperm had on them by renaming it. Names such as "little spermies," "swimmers," "little guys," and "animalitos" are common. We've noticed a tendency in the English language to refer to individual sperm in the masculine, which is interesting since 50% of sperm have male chromosomes, while the other 50% have female chromosomes. Our culture portrays the egg as patient, immobile, receptive, and "feminine," while sperm are individual, competitive, powerful, dynamic, and "masculine," even in scientific writings. Recently, scientists have found that a large number of sperm must act cooperatively in order to achieve conception. Perhaps some of us would find it easier to embrace the sperm's role in conception if it weren't portrayed through a sexist perspective. Reenvision it for yourself if you need to.

Internalized Homophobia and Deservedness Issues

As discussed in Chapter 2, internalized homophobia is a powerful force. Many of us believe we're not as fit to be parents as heterosexual women are. Sometimes this deep-seated belief isn't even recognized until a woman is long into the process. Often our religion, family, or friends have told us directly that we're not fit to parent. Unfortunately, often we've internalized this common sentiment, which is one of the reasons it takes many lesbians so long to get to the point of actually deciding to parent. Internalized homophobia continues to undermine women throughout parenthood by causing self-doubt and insecurity.

Accepting the fact that we do indeed deserve to have children in our lives can be a long and painful process that often requires support. Part of the process includes tackling fears that your sexual orientation will be a disservice to your children. Reread the first section of this book. Try to find a gay-friendly therapist or consider joining or forming a prospective queer parenting group in your area. Talk to other parents in your community, contact Children of Lesbians and Gays Everywhere (COLAGE), read some books, or investigate any of the numerous lesbian-parenting Web sites.

Many studies show that not only are our children well adjusted, but they also have higher-than-average verbal capacities. Studies also indicate that our children have higher-than-average stress loads, but they also suggest that our children have more coping skills to deal with their stress. There have been no studies to date showing that our children are maladjusted in any way.

You deserve to have a child. If you are able to bring a wanted child into a loving home, what more could a child ask for? This doesn't mean you won't encounter challenges along the way. It just means those challenges are simply that: challenges. And all parents, gay or straight, face challenges.

There are many reasons why you may feel you don't deserve to be a parent. Feeling undeserving can be related to your sense of self-esteem, which often comes from a place of guilt: "I can't be a parent until I have more money, own a home, have a stable relationship, am more emotionally stable, am younger, am older, am thinner, have gotten over my body issues, have smoothed out my relationships with my family of origin, have more education, am healthier..." The list goes on and on.

Once you recognize it, you may notice this theme running through your whole life. This may be a good time for you to enter therapy. These feelings often stem from past formative experiences and from growing up female. Gloria Steinem, in her book *The Revolution From Within*, speaks in depth on the intricacies of self-esteem and the feminist process of reclaiming it. Overcoming feelings of undeservedness allows you to feel much more confident, secure, and content. What an opportunity to have more happiness in your life, with or without children!

Sex Preference/Selection

Although both science and folk wisdom have devised many methods of influencing the conception process, none of these methods can guarantee that you'll conceive a child of a specific sex. Therefore, *before you get pregnant* it's extremely important that you closely examine the reasons why you think you must have a boy or a girl.

Women who want to influence the sex of their child often have fears or concerns about raising a child of the "undesired" sex. Some are afraid of passing on sex-specific diseases to their child. Some are afraid of raising daughters; some are afraid of raising sons. Some hope to "balance" their family. We encourage you to seriously consider what you'll choose to do about continuing the pregnancy if you discover that the fetus is not of the desired sex.

It no longer seems to be true that lesbians are giving birth to a disproportionate number of boys. According to current sperm bank statistics, and those of our own practice, it seems to be balancing out, with female births and male births being about 50/50. It is, however, slightly more common to give birth to a girl when using fresh sperm and slightly more common to give birth to a boy when using frozen sperm.

Exercise

Whether or not you have a preference about having a boy or a girl, take some quiet time to explore the following questions and the feelings they bring up. Allow yourself to write freely and completely. No one has to see these pages, so try not to censor yourself.

- What is a girl to me?
- What is a boy to me?
- Which do I want to have? Why?
- What exactly am I looking for in my child?

Part of this discussion concerns our own histories and how our personal experiences have informed our desire to have a child of a specific sex. It's important to explore our enculturation as female and our experiences as lesbian and bisexual women. Exploring the sexism involved in our histories is often particularly poignant for women who consider themselves butch. Continue writing for a few minutes (or more) on your history as a female and as a lesbian or bisexual woman. We have great power to change the labels and differences in treatment of males and females if we start exploring these issues in ourselves before we conceive. Gender enculturation begins in the womb. We can choose if and how we would like to buy into this concept.

Conversations about gender often reveal past wounds and unexamined internalized sexism and homophobia. We feel it's equally important and equally challenging to raise feminist boys as it is to raise feminist girls. It's important to note that sex is the physiology we're born with. Gender is each culture's meanings and perceptions related to physical sex. With the growing recognition of transgender identities in our culture comes a greater understanding of how complex gender is and how someone's gender identity doesn't always match the sex they're born with physically.

When we enter into these conversations with women, we frequently hear things such as "I want someone I can play football with" or "I want someone I can dress in pretty clothes." Other comments women have shared with us include:

• They're separatists and believe they'll be kicked out of their community if they have a boy.

• They have an unexplainable, tremendous dislike of one gender or the other.

• One partner has threatened to leave if the other partner births a baby of the "wrong" sex. In this case it's your relationship that needs examination. Are you ready to have children together if such a threat is involved?

Please talk to as many parents as you can about their experiences in parenting children of any sex. If you want to nonmedically increase the chances of giving birth to a baby of a particular sex, read the following section for ideas. Do think carefully, however, about the above questions and how you'll feel if any techniques you try don't result in your having a baby of the sex you prefer. If, after exploring your feelings and the sources of your feelings, your preferences remain unwavering and a child of the undesired sex is unappealing, perhaps adoption is more appropriate for you.

Sex-Selection Techniques

What Determines the Sex of the Baby?

The sex of a baby is determined at the time of conception by the sperm cell that fertilizes the egg. If the sperm carries a Y chromosome, the baby will be male. If it carries an X chromosome, the baby will be female. Because the X chromosome contains more genetic material, "female" sperm are larger, heavier, and slower swimmers than "male" sperm, but they're also thought to be hardier and to live longer.

Caution: Most of the methods outlined here decrease the likelihood of pregnancy. Douching just before insemination, limiting your number of inseminations to only a few days before ovulation or the day of ovulation, and chemically or physically altering sperm will all decrease your chances of conceiving.

Folk Wisdom and Conceiving a Girl

1. Diet: Both partners should eat plenty of fish and vegetables. (A diet high in calcium and low in salt and potassium for six months prior to conception has been shown to dramatically increase your chances of having a girl, but this isn't necessarily sound nutrition or a healthy pre-pregnancy diet!)

2. Cravings: The woman should give into her chocolate urges.

3. Timing: Inseminate between one day (24 hours) and four days (96 hours) before ovulation and then don't inseminate again during that cycle. Inseminate in the afternoon. Inseminate only on even days of the month.

4. Moon cycle: Inseminate when the moon is full and when the moon is in "feminine" astrological signs.

5. Insemination: With intercourse, try face-to-face positions, especially the missionary position and shallow penetration at time of male ejaculation. With insemination, deposit the sperm in a shallow part of the vagina.

6. Acidity: Before insemination, douche with an acidic solution to increase the acidity of the vagina. (two tablespoons white vinegar to one quart water). The inseminating woman should not have an orgasm at the time of or immediately before insemination to avoid increasing the alkalinity of the vagina.

7. Sperm: The donor or father should *not* refrain from ejaculation in the days before insemination. Also, he should wear briefs to reduce his male sperm count. (Keep in mind that this will also reduce his overall sperm count.)

Folk Wisdom and Conceiving a Boy

1. Diet: Eat meat, the redder the better. (Some research has shown that a preconception maternal diet high in salt and potassium, and low in calcium will dramatically increase your chances of having a boy, but this isn't necessarily sound nutrition or a healthy pre-pregnancy diet!)

2. Cravings: Mom can eat lots of salt, and donor/father can drink lots of soda.

3. Timing: Inseminate at the time of ovulation or immediately (but not more than 12 hours) before. Inseminate only at night and on odd days of the month.

4. Moon cycle: Inseminate when there's a quarter moon in the sky or when the moon is in "male" astrological signs.

5. Insemination: With intercourse, vaginal penetration from the rear and deep

penetration at time of male ejaculation to deposit the sperm at the cervix so that the sperm won't have to travel far through the vagina (which is not as hospitable to male sperm). With insemination, place the sperm near the cervix. Lie down for a while after inseminating to give the male sperm a chance to outswim the slower female sperm. Some people swear that pointing the mother's head toward the north during sex or having her sleep to the left of her partner will ensure her having a boy.

6. Alkalinity: Use a baking-soda douche (two tablespoons baking soda to one quart water) prior to insemination to increase the alkalinity of the vagina. Also, the mother should orgasm prior to insemination to increase the alkalinity of the vagina.

7. Sperm: To increase their male sperm count, donor or father should not ejaculate for at least a week prior to insemination, nor should he wear briefs.

Gender-Preselection Medical Procedures

Several medical procedures used for sex preselection are available from fertility specialists. The most proven medical method available is the Ericsson method, in which a two-step, two-layered albumin (protein) separation procedure is performed. With the recovered sperm an intrauterine insemination is done the day after the luteinizing hormone (LH) surge. If the couple is trying to conceive a girl, the woman must take an ovulation-enhancing drug called clomiphene for several days during her cycle. For an unknown reason, the combination of this drug with the albumin separation procedure increases the chances of having a girl by 20%. In 1995, 244 births resulted from this procedure, with a 72% female birth rate. **Note:** The side effects of ovulation-enhancing drugs include an increased chance of multiple births and increased possible chance of later developing cervical or ovarian cancer. See Chapter 14 for extensive information about clomiphene.

If a woman is trying to conceive a boy, the sperm will be separated as above and an intrauterine insemination will be performed, but the mother will not take clomiphene. On average, about 75% Y chromosome sperm result, which are then used for intrauterine insemination in concentrated form. As of 1990, there were 698 babies born from women inseminated with albumin-separated sperm. The male birth rate was 74%. There's a newer variation on this procedure, which can be done with semen samples with sperm counts of 150–200 million. In this procedure, laboratory Y-chromosome counts were about 80-85%, and the actual birth rate was about 79.8% male. This procedure is also linked to lower rates of birth "abnormalities."

Another medical procedure, called centrifugation, involves layering semen over 12 layers of Percoll, a gel made of fused silica, which is placed in a tube and spun in a centrifuge. Because male sperm are lighter than female sperm, they rise to the top. The heavier female sperm collect at the bottom. Intrauterine insemination is then performed using the preferred sperm. Centrifugation isn't considered as successful as the Ericsson method, and reliable statistics haven't yet been published.

The most successful gender selection method is also highly controversial and not yet available to the general public. This method, called flow cytometry or MicroSort®, was developed originally for farm animals and hasn't received FDA approval for human use. Flow cytometry uses fluorescent dye and a laser to sort sperm. The long-term effects of this procedure on human DNA are unknown at this time. The sorted sperm are used to inseminate eggs that have been harvested from the mother. After the embryos have grown to an eight-cell stage in a petri dish, they're genetically tested. Then only the embryos of the desired sex are introduced into the uterus. The parents must decide what they want done with the remaining embryos. This method is highly invasive and is currently available only to parents with genetic or reproductive disorders, and is considered experimental.

Past Pregnancies

If you've been pregnant before, you'll have a different history in your body than women who haven't been. It's important to explore your feelings about that part of your past. It's also important to explore your body memories about these past times.

Those of you who have been pregnant and given birth before may have given birth during a time in your life when you were straight. If you've raised your child or children, you may wonder if it's fair to want children again. If you haven't raised the children you gave birth to, you may question your capacity and deservedness to parent again. If you've given birth and given a child up for adoption, thinking about getting pregnant again may bring up suppressed guilt and other feelings about that time of your life. From a body-memory point of view, your body may still be weeping from that loss. We've seen women effectively prevent future pregnancies by experiencing "infertility," which ceases to be a problem after they're able to finish the emotional processing of that loss/choice/set of experiences.

If you've had past abortions, the experience can be similar to having given up a child. Often there are overlapping issues: *If I chose no before, do I deserve to choose yes now? What if that was the one opportunity I was given? Will I now be punished for not wanting that baby?*

Many women have developed ovarian and uterine symptoms after abortions, unwanted pregnancies, and miscarriages. Examples of this include endometriosis, ovulation pain on one side of the body, and ovarian cysts. Painful reproductive cycles are often related to suppressed anger, sadness, and feelings of betrayal. This is not to downplay in any way the seriousness of these situations, but rather to emphasize that we live in our bodies our entire lives, and the experiences we have are recorded like a map. Roadblocks come from areas of stagnant energy. Releasing those energies through movement, either emotional or physical, can free the pathways again.

Exercise

If you've been pregnant before, take some quiet time alone and allow yourself to write freely about this time in your life. Write about how you feel now, emotionally and physically. Is there anything you'd like to say to those babies or potential babies, born or not? Is there any healing you'd like to give yourself? Hold yourself in your heart and visualize yourself getting all the healing and support that you needed then and may still need now.

Past Surgeries

Our bodies need to recover from the traumas of surgical procedures that have helped us heal. Due to anesthesia, it's logical that the body may retain memories of trauma that the mind might not remember. Because we don't remember the pain of the incision and internal manipulations, we often don't realize the long-term impact surgery may have on us.

Doing bodywork, meditating, spending time rubbing the part of your body that was cut, and writing in a journal are all helpful methods of clearing stress. Once again, the theory is that when your energy is not tied up elsewhere, you'll have more available energy for pregnancy. Cut down on the many messages your body is receiving and make pregnancy your focus.

Getting Comfortable in Your Body

Pregnancy is, of course, an extremely physical experience. Getting comfortable in your body helps to prepare you for a healthier, easier pregnancy. It's a great time to receive massage, start exercising, take a dance class, do yoga, make love, or masturbate. It's a great time to touch your own body lovingly, give self-massage, use lotions, and appreciate your body for the wonder it is. Do what makes your body feel good!

By focusing on nurturing your body, you can come to appreciate how amazing this female body of ours is. Can you believe you actually have the capacity to make and grow a complete human being inside your body?! Celebrate this amazing truth prior to conception by fostering activities that connect you with the strength and beauty of your body. Doing so helps temper the emotional elements of self-doubt that can creep into an extended conception period.

Lesbian Conception

Some lesbians feel a strong initial aversion to the idea of lesbian conception. The idea of "autonomous" conception threatens the core of male-dominated society. If women can buy or borrow sperm, we can essentially conceive on our own. This threatens the fabric of our society and may feel disquieting. We have, however, the power to define conception in whatever way we choose. This realization can feel just as life-changing and difficult as coming out. For some women coming out is painful and earth-shattering. For others, the transition is more gentle.

Allowing the mind to entertain the idea that you can conceive in any way that feels right to you—and that sexual intercourse with a man is not the only or "right" way—can take time. Often heterosexist ideas are so deeply ingrained in us that we don't recognize them.

Take the time you need to explore these ideas until you feel comfortable with the idea that there are a myriad of equally valid ways to conceive. Once you've achieved this, you'll be ready to imagine how you'd like to conceive.

Photo © Cathy Cade

What Exactly Is Conception?

Once you've established where you'll obtain sperm, you're ready to conceive. So what exactly is conception? The actual act of conception isn't discussed much in our culture. This silence appears to be linked not only to sexual taboo but also to cultural taboos surrounding life, death, and spiritual mysteries that prohibit us from talking about the unknown. Women who have intercourse with men often get pregnant "by accident." This may happen with lesbians who sometimes have sex with men, but more frequently lesbians fall to the other extreme: delaying pregnancy by painstakingly planning it. All women who get pregnant have conceived, yet serious consideration is rarely given to how we'd like to conceive, to the act and meaning of conception itself.

Before you consider where you'd like to conceive or which method you'd like to use, spend some time examining your beliefs about conception. From a spiritual place, a religious place, a scientific place, what is conception to you? How does it happen? When does it happen? What are the answers you find inside yourself? Each culture and religion passes down a set of beliefs about when and how life becomes, and science adds a whole new dimension to it. But what holds meaning for you?

In Tibetan tantra, a baby is called into your body by your desire; it comes into your body through an energy vortex down through your head. Scientists say sperm from a penis reaches an egg in a fallopian tube, union occurs, and cell division begins. Some Native American traditions believe that babies were once little stars in Spiritland. And Australian aboriginal culture explains that babies come from the Earth itself. Some cultures believe a baby can only be conceived when two people have simultaneous orgasms. Others believe the entire future of a baby is determined at conception.

Some people think conception can't occur until a number of hours after insemination, because it takes time for the sperm and egg to meet. Yet others swear they feel it happen the moment sperm enters their body, or even just before. What do you believe? Have you thought about it?

Although you might not approach making a baby from a spiritual place, bringing life into your body often brings up these questions. Why is it that sometimes you succeed in conceiving, and other months you don't? Are you the one who controls your conception through timing, health, and a good sperm source? Or does something outside you determine this? Is it predetermined? Or is it just chance?

How you approach conception initially is often quite different than how you approach conception after you've been trying to get pregnant for many cycles. Your experience, your ideas, and your ideals all change. There's no predictable quality to this change, but your approach to conception will more than likely deeply transform over time.

It's helpful to review your beliefs about conception if it's taking you many months to conceive. Doing so can give you new insights, deepen your faith, and help you remember things you may have forgotten.

Exercise

Take a moment to write in your journal about your ideal conception. If you were to conceive right now, what would it look like for you? Where are you? Who's there? What does it feel like? What time of day is it? Note any details, emotions, and sensations. Be open to surprises. Write quickly, in the flow of consciousness, without scrutinizing or judging what comes out. If you're partnered, have your partner do this as well. It's often nice to do it at the same time, or at least to share only after both of you have completed the exercise separately. When you're finished, examine what you've written. What does your heart say? Does that differ from the intellectual choices you've made about where and how you'll conceive? Be sure to include this completed exercise in your fertility journal, so that you can refer back to it at a later time.

If you'd like a further discussion of preconception emotional/mental/spiritual preparations and how they influence conception, see the resource page at the end of Chapter 14 for books by Niravi Payne and Carista Luminare Rosen.

As lesbian and/or single women, we almost invariably have limited access to sperm. This is sometimes the case for bisexual women as well. As a result, many of us choose to spend large amounts of money to procure this vital elixir. How much sperm you have available, however, doesn't matter unless you inseminate at the right time of the month for your body. Therefore, timing is everything. This chapter covers in detail the steps you can take to make sure you're inseminating at the optimal time each month.

Female Anatomy, Conception, and the Menstrual Cycle

To track your fertility effectively, it's important to have a working understanding of your anatomy and menstrual cycle. This will allow you to have the same basic understanding and working vocabulary as that of the fertility health care providers you may encounter. Many of us are carrying around limited, misguided, old, or incomplete information about our menstrual and fertility cycles. For example, plenty of women don't realize that all women don't ovulate on day 14 of their cycle. By studying and claiming our own fertility, we take control of our most valuable resource: ourselves. By familiarizing ourselves with the information our bodies have to give us, we can come to trust ourselves and our decisions more fully. Your fertility cycle is so individual that the only way you can reach a comprehensive understanding of it is to explore your own body and its changes. You, and only you, have the ability to be the expert on your fertility. Don't abdicate this right—claim it!

We'll provide an overview of anatomy and the menstrual cycle, then discuss the tools you'll need to more deeply explore your own fertility cycle. You may wish to examine the diagram on page 244 before you read any further, in order to maintain a visual image of the inside of your body. It may also be helpful for you to rent *The Miracle of Life*, a beautiful and informative video on conception filmed with the use of special cameras.

Anatomy of Conception

Let's start by describing your reproductive organs. Inside your vagina, if you reach deeply with your finger, you'll feel something slightly firmer than the rest of your vagina. This firm, round protrusion is your cervix, the opening of your uterus. The opening of your cervix is called your os. When you put sperm into your vagina, it will swim up through your cervix and into your uterus. Your uterus is an upside-down pear-shaped organ, usually the size of an apricot, that will become the home for your baby when you're pregnant. Your uterus grows as the baby grows.

At the top of your uterus on the right and left sides is a narrow area from which the fallopian tubes branch forth. These tubes are 4–5 inches long but are extremely narrow, and they are open at the ends. Floating close to the ends of each tube are your ovaries. Each ovary is about the size and shape of an almond. Your ovaries contain all the eggs your body will ever release. In fact, as a fetus inside your mother's body, you had all the eggs you were born with. Eggs mature over our lifetime, but we never create more eggs. Each month many eggs begin to mature in each ovary, each within its own follicle. As the follicles grow, one follicle ripens most rapidly and becomes the dominant follicle. When the most dominant follicle is ready and an egg within it matures, the egg is released from the ovary. Ovulation is the moment the egg bursts forth from the follicle. Following ovulation, the egg is outside the ovary in the pelvic cavity, where it's immediately swept into the fallopian tubes by small feathery protrusions from the tubes called fimbria. The egg is then guided along the fallopian tubes into the uterus by tiny hairlike fibers called cilia, which line each tube.

Conception occurs after ovulation, usually inside the fallopian tubes. The egg is gently pushed through the fallopian tube, and the sperm swims into the tube via the uterus. Here they meet. If conception occurs, cell division begins and the embryo travels all the way down the tube and into the uterus, dividing cells and growing rapidly as it does. This takes a number of days. Shortly after the embryo enters the uterus, it implants into the uterine wall.

Every woman has a slightly different menstrual cycle. For some women, the first part of their cycle is longer or shorter than average. For others, the second part of their cycle is longer or shorter than average. For still others, their menstrual cycle is a varying combination of lengths depending on multiple factors. A normal menstrual cycle varies from about 24 to 35 days. For the sake of keeping this information simple, we've chosen to describe a 28-day menstrual cycle with one ovulation. The following is an overly simplified yet working overview of the menstrual cycle.

Many hormones in the brain and ovaries affect our fertility cycle. Four basic hormones, however, are at play in the menstrual cycle: follicle stimulating hormone (FSH) and luteinizing hormone (LH) from the brain, and estrogen and progesterone from the ovaries.

FSH causes the egg to ripen and mature. Estrogen is at play predominantly in the first half of the cycle and helps regulate the release of FSH and LH. Progesterone is at play primarily in the second half of the cycle. It's secreted from the corpus luteum in the ovary and, coupled with estrogen, prepares the uterine lining to receive the fertilized egg. Progesterone maintains the lining of the uterus after conception and implantation until the placenta is formed at around eight to 10 weeks of pregnancy. At that time the placenta produces the majority of the necessary progesterone to support the pregnancy.

FSH gives the signal that encourages the follicles in the ovary to begin to mature. These follicles in turn secrete estrogen. Over the next seven or so days the follicles ripen and secrete more estrogen into the bloodstream.

Estrogen signals the uterus to prepare its lining to receive and nourish a fetus. It simultaneously signals the cervix and cervical mucus to change and become receptive to sperm. Estrogen also sends the message back to the brain that the ovary heard the message from the FSH to begin follicle maturation and is responding.

Mid cycle, around day 14 for many women, a sharp increase in estrogen causes a surge in LH. This hormonal dance then stimulates ovulation of the body's ripest egg. This first part of your cycle, which is high in estrogen, is known as the follicular phase, which can vary in duration quite a bit, depending on how long it takes your body to reach its estrogen threshold.

After ovulation the luteal phase begins, marked by high levels of progesterone. This phase usually lasts 12 to 16 days. Following ovulation, LH signals the body to initiate the formation of the corpus luteum, which is the gland formed by the ruptured follicle following ovulation. The corpus luteum continues to produce progesterone to support an early pregnancy until the placenta is formed. If egg fertilization does not occur, the corpus luteum degenerates within 12-16 days and thus starts a new menstrual cycle.

The luteal phase is more finite in length if your body produces adequate progesterone. Just as estrogen begins the preparation of the womb to receive a potential fetus, progesterone completes it. Over the next two weeks the uterine walls thicken. If pregnancy and implantation do not occur, progesterone levels fall, the uterus sheds its lining, and your period begins.

Interior View of a Nonpregnant Female

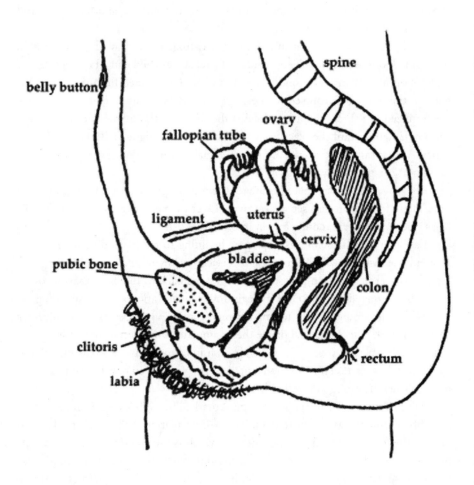

Outside View

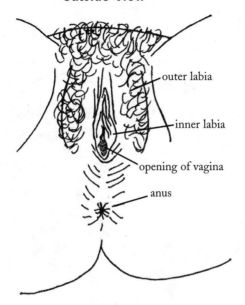

A female
who hasn't
given birth

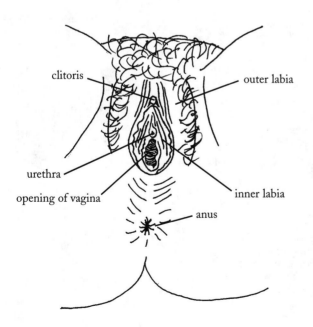

A female
who has
given birth
vaginally

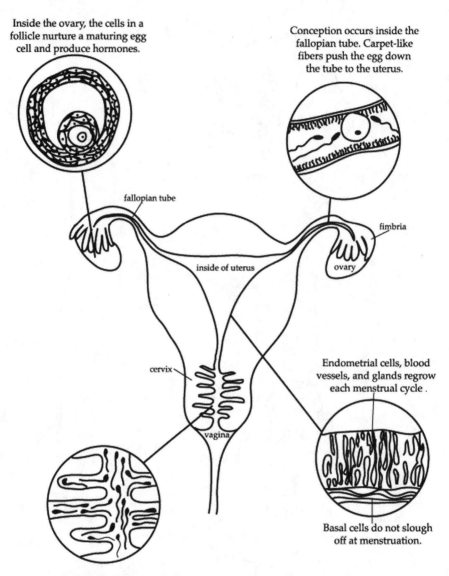

Inside the ovary, the cells in a follicle nurture a maturing egg cell and produce hormones.

Conception occurs inside the fallopian tube. Carpet-like fibers push the egg down the tube to the uterus.

fallopian tube

fimbria

inside of uterus

ovary

cervix

Endometrial cells, blood vessels, and glands regrow each menstrual cycle .

vagina

Basal cells do not slough off at menstruation.

The cells that line the channels branching off of the cervial canal produce fertile mucus. After insemination, many sperm live here until they find their way to the fallopian tubes.

Getting the Most Out of Fertility Monitoring

Once you have a working understanding of the female body and the menstrual cycle, you can move on to learn the Maia approach to monitoring and recording your personal fertility information. Fertility awareness allows you a profound understanding of the workings of your own body and your unique fertility and menstrual cycles. The methods we outline are highly accurate and effective in identifying your fertile days. When you effectively chart your body's fertility signals, interpreting your chart and deciding when to inseminate can be approached in a straightforward manner.

For most lesbian and single women—as well as for bisexual women who aren't partnered with a man with whom they wish to conceive a baby—good charting and proper interpretation are crucial to achieving pregnancy. This is because you'll only be inseminating one to three times a month, compared to the multiple times that partnered heterosexual women might have sex. We strongly encourage you to start charting as early as possible—ideally at least three months prior to insemination—in order to maximize its value.

Fertility Awareness Can Be Empowering

Fertility monitoring and charting is something you do in the privacy of your own home. You're the only one needed to gather this information. You aren't dependent on anyone else to recognize your signals of fertility and how to interpret them. Despite this, many women find themselves relying on doctors to tell them when they're fertile. A doctor, however, can only know the fertility information of the generic woman. You are not generic, and with a brief amount of self-study, you can become the true expert on your fertility and thus an active participant in your health care.

Unlike so many other aspects of this process, such as finding your source of sperm and interacting with health care providers, tracking your fertility cycles is entirely personal and self-contained. Discovering more and more information about your body can be deeply empowering.

Adequate Charting Is Crucial

Ninety percent of the women that we see don't chart anywhere near enough, if at all. You'll probably need at least three months to gather vital and appropriately useful information about your body. You should allow up to six months if you have irregular cycles. This means it's most valuable to begin thorough fertility tracking up to half a year prior to the time you plan to start inseminating. You can make any other decision about insemination overnight, if you have to. Fertility awareness, however, is not a decision. It's a simple system of gathering information about your body that, to be most effective, requires months of research.

Charting well from the beginning is the single most important tool you have to shorten the time it will take for you to get pregnant. Thus, even if you're certain you're incredibly fertile and that you'll get pregnant on the first try, chart anyway. If you don't get pregnant the first time, by the time you're ready to start charting you'll have already lost valuable months of gathering information about your fertility cycle.

Charting is invaluable and must be done every cycle in which you plan to inseminate. Ovulation rarely occurs on the same day of a cycle from one cycle to the next—even in the most regular of menstrual cycles. So the most valuable information is always your most current information.

Gathering Information

There are many ways to gather this information; some will be more comfortable for you if they resonate with your approach to life. Others can seem, at first, to be contrived or more of a hassle if they're not your usual approach to learning or gathering information about yourself. We encourage you to choose the approaches that are most comfortable to you but also try to incorporate new and perhaps less instinctive methods.

What Should I Track?

The purpose of charting is to try to ascertain not only when you ovulate, but also the signs from your body that indicate approaching ovulation. When three of these signs line up, you're in a peak window for insemination. You'll want to know when your egg comes out and what happens in your body to forewarn you that the egg is about to be released. Many women have an innate sense of their own fertility. Others don't have any sense of this at all. In the next section we'll examine the various signs of female fertility—outlining for each how to observe and chart it— and examine the practical challenges and advantages of tracking each signal. We'll teach you to monitor cervical changes, mucus changes, ovulation predictor kit/monitor results, basal body temperature, ferning patterns observed on a fertility lens, phases of the moon, libido, breast changes, ovulation sensation, feelings of fertility, and your dreams.

Is There Such a Thing as Objective Charting?

A fertility chart is a reflection of your personal fertility cycle. Therefore, your chart is inherently subjective. There's an illusion that certain signals are more objective and therefore somehow more valid than others. The signals that the medical profession tend to validate as being the most important are basal body temperature and the results of ovulation predictor kits. Because these signs are externally obvious, they're somehow deemed more objective and therefore more valuable. As you'll see, these signs are no less subjective than other signs you'll monitor. Yes, the average woman does experience a dip and a rise in her basal body temperature. And the average woman does experience an LH surge that can be detected by ovulation predictor kits. But what these signs indicate in terms of each woman's fertility cycle is different. There is no standardized woman. Thus, we recommend charting many fertility signs to see which ones prove the most helpful and revealing for you. Ovulation-predictor results and basal body temperature changes may be useful indicators for you in combination with other fertility signals, but they may not be useful on their own. Remember, you are not generic! Your experience is subjective, and this is what makes it your experience.

How Much of the Month Do I Need to Chart?

It's essential that you chart for the full month. For a chart to be most helpful, you need to be able to see your low, high, and peak fertility signals, as well as learn the signs that indicate that you've ovulated. As some women ovulate more than once a month and some women's cycles vary significantly in length, it's important to continue charting until you once again see your menstrual blood. Once you've charted in this complete fashion for three full cycles, you'll most likely be able to narrow your charting window to a 10–14 day period.

Separate Documenting From Interpreting

When you log everything you feel, notice, and observe, resist the urge to interpret the data as you go and discard your sensations as invalid. Record your complete experience without censoring it. Interpret it later as a second, separate step. When it's time to interpret your chart you can reengage the discretionary part of your mind and determine what all the information means.

Don't Limit What You Write Down

It's important to write down everything—both significant and what seems insignificant—when tracking your fertility. In our midwifery practice we've worked with so many women who've conceived at unexpected times that we've come to appreciate the true breadth of fertility and understand that each woman's body is unique. Many of the straight women we've worked with have gotten pregnant when they were menstruating, because they'd assumed that menstruation afforded them a window of safe sex. How could they be ovulating when they're bleeding? It's remarkable how many women get pregnant when they're bleeding or at other unlikely times of the month. This phenomenon is caused by double ovulation.

249

Double Ovulation

According to the Western medical interpretation of female fertility, ovulation only happens once mid-cycle. Although it's recognized that some women ovulate twice in one month, it's only considered possible within 24 hours of a woman's first ovulation. Our experience has proven otherwise. We, and many other practitioners around the world, have come to realize that for some women, and for some cycles, ovulation occurs more than once a cycle, often seven to 10 days apart.

We've heard many women say, "Sometimes I have signs of fertility such as fertile mucus when I don't expect it, so I figure I'm checking it wrong." While showing our client Denise her cervix with a speculum one day, we observed a very open os with copious fertile mucus. When we asked her if she thought she was ovulating, she replied, "No, it's day 8." Then with raised eyebrows she looked at her partner and told us, "I always get fertile mucus on day 8 and just ignore it, figuring I'm doing something wrong. On day 15 it returns, and I inseminate." Denise went home and ran her ovulation predictor kit out of curiosity: It was positive! It turned negative again and then turned positive once more with the return of her fertile mucus on day 15. She'd been charting for a year and a half and had managed to convince herself each month that on day 8 she had forgotten what she was doing. We recommended that she expand her thinking, begin to document *everything*, contemplate the fact that she probably had a double ovulation cycle, and inseminate at each fertile window.

Using the Maia Chart

At the end of this chapter we've included a copy of the Maia fertility chart. We feel that this chart is the most comprehensive and effective method of documenting your fertility cycle. Many women note their fertility signs in their datebooks or on scraps of paper. Visually reviewing a comprehensive, condensed, and consistent record of your fertility signals will allow you to interpret the information more effectively. It also makes it easier for an outside professional to review. We recommend that you make photocopies of this chart and use it to monitor your cycles for at least three to four months before deciding whether it's useful for you. Women with computer skills have found they can tailor our chart to their specific needs. We also recommend that you save all of your charts in a folder or binder.

Specific Fertility Signs and How to Chart Them

Begin a new chart on the first day of your menstrual period. This day you'll call day 1 regardless of the date.

Basal Body Temperature (BBT)

In the follicular phase of your cycle, the time leading up to ovulation, your body temperature is on average lower than your temperature during the luteal phase of your cycle—the time following ovulation until your next menses. Basal body temperature (BBT) is your body's resting temperature. Use a regular digital thermometer or BBT glass thermometer. It's essential for you to take your temperature at the exact same time every morning before you fully wake up, talk, or move around. Many women set an alarm, take their temperature, and go back to sleep. Although it's important to take your temperature daily, it isn't necessary to take your temperature on the days of your menstrual cycle.

Some women notice a dip in their temperature with or preceding ovulation. Not all women experience this dip. The vast majority of ovulating women, however, experience a rise in temperature following ovulation. Tracking your BBT can be useful for a number of purposes.

Benefits

You can use a BBT chart to determine when ovulation has occurred. The chart is most helpful retrospectively as a means of confirming and validating your other preovulatory signals. Women who are able to use this tracking method find it an easy means of monitoring their fertility. For most women, BBT readings alone, however, are not a useful means of planning insemination because a woman's body temperature usually rises once she's ovulated, which is often too late. But if you've done additional corroborative monitoring of your fertility and have found that your dip in temperature correlates consistently with the day that your ovulation predictor kit or fertility monitor reads positive and the day when your mucus is most fertile, then perhaps you can use this information for timing purposes.

You can also use your BBT readings to confirm that you do indeed ovulate. If you consistently experience a rise in temperature that stays elevated for 12–16 days, you can feel quite confident that you're ovulating.

Identifying a Short Luteal Phase

Likewise, you can use your BBT reading to determine whether you're experiencing a short luteal phase of your cycle. Women whose BBT stays high for fewer than 12 days more than likely have a short luteal phase (the time from ovulation to menstruation) and may have trouble sustaining a pregnancy to the point of implantation. This most frequently indicates a progesterone imbalance. This is critical information, as you may not have any problem conceiving but may have difficulty maintaining a pregnancy. See Chapter 8 for recommendations on treatments for short luteal phases.

Identifying Pregnancy and Early Miscarriage

Some women track their basal body temperature to try to determine whether they're pregnant or about to get their period. If your temperature remains high and does not dip when you'd ordinarily expect your menstrual blood, you're probably pregnant. If you experience a dip when you're expecting your menstrual blood, you'll most likely begin bleeding within 24–48 hours.

If your temperature has been consistently elevated for 18 consecutive days, you can safely assume that you're pregnant. Although it's always terribly disheartening to miscarry, if you find that your temperatures drop significantly following more than 18 days of elevated temperatures and that you start to bleed, you'll be able to know that this is a miscarriage and not simply a late period.

Identifying a Thyroid Imbalance

Many women's BBT is in the low 97 range, not 98.6 degrees. If your temperature is usually in the 96's, your thyroid level may be a little low, which can affect fertility. A blood test can easily determine this.

Drawbacks

Although tracking BBT provides clear, readable charts for some women, for others it doesn't provide anything other than a confusing and seemingly random set of points. This variability is usually due to the numerous influences that can significantly affect temperature readings for some women. For example, to have accurate readings you may need to: 1) go to sleep at the same time every night and wake up at the same time every morning; 2) sleep soundly through the night; 3) not sleep with pets that are in and out of your bed during the night; 4) sleep in the same bed throughout the week; 5) sleep in a room with consistent air temperature; 6) not get up to urinate; or 7) not drink alcohol before going to sleep. Unless these factors are consistent, there's a good chance that when you look at your chart you might not see a meaningful pattern.

Because BBT tracking is such a widely recognized method of monitoring fertility, many women feel like failures if it doesn't work for them.

Don't lose heart. A random-looking chart doesn't necessarily indicate that you aren't ovulating. More than likely it simply means that temperature charting doesn't work for you, which isn't uncommon.

At Maia we don't consider BBT tracking to be one of the most useful fertility signs to chart to determine when to inseminate, especially as resting temperatures aren't reliable in predicting ovulation or preovulatory fertile days. Many women who do experience a dip in their temperature aren't able to know if they're at the bottom of their dip until a rise occurs a day or two later, by which time they're no longer fertile. Others experience more than one dip and are unable to know which one is the most significant until after the fact. Thus, the best use of basal body temperature tracking is to confirm that ovulation did take place. If your cycle is extremely regular—which isn't true for most women—you can make an educated guess as to when ovulation may occur during your next cycle.

Insemination Recommendations

The majority of women seem to be most fertile during the days preceding and the day of their deepest temperature dip. These are the best days to inseminate. For most women, though, resting body temperature readings aren't a primary fertility signal and are best used in conjunction with other fertility signals when deciding when to inseminate.

Phases of the Moon

Although most women are unaccustomed to tracking the phases of the moon, they play an important role in cultures with strong lunar ties. Moon cycles are useful in determining many things, including insemination timing and the preselection of a baby's sex.

The Czech Psychic Institute has used the scientific elements of astrology to time ovulation and lunar fertility cycles. This methodology is built upon the belief that a woman ovulates not only mid cycle, but also when the moon is in the exact phase it was in when she was born. For example, if you were born two days after the full moon, then every month, two days after the full moon you are particularly fertile. They've also discovered that if you're menstruating at this same time, you're highly, highly fertile and even more likely to conceive. (Perhaps this is why so many heterosexual women conceive when they're menstruating.) If you choose this method, you must ask an astrologer which day of the moon cycle you were born on.

This same research strongly indicates that if you inseminate during "feminine" moon signs, you'll carry a girl, and if you conceive during "masculine" moon signs you'll carry a boy. These moon signs relate to the astrological sign that the moon is in during the actual time of conception, not the moon sign when you were born.

We share this information with you because often in Western culture it isn't easy to access information about radically different means of fertility monitoring and insemination timing. Perhaps this information will open up new possibilities for you. Charting this is optional but can be remarkably useful.

Mid-Cycle Bleeding

Take special note of any bleeding you experience during the month. If you bleed at any time of the month other than menstruation (such as after sex or during the middle of your cycle) write down when it occurs, its color and quantity, and the days when you spot. This information may later be useful if you're unable to get pregnant right away.

Ten percent of all women experience mid-cycle bleeding, for which there are a number of causes. Mid-cycle bleeding can be as simple as a little spotting following ovulation, or it may indicate something more significant such as endometriosis, a sexually transmitted infection, a hormonal imbalance, or cervical cancer. When you've inseminated and are newly pregnant—even if you don't necessarily know it yet—you may experience mid-cycle spotting following embryo implantation into the uterus. This is perfectly normal. It's also common to bleed following an office procedure such as a Pap smear or sometimes following an intrauterine insemination. If you regularly bleed at times other than your menses, you may wish to get an initial hormonal panel before you begin inseminating to ensure that your hormones aren't significantly imbalanced. For safety's sake, you should bring any unexplained bleeding to the attention of a medical doctor.

Often, acupuncture or fertility herbs such as Vitex are all that you'll need to rebalance your cycle. (See Chapter 8 for more information.) If endometriosis is the cause and it's severe, you may need minor surgery to clear out the buildup causing the bleeding. Always share information about your bleeding with your fertility specialist.

Ovulation Sensation

Women experience ovulation sensation in a number of ways. Many women are more sensitive to the feelings of ovulation on one side of their body than the other. A lot of women don't think they feel anything that indicates that they're ovulating. But when you begin to focus more deeply on body awareness through the fertility monitoring and charting process, you may be surprised to note that you actually do experience ovulation sensation.

What Does Ovulation Feel Like?

Some women are aware of approaching ovulation because of certain sensations in their body. Some feel only the actual ovulation, whereas others are aware of the impending ovulation several days prior. For some women, ovulation is simply an open feeling or awareness of the area of their body near their ovary. They may experience an awareness or a buildup of sensation that lasts moments or increases over hours or even days. This may be a physical heaviness or ache, which is actually a response to the rapid growth that the dominant follicle is doing over the 24 hours preceding ovulation. Other women perceive this sensation on a more spiritual level.

Some women feel a twinge or a small sensation of release. Some feel this on both sides, some on just one side. This appears to be a distinct form of intestinal awareness for a brief period of time and often is associated with the sensation of ovulation. More than one woman we've worked with has reported a momentary but intense depression accompanying ovulation. Still other women feel an intense high.

Some women experience cramping with ovulation. Ovulation occurs when the egg breaks through the wall of the ovary, which can cause cramping from the little bit of blood that gets into that peritoneal space surrounding the ovary. For some women this cramping is momentary, but for others it can last a few hours. The pain can range from slight to intense. **Ovulation sensation is a primary fertility signal.**

Notice and Validate What You Feel

When you start to notice and write down the feelings you experience, without censoring yourself, you may become aware of many sensations you'd never noticed before. Many women note in their chart comments such as "Day 16: sharp twinge on right side; might be gas"; or "Day 18: slight achiness on left side. Day 19: lots of achiness on left side increasing as the day progresses." When you pay attention in this way you'll most likely discover a wealth of information that can help you determine which signals may indicate ovulation. Don't be confused if you don't feel that the side you ovulate from alternates monthly. Some women ovulate in an alternating fashion, but many don't have any distinguishable pattern.

Likewise, if you don't experience any conclusive ovulation sensations, don't worry—if you have other strong fertility signs, you probably ovulate when you're sleeping.

Insemination Recommendations

Women who feel physical sensations leading up to or with ovulation can easily time inseminations for that period. We caution you not to use these sensations as your sole indicator of when to inseminate, as you may not have enough warning to coordinate the logistics, or it may come when you're sleeping and you may miss it altogether. If you could plan your final insemination around your ovulation symptoms, you would absolutely be in your peak fertile window.

Cervical Changes

The cervix, located inside the vagina, is the neck of the uterus. In the center of the cervix is an opening, called the os, that leads to the uterus. If you've never given birth, your os will look like a round opening. If you have given birth, your os will be more of a slit or an L shape. The os undergoes monthly changes that are obvious when viewed with the assistance of a speculum, or are palpable to the touch if you're monitoring your cervix by feel.

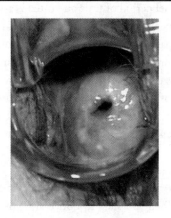

This cervix, viewed through an open speculum, shows signs of fertility: abundant clear mucus and an open os.

The influence of increasing estrogen, which peaks at the time of ovulation, causes the cervix to both soften and to slightly dilate or open. Simultaneously, the cervix produces fertile mucus that can be seen pouring out of the os during your most fertile days.

The changes in your cervix are concrete and are an accurate, inexpensive way to monitor your fertility. **Because this information is so amazingly helpful, monitoring cervical changes, particularly via speculum is a primary fertility signal.**

How to Monitor Cervical Changes

There are two ways of monitoring your cervical changes: by feel with a finger or by viewing with a speculum. The first month that you start to monitor your cervix, it's best to start immediately following the arrival of your menstrual blood and to continue daily until you bleed again. Once you've isolated your usual fertile window, you'll be able to limit your cervical monitoring to an approximate 10-day period. Many women, however, find this sign so incredibly valuable that nearing ovulation and insemination they may monitor their cervix several times a day.

Your cervix will be softer and more open when you're fertile. Most women find that it pulls up high and out of the way when they're fertile and is easier to reach and closer to the vaginal opening when not fertile. Because these changes are what you're hoping to track, it's important to begin your monitoring each month before your cervix begins to open and soften so that you can fully note its changes. Some women's cervices are lower in the vagina and some women's are higher. Sometimes the cervix will alter its placement in the body from month to month. This is normal and nothing to worry about.

Monitoring by Touch

Monitoring your cervix with your fingers is easy, once you've learned to identify where your cervix is and to feel the opening of the cervix. This is most readily done in the squatting position or with one leg raised on the side of a bathtub or bed. You may find, however, that your cervix is too far back for you to monitor with your own fingers. In this case you'll either need someone else to feel it for you, or you'll need to use a speculum. Always wash your hands with soap before checking your cervix. Likewise, for consistency of feel, always check your cervix in the same position each day.

What you should record each day is how easy your cervix is to reach, how far back or high up it is, what direction it's facing, how soft it is, and how open it is. Your cervix will open as your fertility increases and you're about to ovulate. Immediately following ovulation, it closes. This monitoring is incredibly useful, since you can familiarize yourself with these internal changes. You may also notice the quality of mucus remaining on your finger after touching your cervical os.

Monitoring by Speculum

Monitoring your cervix with a speculum is an easy, inexpensive, and amazing fertility tool. It is, however, quite an emotional leap for some women to imagine choosing this option willingly. Because of the amount of information monitoring by speculum provides, many women overcome their ambivalence and learn to use a speculum. **Speculum monitoring is a primary fertility signal.**

Looking deep inside your body is an incredibly intimate experience. It can feel overwhelmingly vulnerable to think of doing so. For women who are uncomfortable with vaginal penetration, or for women who have a history of sexual abuse or assault, it can feel scary. You're not a failure if you choose not to use a speculum to monitor your cervix. There may be another time in your life when it's much easier and exciting. If you do have a lot of anxiety about vaginal issues, however, this may be the perfect opportunity, in the safety of your own home, to become more comfortable with your vagina. It's always helpful to work on your vaginal anxieties when you're planning to give birth and is much easier to do before you're pregnant.

Many women find that looking inside their bodies with a speculum is the most concrete form of feedback they can obtain about their fertility cycle. Being able to see your cervix opening and watching the fertile mucus pour out can seem so much more simple than charting the phase of the moon, observing little changes in this or that, urinating on a stick, or taking your temperature. Many women wonder why they would do those other things when they can just look inside themselves and see when they're about to ovulate.

How to Use a Speculum

To use a speculum, you'll need pillows, a flashlight, a mirror, lubrication, and a speculum. Using a speculum for the first time can take a little while to get the hang of. One of the most important elements to success is being able to relax your body. Lie down on a bed or on the floor; many women find that the firmness of the floor makes observing the cervix much easier. Place supportive cushions underneath your knees. This allows your leg and pelvic-floor muscles to relax.

With your finger you may want to locate the placement and position of your cervix before inserting the speculum. This can help you know in which direction to angle the speculum. Hold your labia apart so that the speculum doesn't pinch your skin. We suggest that you use a fair amount of lubrication, such as KY, when you're using a speculum for the first time. Hold the speculum fully closed with the handle facing the ceiling. To slide it into your body most comfortably, it's best to angle downward toward your backbone.

Near the opening of your vagina is a really strong muscle band. Easing the speculum in over this band is usually the most uncomfortable part of inserting the speculum. Be sure to slide the speculum over that band and all the way in or it will remain uncomfortable. If you don't insert the speculum fully, it will feel similar to partially inserting a tampon. If you're having difficulty with the insertion, use your breath to help you relax more deeply. If you spend a few moments directing your breath to your vaginal muscles with the intention of relaxation, they will soften and stretch. Push the speculum in as you exhale.

Once you've inserted the speculum, take a deep breath or two before you open the bills of the speculum. When you're ready, gently push the bills open. If you're doing this by yourself, you'll need to click the speculum open and shine the flashlight directly into the mirror. This will make it easier to see than to angle the light into your body. Adjust the angle of the mirror until you can see clearly into your body. Whether you're looking for your cervix on your own or with the help of another person, it can take a few minutes or even a few tries with the speculum before you're able to see your cervix. You'll usually need to pull the speculum out a bit, always in the closed position, angle it in a slightly different position, reinsert, and reopen. Eventually your cervix will come into view.

When you're ready to remove the speculum, be sure to close the bills of the speculum before you attempt to take it out of your body. So as not to pinch your cervix, you may want to slide it partially out first and then close it. The cervix is sensitive, so if it gets touched, it will move right out of the way. Likewise, sometimes you'll be up against the edge of it and won't see the opening, so you won't necessarily know that you're there. Have patience; learning to locate your cervix is a skill that often takes time to develop. Once you get used to doing it, though, it will take less time and you'll become familiar with the color variations inside your body. Locating your cervix will also become easier. It's helpful to know that the rugae—the folds of the vaginal walls—look different than the cervix does. The rugae are textured, whereas the cervix is smooth and shiny and often a slightly lighter shade of pink than your vaginal walls.

If you're having difficulty locating your cervix, remove the speculum, stand up, and jump for 30 seconds. This will bring your cervix down and relax your pelvic floor. Remember that feeling first for your cervical placement with a gentle finger can help you find the needed angle. Sometimes when you insert the speculum, open the bills fairly widely, then wait patiently for a few seconds, the cervix will naturally slide its way into view. Likewise, some women find it's helpful to bear down a little or to cough in order to bring the cervix into view. If you still can't find your cervix, you may want to call a midwife or nurse practitioner and ask them to guide you to finding your cervix on your own.

If You See or Feel Bumps or Redness on Your Cervix

In general it's normal to have some bumps on the end of your cervix. These are small cysts and are generally considered harmless. If you notice such cysts and haven't had a recent Pap smear, it's always best to have a Pap smear so that you can feel more relaxed when doing cervical monitoring. An excellent book to help you become more fully informed about female anatomy, with fantastic diagrams and photographs, is *A New View of a Woman's Body* (Federation of Feminist Women's Health Centers, 1991).

Insemination Recommendations

After monitoring your cervix through several cycles, you'll be able to recognize when it's the softest and most open. The peak fertile window is when your cervix is wide open and fertile mucus is coming forth. For many women, this is a one-to-three day period, allowing them time for multiple inseminations.

With frozen sperm, it's best to time your insemination as close to your time of ovulation as possible. Thus, becoming familiar with your cervix will allow you to inseminate on the day when your cervix is most open and has the most fertile mucus. If you're inseminating twice, the inseminations should be 12–24 hours apart.

When you're using fresh sperm, you have a much more flexible window for inseminating since fresh sperm lives longer. There's less of a need to analyze if your cervix is as open as it can be. Once your cervix begins to open and your mucus is fertile, you're in a peak fertility window to inseminate.

If you plan to use IUI as your method, or one of your methods, of insemination, it's not as crucial to plan around your fertile mucus. But you do want to make sure you don't miss your peak fertile window by waiting too long to inseminate.

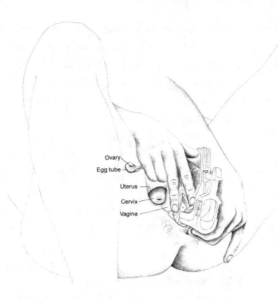

A woman inserting a speculum

A woman opening a speculum

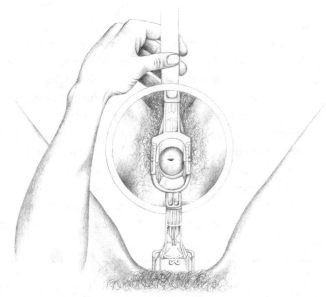

A view of the cervix in a mirror

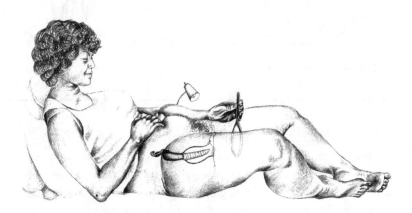

A woman using a desk lamp, hand mirror, and speculum to look at her cervix

Fertile Mucus

Fertile mucus is produced by your cervix and serves as a natural filtration system that allows healthy, well-formed sperm into the cervix. The fertile mucus comes out of the cervical opening and pools in the bottom of the vagina. The mucus then guides the sperm into the cervix. It provides a comfortable pH for the sperm and gives them the energy they need to keep swimming.

Understanding the role of fertile mucus often helps women relax during vaginal inseminations. Our bodies are perfectly designed to guide sperm into our cervix during our fertile periods and keep sperm out of our cervix during rest of the month. Once the sperm has been guided into the cervix, it's stored and nurtured there, where there are special crypts in which the sperm are nourished and then time-released into the uterus. Thus, fertile mucus serves an invaluable role in conception.

Nonfertile Cervical Mucus

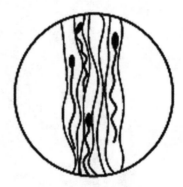

Fertile Cervical Mucus

The Value of Tracking Fertile Mucus

Because fertile mucus is so vital to conception, when having intercourse or performing vaginal inseminations, tracking the progress of your fertile mucus is of great value. By monitoring your fertile mucus, you'll be able to effectively time your inseminations based on the organic processes that facilitate the transportation of sperm in your body. Within 12 hours after ovulation, your fertile mucus has decreased by 50% and is replaced with cloudy, sticky secretions. These secretions form a thick, impenetrable net that prevents sperm from moving into the cervix. Therefore, you must perform your vaginal inseminations when you're producing fertile mucus. **Tracking fertile mucus is a primary fertility signal.**

How to Track Fertile Mucus

There are two ways to check your fertile mucus; one is by touch and the other is by speculum exam. What you monitor is the progress of your mucus throughout the month. You don't need to check your mucus when you're menstruating. Likewise, you can't accurately check your mucus when you're sexually aroused. Note the color, consistency, and amount of your mucus. Usually there are a number of preovulatory days when the mucus becomes cloudy white or yellowish and is sticky but not stretchy. Then, immediately before ovulation, are the "wet days"—when your mucus increases in volume, is extremely slippery and stretchy, and has an egg-white consistency. These are your most fertile days. To determine the most fertile of these days, it's valuable to actually stretch the mucus between your fingers and measure the distance it stretches.

As some women grow older, they produce less mucus. Many women of all ages—especially those who don't eat dairy products or are using antihistamines—don't find any mucus in their underwear or feel any mucus when they reach inside. Other women find that their fertile mucus gets mixed in with their vaginal secretions and is difficult to isolate. If this is the case for you, looking at your cervix with a speculum will help you clearly see the mucus that's secreted from your cervix. You can then use a Q-tip to see how far the mucus will stretch, or when you take the speculum out there may be fertile mucus on the bills that you can touch and stretch. It's best to check your mucus in the same manner each day, whether by checking your vaginal opening, touching your cervix with your finger, or using a speculum.

Too Little Fertile Mucus?

If you find you're not producing much mucus that is clear, wet, and/or stretchy, then this may actually be inhibiting your fertility. This is certainly not the case for all women. Many women don't readily find fertile mucus yet get pregnant after their first insemination. But if you feel that the quantity of your mucus is inhibiting conception, there are a few approaches you may take. Consider discontinuing any antihistamines you regularly take. Likewise, if you haven't eliminated sugar and refined flour from your diet, now is the time to do so. Many nutritionists have found that Vitamin A and potassium supplements can help dramatically. We've seen acupuncture and Chinese herbs have a marked affect on increasing fertile mucus production. Some women swear by the assistance of room-temperature egg whites inserted into the vagina prior to insemination or intercourse. This is one of the only mediums that's friendly to sperm and enhances its motility. If you see a medical doctor about this problem, he or she may prescribe estrogen supplements. If you choose, you can simply bypass the need for fertile mucus and proceed directly to intrauterine insemination.

Insemination Recommendations

The days when your mucus is the wettest, clearest, and stretchiest are your high-fertility days, the last day of clearly fertile mucus being the peak day for vaginal insemination or intercourse. Your peak fertile days are usually one to two days before your temperature rise. We could easily argue that fertile mucus is the single most significant fertility signal.

Fertility Lens

A fertility lens is a pocket microscope that can be used to monitor your fertility. On the days of your cycle when estrogen is prominent—during your most fertile days preceding ovulation—your body produces a fernlike pattern in both your fertile mucus and

Fertility Lens

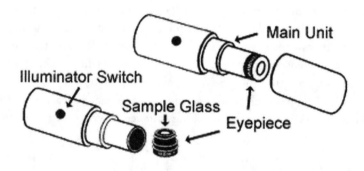

Sample Ferning Patterns

Fertile

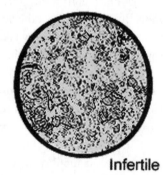

Infertile

Illustrations courtesy of OvuTec, www.ovu-tec.com

saliva. This pattern can be observed on a lens or with a 50x microscope. If you observe the pattern of your mucus or saliva throughout the month, you'll see that it changes. Around the time of ovulation, the entire screen is actually filled with a crystal pattern that looks exactly like fern leaves. Then, immediately following ovulation, usually within 12 hours, it's replaced with a bead-like pattern with only a few ferns remaining.

Monitoring Your Ferning

Each woman has a slightly different ferning pattern. Many have slight ferns creeping into the screen of the lens for a few days before the entire screen is covered. This usually correlates with the time of increased mucus that's just beginning to become clear and stretchy. Then, depending on your body, you may find that you have one day of full ferning or several. These day(s) usually correlate with your peak day(s) of fertile mucus. It helps to replicate with a sketch what you see on your chart so that you can easily track your ferning from month to month.

A clear and obvious ferning pattern is a primary fertility signal. Some women, however, are either unable to detect ferning or have full ferning for seven or more days. In these instances, the usefulness of the lens as a fertility tool decreases since it isn't specific enough.

Insemination Recommendations

When your lens is completely covered with ferns, you're highly fertile. This is your peak fertile window. If you fern fully for half a week, however, you'll need to match up this sign with others for it to be most useful.

Ovulation Predictor Kits (OPKs)

Ovulation predictor kits (OPKs) monitor the level of luteinizing hormone (LH) in your urine. Most women experience a surge of LH in their urine 18–36 hours prior to ovulation. Thus, if you use a sensitive predictor kit, you'll have a sign that indicates a hormonal shift in your body that precedes ovulation. Many women love this method since it appears to be so easy and objective. As with a pregnancy test, you simply pee on a stick and it tells you whether or not your LH level is above the control level. But that's the full extent of what it tells you. It doesn't tell you when you're going to ovulate or if you've already ovulated. OPKs show a positive reading when the amount of LH in your urine exceeds that of the control line, but this is a generic level of LH to which your urine is being compared. You are not a generic person.

Effective Use of OPKs

To get the full benefit from your OPK, it's important to follow a few instructions that aren't always included in the kit manuals. First, begin testing early enough in your cycle to gain the information you're looking for. If your kit shows a positive or almost positive reading the first time you test, you've begun testing too late in the cycle to gain complete information. Begin your testing earlier in your cycle next month.

Second, if you plan to use these kits, we recommend that you only use them if you're willing to test your urine twice a day. If you test your urine only once daily, as is generally recommended, and you have a negative result the first day and a positive the next, you have no way of knowing how long your LH has been surging. If you started to surge a few hours after your first test, it's possible that by the time you get a positive the next day, you've already ovulated, as most women ovulate 18–36 hours following an LH surge.

Third, use the same brand of kit, and ideally sticks from the same kit, for a complete cycle. If you mix and match, you can't accurately interpret the information you're getting. Likewise, stop testing once you get a positive reading. The first positive is the only valid positive. The LH may remain in your urine for longer, but that information isn't useful in any of your decision making. Always try to test your urine at the same time every day.

When used with these guidelines, we consider this method to be a significant fertility signal, if tracked in conjunction with other fertility signs to help you to narrow down your peak fertility window. By no means, however, do we consider this method to be more valid than the other aforementioned signals.

Drawbacks

In our experience, many women inseminate too late. One of the primary reasons this happens is that they're waiting for their OPK to turn positive. All their other signs may have lined up beautifully, but they're reluctant to inseminate until after their results turn positive. By that time many women are no longer in their peak fertility window, and many of them may have already ovulated by the time they inseminate.

Another significant drawback is that these kits are expensive, ranging in price from $10 to $60 for a five- to seven-day kit. Due to both of these drawbacks, many women choose to use the kits for only a few months in order to see how the information they're gathering from their other tracking methods line up with their LH surge.

Other important things to consider include that some women experience mini LH surges preceding their actual surge, which can make the readings inaccurate. Likewise, some women approaching menopause have increased LH but aren't necessarily ovulating. Also, some fertility medications skew OPK results. If you're taking fertility drugs, check with your health care provider and the manufacturer about any possible interference. And lastly, although the control level of the kits reflects the "average" amount of LH for most women under 40, your body may release slightly higher or slightly lower levels of LH into your urine. This would skew the value of the ovulation predictor kits, as they wouldn't provide an accurate positive reading.

Insemination Recommendations

The most important thing to remember about OPK results is that they're not more significant than your other signs. Remember, you're looking for any three signs to line up at the same time. When they do, it's best to inseminate right at that moment. We've found that the best time to inseminate for many women doing vaginal inseminations is 12 hours *before* their OPK results turn positive and also at the time they actually turn positive. Insemination past that time for some women is often too late. Likewise, other women, especially those using IUI, don't need to inseminate until 12–36 hours past a positive reading. Therefore, don't use OPK results alone, as they won't provide you with enough information to time your insemination accurately.

Ovulation Predictor Monitors

If you'd like to make a larger financial investment ($200–$400) toward tracking your fertility, a fertility monitor may be right for you. The monitors are personal computers that track levels of LH and estradiol in your urine. According to the information that is gathered from your body's urine and your unique rhythms, the monitor displays a daily reading of low, high, or peak fertility. This is a nice benefit, because it's attuned to your personal levels of hormonal surge and can detect that surge for you. Often you can rent these monitors from companies if you can't afford to purchase one. For more information on price and how to order a fertility monitor, visit www.clearplan.com or www.zetek.net.

Benefits

This method of tracking fertility is often more accurate than using monthly OPKs. Many women find the "peak" reading to be affirming. Your daily urine results are interpreted for you, so you don't have to squint at color variations on a stick and interpret sometimes subtle shifts. The monitor calibrates itself against your test month. Thus, your highest LH surge will show a "peak" reading even if it's lower or higher that what the OPK might call positive. Thus, it truly is personalized to your body and not that of an "average" woman. Many women inseminating with fresh sperm find this method effective, as not only the peak but also the high fertility windows are more clearly defined than they are with OPKs.

Drawbacks

As mentioned, these monitors are quite expensive, although if you end up using one for more than a few months, they can end up being more cost effective than OPKs. The sticks that are needed each month are often difficult to find in stores, so most women need to mail-order them or order them over the Internet. Likewise, you can only test once a day. This leaves you with the same possible scenario as with OPKs: not knowing when your surge actually happened within a 24-hour period. Most monitors read "peak" for two days. For, some women, however, their ovulation coincides with their first peak day. **Overall, these monitors seem to be more helpful than OPKs and could be considered a primary fertility signal.**

Insemination Recommendations

It's best to time your frozen sperm insemination within six hours of the monitor reading "peak" and 12–18 hours *before* it reads "peak." Knowing when your monitor will read "peak" is impossible to definitively predict; therefore, you should use your other fertility signs as well. If you're using fresh sperm, your final insemination should be timed for within six hours of the monitor's peak reading. You can start to inseminate as soon as the monitor says "high."

Fertility Drugs

If you're taking fertility drugs, it's important to note this in your chart. Fertility drugs can significantly alter your fertility signals. Depending on the medication, your fertile mucus may be significantly reduced or may be greatly increased. Likewise, your peak fertility window may be shifted by multiple days in either direction. At Maia we've seen numerous women informed by their doctors to expect their ovulation around day 17 to day 21, when in fact some women actually ovulate much earlier while taking the drug Clomid—around day 10 or 11. Be sure to monitor your fertility signals from the time that you stop bleeding, as you don't know how your body will respond to the medication during each new cycle.

Mood Changes

Some women find it helpful to chart their mood cycles throughout the month. Many women are familiar with the premenstrual mood changes they experience but have never noticed if they experience predictable mood changes prior to ovulation. When paying attention to this, many women find they're assertive, energetic, creative, and confident around their time of peak fertility, while others feel internal and introspective. Still others experience brief but intense depression at this time, lasting a few minutes to a day or two.

Sex Drive

Tracking your sexual desire is also useful. **We consider libido to be a primary fertility signal.** Many women experience significantly increased sexual desire on the days immediately preceding and during ovulation. Women who have a high libido all the time often report a distinct shift in the quality of their desire or in the kind of sex they're interested in around the time of ovulation.

Although you may not act on your sexual desire, you may notice that you feel sexier at this time of month. Many women report having sexual dreams as they near ovulation. Some lesbians report having sexual fantasies involving men around this time of the month. Tracking your sexual desire will give you essential information, so be sure to write down your feelings, even if they're subtle. Numerous studies document that a woman's increased exposure to pheromones increases her chances of conception. Pheromones are smells that we emit that are probable instigators of sexual attraction; they've been called the "flames of desire." In fact, some experts say that a woman's sense of smell is 100 times as sharp as normal during her time of peak fertility. Likewise, frequent sexual activity increases a woman's fertility. And perhaps the most compelling of all the studies are those that have documented spontaneous ovulation in response to sexual desire.

Insemination Recommendations

Using your sex drive to help confirm your timing is indispensable. When your sex drive or feelings of sexiness increase, your fertility increases. If you're using fresh sperm, we recommend inseminating when your libido increases, especially if your other signs corroborate this timing.

If you're using increased sexual desire as a fertility signal, you'll discover that it often precedes your other signs. Therefore, if you're using frozen sperm you should probably wait to inseminate until you show strong signs of fertile mucus, whether or not your sex drive is high.

Appetite Changes or Food Cravings

Some women have predictable food cravings during their menstrual and fertility cycle. Many women are aware of their food cravings around the time of the month that they menstruate but have never paid attention to their cravings at other times of the month. In fact, many have just as distinct cravings for a few days nearing their time of ovulation. Some women crave comfort foods; others crave salads and fresh vegetables. Some crave chocolate; others notice a general appetite increase. Since you're noticing and keeping track of so many other things throughout the month, pay attention to these cravings as well to see whether there's a pattern to them.

Breast Changes

Some women notice that their breasts become more physically and/or sexually sensitive preceding ovulation, and many notice that their nipples actually darken when they're fertile. For some women, these breast changes are so significant that they're able to use this information as a primary fertility signal. Other women notice no or only subtle shifts that wouldn't constitute primary information.

Stress

In your charts, it's important to document times of increased stress. Stress can greatly affect your fertility. See Chapter 9 for more information.

Dreams

Many women report having dreams that are highly sexual, "technicolored," or filled with fertility symbols. Women have told us that their dreams are particularly vivid or memorable when they're fertile. Pay attention to your dreams; for some women this is one of the clearest signals that ovulation is approaching or even occurring and can be used by some as a primary fertility signal.

Fill in Your Own Selections

Since you're focusing on your monthly cycles and rhythms, feel free to add additional entries to track. Some women like to track their headache cycles, others track constipation, and still others track their arguments with their partners. You can learn so much about yourself through careful charting that it's helpful to track anything that might give you additional insight into in your body and life.

Charting for Partnered Women

Women who are partnered don't always want to share every detail of their bodies with their partners. It's certainly not every woman's dream to have her partner ask her about the consistency of her vaginal discharge on a daily basis. On the other hand, the partner who isn't inseminating can feel frustrated if her partner is not charting thoroughly or if they disagree on how to interpret body signals. This can lead to uncomfortable or unhealthy relationship dynamics if left unchecked.

Many women are reticent to do speculum exams to observe their cervix, since they're afraid that if their partner sees their cervix with a speculum and has to interact with them in a more clinical or scientific manner, it will take the magic out of conception and birth or from their sexual/romantic relationship. Many women, however, are thrilled to look at their cervix but feel offended if their partner is reticent to share the experience with them.

Both Women Charting in a Partnership

We encourage partnered women who menstruate to each keep a chart, even if one is not planning to conceive. You can both see how your overlapping cycles influence your relationship fluctuations. This can become a shared project of self-exploration. It also takes the burden off the woman who's inseminating and turns it into a shared project. It can become a journey for both of you to learn about yourselves and each other.

Charting for Single Women

It can be emotionally challenging for single women to find the desire to continue charting month after month. This is by no means due to lack of initiative, but rather because the shared aspect of learning is absent. As a result, we recommend that single women find another woman in their life with whom to chart. This doesn't have to be someone who's planning to get pregnant. Many women are excited to learn more about themselves and their bodies and would love to do this kind of project with you, sharing both discoveries and frustrations. Charting buddies inspire each other and compel each other to continue charting because they have a shared commitment.

Why Don't Women Chart Enough?

Emotional Aversion

Often women don't chart enough because they feel an aversion to the entire process of fertility awareness. Keeping track of your fertility signals and documenting them on a chart can evoke many surprising emotions. Therefore, understanding your emotional responses is key to charting well. Women who aren't aware of their underlying issues often resent charting and therefore only chart sporadically and ineffectively.

It's often a new and emotionally evocative experience for lesbians to reconnect to their sexuality and their fertility. At first it can seem quite contrived to have to focus so much attention on the details of your menstrual cycle. Many lesbians have prided themselves on being able to be distanced from fertility, having had no need to focus on pregnancy prevention when having sex. Reconnecting with fertility can evoke uncomfortable memories of their body image, sexuality issues, coming out, and homophobia. In the process of reclaiming the option to procreate, many lesbians experience numerous emotions that are beneficial to explore. Some of the common emotional responses to focusing on your fertility cycle include anger, resentment, and self-doubt.

271

Anger and Resentment

One of the initial reactions that most lesbian, single, and bisexual women have to charting is to get angry that straight women (i.e., partnered straight women who don't experience infertility) don't have to go through the ordeal of scrutinizing their bodies in order to conceive. Charting makes women acutely aware that they don't have the heterosexual privilege of sperm being available to them any time they need it or desire it. This anger can make the process of fertility awareness seem unfair.

Likewise, a lot of resentment can arise about having to focus so intimately on yourself and your body. Some women experience this level of self-observation as demeaning. Women don't necessarily like to look at their bodies this closely, since it can make them feel objectified and scrutinized. Likewise, many women feel they're being judged and rated on a fertility scale.

If you'll feel angry or resentful about charting, we suggest that you explore your feelings fully and then release them. It's not a life-enhancing stance to feel victimized by your fertility. Take back your power. Fertility awareness is your key to achieving pregnancy. Claim it and chart your fertility signals with pride. This may require an intentional attitude shift, but doing so will be well worth the effort.

Women also may feel outrage when they learn new information about their bodies. They may feel angry that they were never taught these things about their body by teachers, parents, or doctors. Learning more about your body can evoke feelings of fury and confusion. These feelings are legitimate, feminist, and political, and as a result you may want to educate your friends and families about the wonders of the female body. Likewise, you may find it powerful to commit to raising your daughters (and sons) with all of this information available to them from the start. When used productively and as a motivator, anger will usually quickly transform into excitement and motivation.

Self-Doubt

Many lesbians never felt any need to focus on their ovulation since they ran no risk of getting pregnant. It's common for self-doubt to arise when you're beginning to chart. Women are often afraid of discovering that somehow, by not having focused on it, perhaps they don't actually ovulate. Self-doubt can also manifest as fear that you'll discover that you don't actually have the fertility you've taken for granted. This self-doubt can lead women to avoid charting altogether.

Seems Too Technical

Some women are resistant to chart because they think it's too mechanical. They want getting pregnant to be more of an "in the moment" organic experience, and feel that charting would remove a vital element of spontaneity. This is an important form of thinking to examine, as it often stems from internalized homophobia: having underlying beliefs that the only "natural" way to get pregnant is to have spontaneous sex with a man. Explore if this feels true for you, and don't let it prevent you from conceiving by preventing you from charting.

Charting may also remind you of your relationship to science. If your feelings about science are negative, you might be afraid that you won't be able to chart successfully, since you believe your brain isn't designed to look at yourself this way or you fear you won't be able to read the chart. Charting is actually easy and doesn't require any knowledge of science, but beware of negative internal messages that can undermine your confidence. If you were confused by our descriptions of fertility hormones earlier in this chapter, don't be intimidated. You can chart your fertility whether or not you know the names of these hormones.

When You Find That You Aren't Charting

Remember, many women find charting to be a difficult process. If you find you're not charting more than one or two signs, you've lost your chart for the third time, or you can't remember the last time you wrote on your chart, then it's time to evaluate what's preventing you from charting. Although charting is optional, it's the single most significant thing you can do to increase your chances of getting pregnant swiftly.

In addition to the emotional reasons that prohibit women from charting, there are other issues that cause some to refrain from charting adequately. The following exercise will help you clarify what may be stopping you from charting effectively.

Exercise

If you're not charting sufficiently, it's helpful to examine what underlying issue is preventing you from doing so. Because not charting well is self-defeating, we suggest that you consider your lack of charting to be an indication that something is not aligned in your process at this time. Write down your answers to the following questions:

- Is there something I'm uncomfortable about when I think about getting pregnant? What could help me feel more settled in relation to this issue?
- Am I clearly communicating my needs to the relevant people in my life about what I want from them?
- What am I afraid of?
- What can I do to make myself less scared about this?
- Am I ambivalent about parenting?
- How can I explore these feelings and still log my fertility experiences?

• Have I done things in the past to undermine my own happiness or to make it more difficult for me to get what I truly want?
• Are there ways that I'm continuing this behavior in this process?
• How do I feel about charting?
• What would help me chart more thoroughly and consistently?

When you write freely in response to these questions, you'll most likely discover why you're having difficulty charting.

Timing

Now that you've learned how much information you have readily available to you about your fertility, it's important to know how to use the information in your charts. This next section looks at the fertility chart from the view of a woman who's on the verge of inseminating. How can you interpret all the data you've gathered? Depending on your method of insemination, the number of times insemination will be attempted, and whether your sperm is frozen or fresh, each chart may need to be interpreted slightly differently.

Most Women Inseminate Too Late

Insemination timing is vitally important to achieving pregnancy. The medical field once held an understanding about fertility that is now outdated. Nonetheless, many fertility specialists still recommend that women inseminate at or after ovulation, despite current research concluding that this is too late. From working with hundreds of lesbian, single, and bisexual women, we've discovered that the peak fertility window is before and up to ovulation. This means you're much, much more likely to conceive if you inseminate prior to or at ovulation than following ovulation. Although it's thought that egg may remain viable for up to 24 hours after ovulation, most studies reveal that this time frame is more commonly closer to six to 10 hours.

Early on in our practice, we'd meet women who'd been inseminating for months or even years without achieving pregnancy. When we examined their charts, we'd often discover they had clearly charted their signs of peak fertility but were inseminating 24 to 48 hours later than we recommend. **All too frequently, perceived infertility is nothing more than repeated incorrect timing.**

Interpreting Your Fertility Chart

There are four sets of valuable information that your chart can reveal about your fertility cycle: 1) the signs you experience that let you know your fertile window is beginning; 2) your signs of peak fertility; 3) your ovulation symptoms (which will most likely coincide with your signs of peak fertility); and 4) the signs that indicate that you've already ovulated.

It's important to be able to recognize the onset of your fertile window so that you have ample time to arrange all of the necessary logistics. You might need to forewarn a long-distance donor, give a local donor a first-alert call, order your sperm from the sperm bank, make medical appointments, or keep the anticipated time frame in mind when scheduling your work for the next week.

You'll want to know your signs of peak fertility so that you can inseminate at this time. Peak fertility days are the days immediately preceding ovulation but not after it. Your peak fertility ends with ovulation.

Noting when your body indicates that you actually ovulate is important so that you can time your final insemination. This information can also help confirm your understanding of your peak time in case you don't conceive and want to reevaluate your timing. Signs of ovulation include a rise in your resting temperature and the cessation of strong ovarian awareness and cramping, or the feeling of a localized twinge.

Recognizing the signs that indicate that you've already ovulated also allows you to evaluate your timing and to discontinue inseminating for that cycle. These signs include a basal body temperature that has clearly risen, a cessation of ferning on your lens, a decrease of fertile mucus, a "low" reading on your fertility monitor, and a closed cervix.

Signs of Peak Fertility

Each fertility signal will indicate a peak time of the month, which we've outlined in the previous section. The goal is to have three signs line up at the same time. Because your body is different from month to month, it's important to track more than three signs so that you can see which signs indicate optimal fertility for that cycle. You must chart each month that you inseminate, since your fertile window can shift by a few days in either direction. This is a normal and healthy part of being a woman. Therefore, do not rely on the day of your cycle on which you inseminated last month to determine the day on which you'll inseminate this month. It may help you to predict the probable week you'll be inseminating, but you can't possibly know the exact day ahead of time. When you're charting sufficient information, you'll more than likely discover what is clearly the best time to inseminate.

Why It's Essential to Inseminate at or Prior to Ovulation

Because fertile mucus plays a key role in not only nourishing but also transporting sperm from the vagina into the uterus, common sense would dictate that you should inseminate when you have abundant fertile mucus. Within hours of ovulation your mucus loses its fertile properties. Thus, if you're inseminating vaginally, the carrier system for the sperm is eliminated and is replaced with a barrier system that's designed to keep sperm out of your cervix and uterus. **Unless you're using IUI as your means of insemination, your inseminations should always be timed for when you have fertile mucus.**

Overall Timing Recommendations

For most women, the majority of their peak fertility signals occur within 24 hours of one another. An ideal picture of a day to inseminate would be when you experience: a basal body temperature that hasn't yet risen or is just starting to drop—depending on your body; an open cervix; your OPK is just becoming positive or just turned positive, or your fertility monitor has read "high" for a few days or just read "peak"; your sex drive has increased; you're feeling creative; and you haven't yet felt your ovulation sensation.

It's best to time at least one of your inseminations to occur at night so that you can make sure you'll have plenty of rest after your insemination. Studies show that there's also a seasonal influence to the timing of ovulation. In the springtime, 50% of all women in the northern hemisphere ovulate between midnight and 11 A.M.; in the fall and winter 90% ovulate between 4 and 7 P.M.

If you haven't fully understood our recommendations they are: 1) Inseminate at your signs of peak fertility; and 2) Don't delay while holding out for temperature or a positive ovulation predictor kit while the rest of your fertility signals are screaming "peak." This is the worst trap you can fall into.

Always inseminate more than once a month. We feel this increases your chances so significantly that it would be better to skip every other month and inseminate twice than to inseminate just once a month.

Timing Recommendations for Frozen Sperm

Frozen sperm is only viable for 18–24 hours. Likewise, each semen sample is purchased in such a small quantity that you'd need to purchase four vials to roughly equal one full ejaculate. Thus, because both the life span is shorter and the quantity is significantly smaller than when using fresh sperm, it's even more essential to chart meticulously so that you can maximize your chances of conceiving. Remember, whenever possible, inseminate when three peak fertility signs line up. Unless extenuating circumstances arise and you feel you may have timed your first insemination early, don't separate your frozen inseminations by more than 24 hours.

Some women choose to inseminate with two vials at a time, thereby increasing the quantity of sperm swimming toward their egg. It can sometimes be ineffective to vaginally inseminate with frozen sperm, since if you were to time your inseminations by your increased sex drive or even the onset of your fertile mucus, you may be inseminating too soon. If this is the case for you, and your fertility signals span many days, you may chose to do one IUI per cycle. In addition, it's vitally important to track your signs of *peak* fertility—not just high fertility—when using frozen sperm.

Timing Recommendations for Fresh Sperm

Fresh sperm lives in your body for two to three days. Therefore, it's safe to start inseminating with fresh sperm as soon as two of your signs line up. You do, however, want to save your final insemination for as close to ovulation as possible. Most women using a known donor inseminate two to three times a month. But if you're inseminating only once a month, wait until three signs line up or until your intuition strongly guides you. It's a good idea to separate your fresh inseminations by 24 hours each time. This is not, however, a hard and fast rule. There's plenty of flexibility when using fresh sperm, so feel free to begin inseminating at your first signs of high fertility. Many women choose to cover as much time as possible in a cycle by inseminating every other day.

Timing Recommendations for IUI

Timing for an IUI is much more specific than timing for a vaginal insemination. Because it's believed that sperm deposited directly into the uterus lives for a significantly shorter period than sperm from vaginal inseminations, it's essential to inseminate as close to ovulation as possible. Ideally, you should perform an IUI within eight hours of ovulation. Because this window is so narrow, it's best to have a thorough understanding of your peak fertility signals.

It's our overall recommendation that when using IUI you also perform one vaginal insemination per cycle. Some women, however, don't wish to do vaginal inseminations. If this is the case for you, don't decide to inseminate just once a cycle. Instead, do two or more IUIs per cycle. One recent study shows that statistically there's only a 15% chance of pregnancy when performing one IUI per cycle, whereas there's a 39% chance of pregnancy with two IUIs. This should be a compelling enough reason to choose two over one.

Working With Your Fertility Specialist

Many times when you look at your fertility from the perspective we offer, you'll discover that your view of your peak fertile days does not coincide with your health practitioner's view of when you should inseminate. Most health care providers have a generic formula that they recommend to all women in their office such as, "Call me when your ovulation predictor kit turns positive, and we'll inseminate you the next day, or even the day after if it's the weekend or we're too busy." More often than not, this will be too late. Likewise, most practices recommend inseminating just once per cycle. This significantly reduces your chances of conceiving.

If your sense of when to inseminate, based on either our information or your intuition, differs from that of your fertility specialist, you have several options. You could try alternative approaches for timing each month, instead of trying to reconcile two approaches in the same month. Or you could follow your intuition, if you're able to identify your intuition in the midst of all the recommendations that you're receiving. Some women follow their own timing rather than the advice of their doctors. Ideally, you'll find a practitioner with whom you can work well as a team.

Frequently Asked Questions

I Have Varying Cycle Lengths. Can Fertility Awareness Help Me?

Absolutely! In fact, when you have irregular cycles, fertility awareness is the best means of knowing when to inseminate. Whether you ovulate on day 9 or day 27, recognizing your fertility signs is all you need to correctly time your inseminations. The medical field offers you the approach of monitoring your body through ultrasound to confirm whether and when you ovulate, but with irregular cycle lengths you may have to get daily sonograms for weeks to determine this each cycle. This can be practically and financially impossible. If you're doubting your signs, you may, however, consider getting ultrasound confirmation of your ovulation when you believe it's approaching.

What Do I Do When My Intuition Says I'm Fertile But I Don't Have Three Matching Fertility Signals?

It is the Maia approach to validate your internal knowledge. **Your intuition is definitely a primary fertility signal!** If you're using a known donor, it's appropriate to time at least one insemination as your intuition guides you, regardless of other corroborating information. Remember that fresh sperm can live in your body for days. On the other hand, if you're using frozen sperm and don't have three matching signs, you may choose simply to note your strong intuition in your chart and examine it at the end of your cycle to see if it indeed was an early fertility signal. Or you may choose to perform one vaginal insemination at this time.

What Do I Do if None of My Signs Match Up?

When you say that none of your signs match up, do you mean they're not all on the same day? Are they clumped together in the same three-to four-day period?

When you've tracked your fertility signals for at least three months, you'll have enough information to compare and see if you find observable patterns. For example, many women experience an increase in libido for a day or two (let's say days 12 and 13) prior to the time that their cervix is the most open and they have the most fertile mucus (night of day 13 and morning of day 14). Their predictor kit might also read positive the next day (day 15) with a slight rise in their temperature, followed by a more significant rise the next day (day 16). This is extremely useful information, as it shows that they probably ovulated somewhere on day 15/16, most likely the night of day 15.

• **If a woman inseminates with fresh sperm:** She should perform one insemination on day 12 or 13 when her sex drive increases, and one insemination the night of day 14 when her cervix and mucus indicate peak fertility.

• **If a woman inseminates with frozen sperm**: She should inseminate when her cervix is the most open, on the night of day 13 or the morning of day 14 and then she could time the second insemination in a number of ways: 24 hours later or as soon as her OPK reads positive, depending on the other more subtle signs she's tracking.

• **If a woman is using IUI:** She should time the IUI for as late as possible, ideally after performing a vaginal insemination when her mucus is copious and her cervix is wide open. The IUI could then be performed as late as mid-morning on day 15, but no later, since her cervix has passed its most open point, her temperature appears to be increasing already, and her OPK reads positive.

If a woman truly has no signs of fertility matching up within the same few days, it might be useful to get a hormonal blood panel to rule out any gross imbalances. Likewise, we highly recommend acupuncture and herbs to help fine-tune the fertility cycle. See Chapter 8 on fertility inhibitors and enhancers for recommendations.

Resources

Books

The Fastest Way to Get Pregnant Naturally, Christopher D. Williams, Hyperion, 2001

I Got Pregnant, You Can Too!: How Healing Yourself Physically, Mentally, and Spiritually Leads to Fertility, Katie Boland, Underwood Books, 1998

A New View of a Woman's Body, Federation of Feminist Women's Health Centers, 1991

Taking Charge of Your Fertility, Toni Weschler, MPH Harper Perennial 1995

The Whole Person Fertility Program: A Revolutionary Mind–Body Process to Help You Conceive, Niravi B. Payne, Three Rivers Press, 1998

Ovulation Predictor Monitors
ClearPlan Easy Fertility Monitors
(800) 931-1122
www.clearplan.com/fertilitymonitorovulationpage.cfm

Cue Ovulation Monitors
(800) FOR-CUES
www.zetek.net

Speculum and Fertility Lens Ordering Information
Maia Midwifery and Preconception Services
1676 University Ave.
Berkeley, CA 94703
(510) 540-0682
www.maiamidwifery.com

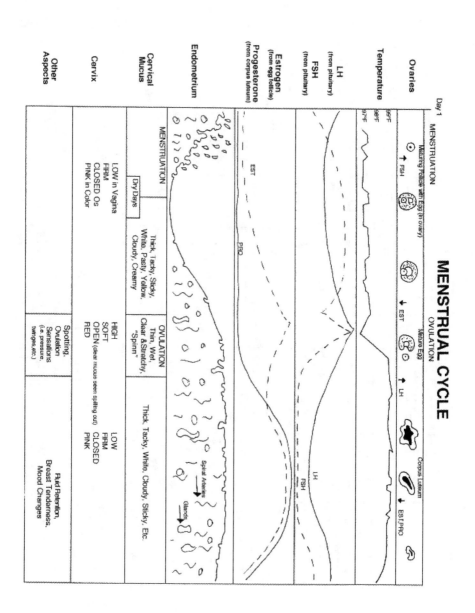

MENSTRUAL CYCLE

Chart One

This woman has never been pregnant. She's 29 years old and has inseminated three cycles with frozen sperm from a known donor. This is her third cycle. She chose to use four vials of sperm this cycle. She had used less during the previous two cycles. She conceived this cycle.

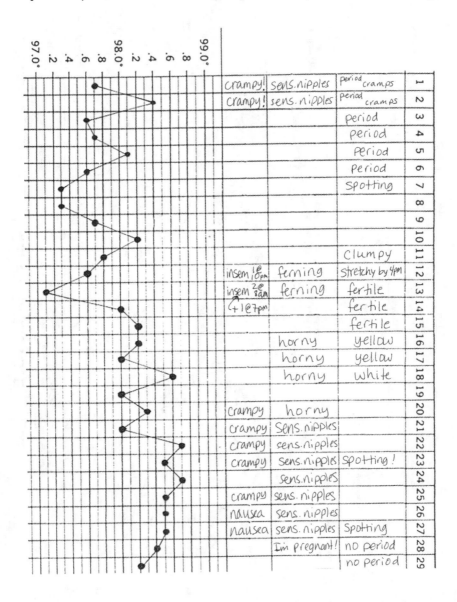

			Day
crampy!	sens. nipples	period cramps	1
crampy!	sens. nipples	period cramps	2
		period	3
		period	4
		period	5
		period	6
		spotting	7
			8
			9
			10
		clumpy	11
insem 1 @ 8pm	ferning	stretchy by 4pm	12
insem 2 @ 8am	ferning	fertile	13
(+1 @ 7pm)		fertile	14
		fertile	15
	horny	yellow	16
	horny	yellow	17
	horny	white	18
			19
crampy	horny		20
crampy	sens. nipples		21
crampy	sens. nipples		22
crampy	sens. nipples	spotting!	23
	sens. nipples		24
crampy	sens. nipples		25
nausea	sens. nipples		26
nausea	sens. nipples	spotting	27
	I'm pregnant!	no period	28
		no period	29

Chart Two

This woman has never been pregnant. She's 42, using frozen sperm, and has inseminated for six cycles by IUI. Her charts show a number of signs of low progesterone. The lens shows ferning in the second half of the cycle; her temperature doesn't remain high; and she spots for five days before actual regular menstrual bleeding starts, preceded by two days of fertile-like mucus. Her cycle length is only 22 days, although the second half (the luteal phase) is close to 14 days long. She did not become pregnant this cycle.

Fertility Chart — Month(s): MARCH/APRIL   Year: 00   Cycle number: 12   Length of cycle: 22 (days)

Day of Cycle	Date	Bleeding	Inseminations/Intercourse	Ovulation	Ovulation (pain, pressure, sensation, which side)	Cervical changes (high/low, open/closed, soft/firm, color)	Mucus color & consistency	Lens (ferning)	Ovulation Predictor Kit/Monitor	Fertility Drugs
1	31	yes								
2	1	yes								
3	2	yes								
4	3	yes								
5	4	yes/spot								
6	5	spot								
7	6					closed	slippery	I	I	¾ I
8	7					little open	stretch	+	+	¾ +
9	8		24	↑3 +3		open	stretch	↑+	↑+	¾ +
10	9			13 +3		less open	slippery	+		
11	10				I	high	sticky	I		
12	11				I	high + soft	sticky	↑		
13	12					—		I		
14	13					closed	sticky	I		
15	14					closed	—	I		
16	15						slippery	+		
17	16						little stretchy	+		
18	17	spot						+		
19	18	spot						+		
20	19	spot		·~				+		
21	20	spot		·~				+		
22	21	light spot						+		

Temperature scale: 97.0° and 98.0° (marked in tenths). The recorded temperatures are plotted as a graph to the left of the chart and do not remain elevated in the second half of the cycle.

Chart Three

This same woman started using a sublingual progesterone supplement this month for the second half of her cycle. She started drinking daily a fertility tea mix at the beginning of this cycle. She conceived this cycle. Notice the changes between this cycle and her previous one.

Month(s): APRIL/MAY Year 00 Cycle number 13 Length of cycle Pregnant! (days)

Day of Cycle	Date	Day	Insemination/Intercourse	Bleeding	Ovulation (pain, pressure, sensation, which side)	Cervical changes	Mucus color & consistency	Ovulation Predictor Kit Monitor
1	22	S		X			blood	
2	23	S		X			blood	
3	24	M		X			blood	
4	25	T		X			blood	
5	26	W		x			spotting	
6	27	T		x		FIRM	spotting	
7	28	F				MEDIUM	dry	
8	29	S				MED.	dry	1¾
9	30	S	Full L+R			SOFTER	sticky	1¾ 1¾
10	1	M		crampy L		SOFT	sticky-e.w.	+1¾ 1¾
11	2	T		crampy L		SOFT	egg white	+1¾
12	3	W				SOFT	sticky-e.w.	
13	4	T				SOFT	sticky	
14	5	F				MED.	sticky	
15	6	S				MED.	sticky	
16	7	S				MED.	sticky	
17	8	M				MED.	sticky	
18	9	T					sticky	
19	10	W					dry	
20	11	T				FIRM	dry	
21	12	F					dry	
22	13	S					dry	
23	14	S	x				spotting	
24	15	M					dry	
25	16	T					dry	
26	17	W					dry	
27	18	T			preg test −	FIRM	sticky	
28	19	F	x			FIRM	spotting	
29	20	S	x		preg test +	FIRM	spotting	
30	21	S					dry	
31	22	M			preg test ++		dry	
32	23	T					dry	
33	24	W						
34	25	T						

Temperature grid (°F): 99.0°, 98.0°, 97.0° with tenth-degree gradations, showing the daily basal body temperature plot across the cycle.

Chart Four

This woman is 37 years old. She conceived on her seventh cycle, inseminating vaginally with frozen sperm, and miscarried at six weeks. She inseminated for three more cycles, twice each cycle, with frozen sperm. This cycle she inseminated once vaginally with fresh sperm from an anonymous donor in an infertility clinic. Although her chart suggests, based on her ovulation predictor results alone, that she may have inseminated too early, she chose this day because intuitively she felt the most fertile. She had the option to inseminate the following day as well but chose not to, confident that she had just conceived.

MAIA
Midwifery & Preconception Services
Fertility Chart

Month(s) _____ Year _____ Cycle number _____ Length of cycle _____ (days) Days of Insemination _____

	1	2	3	4	5	6	7	8	9	10	11	12	13	14	15	16	17	18	19	20	21	22	23	24	25	26	27	28	29	30	31	32	33	34	35	36	37	38	39	40
Day of Cycle																																								
Date																																								
Day																																								
Phase of the Moon																																								
Inseminations/Intercourse																																								
Bleeding																																								
Ovulation (pain, pressure, sensation, which side)																																								
Cervical changes (high/low, open/closed, soft/firm, color)																																								
Mucus color & consistency (dry, wet, slippery, fertile, stretchy, sticky, clear, yellow, white)																																								
Lens (ferning)																																								
Ovulation Predictor Kit/ Monitor																																								
Fertility Drugs																																								
Mood changes (anger, contentment, creative, defensive, ecstatic, insecure, intuitive, irritable, voluptuous...)																																								
Sexual desire (increase or decrease in libido, masturbation, sex with partners)																																								
Appetite or food cravings																																								
Breast changes (tenderness, swelling)																																								
Cramping																																								
Stress																																								
Sleep changes & dreams																																								

Notes/Comments/Details/Dreams (also see back) _____

Chapter 12 The Turkey Baster Myth:

Locations and Methods of Insemination

This chapter provides information on home and clinic settings for insemination, and describes the insemination methods available in each location. Detailed guidance about how to do home vaginal inseminations will help put you at ease if you choose this method. We'll explore ways to make your insemination comfortable and empowering no matter where and how it's done. The goal of this chapter is to assist you in finding your most appropriate combination of locations and methods, taking into consideration your donor choice as well as your legal, emotional, financial, medical, and spiritual concerns. The main body of this chapter is organized into two parts: home inseminations and clinic inseminations. We recommend reading the entire chapter, as you may find it best to use multiple methods and locations within each cycle. Furthermore, if you don't conceive within your first few cycle attempts, you may find yourself changing your plans about donors, your method of insemination, or your location of insemination. However your insemination occurs, our hope is that it is joyful, safe, and comfortable for you.

Insemination: Many Choices, Many Decisions

Deciding Where to Inseminate/Conceive

Sometimes when a woman inseminates in an environment that feels wrong or unsafe, she won't conceive. A change in environment may correct this. We've seen this scenario so many times that it's become painful to watch. Women who've even gotten to the point of high-tech in vitro fertilization and not conceived have gotten pregnant later through careful tracking and self-inseminating at home. Likewise, women who've spent a year trying to conceive within the comfort of their home often conceive the first insemination they attempt at a clinic. Although there's no wrong or right place to inseminate, home and clinic environments are different from each other in many ways.

Conception isn't inherently a medical experience, nor does it need to be medicalized simply because you don't have easy access to sperm. Because of institutionalized heterosexism, however, lesbians—as well as single women using sperm banks and bisexual women who aren't using a male partner as their sperm source—find themselves grouped in the same category as infertile heterosexual couples. Therefore, assumptions are made that they'll need to conceive with medical help; infertility is assumed simply because a woman doesn't have a male sexual partner.

This mind-set is false. All that most women need is *access* to sperm in order to get pregnant. Of course, that access is often limited and sometimes appears to be restricted to the medical world. Thus, for many reasons women inseminate at a clinic or private doctor's office. This doesn't have to be your only option, though, nor does it necessarily increase your chances of getting pregnant. You don't inherently have fertility problems because of your sexual orientation. Nor do you need someone else to inseminate you just because you're not having intercourse to get pregnant.

If you seek information from only your ob-gyn or family practitioner, you may be steered in the direction of clinic insemination simply because that's the environment that they're more knowledgeable about or familiar with. If this is the case, you may trust your doctor to decide when and how you should inseminate without even realizing you have additional options. Our goal is to have all women explore their preferences and options and make decisions about their bodies based on what's right for them. Allow the choices you make to feel life enhancing. If your choices feel depleting or if you feel uncomfortable when you think about your choices, examine why. You may have made the wrong decision or you may need to do more internal work to feel comfortable with your choices.

For example, if you decide it's important for you to inseminate at home in your bed, you may choose to use frozen sperm or have your known donor come to your home despite the possible legal ramifications. But if you hadn't taken the time to explore your feelings about insemination and conception, you might have inseminated in a clinic without thinking twice. Who's to say if it would have affected your chances of getting pregnant one way or the other? It's safe to say, though, that it will affect how you feel about the experience.

Likewise, you may realize that although you'd prefer to inseminate at home, you ultimately will choose to inseminate in a clinic because it affords you the greatest legal security. In this instance it may take you a while to come to terms with this decision, so that you can feel comfortable with your decision, despite making a choice that doesn't feel ideal to you.

So the question is, where do you want to conceive? Where you *want* to conceive may be a different question than where you'll *choose* to conceive. We've found that feeling connected to yourself—and your partner if you have one—feeling comfortable in your body, and feeling in alignment with your own spirituality are equally effective in increasing your chances of getting pregnant as making decisions based solely on statistics and your age.

Sexual Expression and Conception

Many cultures believe that conception is an inherently sexual experience. Although this is obviously heterosexually based, science has lent some validity to it. Studies show that if a woman has an orgasm just prior to insemination/male ejaculation, the uterine pull of the orgasm, in tandem with the chemical release of endorphins and other relaxing hormones, actually draws the sperm into the uterus.

Studies also suggest that frequent exposure to pheromones—biochemicals we secrete and react to physically from others—increase fertility and help regulate menstrual cycles. Being sexual with others is a common way to have intimate contact with the pheromones of other people, so the studies examined the effects of sexual activity on fertility. Indeed, they found a correlation. Interestingly, one study determined that lesbians need three times as much regular sex as do heterosexual women to achieve an influence on their conception rates. Sex with men is defined as intercourse, and lesbian sex is not defined. Anecdotally, a number of single women have reported to us that when they're dating and having regular sex, their cycles are more regular, approaching 28 days in length.

Even though regular sex increases fertility, and sex at the time of insemination can spur physiological and hormonal changes that increase conception rates, not all women want to be sexual at this time. Numerous women don't feel any inclination to have a sexual experience involving sperm.

For other women, it's a natural and logical union. It's simply one they may never have considered. In fact, many women fear that sex might interfere with the process. Do what feels right for you, but feel free to be sexual if you want to! Following insemination, however, it's important to refrain from any sexual activities that include vaginal penetration. Anything put into the vagina can disturb the sperm as they swim into the cervix. Pain around or in the uterus can release hormones called prostaglandins, which are unfavorable to conception. When being sexual before or following insemination, don't use lubrication or introduce any foreign substances into your vagina that might have a chemical interaction with the sperm. Also, if you have particularly "explosive" orgasms, the force of your orgasm may expel the sperm from your vagina. If you think this may be the case for you, having an orgasm just prior to insemination might be better than immediately following insemination.

Logistically speaking, sex just before insemination can be a little tricky. If you're using frozen sperm, you might want to start being sexual before you defrost it. But you'll also want to keep an eye on the time to make sure you don't leave the sperm out too long. Be sure to keep the vial on or under one of your bodies so that the temperature can stay constant. If your donor is in your house, you may feel comfortable being sexual while he's in the other room providing a sperm sample for you, or you may feel awkward. If you feel uncomfortable, wait to be sexual until after he's gone.

Some women like to use a vibrator before and/or after insemination. Others feel the electric currents might interfere with conception. No studies have been done on the effects a vibrator might have on conception. Do what feels right to you.

Be careful—if you're being sexual with a female partner, make sure she doesn't get pregnant! After handling sperm, wash your hands before becoming sexual with each other. Also, make sure she wears underwear if you're planning to snuggle immediately following insemination.

It's easy to feel pressured to have an orgasm on a time schedule. Also, the excitement and nervousness surrounding insemination can make it hard for you to feel aroused. Therefore, for some women being sexual before or after insemination feels too contrived. For others, however, it's a wonderful way to release the anxiety surrounding insemination and feel connected their body and partner. Remember, do what feels right, what makes you feel good in your body. Laughter releases endorphins into your system as well, so whatever you do, have a good time doing it.

Spirituality and Conception

If for you, conception is a spiritual experience, it's important to explore this. What does this mean to you? Will your beliefs influence the location or methods of insemination that you feel most connected with? Will you need to have a certain ritual for the insemination experience? Do you need to feel connected with your egg and the sperm to allow for a more conscious union? Does everything have to "feel right" for it to work? Do you believe that anyone who's with you or touches the sperm will somehow affect the conception and, ultimately, the baby?

We've worked with many women who feel deeply connected with the spirituality of conception. This has meant something different for each person. For some women, this spiritual outlook precludes them from wanting to conceive anywhere but at home. It also often precludes a woman from wanting to take fertility drugs, which can be perceived as a negative chemical influence in a divine process.

For others, spirituality isn't tied to location or method of conception but rather to a place they enter inside themselves. For these women, insemination is an act of prayer. And still others who feel that conception is a deeply spiritual and personal experience don't feel it's in the least way connected to insemination.

Embodiment and Conception

Something people rarely think about, but which we find to be vitally connected to conception rates, is how a woman feels in her body when she's trying to conceive. In our experience wherever you inseminate and whatever method you use, your chances of conceiving are much greater if your body is relaxed, open, and welcomes the experience. If you're uncomfortable or "checked out," your insemination will probably not be enjoyable and will also be less likely to work.

This brings us back to the question of how you make your decisions. If you check in with how your body responds to each of the decisions you make, you'll be less likely to make decisions that ignore the comfort of your body. And you'll be less likely to make decisions based on recommendations from others or what statistics say.

If you find yourself in an environment in which you're scared—be that your home, your donor's home, or a clinic—and you feel strongly that you don't want to switch environments—then it becomes all the more important for you to make peace with your decision. If your decision still doesn't feel right after you do this inner work, you may want to reexamine your choice.

Self-Insemination, Vaginal Insemination, and Intracervical Insemination

The following are brief descriptions of the various insemination methods, followed by an in-depth exploration of the pros, cons, how-to's, and other considerations related to each method (and inherent location) of insemination.

• **Self-Insemination:** Vaginal or self-insemination simply means inserting the sperm into your own body without the assistance of a medical care provider. The sperm is inserted via a syringe without a needle. This method is the most similar to sexual intercourse in terms of the distribution of semen into your vagina. This is the most simple method available. Intracervical insemination (ICI) is the medical term for vaginal insemination, although sometimes it involves using a speculum to locate the cervix.

• **Sexual intercourse:** Sex with a man for the purposes of conception is less common in some lesbian communities now than it has been historically but is still an option many women consider.

• **Intrauterine insemination (IUI):** Intrauterine insemination places the sperm directly in the uterus through a sterile tube that is passed through the cervix.

Self-Insemination/Home Insemination

Any woman can self-inseminate; there's nothing to it, as long as you know where your vagina is. And even that is easily taught! The following section explores everything you need to know about at-home self-insemination.

Advantages

There are many advantages to inseminating at home in a nonmedical environment. One of the primary benefits is that you're the one determining your environment and controlling your experience. You have the freedom to inseminate whenever you want in an unrushed manner, whether it's early morning, late at night, or the middle of the day. You have the freedom to include romance, relaxation, sex, ritual, food, pets, privacy, or friends. You can make it a comfortable, family-centered celebration. At home all emotions are safe; you can giggle, cry, have an orgasm, or even argue. You don't have to worry about being touched by anyone you don't know or trust. At home, you may find it much easier to feel comfortable and safe in your body than you would in an office. For women who have sexual abuse histories this can often make a huge difference in how they feel about the experience. We will discuss this later in the chapter as well.

A main reason women choose to self-inseminate at home is that they wish to receive the benefits of using fresh sperm. For some women, these benefits outweigh the potential health or safety risks. (See Chapter 5 for more information on the pros and cons of using fresh sperm.) In addition, many doctors won't help a woman inseminate with fresh sperm in a clinic unless the sperm comes from her husband, since they don't want to be liable if she contracts a sexually transmitted disease. Finally, women often choose self-insemination at home because it's nearly cost-free. The only cost is your sperm if you're using a sperm bank.

Challenges

There are two fairly significant challenges to inseminating at home. One is severing your donor's paternity rights if you use a known donor who comes to your home. The other is finding a medical doctor—if you choose to do so—come to your home and be present at the insemination. A third challenge, but one that's more easily remedied, is that you need to feel confident that you know how to do the insemination.

Legal Security and Known Donors

Legal security for our families is still new territory, and the precedents are still being established. Each state has different statutes governing insemination and paternity rights. In California, for example, according to the National Center for Lesbian Rights (NCLR), when using a known donor, the safest way to ensure sole custody of your children is to inseminate in the presence of a medical doctor. At the time of insemination, if the semen passes through the hands of a doctor before going to the mother-to-be and if a waiver of responsibility is signed, the donor relinquishes any claim to that sperm. To solidify that, however, the sperm donor must sign additional legal papers after the baby is born in order to abdicate any further responsibility for—or claim to—the child.

Women handle this legal issue in many ways, some within the letter of the law and some possibly on the fringe of it. Many women we work with who use known donors choose to inseminate in a clinic; they say they feel this assures them full custody. Some have a doctor friend come to their house for the insemination or get a monthly signature from a doctor who isn't actually present for the insemination. Other women we work with feel that in order to choose a known donor in the first place, they have to know him well enough to trust him with a signed contract of intent to relinquish paternity. They then inseminate at home without doctor supervision and plan to sign the papers after the baby is born. Some women inseminate at home by default since they want to use a known donor and no clinician will assist them due to the risk of being sued for malpractice. And still other women don't even

Photo © Cathy Cade

sign contracts with their donors. Of course, it's a very personal decision. Research the current laws in your state and make a legally informed choice about your location of insemination. The NCLR is an excellent resource.

Is It Possible to Perform an IUI at Home?

We explore intrauterine insemination in depth later in this chapter in our discussion on clinic inseminations. We only mention it here because practitioners will occasionally—but rarely—perform it in your home. If you desire this, it may be worth your while to ask local obstetricians, general practitioners, midwives, and nurse practitioners to see if any of them might be open to the idea. Also, a growing number of women are teaching themselves how to do IUI for their partners. Many women want to do IUI but are unable to find a provider to perform it at home. Thus, they choose to do one IUI per cycle in a clinic setting and one at-home vaginal insemination per cycle to secure the benefits of both. IUI is further discussed in Chapter 14.

Self-Inseminating With Fresh or Frozen Sperm

Although it's quite easy to perform a self-insemination, environmental and logistical elements must be considered and planned in advance.

Making and Setting the Space

Insemination is a prayer. It is praying to get pregnant, to make a baby, to become a parent. When you look at it in this light, it's easy to focus on what kind of mood or environment you might like. Some women set up a beautiful environment in a special place in their home, often the bedroom, that includes flowers, candles, or incense. To them beautifying the space is a way of focusing their intention on conception. Other women are less energetically inclined and don't need to tinker with their environment. The possibilities are endless; it's up to you. Here are some practical suggestions:

- Urinate before you begin the insemination so that you can comfortably stay reclined afterward.
- Have plenty of pillows, a blanket, food, and water within reach.
- Disconnect the phone.
- Take care of your pets ahead of time.

Fresh Sperm Logistics

Sperm-Friendly Containers

If you're working with a known donor, he needs to ejaculate into a small jar with a lid, if he isn't donating the sperm in your home. The jar doesn't need to be sterile. It just needs to be clean and dry, with no water left inside from washing, since sperm don't thrive when in contact with plain water. Many women give their donor a clean glass artichoke-heart or baby-food jar. Some use sterile urine specimen cups from a doctor's office, but some prefer not to use plastic. Make sure the receptacle size will work for your donor.

Fresh Sperm, Unknown Donor

Arrange for your liaison to deliver the sperm to your home. Prearrange a system where they have a special knock and leave it on the doorstep, or arrange a simple hand-off. Since time is so clearly of the essence, it's important not to spend time making niceties. Say all of your thank-yous in advance.

Where Will He Ejaculate?

In a Separate Location?

If you're going to inseminate in your home, you need to decide where you'd like your donor to ejaculate. Some women can't imagine a man masturbating in their home. If this isn't a viable option for you, your logistics have to be well thought out. Does your donor live close enough that you, your partner, or friend could pick it up and bring it home? Could he use the nearby home of a friend or neighbor? Is there a local hotel he could use? Would you like him to deliver the sample? Would you prefer to pick it up? Would you like it to be left your doorstep? How inconvenienced is he willing to be?

In the Same Location?

When you and your donor will be in the same location for the ejaculation and insemination, it's helpful to preconsider the dynamics. Although you'll improve this process through trial and error, we've found that discussing some things in advance will make the process smoother. For example, if your donor comes to your home just after work and rush hour, he probably won't want to run to the bathroom and masturbate as soon as he arrives. Do you want to allow for some down time together? Share some food? Talk a bit? It's common to spend 15 minutes to an hour chatting. If this isn't something you want, however, clarify your expectations in advance.

Show your donor what room you would like him to use and where the sperm container is. Be sure to give him privacy when he enters that room. If possible, try not to be in the next room. The more relaxed and sexually aroused a man is, the higher his volume of ejaculate will be. So if he feels you're hovering by the door, the sample probably won't be as large. One trick in a small apartment is to put on music and involve yourself in something so he won't think you're watching the clock and listening for him.

Ahead of time, think about and discuss how you would like the handoff to be.

Some women feel guilty if they don't extend hospitality after the donor ejaculates, yet feel torn since they want to get to the insemination as quickly as possible. Decide if you would like him to knock on the door and leave the container, bring it to you in person, or stay to chat. If he's from out of town and is staying with you, be sure to have discussed these details with him too. You can avoid awkward situations by being clear and direct ahead of time. Many women we've worked with have felt the most comfortable with a quiet handoff and the donor immediately going out for a walk or to another part of the residence. They discussed this plan in advance and said their thank-yous and goodbyes before the donor went to ejaculate.

Donor Masturbation vs. Sex With His Partner

Because sperm volume is often much lower from donors who masturbate than those who are sexual with their partners, you might agree to invite his partner if he has one. Some women feel fine about this and like that it's less mechanical and more organic. Others don't want to think about the donor's sex life so intimately. It's up to you.

Frozen Sperm Logistics

Frozen sperm is extremely cold. Use a glove or cover your hand with something when removing the vial from the tank or dry ice. If your sperm comes in a liquid nitrogen tank, the sperm bank will give you instructions on how to open it easily. The sperm will then need to thaw so that it's at body temperature. After a minute or two it will still be frozen but not too cold to touch. You or your partner should hold the vial of sperm next to your body until it's warm, at which point you should gently turn it and look to see if it's all liquid. Wait until the sperm has completely liquefied before drawing it up into the syringe. Avoid turning the vial upside-down as this will disperse the sperm too widely for optimal collection.

You may be advised to immerse the vial in a bowl of slightly warm water. It's more difficult, however, to keep a bowl of water at human body temperature than it is to put the vial under your arm or in your bra. Placing the vial in water that's too warm can overheat the sperm. The sperm survive the thawing process best if they thaw as quickly as possible. Therefore, don't leave the sperm sitting on the counter to slowly defrost. During the time you warm the sperm, you can be sexual (or not), focus on the baby, get centered, etc. A vial of frozen sperm usually takes 8–15 minutes to thaw.

How to Inseminate at Home With Fresh or Frozen Sperm

If you're using frozen sperm, the sperm bank should provide you with a non-latex 1-cc (tuberculin) syringe. If your sperm is fresh, use a 1-cc, 3-cc, or 5-cc nonlatex syringe. Use a needle only if the tip of the syringe isn't small enough to draw up the entire sample. Using a 1-cc syringe for fresh-sperm inseminations often requires a few fillings and insertions to use up all of the semen. Before drawing the sperm into the syringe, make sure that the cap is off the syringe and that you've expelled any air from it.

Prop up your bottom slightly on a pillow so that your hips are tilted up. This doesn't need to be a tall stack of pillows that makes your back hurt; you just need to be tilted up. Now it's time to insert the syringe. Take a deep breath and exhale slowly and fully. Relax your body and vaginal muscles. Get ready to welcome the sperm and your baby into your body.

Next, guide the syringe into your vagina yourself, or let a friend or your partner slip it in for you. Slide the syringe deeply into the vagina. You don't want to put the syringe directly up to the cervical opening and squirt it forcefully. The sperm needs to find its own way through the cervix; if it doesn't, the fertile mucus inside won't appropriately filter it. The risk of accidentally doing this is minimal, in fact virtually nonexistent, if you push the plunger of the syringe in gently. The more slowly you push the plunger, the less likely it will be that the sperm will run out of your body again. Fertile mucus pools in the back of the vagina and guides the sperm into the cervix, so aiming the syringe is not necessary. If you use a speculum, much of the sperm will get pulled out to the opening of the vagina as the speculum is removed. Therefore, it is not wise to use a speculum. When you're done, remove the syringe slowly from the vagina.

After the sperm has entered your body, relax, breathe, and notice what you feel. Some women can feel the aliveness of the sperm. You should remain lying down for at least 20 minutes; up to a few hours is ideal. After the first 15 minutes or so, very slowly roll over. Spend five minutes on each side and your stomach. Then very slowly roll back. In this way, if your cervix happens not to be angled directly into the pool of sperm and mucus, slowly rolling will ensure that it gets coated with sperm regardless of your position. If you know or have a sense of which ovary you're ovulating from, roll to that side first.

Slight cramping after insemination is normal. If you experience severe cramping, which is highly unlikely, contact your health care provider immediately.

You Don't Need to Rush

Sperm doesn't lose much motility in the first hour after ejaculation. Try not to feel rushed. Sperm thrive in a warm (not hot) temperature and may be somewhat sensitive to light and air. Before insemination, keep the sperm container covered and warm inside your shirt against your body until you're ready to use it. If you're using frozen sperm, thaw it just before you use it, if possible. If you need to wait a little while to inseminate after it has thawed, keep it warm and out of the light against your body and inseminate within the hour.

Partner Issues

If you're planning to parent with your partner, please do everything you can so that both of you are present for all inseminations. We've seen relationships damaged when both partners weren't able to be together for inseminations on a regular basis.

We encourage you to make each insemination a beautiful and memorable experience for both of you. Whether or not you get pregnant, each month you inseminate you're solidifying your love for each other and building memories. By claiming these moments as powerfully intimate experiences, you won't let them take over your lives. Instead you'll be left with your love for each other and your desires to expand that love into a bigger family.

To those ends, sharing silence, laughter, massage, and rest in bed are all intimate post-insemination acts. Even if one or both of you have to return to work, take at least a half-hour after the insemination to connect with each other. It's worth it!

Single Women

There is great beauty and power in being able to say you made a baby all by yourself. It's also a lot of energy to have to hold all by yourself. As mentioned, it's helpful to decide ahead of time whether you'd like a friend to be with you when or right after you inseminate. If not, just make sure you have all of your items of comfort gathered so you won't have to get up after you inseminate.

Many women have shared with us the beauty of the inseminations they've done alone in their homes. The depth of union with yourself and all that comes with can be amazing. More than one woman has described feeling like she was making love with the world. You've chosen to intentionally create new life in your body, so go for it in the ways that are most meaningful for you.

Insemination Tricks and Gadgets

Sperm Cups

Some women and medical providers use a sperm cup to hold the semen close to the cervix. A sperm cup is like a cervical cap or small diaphragm with a tube that can be attached to the bottom. Once the cup is placed on the cervix, the semen is pushed from a syringe up the tube and into the cup. Then the tubing is removed. The cup remains in place, and you can remove it a few hours after inseminating. Some women use a contraceptive cervical cap or menstrual cup at home to inseminate. It's best not to use ones that are made of latex, since studies show that it is detrimental to sperm.

From the clinical studies and anecdotal information we've examined, we feel comfortable in our conclusion that if you have enough time to rest lying down immediately following insemination, a sperm cup lends no advantage. The vast majority of sperm will travel into the cervix on their own within 20 minutes.

Also, we've worked with many women who've had difficulty using sperm cups as well as cervical devices, including the Keeper and Ensure. In a clinical setting, without a sperm cup fitting, just a small syringe will be inserted into your vagina. Many women experience emotional and physical discomfort when receiving vaginal and speculum exams, which are necessary when using a sperm cup in a clinical setting; this may predispose them to feeling anxious about the insemination. In addition, many women experience difficulty, pain, and occasionally bleeding when trying to remove the sperm cup. This can traumatize, although only temporarily, your cervix (not to mention your psyche).

We've found that unless you feel comfortable putting things on and removing them from your cervix, or you absolutely can't lie down for 20 minutes following your insemination, then it's preferable to avoid using a sperm-cup device.

Egg Whites

Some women we encounter fill a needleless syringe and with egg whites and insert it into their vagina before insemination. Egg whites have a similar consistency to fertile mucus, and some believe they mimic fertile mucus and help guide the sperm into the cervix. We have no data about egg white use, just a few anecdotes. Women who use them, however, swear by them.

Robitussin Cough Expectorant

Some people claim that swallowing large doses of Robitussin before insemination helps increase the runniness of fertile mucus. Although we've met women who use this method, we haven't heard that it has helped anyone. If you purchase a cough syrup containing decongestant or an antihistamine, your mucus may actually dry up. We don't encourage the use of cough syrup in this way.

Sex With a Man

Some lesbian, bisexual, and single women choose to have intercourse with a man to get pregnant. This, of course, is an age-old approach to conception. There are numerous advantages and some equally serious potential drawbacks that should be contemplated thoroughly before choosing intercourse as your means of conception.

Advantages

Choosing to have intercourse with a man to get pregnant has some of the same advantages as at-home self-insemination. You're receiving the benefits of fresh sperm, it's a nonmedical experience, and it takes place on your time schedule. You have the freedom to make the experience whatever you want it to be.

Women choose this option for a number of reasons. It may feel more "natural" to or spiritually appropriate to them, or they may not believe sperm is designed to touch air or see light. In addition, intercourse is cost-free. For many women, having sexual intercourse is the logical way to get pregnant. This can be an easy decision for many bisexual or single heterosexual women, as their sexual inclinations embrace being sexual with men. Others choose intercourse because they don't want to use a sperm bank or don't have access to or money for a sperm bank. Some women choose this option by having unprotected sex with a man and not informing him of the pregnancy. Women who conceive this way often feel this grants them legal safety, as the man won't have to know they conceived. If the man later discovers the woman got pregnant, however, DNA tests can prove paternity and he can then sue for custody.

When choosing this method of conception, it's important to feel connected with your sense of who you are and what feels right. It can be challenging as a lesbian to choose to be sexually intimate with a man in order to get pregnant, and it's often not accepted in most lesbian communities as "appropriate." You might not rationally feel it's right, but intuitively and spiritually you may feel it's best for you. Perhaps you feel that male/female intercourse for conception is human design and anything but intercourse is artificial or unnatural. If you're partnered and feel this way, your partner may have a hard time with this perspective, as she may feel a threat to the intimate connection the two of you share and to the very concept that the two of you are trying to conceive a baby together.

For many women it isn't necessarily a sexual or erotic experience they're looking for when choosing intercourse, but simply a means to pregnancy. Others feel the erotic and sexual nature of conception to be intertwined. They feel that a sexual connection with the man who is cocreating the baby-to-be is necessary. This may surprise women who have never had sex with a man or who haven't been attracted to men for a long time. For women who have this conviction, however, all other ways of conceiving seem unnatural.

Challenges

The desire to have sexual intercourse to get pregnant can be a difficult internal struggle for lesbians. We've seen women use this as a place to get "stuck." They feel that having sex with a man is the "right" way, but they don't want to have sex with a man, or their partner won't hear of it. This enables these women not to move on to a stage in which they are ready to conceive. Some women find that their belief is actually an internalized version of heterosexism/homophobia. They don't feel that making a baby any way but the "right" way counts. Since they think this—but can't fathom having sex with a man—they are left childless. Coming to recognize this as heterosexual enculturation is often the first step in feeling free to think about conception in a way that's unique to you. Some partnered lesbians have sex with a man and let the partnership weather it, while others keep staying stuck. Still other couples who are committed to monogamy can't find a way to get comfortable with one partner having sex outside of the relationship and don't move forward toward pregnancy.

Many lesbian communities embrace a specific "politically correct" method of conception that currently is not intercourse with a man. In fact, many people of all sexual orientations assume that if a woman can have sex with a man, it proves she's truly heterosexual and "going through a phase."

Some women choose to have sex with a friend who will be a known donor or coparent. In these situations most women have prescreened the men for communicable diseases, as they would with any known donor. (See Chapter 5 for recommended tests.) When you have sex with a man to get pregnant, however, there's no way to formally sever paternity rights until after the baby is born and the donor has gone through a formal court process to relinquish those rights. From a legal standpoint, it's best to at least have signed a contract of mutual consent and intention—a known-donor contract. The fact that you're having intercourse to conceive, however, may negate any legal standing the contract might have. Therefore, the legal risk of using intercourse as your means to conceive is potentially great.

If you're having sex with someone you don't know well, or at all, or if you aren't telling him that you're trying to make a baby, there are other challenges that are potentially much more serious, such as health risks. Please consider these carefully, as you're inviting this man's bodily fluids into your body. For more information about this and other potential issues related to anonymous sex, please read Chapter 5. When you choose not to tell the man, you face some additional challenges. First of all, will you reveal the man's identity to your family and friends? If so, you run the risk of the information eventually coming back to him, and therefore run the risk of a custody suit. If you don't tell anyone, you'll have to live the rest of your life keeping a secret. Secrets of this magnitude can be hard to keep. If the man was someone you ended up dating for a while or is in your extended social circle, how are you going to make sure he doesn't find out that you're pregnant? This can be a challenge for women in smaller towns. What will you tell your child about his or her conception?

Some people are nagged by feelings of guilt when they're dishonest. Choosing not to tell the man that you're trying conceive poses an ethical dilemma that each woman must confront. Is it ethical to be pregnant and not inform the biological father?

It's important to note that, just as with known donors with whom you aren't having sex, you may form an emotional bond that may surprise you. In fact, some women have fallen in love with the man they had intercourse with. This can be quite surprising, overwhelming, and complicate matters exponentially. Although these feeling usually pass, they can be quite disturbing at the time.

We had a client who was a lesbian in a longtime monogamous relationship. When we met her she had tried for quite some time to get pregnant in a number of different ways. She had used a sperm bank for more than a year. After that failed, she had been using a known donor's sperm for nearly a year. When that didn't work she decided to try having intercourse with a younger man she knew who had a high sperm count. She felt that something in the physiological process of having intercourse might increase her chances of conception.

When she attempted conception by intercourse her partner felt betrayed. Because the partner trying to conceive framed the act as a sexual experience, the non-biological mother felt like her partner was "cheating" on her, and she also felt that it destabilized her concept of their sexual orientation. She felt her partner should try fertility drugs instead. The woman trying to get pregnant felt strongly about not taking fertility drugs. This couple eventually broke up because of this—after having tried together for more than two years to get pregnant.

This client continued on as a single woman planning pregnancy while mourning the loss of her relationship with her long-term partner who didn't understand that she needed a baby more than she needed to be attached to a limited perception of sexual orientation. It was a painful experience for both women.

Because choosing to have sexual intercourse as a means of conception can have many ramifications, be sure to weigh the pros and cons before making this decision, and include your partner, if you have one, in your decision.

Tips for Increasing Your Chances of Conception When Having Intercourse

Some women choose to involve their partner in the sexual experience of conceiving with a man. Others aren't out in regard to their sexual orientation or their plan to achieve pregnancy, and therefore they don't involve their partner in the process. Some partners don't wish to be involved.

Almost all commercial lubricants contain either spermicides or preservatives. They should be avoided when you attempt to conceive. If you need lubricant for comfort, mineral oil is preferable. After the sperm has entered your body, relax, breathe, and notice what you feel. As we've mentioned, some women can feel the aliveness of the sperm. Try to remain lying down for at least 20 minutes; up to a few hours is best. After the first 15 minutes or so, very slowly roll over. Spend five minutes on each side and your stomach. Then very slowly roll back. When lying on your back with your hips slightly tilted, your cervix will always sit right in the pool of sperm, but if your cervix happens to be angled, rolling will ensure that it gets coated with sperm regardless of your position.

Clinic Insemination

Both vaginal (intracervical or ICI) and intrauterine inseminations (IUI) are performed in an office or clinic. In vitro fertilization (IVF) is also available in infertility clinics. This procedure is discussed in Chapter 14.

Advantages

There are many good reasons for choosing to inseminate in a clinic. Some women inseminate in a medical setting because they're using a known donor and feel that, for legal reasons, it's the safest place. Some inseminate in a medical setting because they feel most comfortable there; at home would make them feel too vulnerable or unsafe. Some women live in places where sperm banks will only release sperm to a doctor and the doctor won't allow the women to take it to their homes. Others choose a clinic because they're using fertility medications or receiving medical treatments that are only available in a clinic and they choose to inseminate there as well. Women who choose IUI are frequently only able have this procedure performed in a clinic.

Challenges

As we've mentioned, women are often led to believe that because of their age and, unspokenly, because of their sexual orientation, they have fertility problems and must start on a medicalized track. They're often led to believe in no uncertain terms that a medical approach will shorten the time it takes for them to get pregnant. This frequently involves starting with both IUI and fertility medications.

If you choose to inseminate in a clinic because you're scared not to, examine whether fear is the best place from which to make your decisions. If you decide it isn't, take some time to gather more information about your feelings and the procedures offered, then make your own decisions. Your final decision may be the same, but you'll know you've reached the decision on your own. You'll then be more inclined to remember that the whole process is yours, and you won't be as likely to forget that you continue to have choices every step of the way.

Many women have difficulty feeling fully comfortable in their bodies when inseminating outside of their homes. Some of the most common barriers to feeling comfortable in a clinical setting are those of not feeling you have freedom of sexuality, affection, and expression; feeling the staff is homophobic; reliving past traumas;

feeling paralyzed about asking for what you want; and not feeling in control of your conception or health care.

Often some creative work is necessary to reduce or eliminate any of these barriers. We suggest that you start working on any relevant issues as early in the process as possible. Later we'll address some of the most common issues and then discuss what you can do to personalize your experience if you choose to inseminate in a clinical setting. First, however, you'll need to know what an in-clinic insemination looks like. We'll describe both vaginal insemination and intrauterine insemination before moving on to suggestions for increasing your comfort and empowerment.

Logistics of a Clinic Vaginal Insemination (ICI)

Although there's slight variation from office to office, inseminating in a clinic is a fairly standard procedure. Vaginal insemination, or intracervical insemination, is performed as follows: You'll get up on an exam table, just as you would for a Pap smear. You'll undress from the waist down. You'll most likely be given a paper gown or a paper drape to put over your legs. If a sperm cup is being used, the practitioner will need to fit it manually. This involves finding the correct size cup for your cervix, which can amount to a number of vaginal exams with a little internal movement to get the cup onto and off of your cervix. Then the practitioner may or may not do a speculum exam to see if the sperm cup is placed correctly before he or she performs the insemination. The sperm cup is attached to a tube that comes out of your vagina, to which a sperm-filled syringe will be attached.

Next the sperm is released into your body directly into your vagina via a needle-less syringe or into the tube if you're using a sperm cup. Review the section on home insemination for a discussion of the pros and cons of using sperm cups. A speculum should not be used during the actual insemination, as the semen can pool in the bills and you'll lose some of the sperm. If it's the protocol of your practitioner to use a speculum, request that he or she not use it. Once the insemination is complete, your practitioner may either ask you to rest for a few minutes or to get dressed right away.

Although many women don't feel experience it, slight cramping in the uterus is not uncommon after insemination. Whether or not you've experienced cramping in the past during inseminations or during unprotected intercourse with a man, you may experience it now. Breathe into the sensation, relax, open your body up to the sperm, open yourself up to the pregnancy, and allow the sensation to just be there. If it's extreme, however, be sure to alert the medical staff immediately.

Logistics of a Clinic Intrauterine Insemination (IUI)

Intrauterine insemination occurs as follows: You'll get up on an exam table, just as you would for a Pap smear, and undress from the waist down. You'll most likely be given a paper gown as well as a paper drape to put over your legs. You'll undergo a speculum exam so that the practitioner can locate your cervix.

Sometimes an instrument called a tenaculum is put on the cervix. This may be used if your cervical opening is difficult to view. A tenaculum has two little clamps that hold the cervix in place. If this instrument is used, you may feel a pinching sensation, which some women experience as painful or uncomfortable. If your practitioner routinely uses a tenaculum with every woman, you may ask him or her to attempt the IUI without it.

Once the cervix is in view, some practitioners will wipe it with Betadine, an iodine wash that feels cold and wet and has an astringent-like odor. Next, a thin plastic tube called a catheter is put through the cervix and into the uterus. The catheter is connected to a syringe that contains sperm solution. Ideally, your cervix will be quite open since you'll be inseminating during your window of peak fertility.

Some women don't feel the catheter going through their cervix and into the uterus; others feel pressure or slight discomfort. Still others feel painful cramping. What you feel will depend on the timing of the insemination, the finesse of the practitioner, and the size of the catheter.

After the catheter is inserted into the uterus, sperm is released into the tube and the uterus. Most women cannot feel this directly, though many have a sensation of feeling full. The whole procedure, from the moment the speculum is put into your body until it is released, usually takes between three and 15 minutes. In some clinics women are offered ibuprofen. Some are given antibiotics, prophylactically, to take after the insemination. You may request not to receive any medication. Once the insemination is complete, the practitioner may ask you to rest for a few minutes or to get dressed right away.

Some women feel cramping in their uterus after they inseminate, no matter where they inseminate; others do not. Whether or not you've experienced cramping in the past during unprotected intercourse with a man, you may experience it now. It's a common physical sensation. However, if a woman has a reaction to the sperm, the washing solution, or any hormones in the semen that are not thoroughly washed away, she may feel severe cramping following the IUI. If this is the case for you, promptly alert the medical staff.

Advantages

• **Cervical Considerations:** Sometimes it may be difficult for sperm to get through your cervical mucus, or the chemistry of your vagina may be not conducive for the sperm. Thus, by placing sperm directly into your uterus, you have a greater chance of conceiving.

• **Sperm Considerations:** Some studies indicate that only 5–10% of sperm make it through the cervix after intercourse; the rest remain in the vagina. Although this is not significant with a normal ejaculate containing millions of sperm, it becomes significant to women working with low-count or low-motility sperm or sperm that experiences agglutination (clumping). Frozen sperm often falls into the "lower sperm count" category, as we've discussed. It's recommended that women over 35 use IUI when inseminating with frozen sperm. This, however, is a personal decision. If you're younger than 35 and haven't gotten pregnant using frozen sperm within four to six months with vaginal inseminations, you might consider doing one IUI and one vaginal insemination each month. For reasons of efficiency, some women choose to do IUI with frozen sperm beginning with their first cycle.

For additional information about timing IUIs and the recommended number of IUIs per cycle, see Chapter 14.

Challenges

When performed without a specific reason, combining an IUI with fresh sperm hasn't definitively been proven to increase the rate of achieving pregnancy. Precision of IUI timing is critical, since sperm only live for approximately eight hours once inside the uterus. Once again, if a clinic setting isn't your first choice, IUI may not be the best method for you.

IUI is an invasive medical procedure, and as such, it involves potential risks. The risks, although slight, may include infection and perforation of the uterus. An IUI does not need to hurt. Unfortunately, women often report to us that their in-clinic IUI experiences not only hurt but are often even excruciatingly painful. This does not need to be. If the timing is appropriate and a gentle technique is used during the IUI, a woman should only feel a sensation of slight pressure.

There are some good reasons why you should not participate in a painful insemination. When your cervix or uterus is traumatized, prostaglandins are released that cause the uterus to contract in a way that can push sperm out. Thus, a painful insemination may result only in trauma and not pregnancy. Many women, if they can't find a gentle IUI practitioner, feel that a unpainful at-home vaginal insemination is preferable to a painful IUI in a clinic and will more likely result in conception.

Be aware that most clinics don't have weekend hours, so some months you may choose to inseminate at home rather than miss a cycle or inseminate at the wrong time. Likewise, scheduling can prove to be a constant challenge for some women when using IUI. Often the clinic may have restricted hours or be unable to inseminate you at the optimal time. As we've mentioned, with IUI timing is even more critical than it is with other methods of insemination, so this can be a significant drawback. Finally, IUI can be expensive and most health insurance plans do not cover it.

How Is Sperm Prepared for IUI?

When a clinic prepares sperm to bypass the cervix and be inserted directly into the uterus, it is washed in order to separate healthy live sperm away from the rest of the semen. Semen contains sugars, salts, antibodies, live and dead sperm, and sometimes bacteria or viruses. It also contains various hormones, including prostaglandins, which can cause the uterus to cramp. The fertile mucus in your cervix is a natural filter that guides healthy sperm through and keeps everything else out. If you bypass the cervix and mucus altogether by doing an intrauterine insemination, the sperm needs to be separated from the rest of the semen. Not washing the sperm can result in severe cramping and allergic reaction.

Most sperm banks prepare sperm for an IUI by adding a saline solution to wash the sperm. Then the semen is placed in a centrifuge where it is spun really fast to separate the sperm from the rest of the semen. There's another procedure called the "swim up" method that allows the sperm to rise to the top of the solution and the rest of the sediment and semen to sink. It's thought that this method may retain a smaller number of sperm, thought it's of a higher quality. Often the two methods are combined.

After the sperm is separated from the semen, 1/3 to 1/2 cc is placed in the uterus, which is all it can hold without trying to push the fluid out. If an IUI is done with frozen sperm, 1/2 cc is the quantity you'll have in the vial. A fresh ejaculate contains 2 to 5 cc. When this fresh semen is concentrated and washed for IUI, some clinics waste much of it by concentrating only 1 cc of it and not inserting the rest vaginally.

We've mentioned that many women do one IUI and one vaginal insemination per cycle, whether in a clinic or at home. Now that you have a mental picture of what a clinic insemination may look like, let's return to some of the potential emotional challenges of clinic insemination and explore some possible solutions.

Finding a Practitioner: Initial Questions to Ask

Many women find physicians to be resistant to assisting lesbians or unmarried women. It's not illegal in any state for a physician to provide you with these services; each physician, however, makes his or her own decision about whether or not to provide those services to you. Many practitioners won't inseminate you if you use a known donor to whom you're not legally married. Many sperm banks will only release sperm to a physician directly and not to you for home insemination. Finding a physician to accept this sperm and turn it over to you can be challenging if he or she is only willing to work with married women. Some women actually fly to a lesbian-friendly practitioner who will release sperm to them directly. This means that the woman trying to conceive forgoes the option of IUI and instead secures the option of having sperm shipped to her home on a monthly basis for self-insemination. In areas that are less lesbian-friendly, there are many hoops that woman must jump through in order to get the services they need and deserve. If you're having difficulty finding an appropriate practitioner you may want to contact the Gay and Lesbian Medical Association at (415) 255-4547 or www.glma.org or for referrals.

Many health insurance companies are becoming more savvy with their language when defining coverage limits. You may have to be creative in finding loopholes, or you may pay out of pocket if you can't prove you have a male partner who's infertile. The best bet is finding a sympathetic doctor who'll make an ambiguous note in your chart, or have the office staff call your insurance company to clarify that indeed you don't have a partner who has a viable sperm count.

Initial phone screening will save you time and emotional energy. You might want to do interviews over the phone to determine which clinics have worked with lesbian, bisexual, or single women. If you live in an area where more than one queer-friendly practitioner provides insemination services, take note of how the practitioner and other office staff discuss your sexual orientation, address your partner (if you have one), and address you. If you feel more comfortable working with a woman, seek out a female practitioner.

Perhaps there's only one nearby practitioner or only one covered by your health insurance. If you don't feel comfortable with him or her, you may need to decide what will make you feel the most empowered in the situation. Perhaps you could change insurance plans, travel to a nearby city, or pay out of your own pocket.

Sometimes you may need to continue to work with the provider, letting him or her know your expectations in advance and giving feedback afterward. In some cases, unfortunately, the best you can do is not rock the boat.

Even in the Bay Area, where many lesbian and bisexual women inseminate in medical settings and many doctors specialize in insemination services, we've heard dissatisfaction from our clients time and again. Perhaps the doctor is friendly, but the nurses aren't. Or maybe the nurses are friendly, but the doctor isn't. Having a lesbian practitioner doesn't always necessarily carry over to the office staff being sensitive in their care and inclusion of the partner. Finding a supportive, respectful, sensitive care provider can even be a challenge in urban areas, including queer-friendly San Francisco. The key to a good experience is to find a care provider with a warm bedside manner who treats you and your family with respect, maintains eye contact, and does not dismiss your concerns or questions .

We suggest that you have an initial consultation during which you can meet the fertility specialist and discuss your preferences without committing to any services. At this time you can ask to see the exam room so that you'll be able to visualize where the insemination will occur and prepare for it mentally. You can let the practitioner know how you'd like your conception to be and get his or her feedback.

At this visit you should ask to meet the other practitioners in the practice, especially if you have a practitioner who might be on call, out of town, or on vacation during your insemination. If you can't arrange to meet the other practitioners, be sure to ask about their experience and comfort level when working with lesbian women. It's quite common for there to be weeks or even months when your practitioner is unavailable, so it's important to feel comfortable with your back-up options.

Along these lines, it's important to inquire about the clinic's hours and what your choices are if you're fertile after hours or on the weekend. Because you can't control which days you're fertile, it's helpful to explore whether there's a clinic in your area that provides weekend inseminations.

At the end of your interview ask that your preferences be noted in your chart so that you can reference them to any other staff members with whom you may be interacting. This is a valuable tool that will help reduce the possibility of stress and miscommunication at the time of insemination. For example, if it's noted in your chart that you and your partner are lesbians, that your partner will be in the room with you at all times, and that you'll be inserting your own speculum, you can avoid challenging conversations by just asking the staff member to look at the agreements that are documented. In the medical world, if a conversation isn't documented, it never happened.

At any point, if you're unhappy with the services provided in your area, consider making a longer drive to have the kind of experience with which you feel comfortable. We live in an urban environment and have clients who drive from towns three or more hours away for our insemination services; some of our clients even fly in from out of state.

Things You Can Do to Feel Safe Before You're in the Exam Room

One element that affects how we respond to a "medical" or gynecological experience is our life history. Being inseminated in a clinic can sometimes bring up sexual abuse memories. If you think this may be the case for you, it's best to do some emotional preparation. Perhaps you'd feel safer if you let the practitioner know about your sexual abuse history in advance. Likewise, bringing a partner or a friend to your inseminations can help keep you rooted in the present. Familiarizing yourself in advance with a speculum may help put you at ease as well. (See pages 257–259 for step-by-step instructions on using a speculum.) Practicing relaxation exercises can help you feel more comfortable at the time of your insemination. In addition, having a gentle and reassuring talk with yourself prior to arriving at the clinic can help alleviate any anxiety. Likewise, being aware that you may need to take extra time during the insemination simply to process the situation is helpful in planning your schedule.

Clinic inseminations may also bring up physically or emotionally uncomfortable medical experiences you may have had, particularly in regard to abortions, miscarriage, or pelvic exams. These memories can make you feel out of control. In the past, many women have scrunched their eyes up, gritted their teeth, and held their breath to get through Pap smears or vaginal exams. Many haven't had Pap smears for many years due to past negative experiences.

Although it may not be an altogether pleasing idea, if you address these issues in advance, you may be able to move into a much more comfortable, empowered place, thereby allowing your insemination to be a pleasant experience. This is a novel concept for many women. It isn't a bad or shameful thing for a vaginal exam to be comfortable. On the contrary, comfort with our bodies has been taken away; it's time to reclaim it.

Often, connecting with the "baby" and how you'd like to feel when you conceive and bring the baby into your body may provide the incentive for you to do the emotional work necessary for you to become more comfortable with the process. For some women, using a speculum at home can serve as a way of monitoring their fertility, getting comfortable with their body, and demystifying and demedicalizing speculums. It can help increase your awareness of your vagina and cervix. You can do exercises to control your breathing, relax your muscles, and feel more in control. In the clinic you can then insert your own speculum if it feels empowering to do so. Whether or not you insert the speculum, you will be familiar with its movements and more comfortable with the feelings of insertion.

When you bring a health care provider into your conception process, it may be difficult for you to maintain your decision-making power. Many of our clients share that they never even considered that they had more options than were offered to them. Questioning your care provider or making a decision that doesn't include all the pieces of their plan can often be met with a feeling of disdain from the doctor. This is one of many reasons why it's important to interview practitioners and take note of each practitioner's style and approach. Remember, you can change practitioners at any time.

Feeling Comfortable in the Exam Room

Some women worry that insemination in a clinic will be physically uncomfortable, rushed, or impersonal. This can be true. There are a number of ways to make yourself feel more comfortable in a clinic. Often none of these possibilities are offered to you—you'll have to request them, which you may find surprisingly difficult at first. It's common for women in a medical setting to feel they're supposed to behave a certain way—to be a "good girl" or a "good patient." Our deference to the authoritative medical system is culturally ingrained, and a self-protective element often leads women not to act in an antagonizing manner toward someone who's going to touch them intimately. Remember that you are *hiring* your practitioner to help you conceive your baby. You have the right to make it a comfortable and personal experience.

You may receive a disgruntled initial response to requests simply because you are disrupting the normal routine—not because your requests are impossible to fulfill. The medical assistant, nurse, or practitioner may need a moment to compose themselves after your request. Let them have it, then ask again. Examples of things you may want to request include:

- If you feel uncomfortable/out of control having your feet up in stirrups, you can rest your feet on the edge of the exam table.
- If the room is too cold, you can ask for the temperature to be changed or you can bring a blanket or wear a sweatshirt. You can ask for a blanket if you become cold or nervous while on the exam table.
- You can ask to see your cervix with a mirror. You can ask for your partner to be able to see your cervix as well. Not all offices have hand mirrors, although they should. Bring one from home if you need to.
- You can ask that your partner or a friend be allowed to watch the procedure.
- You can ask for your partner or friend to push the plunger of the syringe in. Remember to go slow.
- You or your partner can insert the speculum and then have the practitioner adjust it.
- You or your partner can insert your sperm cup if either of you feel comfortable doing that and it's something you know how to do.
- You can ask your practitioner to explain exactly what is being done as it's being done, or let you know at the time when something may feel uncomfortable.
- You can keep the top half of your clothes on.
- You don't have to have a drape over your legs if you don't want to. The drape blocks your view of the lower half of your body. There's no reason for the drape other than the idea that it's more comfortable for both the patient and practitioner by supposedly desexualizing the situation.
- Although it's easier to have a speculum inside you if you're not fully sitting up, the exam table doesn't have to be completely flat. It can be raised slightly or you can ask for a pillow so that you'll have a better view of what's happening in your body.
- You can also ask that the practitioner not use a speculum or a cervical cap if you are receiving an IUI.
- You can request to be alone and do a vaginal insemination on your own.

- If your practitioner is rushed and brusque in his or her speculum- or finger-insertion method, you can ask him or her to stop or go more slowly at any time. If your practitioner isn't receptive, change practitioners. A vaginal exam need not be painful. We repeat, a vaginal exam need not be painful.
- You can ask to be allowed to rest undisturbed for 15–20 minutes after the insemination.

Intimacy and Personalizing the Space

This is your insemination, the potential beginning of your pregnancy. Claim the experience. Feel free to bring anything that might make you feel more comfortable. Some women like to bring music.

It's valuable to have practiced quick ways of establishing a sense of connection with yourself and your partner if you have one. When practiced, this skill can be called upon. From helping a number of women inseminate, even in our nonmedical environment, we've found that women often feel vulnerable and even slightly embarrassed at first if they want to have a feeling of sacredness or intimacy during their inseminations. Once they get over their internal self-inhibition, they can be much more affectionate and connected.

Depending on whether the office staff are homophobic, you might not feel comfortable being physically affectionate in any way with your partner. In some cases you might not even be out to your care provider, and your partner might not be present. Or you may be single and closeted and therefore feel you can't be fully present. Although physical intimacy isn't inherently encouraged clinic settings, there are some ways for you to share an intimate connection with your partner.

If your partner or friend is going to push the plunger, you have a built-in opportunity to look each other in the eyes for a moment and say something personal before releasing the sperm. Likewise, if you're the partner or friend of an inseminating woman and choose not to release the sperm, be sure to make physical contact with her. Hold hands and speak soft words of encouragement to her. Remind her to be open and to welcome the sperm. In your time alone after the procedure, take some time to visualize the conception happening and pregnancy beginning. Make this time special and memorable.

If your ideal conception includes being sexually intimate with yourself or a partner, it's important to come to a peaceful place inside yourself and within your relationship about the fact that you probably won't be able to be sexual at the clinic.

You may choose to be sexual before your appointment so that you enter the space of sexual connection with yourself and your partner (if you have one) ahead of time. This established sense of connection will then have a greater chance of being maintained throughout your insemination. Another way is to maximize your time alone in the room. In most offices you'll probably find yourself waiting, both in a waiting room and in the clinic room. This is the time to initiate contact with yourself and/or your partner. Most partnered women become nonsexually intimate at this time, or feel sexual energy without direct physical expression. This can be through holding hands, making eye contact, rubbing each other's back or shoulders, singing silly or meaningful songs, smooching, or doing whatever feels right. Some women choose to be sexual with each other as soon as they get home.

Clinic Insemination and Partner Issues and Roles

When you're partnered it's important to examine, as a team, the choices you're making. Established and practiced ways to feel connected become important resources to call upon when you're inseminating—the emphasis being on having established familiar cues. If you choose to inseminate in an environment that isn't your own, you don't have much time in which to create an intimate bond, and established cues will be important.

Working as a team means communicating clearly before, during, and after each insemination. With clear communication you can either consciously resist falling into roles, or consciously embrace a separation of duties, feelings, and roles. In a clinical environment there's an inherent segregation of roles between someone who's conceiving and her partner, simply in terms of who has their clothes off and is up on the exam table and so vulnerable, and who is fully clothed and upright.

Often with this inherent difference in vulnerability comes an unspoken assumption that the clothed partner is responsible for the physical and emotional well-being and safety of her inseminating partner. Often the woman being inseminated doesn't feel comfortable being assertive, expressing when she isn't happy with the interaction, or giving feedback. This role, therefore, gets delegated to the partner.

A woman may feel very vulnerable—especially when she needs to trust the practitioner with the inside of her body—saying anything that might upset him or her. This may lead to an unspoken expectation that the partner will be the one who expresses anger or frustration about an interaction or who gives feedback. Taking on this role can leave the partner feeling she has to hold all of the negative energy in relation to the clinic staff, and she may not want to shoulder this burden. If the partner is unaware of the expectation, the woman being inseminated can feel let down that her partner doesn't verbalize her feelings for her.

Commonly, the partner who is not inseminating feels ignored or marginalized by the staff. She may also feel blatant or suppressed homophobia from the staff. Often the woman being inseminated is so focused on herself in the moment, which is natural, that she doesn't notice this. This is another reason why it's important to communicate with each other before and after each insemination. This way you can decide as a team how the experience felt and what you might like to change next time—if there will be a next time—and how and when you'll address your concerns with the staff.

It's important to discuss in advance any cues you might want to have with each other in the moment. For example, if you're nervous about vaginal exams (perhaps they trigger past abuse for you), and it's hard for you to speak up for yourself in those moments, you might have a cue for your partner—such as patting her arm twice— that lets her know you need the practitioner to stop. Having prearranged signals allows you to feel more in control of the experience.

Many women decide it's unnecessary for both partners to take time off from work, so the one conceiving will go by herself to the appointments. However, we hear time and time again that these women don't feel as safe or supported as they would if their partner were there, and so they start to feel resentment and loneliness. The women who inseminate with their partners, however, express feeling safer and more connected to the experience. In Chapter 13, we explore how the ongoing process of insemination can undermine self-esteem and relationship intimacy, and why it's vital to be together whenever possible for inseminations.

If there's no possible way you can arrange to be together, we strongly encourage the two of you to establish a special bonding ritual the morning of each insemination. We also suggest that both you and your partner focus on conception during the time of insemination, even if one of you must be at work, and connect by phone just before, during, or after, if you can.

Some women are afraid to go to a clinic with their partner because it would mean acknowledging just how big a step conception is. When a woman can't miss work for financial reasons, there may be an underlying factor of homophobia, both externally feared and internally based. Perhaps she isn't out at work or hasn't told anyone that she and her partner are trying to conceive. It can be difficult to try to reconcile all these areas of our lives. At some point you'll come out, probably, and miss work at the time of the birth, in the first few months thereafter, or if your child is sick. Insemination fits in the same category. This is where partner communication is once again key. If you've established your priorities jointly, while honestly listening to each other, you can decide how to approach these issues. If you don't fully discuss them, you may both be working from inaccurate assumptions. Working together, you can support each other in making decisions that feel right.

The key is to stay honest with yourselves and each other. Allow for your needs and priorities to change and modify as time passes. If you do, you'll be able to feel connected with yourself and each other throughout the process.

Single-Woman Issues During Clinic Inseminations

When you're single it's easy to end up in a clinic for insemination. Many single women express to us that they don't feel as lonely in a clinic. It can feel like you have someone to share with and talk to. Other women don't feel that at all. Instead they report feeling as if the whole world is their partner; they share and ask questions of everyone in their lives. Still other single women we've met have used a team-approach for both insemination and decision making, involving an intimate circle of family or friends for support.

Some women feel empowered by inseminating on their own; it makes them feel more complete. Others feel a loss at such a prospect. If you feel this way, we recommend that you bring a friend or family member with you when you're inseminating in a clinic. Remember that you may also ask a friend to come to your home. Self-insemination is easily done. If you need someone to share with and don't have a friend to talk to, see if a Single Moms by Choice group is in your area, see a therapist, or join a single mothers chat room. Your clinician doesn't have to be your confidante.

Likewise, if you do choose to inseminate in a clinic and go alone, you may feel you have no one with whom to share both the painful and joyful moments. This can bring up the bittersweet nature of single parenting: You get everything for yourself, but you have no one with whom to share it. Have you come out to your practitioner? Or have you chosen to remain closeted? Does your decision affect how you feel in your body during the insemination?

We've spoken with a number of women who started off inseminating at home but soon switched to inseminating in a clinic so they could decide with someone else what they might do differently. Remember that you can consult with a fertility specialist or give Maia a call, get the information and feedback you need, and still conceive at home if that's what you prefer.

Cervical Awareness Increases Insemination Effectiveness

Different women have different levels of awareness and sensation in their cervix. Some have sensitive cervices and others don't. When you're at different parts of your cycle, your cervix is either more or less relaxed. Our cervices are emotional. As midwives we see/feel this all the time in birth. We also experience this when we teach women how to do self-speculum exams. If you accidentally bonk your cervix with a speculum, it will often retract self-protectively.

You can get fairly deep insights into your emotional state by looking at your cervix regularly and simultaneously noting your emotional state. The cervix is the doorway to the center of woman's capacity to create life. It is a sacred doorway. If you don't feel safe, your cervix may be noticeably tense or closed.

We've noticed this phenomena distinctly when we perform IUIs. We've seen how much control women have over allowing something to enter their cervix. An apparently closed cervix can open if you relax and focus on deep opening. This not only makes the insemination much more comfortable and quick, but also most likely increases your chances of conception by lessening the hormonal reaction the cervix triggers when it senses pain. Likewise, common sense suggests that an open cervix will more easily allow sperm to swim into it after vaginal insemination.

Exercise

Each day imagine being open to conception and bringing a baby and sperm into your body. Breathe, visualize, pray. Spend time cultivating this openness. Then imagine you can connect with your cervix. Feel it. Breathe it open. See what message it sends you. It holds our female and sexual histories. Spend time each day checking in with it. It may sound silly or uncomfortable for you at first, but ultimately you'll bring your ability to open your cervix into more conscious control, which will ease not only your insemination but also labor.

First Insemination

A few words of wisdom to share about the first cycle you inseminate: Allow it to be funny—laugh and enjoy yourself. The first month is always comical. You're usually nervous and stressed. If you're at home, your dogs may knock the semen over, you may lock your sperm tank and keys inside your car, you may insert the sperm and watch it come out again. You may have to wait forever for your donor to leave or not have your donor show at all. Also, expect your donor's sperm sample to be meager the first time, if he's nervous. If you're going to a clinic, the first time almost always will be the one when either you or your partner will be stuck at work, the doctor will be busy doing emergency surgery, or the sperm bank will send a vial with a less-than-optimal sperm count. Chalk it all up to gaining experience and laugh at the comedy of it all. Try not to argue and have compassion for yourself if you can't help feeling stressed out.

Partner Tension Cycles

There's often a predictable cycle to the tensions surrounding inseminations. Many couples have either a pre- or post-insemination fight. This seems to be a way of clearing the tension in the air. Crying is also a common component of insemination—especially those performed at home. Maybe it has to do with finding a release that then leaves room for an opening. Perhaps it's about making enough time and space for all of the feelings that come up each time you choose to ask a baby into your body, or perhaps intentional ritual might help ease the building tension and expectation. Maybe simply having compassion for yourself and your partner, regardless of what comes up, is all that is needed.

Make It Meaningful!

Insemination can be done at home or in an exam room; with fresh or frozen sperm; by sex, IUI, or self-insemination. Each woman makes her own choice based on a variety of factors. Wherever and however your insemination occurs, it should feel meaningful, comfortable, and safe to you—even joyful and celebratory! Insemination doesn't have to look any certain way. It doesn't have to be ritualized or sexualized. It doesn't have to take three hours. Take some time to decide what might make it better for you. It seems that the more time that passes without pregnancy, the easier it is to unconsciously prohibit the actual act of insemination from taking up much time or space in your life.

Trying to get pregnant can take over your whole life, making you feel out of control. In some ways the actual insemination is the only part that can be controlled. As a result we've seen women try to take any hope or meaning out of the insemination process itself, relegating it to a task that must be done on a certain day. Resist the temptation to strip your baby's conception of its magic. Claim your conception and make it the internal and external experience you want it to be. Reverse the equation: Instead of controlling the insemination as a means of feeling there's something you have a handle on, use that same ability to control it to reaffirm to yourself, and your partner (if you have one), and to the baby why you want to be a parent. Allow each insemination to be a meaningful and memorable experience.

Part Five
Challenging Conceptions

Chapter 13 The Emotional Roller Coaster Ride

This chapter explores the emotional road map of the insemination period and provides you with tools for making this time of your life more meaningful and enjoyable. Most women find that the excitement of creating a baby dominates the first few months of insemination. Each month that passes without conceiving, however, becomes exponentially harder to weather. The point at which conception becomes emotionally challenging is different for each woman and family. Some women don't feel they're in the advanced stages of insemination until eight months have passed. Others grow discouraged after one or two cycles. How you react depends greatly on your temperament and the outlook you have when you begin to inseminate. Despite the variation in experience, there are some predictable cycles most women go through each and every month of inseminating.

Most women find the insemination process to be stressful, even to the point of consuming all aspects of their lives. Insemination directly impacts your self-esteem, finances, partnership, work life, social life, sex life, your ability to trust, and possibly your relationship with your family of origin. Thus, if you experience a lengthy conception period, you may be in a constant state of chronic stress. Examining the specific stresses involved and identifying strategies for creative stress management is helpful for many women. If it feels unnecessary, or even more stressful, to review these stresses, simply skip ahead in the chapter to the section on tools for weathering stress for helpful actions you can take during your insemination period.

Monthly Cycles

The menstrual cycle structures the emotional cycle of the months of insemination in a way that is both compelling and universal. This is the template upon which is superimposed all other aspects of your life for the entire duration of your insemination period. How you relate to this cycle can change as time passes, but as long as you're inseminating, you're going through the same basic cycle as hundreds, probably thousands, of other women do each month.

From the first month of insemination through the last, the menstrual cycle regulates your life. For most women who are inseminating, not a day goes by that they aren't calculating what day they may be ovulating, what days would be best to inseminate, what day they're scheduled to have their period, or which day they could take a pregnancy test. This mental calculating is often stressful simply because of how much time and energy it takes. Let's look at the phases of this monthly cycle.

Phase 1: Fertility Awareness

Each month, from the time you menstruate until the time you inseminate, your emotions build up, much like the lining of your uterus builds to create a potential home for your baby. This first part of the month up until insemination is the fertility-awareness phase. In the first few months of inseminating, the cycle is usually filled with hope and excitement. If you're partnered, this is usually a good part of the month for your relationship.

As you approach mid-cycle you likely become increasingly more consumed with your fertility signals, trying to correctly time your insemination. The planning required to inseminate at the right time takes a tremendous amount of focused attention, and fertility monitoring may make you feel more like a science project than a person. If you don't get pregnant quickly, fertility awareness can move from an amazing learning experience about your body to a confusing jumble of signals whose meaning you doubt. You can begin to feel like your body is failing you, believing that if your fertility signs were adequate you would already be pregnant.

If you're taking fertility medications or receiving other fertility or infertility treatments, this is the time of month spent shuttling yourself from appointment to appointment. As a result, it's common to feel more job stress during the first half of your cycle, as you may be required to miss work multiple times for doctor's appointments.

In general, over time the fertility awareness phase of the month often becomes increasingly difficult. Each month you may find yourself getting cold feet and needing to recommit to having a child. Perhaps you begin to doubt your ability to parent or the wisdom of your choices. It's the time of the month when fears can loom large. These fears and concerns are a natural part of the process—it's common to question what you're doing. But it's also easy for such concerns to play games with your mind. Some women feel that having *any* concerns about their desire to parent proves that their decision is wrong. Just try to let that go, and if you're partnered, don't allow this to be something you argue about every month. Serious reservations require your attention, but having cold feet is normal.

Phase 2: Insemination

Each month the fertility-awareness phase segues into the insemination phase. How women experience this phase varies greatly, as there are so many insemination methods and approaches to conception. Nonetheless, most women end up feeling some amount of stress from all of the logistics they must juggle. This stress may come from trying to arrange to get your vials of sperm at the right time, trying to arrange for an IUI on the right day, or trying to coordinate everyone's schedules with your body's timing when using a known donor. Despite the stresses leading up to your inseminations, the actual inseminations are, at least initially, usually filled with optimism and hope. For partnered women, insemination arguments are quite common; they're probably an outlet for the stress of trying to coordinate such an important event.

If you inseminate for a number of months, you may feel increasing tension as you approach the actual time of insemination. Some women feel uptight or desperate. Those feeling uptight may have a difficult time relaxing and being comfortable during the insemination. Those experiencing desperation can find themselves obsessing about coordinating the logistics of the process. For example, they may call their donor six or seven times a day, leaving messages trying to reach him. They may check their saliva with a fertility lens every hour at work, trying to ascertain the exact moment they should inseminate. Although most women still feel optimistic and hopeful during this time, many find themselves talking about "next time" moments after they've inseminated. It becomes more and more difficult to remain emotionally open to the possibility of pregnancy and stay in the present.

Phase 3: Waiting

The second half of your cycle is the waiting phase, which is broken into two parts. The first few days are often some of the most exciting days of the cycle. Both in the early months of trying and in the months when you feel your timing is impeccable, these few post-insemination days have a positive, upbeat feeling. The possibility of pregnancy is very real. It's also a crazy-making phase because you'll probably scrutinize yourself constantly for signs that indicate pregnancy. When you focus so much attention on your body, you may discover a plethora of potential pregnancy signs every month—some real and some imagined.

The second half of the waiting period, leading up to your menstrual period (or no period if you're pregnant), is the hardest time for most women. This is when hopes and fears dominate your mental experience. A feeling of depression may set in as many women fear they feel their period coming on or brace themselves for the possibility of seeing blood.

Most veteran inseminators often try hard to ignore this phase of the cycle, hoping to feel less controlled by it. Many women, however, find upon reflecting that it was rare for them to think about possible pregnancy less than 50 times a day. What else in your life do you think about a minimum of 50 times a day? Given the importance that this process has in your life, it may be easier and more meaningful to admit to and honor its significance than to discount it or feel like you're going "crazy."

Women in this phase of the month are also often quite superstitious and don't want to do anything that might "shake the pregnancy loose." So, for example, some women refrain from having sex, exercising, lifting, eating specific foods, and even having certain thoughts or emotions.

Phase 4: Will There Be Blood?

The waiting phase is followed by either the arrival or the absence of the menstrual period. As women's conception journeys lengthen, they often feel lower and lower emotionally with each new menstrual period. Some women cry when they see their blood or feel angry or let down by the universe or God. Others don't feel anything and become emotionally numb. It gets more and more difficult to come up, yet again, from this low phase into the hopeful fertility-awareness phase the new month offers. Over time, this aftermath depression may grow longer and stronger. The emotional roller coaster gets crazier as the highs and lows become more extreme.

If you miss your period, or if you get a positive pregnancy test, you're likely to be ecstatic. It's a moment that words cannot capture. If you've miscarried before as part of this roller coaster ride, then fear may immediately follow this ecstasy.

The insemination cycle is compelling, consuming, and emotionally havoc-wreaking. It's also the monthly pattern of your life until you get pregnant or decide to take a break. Acknowledging this cycle and learning to recognize your emotional responses to each part of the cycle will help you align more easily with the process. Rather than feeling like you're on an out-of-control train, you can become a willing passenger on the ride to parenthood. This acceptance and acknowledgment calms the journey and makes your monthly pattern feel gentler.

Inseminating Affects All Areas of Your Life

In the following section we explore the impact inseminating may have on specific areas of your life, so that you can develop plans for minimizing stress. Likewise, if you've been on this roller coaster for some time, it's helpful to review all of the stresses you're under so that you can appreciate how well you're doing and plan strategies for even better stress reduction. This allows you to anticipate the support you'll need as well as validate the struggles you may be encountering. However, if you need no reminder that inseminating is affecting all areas of your life, you may wish to skip ahead to page 332 for tips on making this time more manageable.

Financial Strain

Conception almost always involves a financial component. For some this can be considerable. In fact, it's not uncommon for us to see women depleting their savings and retirement accounts while trying to get pregnant. It's also not uncommon for us to see less affluent women having to decide between spending money on holiday gifts or sperm, or having to get an extra roommate or a second job to help finance the project. Unless you get pregnant right away, it will most likely cost a considerable amount for you to get pregnant, whether or not you're buying sperm.

It's difficult to embrace starting your parenthood with depleted financial resources, but that's what many of us face. This stress is unique to our situation. Granted, partnered heterosexual women experiencing infertility have to weather the financial strain of fertility treatments. It still remains true, however, that men make much more money on average than women do. Those of us who don't use known donors have to spend significant amounts of money just to have the opportunity to get pregnant in the first place. Many women feel justified anger at these inequities.

Impact on Your Work Life

Insemination can directly affect your work life. The decision to share your plans with your coworkers or boss can be complicated. If you're experiencing an extended conception period, remaining private at work about your conception struggles can feel isolating. Many women are rightly afraid of losing their jobs or suffering in other ways from discrimination or homophobia, whereas others simply want to retain their privacy. It can become even more emotionally challenging if you work with pregnant women.

Inseminating can also affect your job if you have to miss work. The stress of trying to coordinate inseminations with your work schedule can be harrying. Business trips, important projects, presentations, and clients' needs aren't always easy to reschedule. Women receiving fertility treatments often have an even more difficult schedule, sometimes needing to miss work to attend six or more appointments a month. Not only may your managers disapprove, or your coworkers resent sharing your workload, but also vagueness about why you're leaving may make it even harder to get understanding. Missed work is lost money and a possible threat to your job security. This strain can be significant.

Impact on Your Social Life and Support Circle

At times vital members of your support circle may leave or feel "maxed out." Perhaps you've distanced yourself from some of your friends because it's become more difficult to talk about not getting pregnant than not to talk at all. Sometimes your friends simply cannot relate to the depth of your desire to be a parent. They may judge the choices you make in terms of the time, money, energy, or methods you use to conceive. They may choose to withdraw from you rather than share their feelings, or they may choose to share their feelings and then withdraw their support. Other times your friends may try to be well meaning as they provide you with their interpretations as to why you aren't getting pregnant: You're too uptight, you need to relax, your relationship is no good, you need a partner, you're too old, you just need a vacation.

Self-Esteem

Unsuccessfully trying to get pregnant eventually affects your self-esteem. Primarily you're faced with the existential question of "Why?" But you can run yourself ragged trying to answer this question. You may become fanatic about your fertility monitoring, exercise, diet, attitude, etc. Becoming rigid and controlling is a common response to feeling out of control. You may no longer participate in any of the activities you once enjoyed, leaving your life as well as your body feeling barren.

Shame

If you have trouble conceiving, it's very easy to point the blame at yourself and to feel you're defective in some way. This is the most common emotion that arises during a lengthy conception period. Shame manifests in different ways. Many women say they no longer feel like a woman if they can't conceive. Others regret having had abortions in their younger years and may feel they are now being "punished." A woman may also feel she's letting her partner down if she can't conceive. Shame can also spur feelings of internalized homophobia: "Maybe this isn't meant to be because I'm a dyke."

Although there's much to be gained from self-reflection, there can be a misguided tendency to think that if you haven't gotten pregnant it's because you have a psychological or physical impediment. Although you should strive for mental, physical, emotional, and spiritual health, blaming yourself for not being "perfect" will in no way help you conceive.

Anger

The second most common emotion after shame is anger, which may be very strong. You can feel anger at your body for betraying you, at pregnant women on the street, at heterosexual women for having it so easy, at yourself for waiting so long, at the universe for not supporting your desire, at the potential baby for making it so difficult, and at having to pour so much money and emotional energy down the drain. The inability to get pregnant can feel like cruel and unusual punishment.

It's important to recognize and acknowledge these feelings as they arise. Chapter 9 offers numerous suggestions on how to balance and manage stress. Getting out from underneath the sometimes all-consuming emotional chaos of the insemination period can be quite difficult in and of itself. You may need to go through the motions of doing things that are nurturing for you, so that eventually they will help to alleviate some of your stress. There are quite a few chat rooms on the Internet for lesbian moms in which many mothers-to-be find solace and understanding. Breaking free of the emotional isolation and sharing the struggle with friends and loved ones is worth the effort and perceived risk of doing so.

Relationship Stress

The longer that partners are in the preconception phase together, the harder insemination can be on their relationship. This may be especially true if one partner is ambivalent about having children. Because inseminating unsuccessfully month after month can lower self-esteem and increase the likelihood of depression, communication between partners may become more difficult.

Different Responses to Stress Within Partnerships

In most relationships each partner deals with stress differently. Often one woman wants to talk, share, and process frequently. The other may try to ignore the subject and proceed with life as usual. Some women internalize stress, while others release it inappropriately. Of those that engage with it consciously, some work through it quietly and internally, while others work it through verbally. These are polar-opposite approaches. One partner may be an eternal optimist, seeing all physical symptoms as signs of pregnancy every month. The other may be more pessimistic, convinced that everything about the insemination timing is wrong. Some women don't want to discuss the possibility of pregnancy at all, preferring to wait until the blood does or does not arrive.

Early on it's valuable to discuss with each other your approaches to the insemination process. Some women firmly believe that if you just smile and pretend the stress isn't there, it can't get to you. Some feel that if you "give in" to negative feelings and let the disappointment get to you, you're ruining your chances of getting pregnant. Others believe you need to feel, express, and explore every feeling as it arises. There's no right or wrong approach, but if you can understand each other's natural approaches, you'll have more understanding and compassion for the other's needs.

Sex Life

Your sex life can come to an abrupt standstill during the insemination period. Although some women still have sex during this time, it's often inspired not by sexual desire but by the idea that it might increase the likelihood of conception. If you feel your body is defective, it's hard to imagine anyone else wanting it. Likewise, many women find themselves wary of being sexual during the second half of their cycle out of a fear of disrupting a new pregnancy. Occasionally at Maia we find a couple that's able to maintain a wonderful and active sex life throughout this period, but it doesn't appear to be the norm.

Feeling Impotent

Many partners of inseminating women feel their self-esteem erode as well. If they're performing the insemination at home, they can feel impotent if they can't get their partner pregnant. Queer conception has many unexpected twists to it, and this is one of them. Feeling impotent in this way can also decrease sexual confidence.

The Elephant in the Middle of the Room

You'll feel the stresses of the insemination cycle and the desire for a baby are present with you at all times, even when you're not expressing them. This quiet longing, desire, hope, and disappointment is in the air you both share. Many partners try to ignore their sadness or depression and don't realize how stressful this process is for each other and the relationship. The longer it takes you to get pregnant, the harder it is on a relationship. One friend of ours said, "Oh, it's no problem. It's just that we're single-handedly holding up Mount Everest while acting like everything is normal. What a joke!" Most couples say they've never gone through anything more difficult than an extended conception period or infertility.

Role Separations

Even though you're both going through this process together, a definite separation of roles appears for most couples. An unspoken dynamic that occurs in many relationships allows only the woman trying to get pregnant her vulnerability and emotional expression. Although it's a shared experience, there's a mutual understanding that in some ways it's more the experience of the birth mother.

The nonbirth mom is expected to be strong and supportive. She may feel it's inappropriate for her to share her feelings of disappointment, sadness, and frustration with her partner. Being supportive of her partner can mean not breaking down or expressing her emotional needs. Unfortunately, over time this well-meant behavior can undermine the closeness a couple shares. If only one partner is allowed to feel, two-way emotional communication shuts down. This leaves just one partner discussing practical decisions and plans. It's a brave step to decide to be emotionally vulnerable after keeping to yourself for months, but when you do you'll both be thankful for your regained sense of connection.

Pressure From Your Partner if She Also Wants to Try to Get Pregnant

If your partner wants to get pregnant after you do, there's a mutual understanding that the longer you take to get pregnant, the further away her pregnancy will be. Even if she doesn't want to pressure you, she sometimes can't help worrying about it. Sometimes she'll start to share your physical longing for a baby. This particular stress is quite unique to lesbians. It's a sweet possibility to have each of you give birth, but it can also stir up an awkward form of envy and resentment. Keep an eye out for this dynamic.

It may be reassuring to agree upon a date at which point you'll reevaluate your options if you haven't conceived. Still, this agreement alone may not be enough to avoid the serious strain and stress the issue can bring into relationships, especially those in which both women have delayed trying to conceive until they are in their late 30s or early 40s. If this stress is underlying your actions and stultifying your ability to communicate with each other, you should bring this topic to a couples counselor.

Stress From Your Family of Origin

Women commonly experience some stress from their family of origin. Even if you're out to your parents, you may feel the stress of deciding whether to share with them the fact that you're trying to conceive. It's challenging to go through an emotionally draining extended conception period without sharing your news with family members with whom you usually discuss other trying times. On the other hand, if you've told your family that you're trying to make a baby and they aren't supportive, it can be hard on your heart. It can be painful if your family doesn't recognize your partner and therefore *your* family. Some women are fortunate and have supportive families. As lesbian families become more visible, they'll become more accepted and have the deserved experience of having their parenting choices celebrated by their families. For now, however, remember that you're not alone if you're rejected or misunderstood by your family members.

Shaken Trust

We all start out with hope, faith, and trust that if we really want to get pregnant we will. In fact, most women secretly believe they'll get pregnant the very first time they inseminate. This faith in their bodies and the universe is important to them. But if month after month you go through the cycle of waiting with bated breath only to be disappointed, your trust in life may begin to erode. It's difficult to hold on to hope when you're increasingly afraid that your dream won't come true.

A lengthy insemination period challenges many women's spiritual framework. Some women's spiritual beliefs are strengthened through the adversity of a challenging conception. Others feel abandoned by the divine and find little comfort. When you lose trust in all you know to be true, it's hard to find the voice of truth inside yourself that may have helped you to make strong decisions in the past . You may feel like your intuition has failed you. Losing trust in life can happen gradually, but it can also feel like a slippery slope.

Isolation

If you've been inseminating for several months, you may feel like crawling into a private hole until you get pregnant. This desire to self-isolate can be strong and is also a symptom of depression. It helps to meet with others in the same situation. In large urban areas you might place an ad in your local queer paper to meet with other women trying to get pregnant and form a support group at a local bookstore. If you aren't in an area with many other lesbian or bisexual women, you may want to seek out local infertility support groups. Although you may be the only lesbian(s) in the group and not all of the issues will apply to you, the support and understanding you find may be great.

When you're undergoing fertility struggles it can be difficult feeling so isolated in your experience. Unless you tell people, they can't know the level of stress you're experiencing. Your grief and pain about your infertility become a hidden disability. Although the depth of your anguish is often isolating in and of itself, try to resist the urge to experience this process alone. Withholding your feelings can be tremendously stressful to both yourself and your relationship. You'll find that people can support you even if they can't fully understand the depth of your anguish. Share the burden with at least one friend or a counselor. If you're not reaching out for support, examine your self-isolating tendencies and try to find others you can talk with.

If your partner is the one trying to get pregnant, you're in a category that's even harder to get support for. You're under tremendous strain, yet many people don't even recognize your role. They may consider it your partner's struggle, totally ignoring your experience. Once again, reach out for support in one of the ways we've mentioned.

Racing Against the Clock

When you're getting older or your body is showing signs of waning fertility, you may feel an increased sense of urgency. It feels overwhelming to do battle with the internal and medical messages of infertility. Sometimes it's helpful not to get any more hormonal tests for a while and trust that you'll get pregnant, if you can, regardless of the numbers attached to your odds.

The Stress of Infertility Is Said to Be Equivalent to the Stress of a Terminal Illness

It can be validating and poignant to realize that stress experts consider these stresses equivalent. The uniquely difficult aspect of infertility stems from invisibility and subsequent lack of recognition. If you had cancer, you'd receive much more support from friends, family, and neighbors. The inability to get pregnant is often a hidden and personal burden. When you combine it with possible homophobic reactions from others and the lack of compassion others may have for your partner, if you have one, then for lesbians and single women perhaps the stress of infertility is even greater than for other women.

Monitor Your Mental Health

Women who experience challenging conceptions can often feel a serious strain on their psyches. When you're under this much stress and feel out of control, both old and new responses may arise. Many women experience true depression. Please seek professional help and support throughout this journey if you exhibit symptoms of depression. If you have a history of depression, it may be upsetting for you and the people around you to acknowledge seeing some of your old and familiar behaviors.

Likewise, for women who experience anxiety rather than depressive tendencies, infertility and fertility challenges will commonly kick these up in full force. For example, a common fear is that something dreadful will happen if you or your partner doesn't get pregnant. Seek counseling and stress-reduction activities if you recognize your overall state of anxiety increasing. Again, ways to handle stress are discussed in Chapter 9.

The advantage of having a history of depression or anxiety is that you've probably learned numerous coping skills. It's important to prioritize these skills and to ask other people in your life to remind you to practice them. Common tools that many women use to help stabilize their mental health include getting regular sleep; eating regularly; exercising; and doing relaxation, visualization, and breathing exercises. If during your preconception period you're showing signs of depression or anxiety for the first time, you may want to join a support group for women experiencing depression or anxiety or enter therapy to help you develop coping skills.

Life Markers

Certain times of the year and important milestones in life may be exceptionally difficult for you. When thinking about getting pregnant you may often create visions of the future. For example, you might imagine that you and your sister will have children who are the same age or that when you graduate from grad school your partner will be pregnant, or when you move to New York for your new job in two years you'll have a one-year-old child. If you're still trying to get pregnant when these events approach, you may feel quite disheartened.

Tools for Weathering Stress

Now that we've outlined how stressful a lengthy conception period can be, it's important to think about what you can put in place to help you to reduce your reactions to stress and to minimize your stress load. Please review Chapter 9 for general stress-education tools and techniques that will help you through this time. Here we specifically speak to mental, emotional, and spiritual attitudes and discuss specific things you can do to gain support throughout your journey.

Pregnant Until Proven Otherwise

Many women find that one of the most helpful attitudes to adopt is that they're pregnant until proven otherwise. In other words, they honor the entire second half of their cycle as pregnancy whether or not it continues. Although at first this may seem delusional, it can actually be quite validating. In essence it's true that every month you inseminate you could be pregnant, therefore you may choose to act as if you're pregnant during this time. This idea is that one's mental attitude corresponds with her actions, hopes, and dreams.

This attitude allows each return of menstrual blood to be treated emotionally as a miscarriage, which is often truly what it feels like. Therefore, women allow themselves not only more personal room for grief and sadness each cycle, but also permission to take breaks between cycles when needed. If you don't feel this is a healthy attitude for you to adopt, by all means do only what feels right for you.

Use This Time to Enhance the Overall Quality of Your Life

The preconception period is a protected period of your life that you can use to enhance your health and overall well-being, your relationship to your body, and your partnership. As you spend more time focusing on health enhancement not only do your chances of getting pregnant increase, but so does your quality of life.

Two of our clients, Sarah and Jamie, expressed to us that although the nine months they spent inseminating were some of the most emotionally trying months they'd ever been through individually and as a couple, they were also their best. The couple started to take nightly walks together, altered their diets to eat home-prepared fresh and healthy foods, practiced yoga in the morning, felt more connected with each other, and felt healthier than they ever had. While Sarah was receiving acupuncture for fertility, she noticed the treatments relieved her chronic headaches and allergies as well. Although pregnancy inspired them to make these changes, they mentioned to us that they were very pleased with their new selves, whether or not they became pregnant!

Use This Time to Prepare for Parenting

Whether you're single, partnered, or preparing to be in a group family, you can use an extended preconception period as a gift of time to more fully prepare for parenting. Take the opportunity to read books on parenting philosophies and to clarify your views on subjects such as discipline, spiritual upbringing, sleeping arrangements, and approaches to health care. If you've always wanted to learn more about a certain element of parenting or have been concerned about a specific phase of parenting, use this time to read about it, talk to other parents, and develop your personal convictions. This will only strengthen your ability to parent when the time arrives.

Keep Living Your Life

Although it's difficult, it's important not to put the rest of your life on hold as you try to make a baby. Resist this temptation. Try to stay engaged with the things that were important to you before you started to inseminate. Continue to make time for the activities and people that feed your soul and let the other things go. This can ease the feeling that your life has stopped until the unknown time when the baby arrives. When you inseminate month after month, you may feel like you're balancing on the edge of a precipice, ready to jump into parenting but never quite getting the chance. This balancing act is truly exhausting. Have compassion for yourself during this time.

Give Yourself Pleasure

Although masturbation is always great, this isn't just what we're referring to! Intentionally engage in activities that nurture you and give you pleasure. This may be treating yourself to a massage or taking a hike in the woods. It may be spending the day with friends or going shopping. Do whatever gives you joy. There's a tendency for women to avoid pleasure when they're not getting pregnant—which is often a subconscious form of self-punishment. Negative thinking has an addictive quality. Don't foster this addiction; relish the things you enjoy!

Feel the Love You Have

Allow yourself to take regular time to remember why you want to make this baby. Rejoice in the love you already have for this baby. Making a baby is an act of love. Celebrate and grow love in your life. While you're waiting to love this baby in the flesh, allow yourself to feel the love others have for you and the love you have for yourself. Choose to actively love the people who are in your life now; don't reserve all of your love for the baby alone. Many spiritual teachings say love is what brings our babies to us. Include in your daily life a focus on love itself. Living a life that radiates love feeds our souls.

Develop a Spiritual Practice

Making a baby is exciting and amazing. Whenever you feel discouraged, do what you can to keep the energy moving. Make it your goal to expose yourself to new and fresh ideas. Just as you may experience cycles of pessimism, notice the cycles of optimism on your journey. Do what you can to keep an inspirational quality to your quest. Sometimes this means taking an entirely new approach to conception. Try to find books, friends, practitioners, and teachers that inspire you to new ways of thinking. Flowing ideas and flowing energy is renewing. Inspiration—emotional and spiritual—feeds the soul.

Many women we've worked with get trapped in a cycle of negativity during the months in which they're not getting pregnant. They can only talk about or feel the things that are *not* happening in their lives. It can seem impossible to find a way out of the spiral of negativity. We worked with one couple who had been trying to get pregnant for more than two years. During these years they'd suffered through two miscarriages. They had no hope left, yet they were unwilling to take a break or vacation.

When they came back to see us in four months, they were different people. They still weren't pregnant, but they had discovered a Buddhist meditation practice, which they'd been doing together for three and a half months. They talked about how it had changed their lives and reported having renewed energy. They said they felt much more peaceful and more trusting that the pregnancy would happen when the time was right. The changes were obvious. They talked about how "safe" it had been to be so wrapped up in seeing not getting pregnant as a failure and how threatening it had been to let go of that mental stance. They said they both knew that if something hadn't changed when it did, they wouldn't have survived as a couple. When they realized their relationship existed, and the baby did not, they decided to focus on growing what they'd been neglecting: themselves and their partnership.

Through their meditation practice they experienced a complete shift in attitude. Hope wasn't the only thing that returned, though; they rekindled their sex life, they started socializing again, and they started to have fun again. They, like many women, found that focusing on the positive aspects of their lives was an incredibly helpful act. Living in the moment and appreciating fully the good things in your life will help shift your focus from lack to abundance. This shift is key in maintaining a personal and relationship equilibrium.

Visit Your Fertility Altar

Many women find it helpful to create and maintain a space in their home for their baby. Placing fresh flowers or new items on the baby altar and spending time at the altar is another way to spend time with the baby before he or she arrives. This allows you a physical way to connect with your feelings about the baby.

Take Breaks

Even if you go on vacation during an insemination cycle you'll probably still be affected by the day-to-day awareness of fertility or pregnancy signs. A true break requires taking a month or more off from inseminating. Occasionally taking a month or two off is the healthiest and most supportive thing you can do for yourself (and your partner). It's often difficult to allow yourself to take a break, but you'll find it amazingly renewing. If you're able to, take a vacation during this month, or do whatever your heart desires during this time off. You might make the most of your break by putting your fertility charting aside. Although some things that you may be tempted to do during this month are OK, such as taking a hot bath or having a glass of wine or cup of coffee, be careful not to reengage with habits you've taken such care to avoid that either undermine fertility on a long-term basis or are ill-advised for pregnancy—such as daily caffeine intake or cigarette smoking. Enjoy the return of sanity and laughter, if you feel these have been lost along the way.

Treat Your Body as You Would Your Baby

Finally, there's nothing better that you can do for yourself throughout this process of preconception and pregnancy than to treat your body as if it were your baby. Nourish and nurture yourself by giving yourself good food, fresh air, and exercise. Take naps, sleep well, play! Have deep understanding and compassion for your feelings. Give yourself lots of hugs and reassurance. You are a sweet, tender, lovable, and needy baby. Giving yourself the love you need will create a profound and healing shift in your self-esteem and prepare you for the tremendous amount of love you'll give your child.

Chapter 14 What More Can I Try?

Infertility Diagnosis and Treatments

Today's headlines shout that infertility for both men and women is on the rise in the U.S. Current statistics show that one in four women has difficulty conceiving. These statistics include only heterosexual women who have been having unprotected intercourse with men for at least one year and have not achieved pregnancy. How can lesbians and single women relate to this information? We may feel overwhelmed, understanding that we not only share other women's infertility odds, but also have additional fertility challenges because of our limited access to sperm. Our chances of conceiving can often seem minimal at best.

If we choose to enter the medical system for help in getting sperm, we're automatically labeled as "infertility patients." We're treated as infertility patients whether or not we've ever inseminated and without regard to our true fertility status. Many of us are not "infertile"; we simply often have to work much harder to get pregnant than straight women who have access to fresh sperm.

This chapter offers a broad range of information to women having difficulty conceiving, for whatever known or unknown reason. We address how veteran inseminators can reapproach the topics of increasing fertility and fertility awareness, and explore the insemination/donor options we've discussed in earlier chapters—capitalizing on your self-knowledge gained so far. While trying not to sound like a medical textbook, we do extensively discuss causes of infertility, available diagnostic tests, and many of the treatment procedures Western medicine offers, including the risks and benefits of each. We also answer other questions, such as when to change care providers, and if applicable, if and when your partner should start to inseminate.

This chapter should be reviewed whenever you get frustrated and feeling nothing is happening. It's empowering to remember that there are always new things to try. Sometimes making a subtle shift is all that's necessary to regain your hope and inspiration. You may need, however, to reevaluate all of your decisions to date and try a completely new approach. When you haven't gotten pregnant and feel ready for a change, just review this chapter and refer back to Chapter 11 and Part Three for options you may not have tried yet.

We recommend that you don't use this chapter in lieu of the rest of the book. Even if you find this book after you've been trying to get pregnant for a long time, take the time to read the entire book. Many ways to optimize fertility discussed in the past chapters are not reviewed or discussed here. The previous chapters lay the foundation for the following new information.

Address Your Hesitations About Pregnancy

Often women are offended if friends suggest they aren't getting pregnant because they harbor hidden ambivalence. We want to address this head-on, not to "blame the victim," but to acknowledge that many of the women we've worked with who aren't getting pregnant do express to us occasional ambivalence about parenting or pregnancy. This isn't something to be ashamed about, but it is something to recognize and examine. We don't know how the mind-body connection may play into a relationship between ambivalence and infertility, or whether ambivalence simply adds to a woman's stress and confusion. In either case, let's discuss what you can do to acknowledge it and resolve it if you notice it's present, before we move on to the topic of infertility. If you didn't feel ambivalent when you started trying to conceive, we're not suggesting that you just weren't aware of it. Unsuccessfully trying to conceive can create looming fears and doubts you may not have had initially. Writing in a journal and/or talking openly about this issue with friends and/or your partner can help you gain insight. Ask yourself questions such as: What am I afraid of? What's the nature of my ambivalence? What might enable me to wholeheartedly embrace pregnancy/parenthood?

Many times women are afraid they won't be a good mother or that the responsibility of being a parent is too great. Some are concerned that their own experience growing up has left them without positive role models and that they're doomed to repeat negative behaviors from the past. Other women are simply unsure whether they truly want to give up control of their adult lives. And still others are paralyzed by the fear of not having enough time or money to raise a child in the way they see best. Finally, many haven't resolved their internalized homophobia.

These are complex issues that may require counseling or therapy. However, the women we have worked with that address the issues from which their ambivalence stems express greater emotional freedom for having done so. Addressing these issues has also allowed many women to discern the necessary next step to become parents, whether that's through adoption, in vitro fertilization, or other options. The books listed in the resource section at the end of the chapter all address these issues and options in depth.

Ideas You Can Try Without Seeing an Infertility Specialist

In Chapter 8 we explore numerous options for increasing your fertility. We encourage you to reread it for ideas you may not have incorporated into your approach so far. Fertility enhancement is a key component of achieving pregnancy. If you haven't yet incorporated any of the recommendations we make in Chapter 8, begin to wholeheartedly do so now. Renew your commitment to enhancing your body's ability to achieve and maintain a healthy pregnancy.

Striving toward greater health not only increases your chances of pregnancy, but also helps you continue to weather the stresses of monthly insemination. The stress of not getting pregnant affects all aspects of health: physical, mental, emotional, and spiritual. The fertility-enhancement suggestions we make help support your body through the stresses of the preconception period.

When you've been trying to get pregnant for some time, you may feel tempted to discard all of the fertility-enhancement approaches you've been using because they seem ineffective. Resist this temptation. What you've done so far has helped your body prepare for a healthy pregnancy. It's perfectly appropriate, however, to reevaluate the methods of fertility enhancement you've tried so far. Rotate the methods, incorporating new ideas that you haven't tried and discontinuing methods you've come to resent. This will help you continue to optimize your fertility and health—which is vitally important—while giving you a fresh outlook.

More Thoroughly Monitor Your Fertility

Many women have never charted more than one or two fertility signs during the months in which they've been trying to get pregnant. This is often because the doctors they've been seeing only recommend using ovulation predictor kits and/or charting basal body temperature as appropriate means of fertility monitoring. Many doctors go so far as to claim that to monitor more "subjective" signs such as sex drive or fertile mucus is worthless. Keep in mind, though, that most fertility specialists have learned their trade through working with heterosexual women who have abundant access to fresh sperm. They aren't necessarily specialists in lesbian or single-woman fertility. That's our specialty, and through working with hundreds of clients, we've found that a woman will significantly increase her chances of getting pregnant if she monitors a minimum of three signs, but preferably four or more.

Fertility Tracking Is Inherently Subjective

In addition, it's valuable to know that in our practice, we consider information gathered from ovulation predictor kits and basal body temperature readings to be as subjective as any other means of tracking fertility. Working with so many women has clarified our understanding that a positive reading from an ovulation predictor kit test strip gives nonstandardized information. That is to say, there isn't a general way of interpreting what a positive reading means. Some women have already ovulated at the time of the positive reading, some will in the next few hours, and some will ovulate in 36 hours. If you're monitoring your temperature, and you see it dip or start to rise, you may be ovulating, have just ovulated, or be about to ovulate. Furthermore, you may not recognize the dip or rise as such until you compare it to your temperatures on the following days. When your temperature dips, it can be difficult to know whether or not you're at the bottom of the dip. You can only truly tell this retrospectively.

This isn't to discount the value of either of these methods, but to emphasize that fertility signs *are* subjective. You are unique and must come to learn what each fertility sign indicates for your body. Therefore, the Maia approach is to track at least three indicators of fertility each cycle, preferably more. Then, when at least two, but preferably three, signs line up you'll have a clear indication of your most fertile window for that month.

Bear in mind that your body changes month to month. It's very rare that a woman is static in the fertility signs she shows each month. Some months you'll have a lot of fertile mucus for four days; some months you'll have fertile mucus for one day. One month you may have peak-fertility signals on day 12, and the next month on day 15. As you become aware of which side you're ovulating on, it's likely that you'll find a more predictable pattern for each side. Keep in mind that your ovulation doesn't necessarily alternate between your left and right ovaries every month.

The More Signs You Chart, the More Accurate Your Timing Will Be

If you've been charting fewer than three signs or haven't been getting clear information from your charting so far, try charting more fertility signals. Even if you think you're getting clear information from your methods, it's probably wise to try more since you haven't yet conceived. Perhaps you're getting clear information that you're interpreting incorrectly, leading you to inseminate a little early or a little late for your optimal fertile window. This becomes obvious when you begin to track additional signals. The more information about your body that you have, the greater your chances of conception.

So if you've been resisting looking at your cervix with a speculum, or at your saliva with a lens, you may be ready for that now. Since there are so many fertility monitoring methods, keep adding and rotating methods until you get pregnant. Discontinue charting signs that give you no pattern or valuable information, and add any of the numerous fertility signals you aren't tracking. More than likely, this will add vital information to the patterns you're already tracking. Continue to monitor all of the signs that do show a pattern. The more sources of information you have to work with, the more sophisticated your interpretation will be. Use Chapter 12 as your guide to help you track multiple fertility indicators.

Fine-Tune Your Timing

It's best to increase your fertility-tracking methods before you try to fine-tune your timing. This will give you additional information to work with. Even with the most thorough charting, deciding when to inseminate always involves an element of guesswork. For each cycle, it's helpful to write up a short addendum and attach it to your fertility chart, briefly stating why you inseminated when you did. For example: "This month I inseminated twice: once when my cervix was most open, and once when my ovulation predictor kit read positive." This kind of notation is useful to reflect back on when reevaluating your timing if you're not conceiving.

Please, please remember that it's been our experience that women often inseminate too late—in other words, after their fertility peaks. The problem isn't always infertility or the limitations of frozen sperm; you just may be inseminating too late. We cannot emphasize this enough. Please review Chapter 11 for timing recommendations.

Increase Your Number of Monthly Inseminations

Too many women inseminate just once a month. Whether you're using fresh or frozen sperm, *at a minimum you should inseminate twice a month*. This is especially important if you're using frozen sperm, since it is only viable for 18-24 hours. Two vials of frozen sperm do not add up to even one fresh ejaculate in terms of sperm quantity. Ideally you could use three vials of frozen sperm and inseminate twice each cycle. We know this can be expensive, but increasing your number of inseminations will increase your chances of conception. Therefore, it may be better to use greater quantities of sperm and skip every other cycle than to inseminate just once per cycle. When you step back for a moment it doesn't take much to realize that by increasing the quantity of sperm and spreading out its coverage each month, you're increasing your chances of conceiving.

Increasing your number of monthly inseminations is particularly significant if the only insemination you've been doing each month has been an IUI. Remember, sperm deposited into your uterus doesn't live as long as sperm placed into your vagina. Some estimate that IUI sperm only live in the uterus for six to eight hours. So unless you're within six to eight hours of ovulation, by inseminating just once a month you've lost your chances for the entire month. Likewise, although fresh sperm lives for 48 hours and longer, by increasing your number of inseminations per cycle you'll significantly increase the quantity and the amount of time covered and therefore increase your chances of getting pregnant.

A number of women have reported to us that increasing their number of inseminations per cycle freed them from the enormous pressure of timing their insemination perfectly, and therefore made the insemination part of each cycle much more enjoyable.

One Vaginal Insemination and One IUI Each Month

For women having difficulty conceiving, we recommend they do at least one vaginal insemination and one IUI per cycle. The IUI should be the second insemination, timed as closely to ovulation as possible. We recommend this in lieu of only doing one or more IUIs per cycle. Even if it's been suggested that due to your age and overall fertility status you should not do a vaginal insemination, we don't agree with this blanket approach.

There are a number of reasons why adding at least one vaginal insemination to your IUIs will increase your chances of getting pregnant. One key reason is that the life of unwashed sperm is longer than that of washed sperm, so you'll be able to cover a wider window of possible fertility. Likewise, vaginal insemination uses a significantly higher quantity of sperm, whether you're using fresh or frozen. The added time coverage and the additional sperm quantity will greatly increase your chances of getting pregnant. Also, if you're doing your vaginal insemination at home, you may benefit from the dramatic increase of your emotional, physical, and sexual comfort when you're in your own environment. These elements cannot be underestimated in their effect on helping women achieve pregnancy.

If your donor has an exceptionally low sperm count, or very low motility, you may want to try two IUIs per cycle. Some studies show that doing two IUIs per cycle—instead of just one—more than doubles a woman's chances of conceiving. Others show that two IUIs are *not* significantly more effective than one. The choice is up to you.

Change Your Source of Sperm

When You're Using a Known Donor

If you've been using a known donor and haven't conceived, there are a number of things to consider. If you feel confident about your timing and feel fertile, the problem may very well be your donor's sperm. Has he had a recent semen analysis? Are his sperm count and motility high? Is his morphology good? Is he abstaining from ejaculating for at least 72 hours prior to donating sperm?

How do you know when it's time to change donors? If you've been unsuccessfully trying to get pregnant for six consecutive months, inseminating two or more times each cycle with *vaginal* inseminations, then it's time for him to get another semen analysis. Remember that there are different gradations of semen analysis. See Chapter 5 for a fuller explanation. If you've simply gotten the basic semen analysis up until now, you may want to consider finding a practice that can do a Kruger strict morphology as well as a sperm penetration assay, which gives more specific information about the sperm's actual functioning by observing how it moves through your fertile mucus. If the tests come back with good results, try six more cycles with one vaginal and one well-timed IUI each cycle. If you haven't gotten pregnant after 12 cycles, it may be time to change donors.

If your donor starts off with a low sperm count or low motility or if the sperm have a high rate of malformation, you need to take a different, more aggressive approach. (Again, see Chapter 5 for a description of semen analysis.) To begin with, have your donor do all he can to enhance his fertility. (See Chapter 8 for suggestions.) Then it's best to begin inseminating with one IUI and one vaginal insemination per cycle, rather than two vaginal inseminations per month. With this approach you can be sure to have increased time coverage, a sufficient quantity of sperm, and the comfort of a vaginal insemination along with the higher sperm concentration and closer placement of an IUI. After three months ask your donor to get another semen analysis to see whether whatever he's been doing has improved his fertility. If there's no improvement in his semen analysis, you need to decide if you'll try a number of cycles more regardless, if you'll use assisted reproductive technology such as in vitro fertilization to overcome his sperm limitations, or if you'll find a new donor.

We know you may be deeply invested in your donor's participation in your family and that you probably don't have donors beating down your door. Nonetheless, to continue using him as your donor means committing to a possibly long, arduous process with significantly decreased chances of achieving pregnancy, or committing to expensive, invasive fertility treatments. The choice is up to you.

When You're Using Frozen Sperm

If you're using frozen sperm, be sure to rotate every few cycles which donor you're using. Also, be sure to work only with donors whose sperm has resulted in pregnancies before and who have a high sperm count and high motility. Remember, the way to ensure this is to be assertive with your sperm bank. Ask explicitly for the newest samples and those with the highest motility and greatest sperm count. For additional tips about getting the most out of your sperm bank see Chapter 6.

Even with all of this, many women just don't get pregnant using frozen sperm. The advantages of fresh sperm are described below. Do other factors exist that can affect a woman's ability to get pregnant with frozen sperm? We don't know. Many aspects of the conception process are a mystery, especially for us because lesbian conception has barely been studied at all.

It's insightful that so many of the women we have seen over the years refer to fresh sperm as "live" sperm—as in, "If only I could find a *live* source of sperm to use" or "Do you think I should use *live* sperm?" Frozen sperm isn't dead, but clearly to many women's subconscious minds it is. Many women try unsuccessfully for months or even years with frozen sperm and then inseminate once with fresh sperm and get pregnant.

If you've been using frozen sperm with no success, the most effective thing you can do to increase your chances of achieving pregnancy is to find a known donor.

The Fresh Sperm Advantage

Although we describe the differences between fresh and frozen sperm in Chapter 5, we feel they're important enough to review again here. Fresh sperm comes in much greater quantities than frozen sperm. Frozen sperm is purchased in quantities ranging from 0.5–1 cc, whereas an average fresh sperm ejaculation is 3–5 cc. This difference in quantity alone significantly increases your chances of getting pregnant. Sperm swim in groups; together they propel one another forward. Perhaps there's an ideal number of sperm that swim together, and the arbitrary breaking down of semen into freezable and measurable quantities does not always allow for this. There needs to be enough sperm surrounding an egg to biochemically change the environment so that fertilization can occur. Does the fact that we have seen a number of women get pregnant quickly when they inseminate with two vials at a time bear out the quantity argument? Our statistics are too small to prove this definitively. We know that some studies show that during intercourse only 5%–10% of sperm make it through the cervix into the uterus. Out of the millions, only a few hundred actually swim up the fallopian tube. Because of this, for vaginal inseminations, quantity of sperm is directly related to likelihood of conception.

Fresh sperm lives at least twice as long as thawed frozen sperm; some sources even say three times as long. This longevity helps reduce how accurate the timing of your inseminations needs to be. Combine these two facts with the fact that most donors are willing to donate at least two times a cycle and you've exponentially increased your chances of conceiving. Furthermore, aspects of the freezing process, including the addition of glycerol (a buffer), have been shown to decrease sperm's ability to fertilize an egg.

Of course, there are still potential health and legal risks involved in using a known donor, but if you've been using frozen sperm with no success, you should seriously reconsider the fresh-sperm option. See Chapters 5 and 6 for more information.

Fresh Sperm and IUI

In general we don't recommend using IUI when using a known donor. If one or more of the following applies to you, however, IUI may very well help: 1) You've been using a known donor and doing vaginal inseminations with no success; 2) You're working with a donor with a low sperm count; 3) Your fertility is quickly declining; or 4) You're in your late 30s or 40s. Although in these circumstances IUI may improve your chances of conception, many women will have a difficult time finding a practitioner to inseminate them with fresh sperm. Sometimes the practitioner will be willing if you show that your donor has tested negative for transmittable infections, or if you sign a waiver stating that you won't hold your practitioner accountable if you contract an infection from your donor's sperm. If you've been using frozen sperm and doing IUIs up until now, there's no need to do IUI when switching to a known donor unless you fall into one or more of the aforementioned categories. In fact, if you've just switched to a known donor with fresh sperm and you're older or your fertility is decreasing, it still may make sense to inseminate two to three cycles vaginally, assuming the challenge has been the sperm and not you, since IUI may even decrease your chances of pregnancy if your timing isn't accurate.

If you have signs of decreased or decreasing fertility, you may wish to do one IUI and one vaginal insemination per cycle. Adding an IUI is important, since it seems to increase the chances of conception for women with decreased fertility even when the cause is unknown. Remember, a vaginal insemination provides a slow, steady release of sperm into your cervix over a much greater time period than IUI. Therefore it's best to perform at least one vaginal insemination a month, even if your fertility is apparently waning. See the section on IUI in Chapter 12 for more information.

Finding a Known Donor

Many lesbians are in the awkward position of not having close male friends. As a result it can be difficult to think of a man who would logically be your sperm donor. In addition, there are serious health and legal considerations that can serve as deterrents for many women. There often comes a time in this process, however, when you reevaluate your priorities. For many women this comes when they're deciding between finding a known donor and taking fertility medication, or between a known donor and adoption, or between known donor and in vitro fertilization. At these crossroads some women decide to pull out all of the stops and find a known donor, even if it means having more donor involvement than they once thought ideal and taking health risks they were previously unwilling to consider.

Usually after you've been trying for what seems like forever, you'll discover that you've mustered more courage to ask men to be donors—one nice side effect of being a veteran inseminator. So look again at your Rolodex and E-mail list. Put the message out to your friends, male and female, that you need help finding a donor. It works! If you still feel shy asking people directly, send out a group E-mail message or leave messages on answering machines when you know people are at work. Your friends can then respond on their own schedule after they've given the matter some thought. Many, many women end up finding numerous men in their lives who are willing to help out.

When Your Donor's Sperm Doesn't Seem to Be Working

There may come a time when you decide you need to find a new donor. This can be emotionally difficult for a number of reasons. Perhaps you've been emotionally invested in using this man's sperm. Or perhaps you're afraid you may lose his friendship if you choose to use another man's sperm. Perhaps your donor is also going to be a coparent to your child. Navigating the emotional territory can be challenging, but this isn't a reason to continue with a sperm source that isn't working.

If you'd like to continue a parenting relationship with this man, whether or not you use his sperm, then broach the topic with him. Once they get over their attachment to biological connection, many men realize the parenting relationship itself is most meaningful to them. Some women, however, feel they need the opportunity to completely reevaluate their options. This would mean ending a parenting commitment with their current donor and prospective coparent in order to be able to foster relationships with other men.

Change Your Method of Insemination

If you've been using the same method and location of insemination all along and haven't gotten pregnant, it's time to consider other options. For example, if you've only been inseminating by IUI at a clinic or doctor's office, you might want to try inseminating vaginally in the privacy of your own home. If you've only been inseminating vaginally at home, to no avail, you may want to try IUI. Some women prefer to try having sexual intercourse with a man. Likewise, if you've only been having intercourse, perhaps you need to try a new donor or try inseminating instead.

We've worked with women who had inseminated for more than a year doing only vaginal inseminations, then decided to try IUI, and after one IUI got pregnant. We've also worked with women who began trying to get pregnant in their 40s. Aware of their waning fertility, they took fertility drugs and did IUIs from the get-go. Eventually, they ended up in our office looking for a different approach. When we suggested they listen to their bodies, many of them stopped taking fertility drugs and started inseminating vaginally at home. It wasn't unusual for them to get pregnant after one or two cycles. Again, review Chapter 12 for a through discussion of insemination methods.

Changing Care Providers

The fresh energy and perspective of a new care provider may be the missing link you've needed in order to get pregnant. Seriously consider changing care providers, whether you have a primary care provider, obstetrician/gynecologist, or reproductive endocrinologist (infertility specialist) if:

- You feel you've surpassed your provider's skill base.
- You feel your provider has lost hope in your ability to conceive.
- Your provider does not respect your choices.
- Your provider is badgering you into trying something you aren't ready for.
- Your provider has only one way of doing things.
- You feel your provider is homophobic.
- Your provider does not have time to answer your questions.
- You are uncomfortable in any way with your provider.

New energy and ideas are always a welcome change when you've been inseminating for what feels like forever. Remember, you don't need to have a reason to change care providers.

Infertility Technology: Considerations, Diagnosis, and Treatments

This section begins with a discussion of how you might approach making decisions about infertility treatments and procedures. We choose to start with this to provide you with a critical-thinking framework from which you can read the rest of the technical information. Hopefully, this will help you figure out how the information relates to you specifically. After this section, you'll find an introduction to the various causes of infertility. This will help you understand the last two sections on diagnostic tests and treatments.

The information we give is complex. You might find it logical or it might be confusing, depending on your background. Bring this book to appointments if it raises questions for you but you don't feel confident that you'll communicate them accurately to your health care provider. Don't worry if you don't understand all the details right now. You can ask questions of health care providers and look at other less detailed books and pamphlets explaining infertility. We do suggest reading the whole section through once to get a sense of the field of infertility. If you choose any of these tests or treatments, know that some of the simplest may be completely effective for you in helping you conceive and that you may never need to reread the sections on injectable infertility drugs or in vitro fertilization.

Who Will You Be Working With?

You may be used to seeing a nurse practitioner, midwife, or family practice doctor for regular Pap smears. These health care providers are perfectly able to provide gynecological care, but they probably don't do much infertility screening or treatment beyond the first set of blood tests. A regular obstetrician-gynecologist (ob-gyn) may, if experienced, have a practice that prescribes infertility pills and performs intrauterine inseminations or diagnostic procedures and surgeries such as laparoscopy. Most often, to have a comprehensive infertility screening, receive injectable infertility drugs, or have in vitro fertilization performed, you'll need to see an infertility specialist who is an ob-gyn with a number of years of further specialized training. This specialist is called a reproductive endocrinologist (RE). (The "endocrinologist" part refers to understanding the complexities and workings of hormones.)

Some of any of the above doctors will devise a treatment plan that includes trying low-tech options before moving on to more invasive testing or treatments. Others want to do a very comprehensive workup that includes many of the diagnostic tests we'll describe, before providing any kind of treatment. You may just see an obstetrician, you may see an RE for a consultation, and then work with your regular obstetrician to complete the steps of the treatment plan you all come up with, or you may at some point see the RE exclusively. It probably depends on which tests or treatments you're doing, your insurance coverage, your preference, and how far you have to drive to see a specialist.

Infertility specialists are listed in your health care plan, in the Yellow Pages under "Physicians," or through RESOLVE's infertility specialist referral list (see the resource section at end of this chapter for contact information).

Your care provider should:
- give you full disclosure of the risks, side effects, and actual rates of success of procedures and treatments
- be respectful of other healing modalities and practices you feel are useful
- encourage you to remain central in the decision-making process

If your care provider specializes in infertility, he or she should also:
- have an office staff person help you navigate insurance policies and payment plans
- give referrals to support groups and mental health providers specializing in infertility issues

Technology Is Compelling

Assisted reproductive technology (ART) is on the rise and is very big business. Some of the procedures in widespread use have been shown to increase a woman's chances of pregnancy, while others have much more questionable success. A helpful book on the subject is *Beyond Second Opinions: Making Choices About Infertility Treatment* by Judith Steinberg Turiel. The technological advances of our times have allowed many women to get pregnant who would not have otherwise been able to.

Many women who aren't actually experiencing infertility, however, receive infertility treatment, simply because they're lesbians or single women and are assumed to be infertile by the medical establishment. Infertility treatment is often presented to women as if it's a magic pill guaranteeing conception. Lesbian and single women often enter the medical system seeking advice on how to get pregnant. Then, simply because they're using insemination as their means to achieve pregnancy, they're put on the infertility track. Once again, the unexamined heterosexual assumptions of our culture are played out on women's bodies. Because there isn't a separate fertility field for lesbians and single women, they are instead lumped into a category that may or may not pertain to their actual fertility status.

Because the medical approach is the most widely accepted, many women follow the path their doctor or friends recommend, not stopping to evaluate how they feel about these choices. These same women may end up feeling completely out of touch with their bodies and wondering how this feeling of disconnection could have happened. The most important message we have for you is to stay comfortable with your choices. If you feel you're traveling down a path where you're no longer the driver, step back and reevaluate your decisions.

Is Assisted Reproductive Technology (ART) for You?

In lieu of putting yourself on cruise control, take some time to explore whether the medical/technological approach is right for you. There's no universal right or wrong way to conceive, only what's best for you. Some women choose not to enter the realm of technology at all, since they don't feel comfortable with it. For some this is an ethical consideration; they feel that if they can't conceive without the help of technology then it's not meant to be. Others feel that it's not "right" to take conception out of the bedroom and medicalize it. For some women this conviction feels like a spiritual belief.

Others are limited by their incomes. Fertility treatments are expensive and aren't usually covered by health insurance. Even without such grand expenses as that of in vitro fertilization, it's not unheard of to spend more than $50,000 trying to conceive. The price of sperm, IUI, ultrasounds, medications, and lab work can add up quickly.

It's perfectly reasonable to set limits for yourself. In fact, it's necessary. Some things may be fine for you, whereas others you will never try. On the other hand, many women feel comfortable using assisted reproductive technology. Perhaps they aren't attached to their biological relation to the child, but they want the experience of being pregnant, giving birth, and breastfeeding. Therefore, they'd be willing to consider doing in vitro fertilization with a donor egg and donor sperm. Some women are willing to do this especially if their partner is responsive to the fertility medicines that would allow her egg to be used for the pregnancy. Some women are only willing to do ART with their own egg, since for them an important part of choosing to be pregnant instead of adopting is having a genetic relationship with their baby.

Self-Reflection

Before you enter the realm of technology, it's helpful to ask yourself some questions. Take the time to write down the responses you have to the following questions. Also, take note of the messages your body communicates to you about each question. If you're partnered, you may both want to do this exercise then get together and discuss what your feelings about technology and this pregnancy are at this point in your process. Answering these questions for yourself can help you to interact with the medical world in a way that is true to your convictions.

• What are my beliefs about conception?

• Are there limits to what I'll do in order to conceive? If so, what are my limits?

• Are there things I believe are too technical for me?

• How much money am I willing to spend to conceive?

• Do I have a doctor I trust?

If you're partnered:

• Do we have the same feelings and beliefs regarding conception and fertility treatments?

• Are there things we should talk about now to help clarify our beliefs and establish a mutual understanding?

Selective Use of Technology

Remember, you're always the one in control of what's done to your body. This is often difficult to keep in mind in the face of the medical establishment. It's even more challenging to assert yourself if you feel your body has failed you. Nonetheless, remember that you have total choice about your body.

Just because there's a standard approach that your doctor takes for dealing with "infertile" women, you don't have to accept the entire package. It may take considerable effort to assert yourself about what you want. When you do, however, your doctor should respect your choices. If you feel your practitioner is badgering you, consider changing doctors. Many women find it helpful to bring a friend to act as an advocate. You can discuss your preferences with your friend prior to the visit. This friend can then act with a level head and support you in taking your time to make informed choices that feel right for you.

Technology and Partnership Issues

Some women reach a relationship impasse when deciding what to do next. Often the woman trying to conceive isn't ready to give up and wants to go one or even many steps further to achieve pregnancy, while her partner isn't willing to go any further. There are a number of reasons for this. The partner of the woman trying to conceive often feels more distanced from the process. Perhaps she'd like you to stop trying because she thinks that if you aren't able to get pregnant "naturally," then it's her turn to try to conceive. Or perhaps your partner is unwilling to support your trying other options for ethical or financial reasons. Or maybe she's emotionally exhausted and doesn't share the same emotional stake in biological parenting, leading her to feel ready to adopt rather than to keep pushing to conceive.

Sometimes it's the partner who isn't conceiving who wants the mother-to-be to engage with technology and stop trying so long to conceive "naturally." Philosophical differences in approaches to fertility and conception often become highlighted during extended preconception periods. Perhaps your partner places much more faith in medicine, which drives her to encourage you to receive treatments you don't want or feel ready for. Or she may be growing tired of the level of emotional support required of her each month and want to move the process along. Or perhaps she's eager to get her chance to try and is subconsciously rushing you along in the process.

These kinds of struggles can put a serious strain on a relationship. If you reach such an impasse, it's important that neither of you simply acquiesce to the other. Both of you do need to be on the same page in order to stop or forge ahead. If you can't come to a place of peaceful agreement, enlist an unbiased friend or professional to help the two of you navigate this very emotional territory.

Neither of you wants to look back on this time and the decisions you made with resentment toward the other. Harboring resentment and anger, at either yourself for going along with your partner's choice or at your partner for having all the decision-making power, can ruin a relationship. It's valuable to reevaluate the process by which you make decisions in your relationship and to fine-tune it if necessary. To remind yourself about making decisions see Chapter 2.

Causes of Infertility

Infertility problems are fairly evenly divided between male factors, female factors, and the unknown. Sometimes infertility has multiple factors. We'll start by discussing sperm factors. A man may have been born with a structural or chromosomal abnormality that affects his ejaculation or sperm production. Injury, past disease, current infection, toxic exposure, or nutritional deficiency can also affect sperm production. The sperm can clump up—this is called agglutination—so that they can't swim. They may have other problems swimming, be abnormally shaped or low in number, or lack the capacity to do certain biochemical processes in the female body that allow them to fertilize the egg. The man may have antibodies against his own sperm that trigger his immune system to destroy his sperm (or the woman may have antibodies against his sperm that lead her immune system to attack them once in her body).

The other crucial cell involved in conception is the egg. Many infertility challenges are related to ovulation problems. When women run out of healthy eggs that can respond to hormone messages (described in Chapter 3), their fertility decreases and eventually they go into menopause. Some women in their 20s and early 30s experience "premature ovarian failure"—meaning they run out of eggs early. This is, fortunately, not the most common fertility problem. Sometimes there's a problem with the functioning of the pituitary gland, which can affect any of a number of essential ovulation hormones. Other factors affecting these hormones are excess exercise, chronic illness, stress, and weight loss. These factors may affect the delicate balance of hormones in the brain, thus disrupting fertility, without necessarily causing changes in menstrual cycle regularity or length. Sometimes other hormone imbalances hamper fertility, such as those caused by polycystic ovarian syndrome, or those occurring in the thyroid or adrenal glands.

If egg and sperm are both released and functioning well, the next step is for them to meet. Besides the antibodies we mentioned, another potential obstacle is that the woman may not have enough fertile mucus for the sperm to enter the uterus. In addition, both men and women can have blocked tubes. We discuss causes of blocked fallopian tubes in detail later in this chapter.

If the egg and sperm meet in the fallopian tube and conception occurs, the tiny developing bundle of cells we call an embryo must attach itself to the lining of the uterus and start to grow placenta. Sometimes structural problems in the uterus prevent the embryo from having a good spot to implant. These abnormalities that prevent the lining of the uterus from growing rich and thick and nurturing can include anomalies a woman was born with, fibroids, endometriosis, or a hormonal problem such as a "luteal phase defect." There are other more rare situations that we don't mention here. Indeed, this may appear to be such an extensive list that it's amazing anyone can conceive. Yet we know many women do, many even unintentionally or despite their best efforts not to. And in fact, many women with infertility challenges do conceive on their own without "high-tech" interventions if they inseminate long enough. The next section describes a number of standard tests for gathering more information about any of the above challenges that maybe apply to you. We then go on to discuss treatment options.

Diagnostic Tests and Procedures

As mentioned, 40% of infertility cannot be explained. So although we outline some of the available diagnostic options, it's quite possible that you may never know why you aren't getting pregnant.

Blood Tests

If you're reading this chapter because you've been trying to get pregnant for more than six months, and you haven't already had your hormone levels tested, then it's time to do so. This is especially important if you're nearing 40 or have irregular cycles. By irregular cycles we mean cycles that are as short as 24 days or longer than 32 days, mid-cycle bleeding, very heavy or light periods, or cycle lengths that vary dramatically. If you're in your late 30s or 40s, or if you've had questionable levels of any of your hormones in past labs, we recommend that you get your hormones tested two to three times a year.

This information can help you relax if you find you have no significant hormone imbalance or indication of infertility. It can also let you see how rapidly your body is moving toward menopause and help you make decisions that reflect this rate of change. You can use the information to target your fertility therapies as well. The following are common basic fertility tests: FSH, estradiol, progesterone, thyroid, prolactin, and cervical culture for chlamydia. These are described in Chapter 3.

The "Clomiphene Challenge"

The clomiphene challenge involves taking a low to medium dose of clomiphene (described in detail on pages 356–360 of this chapter) to stimulate the ovaries. FSH and estradiol levels are expected to change a certain amount in response to the drug, and ideally at least one ovary should respond by maturing multiple egg follicles. Some physicians feel this is a more accurate test of fertility than simply checking FSH and estradiol levels in the blood during a regular unmedicated ("natural") cycle; other physicians don't consider the test particularly insightful.

Hysterosalpingogram (HSG)

An HSG is a medical procedure in which 3–6 ml of dye is injected into the uterus and fallopian tubes through the cervix. An X ray will show if the dye moves from the uterus into the fallopian tubes and then out the ends. This checks whether the tubes are blocked and whether you have intrauterine lesions such as polyps, fibroids, or scar tissue—any of which may impede conception. Scar tissue blocking tubes internally or tangling them externally is usually caused by pelvic infection (often from gonorrhea or chlamydia bacteria), post-abortion infection, a ruptured appendix, past tubal pregnancy, or abdominal surgery. Interestingly, almost half of the women whose HSG shows pelvic scar tissue or tubal damage have no history of any of these. Many women with scar tissue, though, unknowingly had chlamydia at some point in the past without showing any symptoms.

Some women choose to get an HSG even if they've never had any of these illnesses or conditions, just to confirm that their tubes are clear. An HSG "washes" out the tubes; thus even for women who have no visible obstructions, it's still possible that undetected minor blockages will be cleared through the procedure. As a result, for many women fertility seems to increase during the three months following an HSG.

HSG Considerations

The HSG procedure involves a series of X ray exposures, which are directed at your ovaries and uterus. This is a strong reason to carefully consider whether to choose an HSG without apparent cause. Expert texts suggest that three films (be-fore, during, and after) are sufficient, but many practitioners expose patients to more X rays to pick up details that are probably insignificant to conception. During the procedure, many practitioners performing HSGs prescribe antibiotics that aren't considered safe for pregnancy. This eliminates the possibility of inseminating during the month of the procedure. If you ask, you may find that these antibiotics are op-tional. Likewise, although some women feel only slight discomfort, others experi-ence the procedure as extremely painful.

Biopsy, Ultrasound, and Laparoscopy

An endometrial biopsy is the removal of a very small portion of the lining of the uterus through a narrow plastic tube placed through the cervix. A tissue specialist will examine it for cancerous cells if biopsy is performed to diagnose the cause of ab-normal uterine bleeding. If the biopsy is part of a fertility workup, he or she will ex-amine the sample for its thickness and progesterone level. Most women find the pro-cedure fairly uncomfortable but very quick. This method of assessing adequate progesterone is considered more accurate than a blood test.

The following procedures can help determine whether you have ovarian cysts, fibroids, or endometriosis. A regular ultrasound cannot always determine whether fi-broids, polyps, ovarian cysts, or other obstructions are present. A sonohysterogram, however, is a more detailed or high-resolution form of ultrasound that is better at detecting these problems, as water is injected into the uterus in order to slightly push the walls apart. In fact, a sonohysterogram will often show if the tubes are blocked without subjecting a woman to the X ray radiation of an HSG. A sonohysterogram is done by transvaginal ultrasound, which involves having the patient lie on the ex-amining table with her feet in stirrups and inserting a transducer, which is about the size of a speculum, into the vagina. Immediately an image of the pelvic organs will appear on the ultrasound screen. Some women feel vulnerable during the exam and feel discomfort or pain from the internal pressure of the transducer moving around, as well as from the water placed in the uterus.

If you have pelvic pain, fibroids, endometriosis, and/or unusual bleeding, some-times a biopsy, diagnostic hysteroscopy, or diagnostic laparoscopy is recommended. These procedures can sample or produce an onscreen image of the endometrial lin-ing and pelvic organs. Hysteroscopy involves looking at the inside of the uterus through a fiber optic tube inserted through the cervix. Laparoscopy is surgery that shows an onscreen image of the pelvic organs with a fiber optics tube placed in the abdomen via a small incision. If corrective treatment is needed, instruments can be placed through the incision.

Sometimes you can be asymptomatic yet have obstructions in your uterus that prevent you from getting pregnant. During a laparoscopy, endometriosis tissues and fibroids can be removed. Once these are removed, it may be easier to achieve and maintain a pregnancy. The extent to which endometriosis and fibroids affect fertility, and the extent to which the benefits of surgery supercede the inherent risks of surgery, is a matter of much debate. Many factors are at play, including the size and location of the fibroids as well as the location and severity of endometriosis. Not all of these factors may be fully known until the surgery is actually performed.

Infertility Treatments

Fertility Medications

The use of fertility medications has become so widespread for women who use insemination to achieve pregnancy that it's almost scary. Fertility medications have serious potential side effects that often aren't discussed with the women who will be taking them. Often women are automatically prescribed clomiphene (Clomid, Serophene) or one of the injectable gonadotropins (Repronex, Humagon, Fertinex, Follistim, Perganol) before they begin to inseminate, simply because they're over 35 or 38 years old. If a woman of any age hasn't achieved pregnancy in a few months, all too frequently the blanket recommendation from fertility specialists is to take fertility drugs. This is often recommended instead of suggesting that a woman inseminate more frequently in a cycle or change her insemination timing. These options are rarely, if ever, mentioned, which just goes to show that the field of infertility is heterosexually biased. Fertility specialists often don't take into consideration our special circumstances, such as the decreased quantities of sperm we are often using, and the fact that working with frozen sperm and working with fresh sperm require two entirely different fertility plans and approaches.

Clomiphene

Clomiphene, known by the brand names Clomid and Serophene, is a drug that's usually taken from day 5 to day 9 of the cycle to promote ovulation. Some medical consumer advocates feel clomiphene is overprescribed and that women are underinformed about its potential risks versus benefits.

How It Works

Clomiphene isn't a concentrated fertility hormone like injectable fertility drugs. It's a chemical that blocks cells from recognizing estrogen. The pituitary gland in the brain produces follicle stimulating hormone (FSH) to stimulate the ovarian follicles to mature eggs. The follicles in the ovary, in response to FSH, produce estrogen when stimulated. One of the jobs estrogen has is to let the brain know the FSH message was received. When the brain gets the estrogen signal, it knows it's producing enough FSH to prepare the eggs in the ovary for ovulation. If a woman takes clomiphene, the cells in her pituitary gland can't receive the estrogen message since the drug is connected to the receptor sites (where the estrogen message is received) on the cells instead. Thus, the brain continues to produce higher and higher levels of FSH, "thinking" that the ovaries aren't responding. The effects of clomiphene last longer than the five days during which it is taken, since it stays bound to brain cells for weeks.

If a woman isn't ovulating but has eggs and the ability to make FSH, clomiphene can help stimulate ovulation. There's some thought that clomiphene can also help women who are almost ovulating or whose eggs aren't maturing quite enough before ovulation. This can be a cause of "luteal phase defect" or low progesterone during the second half of the cycle. Clomiphene is routinely prescribed for this.

Be an Informed Consumer

In addition to the aforementioned specific purposes for which clomiphene was designed, the drug is often prescribed to any woman who's having trouble conceiving. Studies haven't shown, however, that clomiphene increases the chances of pregnancy in women who are already ovulating. Clomiphene should be started at a low dose, which can be increased if ovulation or conception do not occur.

Checking FSH and estradiol levels and getting ultrasound just prior to ovulation to check on follicular response are useful in monitoring whether clomiphene is actually helping ovulation occur. Many experts, however, consider it adequate proof if a woman's basal body temperature charting shows a clear temperature rise in a way that indicates ovulation. Keep in mind that clomiphene is much less successful in increasing conception rates for women over 35. Nearly all pregnancies for women over 35 who are taking clomiphene and using IUI occur in the first four months of use.

Side Effects

Although it's called "cheap, safe, and effective" in fertility textbooks, clomiphene has some significant side effects. Five percent of women taking it experience abdominal pain, 1.5% experience vision changes from decreased blood flow to the eyes, and many women experience mood changes. Each woman responds differently to the drug. Although some women don't experience mood shifts when taking clomiphene, many experience depression, uncontrollable rage, paranoia, and hysterical crying. These common side effects are usually downplayed, if mentioned at all, when clomiphene is prescribed. If you experience these emotional reactions to taking clomiphene or any fertility medication, we suggest you mobilize a support network. If you're seeing a therapist or psychiatrist, notify him or her about your medication. It's essential to be cautious about making significant life decisions, such as quitting your job—or murdering your partner!—during these cycles.

Clomiphene can cause ovarian cysts, which usually, but not always, recede after stopping use of the drug. In addition, 5% of women taking clomiphene experience significant ovarian enlargement, since their ovaries are so stimulated. This is called ovarian hyperstimulation syndrome. Hyperstimulation greatly enlarges the ovaries with fluid, which can leak into the abdominal cavity and cause serious side effects, including shock, respiratory distress, kidney problems, and even death. Symptoms may include severe pain in the pelvis, abdomen, and chest; nausea; vomiting; bloating; weight gain; and difficulty breathing. Call your doctor or go to the nearest emergency room immediately if you experience any of these symptoms while taking clomiphene.

Ovarian hyperstimulation can take seven to 20 days to fully resolve. Women diagnosed with it are usually advised to avoid penetrative intercourse, gynecological exams, and exercise until the ovaries return to normal.

Although clomiphene stimulates ovulation, conception rates with clomiphene are surprisingly low. Clomiphene can limit the ability of the cervix and uterus to respond to estrogen just as it does with the brain, which can lead to a decrease in fertile mucus and possible changes in the endometrium.

Some studies have shown an increased risk of certain kinds of ovarian cancer in women who take clomiphene or other fertility drugs. These results are up for debate, but current protocol is not to prescribe ovulation-stimulating drugs for more than six months total. If women take clomiphene for three to four months and then take injectable fertility drugs for a number of cycles, their total number of months of exposure can easily exceed six months.

The only studies on the potential fetal effects of clomiphene have been analyzed with data from observable defects in newborns at the time of birth. There are few if any longer-term studies. It's also important to note that up to 10% of women conceiving with clomiphene have twins.

Clomiphene and Insemination Timing

Usually when a woman takes clomiphene, her ovulation changes from its normal day to anywhere from day 14 to day 21 of her cycle, usually occurring on day 16 or 17. We've seen some women ovulate sooner rather than later, usually around day 10. It can be difficult to predict ovulation and to time insemination when using clomiphene, since a woman's ovulation date will probably occur later than usual, her fertile mucus will be decreased, and the drug may affect the results of her ovulation predictor kit.

Injectables

Injectable gonadotropins (fertility drugs) are useful for women who aren't ovulating because of insufficient hormones, or for women whose eggs need extremely high levels of hormones to respond. Fertility medications are either synthetic or distilled from menopausal women's urine. These medications push your body to mature multiple eggs each cycle.

Fertility drugs can cause discomfort at the injection site. Like clomiphene, they can also cause hormonal mood swings. When taking injectables, it's also common to experience extreme physical tension, and many women on these drugs suffer from very sensitive breasts. In addition, 1%–2% of women taking injectables experience mild to severe ovarian hyperstimulation syndrome, described in greater depth in the previous section on clomiphene.

It's common for a woman to ovulate significantly earlier or later when using fertility medications than during nonmedicated cycles. Fertility medications are very expensive, as are the monitoring tools needed for each medicated cycle. So before you decide to use medications, make sure it's the best choice for you. Some women choose to alternate between a medicated cycle and a regular cycle to give their body and psyche a break.

HCG Injections

Although HCG is a hormone produced during pregnancy, it happens to also function to signal the body to ovulate like LH. Because HCG is easier to concentrate than LH, it's sold by prescription pharmaceutically to be given by injection to trigger ovulation when a woman on ovulation-stimulating fertility drugs has fully mature egg follicles. Some clinics routinely administer HCG shots to help with the timing of insemination; others do not use this technology.

Some women choose to get an HCG shot when they're monitoring their cycles by ultrasound, even if they aren't using fertility drugs. The rationale is that they can tell by ultrasound when the eggs are in the optimum state to be ovulated and trigger ovulation with the HCG shot more accurately than their own bodies would. Although this isn't our general recommendation, it is a way of ensuring that when everything looks opportune ovulation will actually occur, and your inseminations can be scheduled based on when you receive the shot.

On the other hand, women occasionally choose to decline the HCG shot that is routinely given to women using fertility medications. Some women feel there isn't enough conclusive evidence that it will help them conceive. Others feel that the fertility medications they're taking interfere enough with the natural process and that their body will ovulate when it's ready.

It's important to realize that since HCG is the pregnancy hormone that urine pregnancy tests monitor, if you perform a pregnancy test too close to the time of your HCG injection you may receive a false-positive result. Likewise, symptoms of pregnancy may appear as HCG runs through your bloodstream, although you may not necessarily have conceived.

Ultrasounds for Fertility Monitoring

Some women monitor a cycle with ultrasound but decline fertility medication. By following a cycle with ultrasound they can confirm that they're ovulating. They'll also know much more precisely when they're ovulating so they can time their inseminations effectively and correlate the ultrasound information with the signs they've been monitoring to see if their timing has been correct.

Other women decline the ultrasounds early in the month and only use ultrasound closer to ovulation to reduce the amount of time spent in the doctor's office and to reduce their exposure to ultrasound.

Often ultrasounds are ordered for women using clomiphene, not necessarily to time ovulation but to see if the drug is working in the desired way. One scientific article suggests that a woman using clomiphene to ovulate or to overcome a short luteal phase doesn't need an ultrasound to find out if the drug is working if she charts her basal body temperature. If her BBT remains high for at least 11 days after ovulation, this is considered adequate information to determine that the drug is working. If her BBT is questionable, her progesterone level can be checked in the second half of the cycle to see if it's high enough.

Blood Work for Fertility Monitoring

In some fertility practices it's routine to have your blood drawn every other day. This information is used to monitor your hormonal shifts throughout the month and help determine the timing of the HCG shot. This information can be quite helpful as you can gain much information about your body and hormone levels. Some women, however, decline these monthly rounds of labs. Many of these women believe they aren't necessary or are too time intensive, or they're afraid of having blood drawn. Some women will monitor a cycle this way once or twice a year; others monitor their cycle this way whenever they're using fertility medication. And still others decline the medications but feel that the hormone-level information, in tandem with the ultrasound information, is invaluable in helping them diagnose subtle imbalances and more effectively time their inseminations. Pick and choose what feels appropriate to you.

Our Recommendations on Fertility Medications and Monitoring

If you choose to take fertility drugs, it's important to maximize your chances of conception, since each cycle you spend on the drugs carries increased health risks.

Thus, if you're on the fertility-treatment track, be sure to inseminate at least two times each cycle. Consider doing the first of these at home vaginally to increase your time coverage and follow it with a well-timed IUI.

If you plan to take clomiphene, do so for only three to six cycles at the most. Do everything you can during those cycles to optimize your chances of conception: Inseminate more frequently, stay lying down for a longer period of time afterward, and definitely don't compromise on your timing.

Do not take fertility medications without monitoring your cycle by ultrasound and/or hormone checks and/or basal body temperature. Monitoring your cycles by ultrasound can help you to recognize ovarian hyperstimulation early on and can confirm that the medications are indeed working at the dosage being given. Many doctors prescribe clomiphene to any woman who's not getting pregnant, without informing her of the health risks or offering fertility monitoring. We strongly suggest that you request or do some type of monitoring if you choose to take any fertility medications.

After receiving an HCG shot, it's important to get the timing of your inseminations down. All too many fertility clinics recommend a woman inseminate just once in the 36 hours after an HCG injection. At Maia, we feel this is too late for some women. If you're relying entirely on the fertility monitoring of the ultrasound and blood draws as your signs of fertility rather than on your own signs, then the ideal approach would be to inseminate three times: once when you receive your shot, once 18 hours later, and once between 24 and 36 hours after your injection. Or you can inseminate two times, once at 18 hours post injection and once at 24–36 hours post injection.

Many women who are monitoring their own fertility, however, experience a discrepancy between when their body starts to exhibit signs of peak fertility (fertile mucus, open cervix, high sex drive) and when they're told to give themselves their shot. The body usually indicates high fertility earlier than the time recommended for the injection and subsequent insemination. Thus, we recommend that you do an at-home vaginal insemination when your body indicates that it's the best time. Don't fret if this is sooner than your doctor recommends and sooner than the injection is scheduled; this insemination will have viable sperm for the next 18-24 hours. The IUI can be timed according to the shot.

We've worked with many women who got pregnant when they incorporated an at-home vaginal insemination at the time they felt the most fertile and/or an at-home insemination 18 hours post injection. This insemination is in addition to the IUI performed at the clinic.

In Vitro Fertilization (IVF)

In vitro fertilization occurs when conception takes place outside of the body. It's a treatment for a variety of infertility problems, both male and female. Depending on your age and fertility status, either your eggs or a donor's eggs are "retrieved" and then the donor sperm is mixed with the available eggs. The remaining eggs, as well as the extra embryos, are then frozen and saved. Some women adopt other women's embryos and have these embryos implanted into their uterus instead of using their own eggs or a donor's eggs and a donor's sperm.

When it's time for insertion into your body, multiple embryos are placed into your uterus—usually two to four. After implantation occurs, a sonogram will be used to determine how many embryos have implanted. Then, if more than two embryos have implanted, you may choose to have a procedure called selective reduction performed. This is the procedure by which certain embryos are vacuumed out of your uterus so that you are not carrying too many embryos at once.

Women under the age of 35 have a success rate, on average, of 30% for each cycle. Women 39 or older, when using their own eggs, have a 10% pregnancy rate per cycle. The rate of multiples (mostly twins and triplets) is often around 35%, depending on how many embryos are transferred. All these statistics are approximate, since they are influenced by each clinic's protocol and each woman's body.

If you're seriously considering IVF, there's a lot of information available on the subject. See the resource list at the end of the chapter.

Advantages of IVF

Some women feel it's absolutely necessary for them to carry a baby and to give birth. For these women, IVF provides an opportunity to do so when nothing else has worked. If they can afford it, women choosing IVF often prefer to use donor eggs and get pregnant rather than adopt or live without children. These women believe strongly that the bonding with a baby that you gestate, birth, and nurse is radically different than the bonding possible through adoption. This incredible procedure affords them the opportunity to bond with their infant right from the start. Sometimes a lesbian choosing IVF is able to use her partner's eggs. This is a remarkable benefit of infertility—perhaps the only benefit—as it is biologically a way of making a baby together. You grow, birth, and nurse the baby that carries your partner's genes.

Disadvantages of IVF

In vitro can cost $8,000–$25,000 per cycle and even more if you're using an egg donor. Some people actually find that it's less expensive to travel outside the United States to receive IVF. And, unfortunately, despite all the time, energy, and money you may invest, there's no guarantee that IVF will work for you.

Another significant consideration when using IVF is that the process of selective reduction is emotionally excruciating. The women we have worked with who had multiple pregnancies have all reported back to us that they wished they had been counseled more thoroughly about how grueling this decision-making process would be. Some women have reported that they would not have chosen IVF had they known.

Is It an Option to Have Your Partner Try to Get Pregnant?

Some lesbian couples have the opportunity to have their partner try to get pregnant. Not all women, however, are able to get pregnant, and not all women want to get pregnant. It's very common to have a female couple in which one woman has always wanted to get pregnant and the other is thrilled to have her partner get pregnant but would never consider bearing a child herself. There's a cultural belief that anyone with female anatomy automatically wants to get pregnant. This is far from true.

Having Your Partner Try: A Mixed Blessing

Deciding to stop trying to conceive and have your partner try instead is a difficult transition for most women. The dynamic is slightly different if your partner has been wanting to get pregnant anyway but you were planning to have the first baby than if your partner is willing to give it a try even though she's never felt the biological drive, need, or desire to get pregnant. If your partner has always wanted to get pregnant, an underlying sense of competition may permeate your choices. Perhaps you wouldn't choose to stop trying at this point if you were the only one who could or wanted to get pregnant. Likewise, if your partner has never really considered getting pregnant but is willing to offer her body up to the cause, you may feel anger or resentment at her lack of appreciation for the amazing opportunity she's being given.

Either way, when your partner starts to inseminate you're relinquishing the possibility of getting pregnant yourself, at least for now. Letting go in this way can be painful. You may feel tremendous loss as you let go of a dream you may have had your entire life. It's vital to honor these feelings and not sweep them under the rug. This may be a good time to enter therapy or search out other forms of support. Although you'll still be parenting, you won't be pregnant or give birth, and this realization can trigger extreme feelings of loss. If this is the case for you, please read Chapter 15 on child-free living.

Take Time Off Before She Tries

When you come to this decision as a couple, it may be in your best interest to take some time off from inseminating before your partner begins to try. You may hear "internal voices" telling you not to skip a month, since you'll be another month further from having a baby. It's unnecessarily emotionally straining to have your partner get pregnant before you've taken the time to process your own feelings.

Take at least one cycle off, and take a vacation together, if you can. Allow time for the two of you to reconnect. Spend time sharing with her how you feel about letting go and the depth of your loss. In addition, take the time to reflect together on the months that you've spent inseminating so far. Are there fond memories you'll both be taking away from this time? Are there things you may like to do differently in the future? And most importantly, are you sure you're ready to let go? If you're not truly ready, it's essential that you discuss this.

The transition from one partner trying to conceive to the next partner can be wrought with emotions. Take the time now to do your personal and joint emotional work so that you can move freely into the present and the future. You'll be grateful you did.

What Does an IVF Cycle Look Like?

After you ovulate, before your next period, you'll receive injections of a GnRH agonist that calms your hormones. Then you'll get an ultrasound to make sure your ovaries have no cysts before you start your IVF-cycle medicines. At the beginning of your cycle, you'll receive your fertility drug injections, and may take some vaginal suppositories or use creams to make sure you have no yeast or bacteria that could interfere. Your hormones and ovaries will be monitored every other day with ultrasounds and blood tests, starting around day 7 of the cycle. (10%–15% of cycles are cancelled due to inadequate response to the drugs.)

When one main follicle, called the dominant follicle, is large enough in the ovary, as measured by the ultrasound, you'll receive an HCG injection. The eggs are retrieved less than 36 hours later, with a needle guided by ultrasound that is pushed through the back wall of the vagina into the ovary to rinse the eggs out of the follicle with sterile saline into a little tube. For this short procedure you'll be sedated with IV pain medicine or light anesthesia.

The sperm are washed and added to the egg cells in the lab, and when the embryos are 8–10 cells each, 72–80 hours after the retrieval, they're transferred through a small tube into the uterus while you're awake (without much discomfort), much like an intrauterine insemination. Then you'll either take either progesterone injections or suppositories for the next 10–14 days. Your progesterone will probably be checked by blood draws during this time. If your pregnancy blood test is positive, you'll continue taking progesterone and probably have your HCG level measured to check on fetal development until an ultrasound can show both fetal heartbeat and the number of fetuses.

When Your Partner Makes Different Choices Than You Did

When it's your partner's turn, you have the opportunity to reevaluate together the choices you've made to date. For example, do you want to use the same source of sperm? You may find that your partner is inclined to make different choices than you did. This may be due to differences in nature and attitude toward conception. It may also be influenced by the experience you both have already been through. If her choices bring up negative feelings for you, it's best to get this out into the open.

When Your Partner Gets Pregnant

When your partner gets pregnant it may be hard for you to fully embrace the pregnancy with excitement. If she gets pregnant right away, you may feel angry at how easy it was for her to do so. Although surprising, it's perfectly normal to feel resentment and jealousy. In fact, these emotions are often overwhelming. But you can reduce them if you spend time together sharing your feelings prior to insemination. Some women, however, find it difficult to fully recognize or process their grief until their partner gets pregnant.

Once again, resist the urge to sweep your feelings under the rug. They'll explode when you least expect it, or they'll interfere with the intimacy you're able to have with your partner during pregnancy. Use your feelings as a catalyst for self-exploration. Have the motivation to be able to bond deeply with the baby.

When Your Partner Also Experiences an Extended Conception Period or Miscarriage

Another rocky situation to navigate is when your partner experiences conception challenges or miscarriage. If you felt anger or resentment toward your partner when she became pregnant, you may feel guilty if she then miscarries. The miscarriage isn't your fault, of course, but it's easy to feel like you both will always remember the pregnancy as one you weren't ready for.

If she has inseminated unsuccessfully for just as many cycles as you did, you may feel that it's your turn to try again. But just as it may have been difficult for you to stop trying when she started to inseminate, it may also be difficult for her to relinquish now that she is so personally invested.

This can feel like a weird power struggle. You're both supposed to be on the same team trying to work together to make your baby, yet it can feel like a competition over who will actually get to do it. Remember, adoption is always an option. Also remember that you're in an adult relationship, so if the process doesn't feel consensual or fair, stop and reevaluate.

We can't stress enough how valuable personal and joint therapy can be for you at a time like this. Don't let the stress of an extended conception combined with the stress of being unable to get pregnant yourself break up your relationship. Seek support. Remember that you're probably just regaining trust in your own body for not having allowed you to get pregnant. If now your partner has lost trust in her own body, it can feel like the two of you are lost at sea.

Some couples decide to alternate who is trying each month, some set an arbitrary amount of months each partner is allotted to try for, some base it on who has better health insurance to cover fertility problems. Some talk until one of them is ready to actually let go and let the other forge ahead. Some decide to adopt.

Stay Connected to Your Body

If you were to throw all of the "shoulds" to the wind, how would you try to get pregnant right now? It's important to ask yourself this periodically. Take the time to really listen to your answers. Then give serious consideration to what your heart says. This may include trying fertility medication when you had previously thought you never would. This can include giving yourself permission to take a break.

Women come to us to help them find a more "natural" approach to conception. Often all we do is help them listen to their bodies. This can include stepping off the compelling wheel of technology and returning to the privacy of their own homes, with their own emotions and biorhythms initiating a new sense of self-discovery.

For these women, whether they ultimately end up conceiving or not, a healing has taken place so that they feel once again that their body is their friend. Your body is all that will stay with you for this life, and you must befriend it to have a happy life. This isn't always easy when you're experiencing conception struggles. Nonetheless, do all you can to strengthen your connection to your body and to increase your awareness of your body. Your body isn't separate from who you are and how you feel. We *are* our bodies. We must trust our body wisdom. When you listen to yourself, you'll know when it's time to try something new, when it's time to move on, and when it's time to let go.

Resources

Books

Beyond Second Opinions: Making Choices About Infertility Treatment, Judith Steinberg Turiel, University of California Press, 1998

The Fertility Sourcebook, M. Sara Rosenthal, McGraw Hill, 1995

Inconceivable: Winning the Infertility Game, Julia Indichova, Adell Press, 1997

Parenting Begins Before Conception, Carista Luminare Rosen, Healing Arts Press, 2000

Resolving Infertility, Diane Aronson and RESOLVE, Harper Resource, 2001
The Whole Person Fertility Program, Niravi Payne, Three Rivers Press, 1998
Women's Bodies, Women's Wisdom, Christiane Northrup, Bantam Doubleday, 1998

Organizations
RESOLVE: The National Infertility Association
1310 Broadway
Somerville, MA 02144-1731
Call (617) 623-0744 to locate a chapter near you or visit www.resolve.org.

Chapter 15 Adoption and Child-Free Living

Deciding to stop inseminating and move into the next phase of your life is probably the most difficult decision you'll ever make. It can be very scary to choose to stop inseminating. What if pregnancy is just a month away? It's a deep challenge to let go of this hope. For many women their entire sense of self is inextricably linked with being a biological mother. Letting go of this possibility can feel like letting go of an essential piece of yourself. It's common to feel afraid that if you stop inseminating, you'll cease to exist. Despite the agony of relinquishing your dream of pregnancy, it's important to recognize when it's just not happening for you.

Acknowledging that it's time to make a change and move on can be a gradual realization or a sudden understanding. In any event, when you're unable to conceive or sustain a pregnancy, the time eventually arises when you must recognize this. It takes courage and strength to leave the possibility of pregnancy behind. But moving forward, whether toward adoption or toward child-free living, is a powerful step.

When you're single you may delay the inevitable because of the fear that it will mean continuing to live alone, when you were so desperately ready to share your love with another human being. Single women can fear that adoption will not be feasible due to legal or financial constraints, so continuing to inseminate often seems like the only possible route to parenthood.

If you're partnered, it can also be difficult to imagine moving on. After many months or years, the process of the insemination cycle may feel like it is the basis for all aspects of your relationship. For couples who have devoted years of their lives to trying to get pregnant, there's a fear that stopping inseminating may reveal that there's no longer any spark or connection remaining in the relationship. Thus, the thought of moving on can be filled with the fear of this loss. Not only do you face losing your dream of being pregnant and giving birth to your child, and perhaps your dream of having children at all, but also you face the fear of losing your primary relationship. The fear of losing your partner is often sublimated and can unknowingly cause you to continue inseminating for longer than might otherwise feel right for you.

How Do I Know When It's Time to Move On?

Deciding when the time is right for you to move on to the next part of your life is deeply personal. Some women inseminate for three cycles and then choose to adopt or live without children. Others devote years of their lives to inseminating. Their journeys may have included multiple surgeries, multiple miscarriages, and multiple IVFs. Some women will have depleted their entire life savings and become emotionally deadened before effectively being forced to give up. In other words, some women move on as part of a prearranged time line, some move on because the roller coaster of insemination is too emotionally devastating, and some move on only when they've depleted all their available resources. For most women, however,

Claudia and Kenya

For many years, Claudia and Kenya both wanted to be parents. Claudia wanted to experience pregnancy, while Kenya did not. After inseminating for five months, Claudia conceived. They were delighted to be pregnant. Claudia and Kenya went to their genetic counseling appointment to discuss testing for chromosomal anomalies of the baby, because Claudia was almost 39. They chose to have an amniocentesis. The results came back showing that the baby had Down's Syndrome. They decided to terminate the pregnancy, and Claudia had an abortion at 19 weeks. They started attending a support group to work through their grief.

After six months, they felt ready to try again. Claudia inseminated for six more cycles without conceiving. They were feeling pulled apart by the stress of insemination and some unresolved grief about their first pregnancy. They chose to not move into more medical realms of infertility technology, but to take a few months together to focus on their relationship. They both felt reconnected at the end of this time after having done some counseling work. Having moved through those issues, they felt ready to explore adoption, both feeling relieved to share more equally in the process, and both ready to move toward bringing a baby into their lives in a more definitive time line. They applied to adopt internationally, and within nine months went to Vietnam to bring home their daughter.

deciding to move on comes from a place that feels much more vague and is a combination of the above scenarios.

Regularly checking in with yourself is important, since there are no established, universal indications to tell you when the right time is for you to stop. When you're losing hope and perspective and feel you can't take any more emotionally, it's important to step back and reevaluate. This is best done by taking a break from inseminating. During a break you'll find a more accurate reflection of how much more time, energy, and money you're willing to give this dream. In addition to losing hope, there are other signs that indicate that the time may be close for you to stop inseminating. Take note if you're experiencing any of the following:

• You check in with your body, and it no longer feels fertile to you.
• You find the idea of pregnancy has lost its appeal and that you would actually be relieved to move on with your life.
• You're realizing that a child-free life sounds appealing.
• You hardly remember what life was like prior to inseminating.
• You're so depressed that you're having difficulty functioning in daily life.
• Your fertility signs and tests have shown that your body isn't fertile, and you've tried unsuccessfully for more than eight cycles.
• Your partner is threatening to leave if you don't stop inseminating.
• Adoption sounds more appealing than inseminating.

Deciding to Move on Is Not a Failure

Although it's often heartbreaking, deciding to stop can feel empowering. You're never obligated to try for longer than what feels right to you. Likewise, you don't need to stop just because everyone in your life tells you you're crazy for continuing. You must be ready and willing to take the step yourself. If you make the decision to stop trying to get pregnant due to external pressure, you may feel resentful and may be unable to reach resolution with this part of your life. When you decide the time is right to move on, you've completed this phase of your life and it's easier to reach a place of peace.

Pursuing Adoption While Inseminating

Some women have known from the start that if they're unable to conceive they'll become a parent through adoption. If this is the case for you, it's important to inform yourself of potential age and financial restraints so that you won't unknowingly exclude yourself from the option of adoption. Numerous adoption agencies don't allow women to adopt if they're over 40. Common age limits for international adoption are 43-45 years old. Private adoptions often end up costing $20,000-$50,000.

Some women choose to pursue adoption at the same time they're inseminating. Although this is a lot to think about all at once, adoption can be a lengthy process, and sometimes a parallel path feels best. Many women pursue a joint path for a while, while they research what kind of adoption interests them and begin to fill out the paperwork. This way they allow the possibility of conception to occur right until the last minute.

This decision can be stressful, however, because you run the risk of achieving pregnancy just as your adoption is finalizing and thus run the risk of bringing two new children into your life simultaneously or losing a hefty deposit for your adoption. Likewise, it can be expensive to pursue fertility treatments and adoption concurrently.

Many couples find that pursuing adoption and conception simultaneously can help jump-start their relationship, since they once again feel hopeful about building a family. Many adoption agencies provide classes that can help you feel like parents already. The excitement and inspiration of these classes are contagious qualities.

Other women feel strongly that starting the adoption process would dilute their intention to conceive. They prefer to dedicate all of their focus and intention on conceiving. Such women don't allow themselves to even begin exploring adoption until they've chosen to stop trying to conceive.

Often it's a good sign to yourself that you may be nearing the end of inseminating when you begin to look into adoption.

Loss and Letting Go

As we've said, deciding to stop inseminating takes courage and strength. We wholeheartedly validate and celebrate your courage to do so. When you make the decision to stop inseminating you'll find that you're not the same person as when you began. Grief, pain, longing, hope, and disappointment have transformed you permanently. You are a survivor. You've been on a journey that only others who have experienced infertility can truly understand.

At first the pain and grief are devastating, but over time you regain a positive outlook on life and begin anew. Some women have been through the stages of grief and loss while inseminating; they're able to start life fresh the moment they decide to stop. The length of your grieving process is unique to you, but allow yourself a full year to reemerge from your cocoon after you stop inseminating. If it takes less time, celebrate. If it takes longer, seek the support you need.

Many women describe experiencing infertility as feeling like a part of their heart has been shaved off, while a callus has grown over the rest of it. Women sometimes describe feeling defective, dry, barren, or not being a "true woman."

In a partnership, the feeling of being barren isn't restricted to the woman trying to conceive. Both of you have been yearning for so long that you both share the feeling of being let down by the universe. For both individuals and couples, a feeling of flatness can consume your entire existence.

The grieving process of infertility is akin to the grieving process surrounding the loss of a child. Just because you haven't conceived or held a pregnancy to term doesn't mean you're not a grieving *parent*. When you allow yourself to feel the depth of your loss and make room for the grief as you'd expect of any parent who has lost a child, eventually you'll more fully be able to move on. Although extreme feelings are to be expected with such letting go, please monitor your mental and emotional state of being. Seek help at any time, but especially if you're unable to function or feel things are getting worse.

Regaining Trust

After you stop inseminating, it's natural to feel that your body has failed you. If you feel betrayed, whether by your body, medicine, or even God, the journey back to trust may be long. This is important to recognize. When you acknowledge your loss of trust, you're able to have more self-compassion. It's especially important to be aware of your loss of trust if you're quickly moving toward adoption, as it may directly influence your parenting. Don't allow your heart to close down to love, as painful as it may be to stay emotionally open and vulnerable. Love will heal your pain. Closing down will only push the pain further inside.

Whether you decide to adopt or to live without children, dedicate some of your newly available time to rebuilding inspiration and confidence in your life. Start up a new hobby or activity. Perhaps it will be physical activity such as rock climbing or mountain biking. Maybe you'll learn to design furniture, remodel your bathroom, or take a dance class. Give yourself the gift of learning something new. If you're partnered, this may be a wonderful opportunity to take up a new interest together as well as individually. Finding something new to bond over can shift your dominant shared experience away from trying to conceive to a completely new and refreshing focus.

Relief

When you decide to stop pursuing pregnancy, it's also perfectly normal to feel as if a huge burden has been lifted. Many women are surprised by this relief and respond by feeling guilty, because they think it means they must not have really wanted to be pregnant. This is far from true. Relief is a good sign that you're letting go; relief indicates that you're beginning to acknowledge just how intense a project you've been undertaking. Remember, infertility is commonly considered to be as big a stress as terminal illness. Of course, then, you'll naturally feel some relief when you choose to move on with your life.

Kelly and Josette

Kelly and Josette had been talking about having children off and on throughout the 10 years of their relationship. When Josette turned 36, they decided to begin inseminating.

Josette had a history of endometriosis, for which she had been taking birth control pills. She'd had surgery for it when she was 27, which had given her relief for a few years. Her period, when she wasn't taking the pill, was very irregular. She tried to conceive for two years, with much medical intervention but no success. After a lot of discussion they decided that Kelly would try to conceive, and she became pregnant the first cycle. Kelly spotted throughout the first trimester and miscarried at 12 weeks.

Josette felt a lot of guilt about the miscarriage, because she had been feeling ambivalent about the pregnancy. She had expected to be done with her feelings of loss about her own experience inseminating and be thrilled that they'd have a baby with the help of Kelly's body. Instead she felt resentment, estrangement, and more sadness. They sorted out each of their own experiences and felt ready to try again.

Kelly conceived fairly quickly three more times, each time miscarrying between eight and 15 weeks of pregnancy. Each time she miscarried, the fetal tissue showed a different kind of chromosomal abnormality. A perinatal specialist advised Kelly that as she was 42 years old, her eggs were "just too old," and she should look at doing in vitro fertilization with eggs from someone younger. Josette was not a suitable egg donor because she was also considered too old.

Kelly and Josette had relatives who were willing to donate eggs, but they didn't know if they were willing to go through more of this. When they took a vacation together, they remembered all the fun they used to have together, before they had devoted the last four years to trying to conceive. They remembered all the reasons they each had been ambivalent about having children earlier in their relationship. They thought of all the extended family and friends whose children they were close to, and how they could love these children in a way that left them free to do lots of grown-up playing. They decided to live without children and invested the very last of their "baby funds" into backpacking equipment.

Although their friends and family had to go through their own grief process, by the time Kelly and Josette decided not to have children, they felt amazingly relieved and ready to move on.

Allowing Yourself to Feel Happy Again

It can take active effort and intention to permit yourself to feel happy again. Most women who have experienced infertility have become so accustomed to sadness and disappointment, and to monitoring their hope so that they won't feel so devastated month after month, that they don't remember what happiness feels like. This often results in an instinctual response of fear when happiness does come their way. Happiness can be so unfamiliar that they instinctively guard themselves against it. Keep an eye on this tendency. Feeling good and enjoying life does not discount your grief. You're allowed to feel both! Still, you may need some help with this. Being spontaneous in your joy may make you afraid that your sadness will be unleashed. Let go of this control over emotional expression. Practice laughing and smiling. Watch funny movies, do silly things. Through ever-increasing bursts of happiness, joy will return to your life. Happiness doesn't need to be rationed—give in to it whenever you can!

Rebuilding Your Relationship

The journey to and through infertility can seriously impact a relationship. Strengthening and rebuilding your relationship can take time and concerted energy. Some partners have had the foresight to enter therapy together before this point and have worked hard to maintain their intimacy throughout the insemination and infertility journey. Others have not. Regardless as to where you are at this point, it takes dedication to nurture your partnership after having undergone such emotional turmoil together.

Emotional Intimacy

Infertility often causes people to shut down emotionally as a way of handling overwhelmingly difficult feelings. Although this intentional or subconscious tactic can provide a sense of self-protection, it also means separating yourself from having any positive feelings. You become emotionally numb. A side effect of this coping mechanism is becoming distanced from your partner. If this has happened to you, you must slowly find your way back to each other, which can be frightening. Having a satisfying relationship, however, requires emotional availability. If emotional disconnection has been your means to self-protection, it's a good idea to seek support from outside sources as you come back to yourself, since you may find many feelings flooding forth in the beginning. Women find counseling, support groups, and online support groups to be helpful ways of sharing the intensity of their feelings.

Recognizing Limiting Roles

Many couples fall into roles during the preconception process that can become deeply ingrained over time. Often the woman who is to become the biological mother, in her role, needs to be sheltered and taken care of. She is the one whose emotions have been given top priority. Likewise, the nonbiological mother-to-be has usually taken to processing her emotions outside of the relationship in order to allow more space for her partner's feelings. She has often been acting as the "knight in shining armor," taking on a protector role. After a number of months she often stops sharing her feelings both about the conception process and about the rest of her life.

Although these roles seem to serve women through the preconception process, they don't necessarily nurture the relationship in the long run. When you stop pursuing pregnancy, your roles may often be very unbalanced and no longer appropriate. It's important to recognize if the two of you have slipped into any such roles so that you can change your interpersonal dynamic to one that more appropriately reflects your current situation. It takes effort to come together as equals again, and it can take time to relearn how to share emotional and daily issues that don't pertain to pregnancy and fertility.

Sexual Intimacy

Many women stop having sex in the very early days of inseminating. In fact, for lesbians this seems to be the norm. If you've been inseminating for more than six months, the odds are probably low that you're maintaining an active sex life. Regaining a sexual connection can deepen intimacy, togetherness, and even emotional healing. Regaining sexual intimacy can also be one of the hardest things for women to do.

Sex is emotional. Making love can release such strong emotions that we can automatically shut down sexual response when we shut down emotional response. It makes sense that by limiting the vulnerability you're willing to experience, you're able to feel safer and more in control of your world. Ironically, by shutting down this venue of connection you're also shutting out a rich source of comfort, pleasure, and release.

Many couples find that after a lapse in sexual activity it helps to discuss the awkwardness and shyness they each feel. Often the sexual intimacy in relationships disappears for reasons that are complicated and full of history. Although you may feel shame and guilt that you're struggling with this issue, it's very common. Honor that your subconscious intention is to protect yourself, and seek ways that are gentle and safe to explore returning to your sexuality. Dedication and love, including self-love primarily, are the key ingredients to regaining sexual intimacy. Therapy, either alone or as a couple, will probably be very helpful. Self-exploration is key.

It can take time to learn to trust yourself, your body, your partner, and life enough to let go fully. Don't judge yourself for this. A simple first step is to make regular dates with your partner. In the beginning these dates may just be time set aside specifically to touch in a way that feels comfortable, perhaps snuggling and massaging each other or relearning how to open up and share. Often these regular dates, coupled with finding safe ways to communicate honestly, go a long way toward regaining an active sex life. With these steps, you'll be able to regain this wonderful part of lesbian love.

New Beginnings

When you've decided to stop pursuing pregnancy, life opens up with new possibilities. What do you want to do with your life? Although many women know they want to adopt, others aren't as sure about what they want to do. It isn't always easy to decide to adopt or to live without children. Child-free living may mean choosing to live without parenting and without children having primary roles in your life. For other women child-free living means finding other ways in which a child or children can have a significant place in their life.

Whether or not you're clear about what your next step will be, now is a good time to take a break for a few months or take a vacation. Find a way to honor the long journey you've been on and lay it to rest. You're beginning a new chapter in your life. Immediately, or over time, you'll probably be struck by the profound freedom you have to choose what to do with the rest of your life. So much potential feels amazing!

Once you've taken some time away from pursuing pregnancy, you'll usually find that you already know whether you would like to adopt. Allow your heart to show you what you would truly like to do. It's perfectly fine to adopt; it's perfectly fine to live without children. It's your decision—there's no "right" or "wrong" way to live your life.

Once you've decided which path you're going to take, you reach the often overwhelming task of telling all the people who knew you were trying to get pregnant. Many women find that aside from their closest friends, it's easiest to tell people all at once. Some women send a letter or E-mail to any relevant people. Some use this time as an opportunity to acknowledge the distance friends and family may have felt during the latter part of the preconception period by explaining how consuming the process has been. This kind of letter is a broad way of both opening up to support and reducing the number of times you bring up the subject of infertility.

Adoption

There are a few issues that are important to consider when you decide to pursue adoption after having experienced infertility as a lesbian or single woman.

If you choose to adopt, you must be completely clear that you want to adopt and that you're ready to become a full parent in this way. When adoption is your second choice after pregnancy, you may feel that your adopted child is a substitute or second-rate in comparison to a biological child. If you have these feelings, we urge you to seek counseling prior to adopting and throughout the first year after adoption. It's very important that you bond fully with your child and that your child isn't led to feel that s/he is second-rate. Feelings such as these can obviously interfere with your ability to bond with your child. These feelings usually are actually perceptions of self-inadequacy that are projected onto your child and need to be addressed so that you can have the necessary self-esteem and confidence to parent to your highest potential.

Adoption Considerations for Lesbians

In all states in this country it's legal to adopt as a single mother. In most states two partnered women must choose one to be the legal adoptive parent, and then complete a second-parent adoption, if available, for the other parent. (See Chapter 18.) In all international adoptions at this point, one woman adopts the baby as a "single" parent. Once the child is in the United States, you can pursue a second-parent adoption for the other parent, if this option is available. Women choosing to adopt privately must decide whether or not they'll be closeted to the caseworker and the birth parents. Whether or not both women will legally be allowed to be named on the finalized adoption papers, they may choose to be out as a couple to prospective birth parents and adoption agency workers. This lessens their chances of being selected but allows them to be honest about their family structure.

When partnered lesbians pursue adoption there are a number of factors to consider. One of the benefits of choosing to start the adoption process is that the partner who wasn't trying to get pregnant can take the lead for a while and start researching options and making appointments. This can be a huge relief, since the bureaucratic elements of pursuing adoption can be quite time consuming and women who have been inseminating for a long time often aren't ready to undertake such efforts right away. They may be thrilled, however, to have their partner do this work. The woman who wasn't trying to get pregnant can finally feel like she's able to do something practical that will further the process along instead of just having a supporting role.

Another benefit to adoption is that you can be more flexible about how you divide parenting responsibilities, as neither of you will automatically breastfeed. Even if you choose to nurse through a supplemental nursing system (see Chapter 19), you could both choose to nurse your baby if you wanted.

This new flexibility can become complicated if the partner who was trying to get pregnant was planning on being the stay-at-home parent, or primary caretaker, and she doesn't want to relinquish the role although the other partner wants to renegotiate how they share the parenting duties.

Another potential site of renegotiation is who will be legally recognized as the parent. In all but a limited number of counties across the U.S., only one of you starts off initially with this status. This is due to the fact that same-sex marriage isn't legally available at this time. If you wish to share legal parenting rights, you'll need to go through second-parent adoption to secure equal parenting status under the law, if it's available in your state.

This may be tricky emotional territory for both of you if one assumes she'll be the legal parent because she would have been previously, or if she newly understands the feeling of legal insecurity that her partner was preparing to face if pregnancy occurred. Walk softly together through the experience of living in a homophobic society. It hurts and it's scary, yet this is something you—and all other partnered same-sex couples—are in together.

Child-Free Living

Some women want to pursue adoption; others don't have or desire the option. Living child-free after wanting to be pregnant and having chosen to parent is a very painful process. Over time you come to find new focus and direction, but initially your whole life can feel like a void. Some women choose to bring children into their lives in other ways so that they can have the spark and joy that children embody around them. Women do this in different ways. They may become a "super-aunt" to a child of one of their friends or relatives; most parents welcome all the support and help they can get. It's possible to create a situation where you and a child dear to your heart spend one afternoon a week together, have a sleep-over, or take a vacation together. In this way you become involved in this child's life. Many parents would love to have a special aunt like you, and any child would love it! Other women choose to bring children into their lives in a less committed way: They may volunteer as Big Sisters, tutor children at the library, or teach art classes to kids in their home. There are many ways to bring children into your life. Focus on what kind of a relationship you would like to foster and make it happen.

Choosing to live without children is a powerful choice. As life moves on you'll continually find new pursuits and things to explore that you wouldn't have the time for if you were parenting full-time. Enjoy your child-free life. Over time you may even find that you feel lucky!

Resources

Books

Double Take: A Single Woman's Journey to Motherhood, Kathryn Cole, General
    Distribution Services, 1996

Issues in Gay and Lesbian Adoption, Ann Sullivan (eds.), Child Welfare League of
    America, 1995

Lesbian and Gay Fostering and Adoption: Extraordinary Yet Ordinary, Stephen Hicks
    and Janet McDermott (eds.), Jessica Kingsley Publishing, 1998

Web Sites

ACLU Fact Sheet: Overview of Lesbian and Gay Parenting, Adoption, and
Foster Care
www.aclu.org/issues/gay/parent.html

Gay and Lesbian Adoption (lists resources for each state)
www.adopting.org/gaystate.html

The LesBiGay Adoption Page
www.lesbian.org/moms/adopt.htm

For a list of adoption agencies throughout the country that accept lesbian and
gay applicants, consult the adoption directory *Loving Journeys: Guide to Adoption*,
which can be ordered from Loving Journeys at (603) 924-7489.

Part Six
Pregnancy, Birth, and Beyond

Chapter 16 Early Pregnancy and Miscarriage

Whether you've been trying to conceive for two years or two months, the moment you realize or confirm that you're pregnant is a wonderful, exciting, and possibly scary time that you'll never forget. Nothing can describe the overwhelming flood of emotions you experience when you realize you're going to have a baby.

This chapter covers early pregnancy, miscarriage, and how to find a care provider. Because on average every one in four pregnancies results in miscarriage, we feel it's important to include this subject in the initial discussion of pregnancy. The following chapters discuss telling the world about your pregnancy, preparing for birth, being a new mother, and also cover the issues of the nonbirth mom throughout pregnancy and birth. These chapters aren't intended as a complete medical guide to pregnancy—to do so would probably double the size of this already lengthy book! What we do outline, however, are some of the major events and aspects of pregnancy and birth (and their emotional themes), while paying special attention to issues that are specific to lesbian, bisexual, and single mothers. In this chapter we focus exclusively on very early pregnancy and miscarriage.

Signs of Pregnancy

A number of women realize they're pregnant at the moment of conception and actually describe feeling sensations of conception. If you're one of these women and doubt what you feel, remember how long you've focused so intently on your body sensations, and remember that women feel many other similarly subtle events such as ovulation. You may not feel conception itself on a conscious level, either physically or energetically, but within 24–48 hours following insemination you may start to experience symptoms of pregnancy. *Most* women do not experience pregnancy symptoms this early but do feel some new sensations by the last few days preceding their expected period. Sometimes, however, after paying such close attention to your body for many months, you may no longer feel confident in interpreting what you feel anymore and will be taken by surprise the day your pregnancy test reads positive.

Am I Crazy or Am I Pregnant?

Sometimes initial symptoms of pregnancy—such as breast enlargement/tenderness and mood changes—are confusing because they're also signs of PMS. It can be difficult to believe that your symptoms indicate pregnancy, or to receive validation from others around you, until you've missed your period and gotten a positive pregnancy test. People are often reticent to believe that women might experience such a strong response to early pregnancy, so they try to persuade women that they're physically manifesting wishful thinking. Unfortunately, you may find it easy to doubt your unique body experience because our culture commonly resists acknowledging women's intuition. Furthermore, because fully half of conceptions don't progress past the first seven to 10 days, and thus don't ever produce a positive pregnancy test result, you may feel pregnancy symptoms but then receive a negative pregnancy test and experience a seemingly normal period. For this very brief but consuming experience of early pregnancy you may find virtually no external validation of pregnancy.

Pregnancy Symptoms

Hormonal changes during early pregnancy cause breast tenderness and enlargement, nipple sensitivity, and mood changes. Some women get weepy or angry in completely uncharacteristic ways long before their period is due. Others can't even lie on their stomachs or be hugged, due to the sensitivity of their breasts. Many women can't specify how they feel different, exactly; they simply don't feel like themselves—they feel pregnant. These same hormonal changes, incidentally, also cause the basal body temperature to remain elevated.

The next set of noticeable pregnancy symptoms includes appetite changes and fatigue as well as sensitive smell reactions, sleep irregularities, sex-drive changes, indigestion, constipation, and even an awareness of the cell division and initial formation of the embryo. Remember, some women experience all of these symptoms prior to missing a period, whereas others exhibit no signs of early pregnancy other than not starting their period.

Progesterone Suppositories

If you're taking progesterone suppositories as prescribed by your doctor, your menstrual cycle may be unusually extended. This common apparent absence of your period, the side effects of a delayed period, and the effects of progesterone itself can mimic pregnancy. Before discontinuing progesterone each cycle, some women like to have a blood test to confirm that they aren't pregnant. It can definitely be crazy-making to have monthly pregnancy symptoms but not actually be pregnant.

Pregnancy and Menstrual Periods

Some women continue to have menstrual-like bleeding, even though they're pregnant. This is most common during the first month of pregnancy. Usually, this bleeding is lighter and shorter than a normal period. If you're having pregnancy symptoms, or your period is uncharacteristically light, you'll want to take a pregnancy test to make sure you're not already pregnant before you inseminate again.

Pregnancy Tests

Home Pregnancy Tests

Most home pregnancy tests are quite sensitive and can usually detect a pregnancy anywhere from 10–14 days following insemination. These tests monitor the level of the hormone human chorionic gonadotropin (HCG) in the urine. HCG is produced in large amounts within a few weeks of early pregnancy; however, the test needs to detect a certain amount of HCG to read positive. For some women, this HCG level takes some time to show up in their urine: therefore, on rare occasions a positive reading may not come until a few weeks after missing your period. Most women receive a positive reading before they even miss their menstrual period, or within a few days thereafter.

You may choose to wait until you've already missed your period before taking a pregnancy test, since the absence of blood is one of the best signs not only that you're pregnant, but also that the embryo has successfully implanted into your uterine lining.

Although a pregnancy test may read false-negatives if you test too early, it's quite rare to have a false-positive result. Thus, although you're almost certainly pregnant, positive home test results are usually confirmed with a test from your health care provider.

Blood Tests

Blood tests are more sensitive than home tests. They can be used to confirm pregnancy if your home test reads negative even though you've missed your period and feel like you're pregnant. A blood test, however, will only read positive a few days earlier than a urine test will.

Reactions to Pregnancy

Of course, many women react to pregnancy in ways they've expected; they feel glee, elation, and ecstatic joy. Many women, however, are then shocked to discover that after only a few moments they move into numbness, fear, panic, disbelief, and uncertainty. This is normal. It's also normal to feel "crazy" about wanting to get pregnant in the first place, even if it's taken you an exceedingly long time to get pregnant. Pregnancy is a big deal. Don't judge these unexpected feelings: They're a natural part of the adjustment period.

If it's taken you a long time to get pregnant, you may only allow yourself a few minutes of joy before you find yourself bracing for the possible disappointment of miscarriage. When your trust in your body has been so deeply undermined, it's often hard to allow yourself to trust that it will be able to sustain a pregnancy. Try to have compassion for yourself. Let both your joy and fear coexist.

Early Pregnancy Issues For Women Who Have Had Difficulty Conceiving

A number of issues are specific to women who have been having difficulty conceiving or maintaining a pregnancy. We cover a few of the initial considerations in the following section. Even if you haven't had a challenging conception but have accessed sperm or insemination services through an infertility clinic, you should also read the following section. Regardless of why you contacted the clinic, you may be treated as if you've been infertile as well.

Early Pregnancy Management by Fertility Specialists

Women who have sought infertility treatments to assist them in getting pregnant are at an interesting crossroads in early pregnancy. Just because conception was difficult, their pregnancy is not necessarily "high risk." An increasing number of fertility patients, however, continue to see their fertility specialists after conception until their pregnancy has been fully established. The care given during these early days and weeks is dramatically different than the routine care provided by obstetricians and midwives in early pregnancy. Fertility specialists often recommend numerous sonograms and blood tests in the earliest days of pregnancy. Although a limited number of women find these procedures helpful, most find them traumatic. We will explore the advantages and drawbacks to these increasingly common procedures, typical responses to these procedures, and some personal exploration questions to help you decide *in advance* whether these procedures are for you.

Routine Procedures

As soon as pregnancy is confirmed, fertility specialists often recommend that the mother undergo repeat vaginal ultrasounds as well as repeat blood tests that check HCG, estrogen, and progesterone levels every few days. Some of these tests may even begin prior to the woman missing her first period. Some women receive serial ultrasounds until a heartbeat is detected, usually around four weeks after conception. Others receive them throughout the first 12 weeks of pregnancy to confirm normal growth patterns.

Advantages

The advantage to these repeated tests is confirmation that the pregnancy is growing adequately. Likewise, tests can confirm that you're producing enough progesterone to sustain an early pregnancy. If your progesterone numbers are too low, supplementation can be started or increased. Sometimes adjustment of progesterone doses, even at the last minute, can prevent a miscarriage for women who have abnormally low progesterone levels. For women with a history of miscarriage, if the current pregnancy also miscarries, these types of procedures may be able to suggest if this miscarriage resulted from unusual cell division or insufficient hormone levels.

Drawbacks

When you've just discovered that you're pregnant, it may be quite disorienting to have to go to the doctor's office every 48 hours. The initial days of pregnancy are some of the most rapid days of cell division for the entire pregnancy, and ultrasounds may have potential effects on cell division. Ultrasounds may demonstrate that miscarriage is likely due to improper development of the fetus. Ultrasounds can't prevent miscarriage, however, because there's no treatment for an irregularly growing embryo—which is the most common cause of miscarriage. Thus, the value of such ultrasounds is questionable because of the invasiveness of vaginal probe ultrasound, the potential risk to the growing baby, and the inability of the ultrasound to prevent miscarriages.

HCG levels that aren't increasing as much as expected can indicate a pending miscarriage, because they signify that the embryo isn't developing well. Once again, however, having this information cannot prevent a miscarriage from occurring.

Common Responses to These Procedures

Because these procedures are routine for women who consult fertility specialists, most pregnant women don't question their value until they've been done. Numerous women have called us in total panic because their joy of pregnancy has been replaced with the fear that something may be wrong. Many women report phone calls from nurses insisting that they return the next day to have more lab work done, because their results are questionable, but aren't offered a specific explanation until they see the doctor in person.

After receiving questionable results, many women feel like they're in limbo for days while waiting for the next sets of test results to indicate whether their HCG levels have reached the expected levels for this early stage of pregnancy or have remained low enough to confirm miscarriage.

For women who ultimately miscarry, all who have reported to us express firmly that this approach of repeated tests and ultrasounds afforded them no peace, no time to enjoy being pregnant, no time to realize that their body finally conceived. Instead, there was only a moment to experience being pregnant before the pregnancy became a relationship to tests and to numbers. They say this approach removed any sense of celebration of finally being pregnant and replaced it with more guilt that their body didn't work right. Most women with whom we've spoken who did miscarry say this approach was a complete nightmare that they would never choose to repeat.

On the other hand, for women who have had multiple miscarriages in the past, having confirmation that this pregnancy isn't going according to plan allows them to have a surgical miscarriage, rather than wait for an inevitable "natural" miscarriage. Likewise, if this pregnancy is growing in a healthy way initially, it provides these women with assurance that perhaps it will work this time.

Women who get positive results from the beginning have reported mixed reactions to us. Some feel that the procedures carried unnecessary risks and that they would not have chosen these procedures had they known of these risks, whereas other women feel that the positive information they gained about the pregnancy right from the start gave them courage to believe that their body does work and will be able to sustain a pregnancy. They say these tests gave them significant emotional relief.

Questions to Ask Yourself About These Procedures

Before you actually get pregnant, it's valuable to ask your care provider about his or her approach to early pregnancy. Knowing this, you can decide which routine procedures you'd like to receive. Spend some time envisioning how you'd like your initial days of pregnancy to be. Are you the kind of person who'd be reassured by visiting a doctor's office every other day and waiting for test results, or would this medicalized approach drive you crazy?

Do you have enough information about the effect of ultrasound on newly developing fetuses to make an informed decision about whether to undergo repeat vaginal probe ultrasounds? How would these procedures serve you and your pregnancy? What might be the drawbacks of these procedures to you and your pregnancy? If you're partnered, be sure to discuss these issues and concerns ahead of time. Choosing to inform yourself about routine medical procedures in order to decide whether they're right for you is part of being a responsible parent. Declining to receive certain treatments is not a betrayal of your baby. You should never feel guilty for asserting your opinions and choosing the form of care you wish to receive. This is both your right and your responsibility as a parent.

Transitioning From a Highly Managed Conception to a Low-Risk Pregnancy

It's hard to believe that having difficulty conceiving doesn't inherently mean that you'll have difficulty during pregnancy and birth, but it's true. Regaining faith in your body and trust in life itself isn't always easy. Nonetheless, it's important work to be done. Some women who see fertility specialists for conception are immediately transferred to "high-risk" obstetricians for prenatal care. Often, though, those who've been seeing a regular obstetrician gynecologist for fertility care plan to continue seeing the same ob-gyn for prenatal and birth care.

We encourage you to see a practitioner, whether it's a midwife or obstetrician, who can separate your challenging conception process from your pregnancy. Sometimes that means changing doctors during your pregnancy when you come to realize that you're having a healthy "low-risk" pregnancy but are being treated as "high-risk."

Many women who have had fertility challenges find it extremely beneficial to see a therapist, with a partner or alone, throughout their pregnancy to help them manage their fears and move to a place of trust with their bodies again.

Choosing a Care Provider

Take Care of Yourself Before You Choose a Care Provider

Self-care during pregnancy is the most vital part of prenatal care. Whether you've just inseminated and are in the window of possible pregnancy, or you know for certain that you're pregnant, it's important to take good care of yourself. Eat healthy, nutritious foods and pay special attention to your vegetable intake. Take a good prenatal vitamin. Get plenty of sleep and exercise. Feel free to be sexual if it feels desirable; during pregnancy, however, be careful about fisting, using long dildos, and partaking in other penetrative vaginal or anal sex. It's important to be gentle with the cervix during pregnancy. If you feel your penetrative sex is gentle and doesn't roughly bump the cervix, then it's safe for you.

Take the time you need to find the right care provider. There's no reason for you to rush this process. Paying attention to sleep, exercise, and diet are the three primary components of self-pregnancy care.

Choosing Your Place of Birth

To find the right care provider for your pregnancy and birth, you must first decide where you'd like to give birth. Many people end up choosing a hospital by default because they know nothing of the other options, and everyone they know has given birth in the hospital. There are actually three options available in most areas of the U.S.: hospital, home, or birth center. As midwives, we feel it's important for every pregnant woman to explore each of these options before deciding where to give birth. Only through such an approach can you be fully informed in your choice of setting and care provider. It's our goal to have women give birth in the setting that makes them feel most comfortable, with a midwife or doctor well-suited to their needs.

For lesbian and bisexual women this is especially important, since we have unique considerations as a result of our "alternative" family structures. Each option affords different levels of built-in comfort and support for our families. Many women reading and researching the subject prior to pregnancy are surprised to learn that home birth is statistically safer than routine hospital birth for low-risk pregnancies. Likewise, in many Western nations—and around the world—women receive care from a midwife unless their pregnancies are considered high-risk enough to warrant consultation with a doctor.

The books we recommend at the end of this chapter will help you understand the benefits and risks of each location. Once you've informed yourself about the available options, do some preliminary imagining about your comfort level in each specific setting. The following self-exploration exercise will help you learn your body responses to each setting. We recommend reading *Immaculate Deception* by Suzanne Arms before you try the following exercise, especially as representations of birth in mainstream media are often quite unrealistic.

Exercise

The goal of this exercise is to help you clarify your ideal birth vision. Having a vision can help you move toward manifesting the key elements of your vision. Allow your mind to imagine freely. Resist the urge to step in and correct your vision; just let it flow. Imagine yourself in labor. Conjure up your greatest feelings of safety and love. Who's with you? What's the quality of your connection with that person, those people? What are you doing that helps you feel safe and helps you work with the strong sensations and pain you experience? What are you wearing? What are you doing? Where are you? Is anyone touching you? Is anyone comforting you?

How do you see the arrival of your baby? What's important to you? What qualities of contact with your close friends and family are important to you? How about immediately following the birth? What do you see happening? Be specific about the feelings you're having when you envision your first few moments with your new baby. Write down the images and qualities that are clearest to you.

Now that you have a strong sense of your ideal birth, try placing the important qualities of the experience into each setting: home, hospital, and birth center. What do you feel, on a body level, as the advantages and drawbacks of each setting? Are you able to maintain the same quality of connection with your partner or close friend(s) in each setting? Take note of what you feel you might sacrifice by giving birth in each location.

Once you've completed this part of the exercise, write down what you've learned about your vision and how it aligns with your available options. Many women, for

Limor Inbar-Hansen, Indelible Images

example, prioritize intimacy with their partner. They want the physical and emotional comfort of home but can't imagine giving birth there because they're afraid to do so. In this instance there are a few options: One couple might choose a birth center. Another might explore what they could do as a team to ensure that the most important qualities of connection can be maintained in a hospital setting. They might work with a hospital-based midwife or hire a labor assistant to help them maintain the emotional and spiritual qualities that are of primary concern. A third couple might educate themselves further about the actual risks and benefits of both home birth and hospital birth, then choose to birth at home with a midwife.

Keeping your emotional priorities in mind, you can begin your search for a care provider who not only shares your philosophy of birth, but also is sensitive to a pregnant lesbian's specific needs.

Finding a Pregnancy and Birth Care Provider Suited to Your Needs

As a lesbian, bisexual, or single pregnant woman you deserve to have health care that is suited to your specific needs. You have the right to have your family structure acknowledged without judgment. This must remain in the forefront of your mind as you begin looking for care providers in your area. If you know any lesbian parents who live in your area, the best place to start is to ask who their doctor or midwife was and what their experience was like. The Gay and Lesbian Medical Association in San Francisco has nationwide referrals as well. Their contact information is listed at the end of this chapter. Many women choose to find a pregnancy care provider before they're pregnant, expecting that it might be a challenge to find a lesbian-sensitive provider in their area. Also, when you're not pregnant you might feel less vulnerable expressing your needs and desires.

You may be the first lesbian family in your town, or at least the first out family. If so, you'll be the one doing the original research. We recommend a proactive approach: Come out from the start. This is especially vital if you're partnered so that your partner will feel able to participate as a parent and not be regarded as just a friend. If you're out, at the time of birth you can celebrate the birth of your child together. If you're closeted, only one of you will get the recognition of motherhood, and each of you will be relegated to having her own private entry into motherhood rather than a shared experience.

You may never have had to come out in a medical environment before. Even if you're uncomfortable with the actual thought of coming out, it's best to do so at the initial interview visit. When you come out to a care provider, or to anyone for that matter, it's helpful to remember that *your* comfort in discussing your family structure will directly influence *their* comfort in discussing it with you. When you explain the nature of your family it's helpful to follow with questions such as:

- Are you comfortable working with my/our family?
- If not, can you refer us to anyone in the area who may be comfortable working with me/us?
- Have you worked with lesbian clients? If so, do you have any past lesbian clients we could speak with?
- Have you worked with single mothers before?
- If this is a group practice, can you speak for the comfort level of each doctor or midwife?
- Is it best that we interview each of the different members?
- If one of you is uncomfortable with lesbians, how can we assure that this person won't be the one providing us care or be at the birth of my/our child?

Just because someone says they're comfortable working with you, you shouldn't immediately breathe a huge sigh of relief and look no further. On the contrary, you've passed the first hurdle and are now moving into the more subtle arenas. In fact, we recommend that you interview at least three practitioners so that you can compare the nonverbal and verbal comfort levels of each practitioner. Do they say the word "lesbian" or do they skirt around it? If you're partnered, can they look both of you in the eye? How do they refer to the nonpregnant partner? Do you like and feel comfortable with them? Do their philosophies and practices align with your own?

These are all good starting places for screening a care provider. Unfortunately, most care providers aren't as lesbian sensitive as we would like. This by no means always stems from homophobia; it usually comes from ignorance or lack of culturally specific education. Once you've chosen a care provider, you can then decide how much education you're willing to provide the clinic's staff. If you're partnered, after each visit it's a good idea for both of you to talk about your respective comfort levels and whether you should be more or less proactive about your needs.

Midwife or Obstetrician?

In general, midwives spend considerably more time with you during each visit than physicians. Most midwives spend anywhere from 15 minutes to an hour with each patient. Midwives, although not specifically trained in understanding gay culture, are trained in psychosocial issues and do tend to ask personal questions. The combination of their training and the time they spend with you allows you to have the time to educate your midwife about your family structure and to address your unique issues of pregnancy and general concerns and questions.

On average, doctors spend five minutes with each patient. Midwives are women, whereas obstetricians are either men or women. Many women, especially lesbians, prefer to work exclusively with female practitioners. In some clinics a nurse practitioner provides all of the prenatal care, and a doctor, whom you may never have met, attends the birth. This is especially common in urban areas. Although this affords you continuity with the nurse practitioner during pregnancy—which is wonderful—it leaves you with a stranger at the time of birth. If you have a choice, we don't recommend this model of care, because it includes too many unknown and unscreened people at the time of birth.

Remember, this is your pregnancy and birth experience. You don't need to acquiesce when finding a care provider. If you can't find a suitable care provider in your area, search outlying areas. If you find a more sensitive provider, it will always be worth the drive. If you discover that your care provider isn't working out, change providers. You're a consumer purchasing a very expensive product: good care. You have a right to quality and comfort. This is the birth of your child; don't compromise!

What Is Good Prenatal Care?

Good prenatal care:
- recognizes that the pregnant woman is the central decision maker, not the health-care provider
- involves and acknowledges the importance of the pregnant woman's partner, other children, extended family, and community to the pregnancy and birth process
- educates and supports a pregnant woman so she can choose and maintain healthy lifestyle habits
- focuses secondly on monitoring for potential illnesses and complications so that they can be diagnosed and treated, while understanding that for most women, pregnancy is a healthy life process, not a disease state

Why Choose a Midwife?

The midwifery model of care embraces the above components of good prenatal care. On average, in the U.S. midwives spend a total of 50–60 hours with a client from pregnancy through postpartum, compared to the average 4–5 hours spent by physicians. In the five nations with the lowest perinatal mortality rate, more than 70% of pregnant women are attended by midwives. The World Health Organization has called on the U.S. to shift its approach to pregnancy and birth care to a midwife-centered model, incorporating obstetricians only in their rightful role as high-risk providers. The reasoning is that the midwifery model of care is more comprehensive and less expensive, and less often subjects mothers and their babies to unnecessary medical interventions.

Is Home Birth Safe?

For low-risk pregnant women—who are the vast majority of pregnant women—birth at home with a midwife is as safe if not safer than giving birth in the hospital. In fact, numerous studies have shown that these home-birthing women have better birth outcomes than women who give birth in hospitals. They experience fewer severe vaginal tears, Cesarean sections (and therefore fewer surgery complications), postpartum hemorrhages, and birth injuries to babies.

The medicalizing of birth in the U.S. has not been a story based on best practice and has been strongly influenced by lobbyists, economics, power struggles, sexism, and media campaigns. Many women don't have access to accurate information about home birth, nor is home birth accurately portrayed in the media. Home birth, however, offers safety as well as familiarity, comfort, privacy, and family focus.

■ ■ ■

Making it through early pregnancy isn't always emotionally easy. As queer and single women we have many unique issues that extend greatly beyond the universal elements of the first trimester, such as choosing your place of birth and a care provider. We will explore lesbian-specific elements of pregnancy in the next chapter. Before moving on, however, it's necessary to explore the ins and outs of miscarriage because of how common an occurrence it is. Although we hope you're fortunate enough to avoid experiencing a miscarriage, you'll benefit from understanding the process in the event that you do miscarry.

Miscarriage

On average, every one in four pregnancies results in miscarriage. As women age this proportion grows higher, reaching one out of two by age 40. Thus no discussion of early pregnancy is complete without covering the topic of miscarriage. Miscarriage is an occurrence in the lives of most women, yet it still seems to be a taboo subject. In fact, it isn't until a woman experiences a miscarriage that she discovers how many women in her life have also miscarried. Although finding this out may offer you support, it often comes after the fact. Therefore, when faced with miscarriage many women feel like they're the only ones who have ever been through such a trauma, which can seem isolating. Because of the lack of openness surrounding its normalcy, miscarriage has become unnecessarily medicalized.

Signs of Impending Miscarriage

Although some women are warned of an impending miscarriage through HCG lab work or a sonogram, most first become concerned that they may be about to miscarry when they see blood. There are a number of reasons for bleeding in the first trimester, many of which are normal and resolve on their own. Therefore, when you first see blood on your toilet paper or underwear, it doesn't necessarily mean you're miscarrying. Sometimes you may bleed or spot for a couple of days or even weeks and maintain your pregnancy. In fact, 50% of women who bleed during early pregnancy continue to grow a healthy baby. If cramping begins, however, it is more likely that you are beginning to miscarry..

Preventative Measures

Unfortunately, there are few preventative measures for miscarriage. Most miscarriages are caused by improper cell division that makes the pregnancy no longer viable. But living a fertile lifestyle may help prevent miscarriage to a certain degree.

See Part Three of this book for ideas. If you're bleeding or spotting, immediately lie down and relax. If anything can prevent a miscarriage, it is often relaxation. Take the Bach Flower remedy "Rescue Remedy"—available at all health food stores—every few minutes to few hours, as it has a calming affect on the uterus.

Although bed rest may not ultimately prevent your miscarriage, it will allow you time to feel your feelings and pay attention to your experience. Above all, it's vital to remain connected to yourself during trying times.

If you have been pregnant for less than 10 weeks and begin to spot, taking a progesterone supplement can be of great assistance in preventing a miscarriage. If you're not already taking oral progesterone or progesterone suppositories, a topical progesterone enhancer cream can be purchased at your local health food store and used until you can secure a stronger form. This supplementing will only help if the bleeding is related to a progesterone deficiency.

Treatment Options for Miscarriage

Most women don't have a midwife or a doctor at the time they miscarry. As a result they feel like there's no one to call to ask what to do. Even if you do have a midwife or a doctor and you call their office, you'll likely reach their answering service or a receptionist who will be unable to give you the information you're looking for. Therefore, unfortunately, most women end up in the emergency room.

Medicalized Miscarriage

If you see a doctor when you're miscarrying or think you're miscarrying—whether in the emergency room or in a private office—they'll perform an ultrasound to check whether the baby has a heartbeat. If there's a heartbeat, they'll send you home and tell you to come back if you start to bleed heavily or your cramping becomes severe. If there's no heartbeat, they'll most likely perform a surgical procedure to remove the contents of your uterus.

Miscarrying in the emergency room can be traumatic. In the overwhelming majority of cases, miscarriage isn't an emergency; thus, you may wait for hours to be seen. Being in the hospital when you're losing your pregnancy can be emotionally painful, since an extremely traumatic—yet normal, private, and healthy—experience is taking place in your body, yet you're in public and don't know exactly what is going on. You're going through a huge internal crisis and navigating the medical world at the same time. Unfortunately, in the hospital there's rarely any acknowledgment of the intensity of your grief about losing your pregnancy.

While in this crisis, you may also need to decide how to represent your family structure, and you may have to filter through possible homophobia or judgments about single mothers, which, more than likely, will only add to your stress.

Nonmedical Miscarriage

On the other hand, if you choose to miscarry at home, you may appreciate the emotional safety and privacy that isn't afforded in the hospital. At the same time, some women don't feel completely safe being unattended, due to the blood loss of miscarriage. Miscarriage is very much like the pain of a mini-labor with the bleeding of a heavy period. The pain of a miscarriage, however, is intensified by grief and fear.

Most women don't know what a miscarriage feels like—what amount of pain and bleeding is normal. If they did, more would choose to miscarry at home. Many home-birth midwives provide the valuable service of assisting women, both in person and over the phone, to safely miscarry at home.

A miscarriage is the body's way of emptying the uterus of a nonviable pregnancy and is a very normal physical process: a combination of cramping and bleeding. Cramps—the sensation of the uterus rhythmically contracting—have a wavelike sensation, may be quite strong, and may last a number of hours. Many women find themselves rocking on the toilet for a few hours and then feel much better. Some women cramp for up to 12 hours. Again, for most women, the bleeding is like that of a heavy period, with a couple hours of concentrated cramping and bleeding.

Not all miscarriages are safely conducted at home; thus, if you completely soak more than one maxi pad per hour for more than two hours, it's best to contact a medical professional immediately. Likewise, because blood loss is involved, we don't recommend that you miscarry without a partner or friend in the house.

What Did I Do Wrong?

After a woman miscarries, it's common for guilt and self-blame to arise. Women often wonder what they did wrong. If they're partnered, they may feel their partner will blame them for not being able to maintain the pregnancy. The need to point to something that caused the miscarriage can feel more settling than living with the fact that it was unpreventable.

Many women go to all lengths to blame themselves or their partner for the loss of the pregnancy. "It was that fight we had." "It was the spicy food we ate the other night." "It was the sex." "It's confirmation that I don't work right." "It's because I'm too old." "It's because I'm gay." Miscarriages happen. This desire to place blame comes from feeling out of control and is a signal you can use to recognize that you may have underlying feelings that need to be addressed.

Grieving

Grieving is a deeply personal process and varies in duration for each person. It isn't something that can be rushed. Usually, the longer the duration of pregnancy before the loss, the longer the grieving period. It's important, especially if you're partnered, to recognize that everyone grieves differently. Having compassion for each other's style and time line for grieving will help deepen your relationship and compassion for each other. Trying to hasten a grieving period can breed resentment.

If you're partnered, it's best not to try to get pregnant again until you're both ready. After a miscarriage, you may not want to try again, since the process may be too grueling. Some women follow miscarriage with adoption, knowing they couldn't withstand more loss. Others don't feel emotionally prepared for many months to resume striving for pregnancy. In fact, it's common to want to wait until after the estimated due date of the pregnancy you lost.

Grieving takes on an additional dimension when you realize you're basically starting all over when you inseminate again. You begin at the first cycle, knowing that once more it may take up to a year (or longer) for you to get pregnant. This can feel overwhelming.

Other women aren't as consumed by the grieving process and are ready to begin inseminating again as soon as possible.

How Long Do I Have to Wait Before Starting Again?

The answer varies. If you were only a few weeks pregnant and miscarried at home, it's probably sufficient to skip a full menstrual cycle and then resume inseminating. If your period is abnormally light or heavy, it's best to wait until your cycle is normalized. If you had a medical miscarriage, it's best to wait at least two full menstrual cycles to allow your uterine lining to build up again.

Because of the hormonal changes during early pregnancy, a frustrating side effect of miscarriage for many women is that their cycles change. Your body may not menstruate for two to eight weeks after you miscarry. After any pregnancy, no matter how brief, your cycle can change dramatically in length and nature. Women often go from a 32-day cycle to a 28-day cycle, or from having no fertile mucus to having a lot of fertile mucus, seemingly overnight. This can be disconcerting. You may feel like you've just gotten the hang of reading your body and now it's totally different.

Celebrate the Fact That You Were Pregnant

One thing we like to celebrate with women, although it can be very difficult to do, is that they *did* get pregnant. This is really, truly wonderful and may get lost amidst the grief. Each woman relates to her pregnancy and miscarriage differently. Women may refer to "my first baby" or "my first pregnancy" or "my 12-week pregnancy," or may base everything in relation to the pregnancy—"after my miscarriage" or "before my miscarriage." Pregnancy loss is a big marker in women's lives.

One of the support groups we led decided to adopt the idea that pregnancy, no matter how long, is an accomplishment worth honoring and celebrating. They discussed trying to hold the attitude of self-support when facing pregnancy loss: "Good job, body! Way to go! The baby wasn't developing right, and you knew just what to do."

Serial Miscarriages

The vast majority of women who miscarry twice in a row don't miscarry a third time. If a woman miscarries three times, many tests can be done to try to determine the cause(s). This area of obstetrics care is new but quickly growing. Many theories are controversial, and treatments go in and out of vogue rapidly. If a woman chooses to see a high-risk specialist, we encourage her to take a team approach in which she also sees a practitioner who can evaluate her diet and overall health, as well as a therapist or other emotional support provider.

Resources

Books

Coping With Miscarriage, Mimi Luebbermann, Prima Publishing, 1995

Ended Beginnings: Healing Childbearing Loss, Claudia Panuthos and Catherine Romeo, Bergin & Garvey, 1984

Hearts and Hands: A Midwife's Guide to Pregnancy and Birth, Elizabeth Davis, Celestial Arts, 1987

The Midwife's Pregnancy and Childbirth Book, Marion McCartney and Antonia van der Meer, Harper Perennial, 1990

Natural Healing for the Pregnant Woman, Elizabeth Burch and Judith Sachs, Perigree, 1997

The Natural Pregnancy Book, Aviva Jill Romm, The Crossing Press, 1997

The Pregnant Woman's Comfort Book, Jennifer Louden, Harper San Francisco, 1995

Prenatal Yoga and Natural Birth, Jeannine Parvati Baker, North Atlantic Books, 1986

Silent Grief: Miscarriage—Finding Your Way Through the Darkness, Clara Hinton, New Leaf Press, 1998

Trying Again: A Guide to Pregnancy After Miscarriage, Stillbirth, and Infant Loss, Ann Douglas et al, Taylor Publishing, 2000

The Ultimate Guide to Pregnancy for Lesbians, Rachel Pepper, Cleis Press, 1999

Wise Woman's Herbal for the Childbearing Year, Susun Weed and Janice Novet, Ash Tree Publishing, 1986

Miscarriage Support Groups and Online Resources
Helping After Neonatal Death (HAND)
P.O. Box 341
Los Gatos, CA 95031
www.h-a-n-d.org

Mothers in Sympathy and Support (The MISS Foundation)
P.O. Box 5333
Peoria, AZ 85385
www.misschildren.org

Pregnancy After Miscarriage (PAM)
www.pam.sakurazone.poznan.pl

SHARE Pregnancy and Infant Loss Support
St. Joseph Health Center
300 First Capitol Drive
St. Charles, MO 63301-2893
(800) 821-6819
www.nationalshareoffice.com/index.html

Organizations
Gay and Lesbian Medical Association (offers a GLBT physician referral list)
459 Fulton St. Suite 107
San Francisco, CA 94102
415-255-4547
www.glma.org

If you are a health care provider, the midwives at Maia invite you to contact us for cultural competency trainings we offer on lesbian and bisexual women's reproductive health needs. Reach us at www. maiamidwifery.com.

Chapter 17 Pregnant Life

Pregnancy is a joyous and phenomenal time of creation. The idea that you can actually create another human being is a miraculous concept! Layered within this joy, however, are innumerable physical discomforts and hormonally induced emotional fluctuations that are an inherent to pregnancy. Add to this blend the issues specific to being a lesbian and the ways that pregnant lesbians must navigate the straight world, and you have a very consuming and complex phenomenon. Welcome to lesbian pregnancy!

This chapter explores issues that may arise for pregnant lesbians, bisexual women, and single women of any orientation. Some issues are just added twists to the universal themes of pregnancy, while others are unique to a lesbian pregnancy.

Sharing the News of Your Pregnancy

Telling people the exciting news of your pregnancy can fill you with many conflicting emotions. You may be concerned about what exactly you'll tell people. You may be afraid of receiving a negative response to your wonderful news. Of course, you'll want the people in your life to be as excited as you are about the news. Living in a straight world, however, has probably taught you to proceed with caution when discussing lesbian issues or publicly displaying your love. This is a challenging dichotomy. It's helpful to explore in advance the emotional and practical elements of telling others that you're having a baby so that you can, as much as possible, prepare for this sometimes awkward phase of pregnancy.

Telling Immediate Family Members

No matter how you choose to tell your family, it's normal to feel nervous about sharing the information. Often at least one person won't receive the news wholeheartedly or with the enthusiasm you'd like. On the flip side, we've found that most lesbians have at least one supportive family member who has been following the progress of their family-making and eagerly awaits the pregnancy.

Many gay women have shared with close family members their desire to parent from the beginning of their process. These women are blessed with open and progressive families who acknowledge and support their relationships and choices to raise children. For these families, the news of the pregnancy is welcomed with glee. As a result, these women usually tell their families as soon as they find out they're pregnant. An embracing family provides these women the wonderful and much deserved experience of having their loved ones react to a planned pregnancy with excitement.

Unfortunately, not every lesbian or bisexual woman, by any means, can rely on receiving a positive response from their entire family. Many women have mentioned to their family, prior to pregnancy, that they plan to raise children, but have chosen to keep private the intimate details of their conception period. If this is the case for you, the news of your pregnancy may come as a surprise to family members who didn't really understand that you were serious about becoming a mother.

We've worked with many women who have guided their parents and other family members through the "appropriate" response to the news. For example, Marina and Jennifer told Jennifer's mother over the phone in this way:

> Hi, Mom! Marina and I have some really exciting news to share with you. We wanted you to be the first to know because we know you'll be as excited as we are... I'm pregnant! We're thrilled! We thought you might want to tell Dad yourself, but what do you think is best?

In trying to elicit the desired response, some women choose to tell their parents and other pertinent family members first by letter or E-mail. Although this may feel too formal or distanced for some, others feel it allows their family members to have their individual responses alone and to adjust to the news before responding. Women who choose this tactic often expect less-than-thrilled responses and feel the situation will be mitigated best by allowing family members the time and space to react before responding.

When Your News Is the First They've Heard of Your Desire to Parent

Many lesbian and bisexual women choose not to inform their family members that they're trying to get pregnant or even that they're hoping to parent. Some delay telling family members until after the window for miscarriage has passed or until genetic tests have confirmed that the pregnancy is one they wish to continue. Letting family members know at this point in the process has distinct advantages and disadvantages.

We've found that women choose to keep their family out of the loop during their preconception period primarily because they feel the news will be met with a negative response and they want to delay that response for as long as possible. These women hope that when their pregnancy is clearly established, their family members may feel less comfortable voicing negative opinions, since the decision has already been made and it would be rude to do so. Thus, by not disclosing their intention to parent until pregnancy, these women are able to protect themselves emotionally during the sensitive periods of conception and early pregnancy.

Unfortunately, waiting to tell family members until the pregnancy is underway often backfires. Often close family members are hurt when they discover they haven't been included in such important elements of their daughter/sister's life. Even if they're also homophobic, they may feel hurt by being left out. Likewise, some people have such an enormous amount of processing to do about the concept of a lesbian pregnancy that finding out about the pregnancy may have successfully delayed the overwhelming reaction but only served to concentrate it during pregnancy. Such family members may be unable to appropriately contain their reactions and fears from the pregnant woman and/or her partner. This can lead to a *highly* stressful pregnancy.

With time, most family members will come around to accepting that you're a mother. Nonetheless, there are the few who may excommunicate you for your decision. Some families will never acknowledge that you're a parent if you aren't the one giving birth. Biology means everything to them. And there are some families who will accept you as a single parent but refuse to acknowledge your partner as a parent. In some families this process takes years or even an ultimatum that they'll lose their relationship with you if they don' t acknowledge your entire family of choice. It has been our experience, however, that most families will come around in time.

If you choose to delay letting your family members know of your intentions to have children until you're pregnant, you're also delaying the time it takes them to integrate and process this information. When you do tell them, you may want to provide them with books and resources on the subject so that they can process this information on their own and not feel the need to do so with you exclusively.

When One Side of the Family Is Welcoming and the Other Isn't

When you're partnered it's particularly hurtful if only one partner's family accepts the child. It's especially difficult if the nonbirth mother isn't acknowledged as a parent, because she is less likely to be recognized in this way, whereas the biological mother is always seen as a mother. Each lesbian family deals with this issue in their own way, but it's often difficult to live in a culture that doesn't recognize our family structures as valid and to live with that same homophobia in our immediate families.

When the Nonbirth Mom Isn't Recognized

We recommend being direct in your communications with your immediate and extended family members, clarifying the significance of each of your roles and setting out parameters for how you'd like each parent to be treated and named. If your family still insists on not recognizing that both of you are equal parents to your growing child, you have some tough decisions to make. Many families choose to discontinue contact with these family members until they're willing to recognize their family as valid. Others encourage their families to accept their family before making such a big decision, knowing that growth sometimes requires time.

It's particularly painful if your own parents reject the notion that you're a parent. We've met more than one nonbirth mom whose family completely ignored the fact that she was a parent until the formal second-parent adoption went through. After she had completed the adoption, the family recognized her parental status because the state recognized it. Having your parents reject your parenthood is one of the deepest wounds you can receive. If this is the case for you, don't hesitate to seek counseling to help you through this time.

When the Pregnant Mom Isn't Accepted by Her Family

When you're pregnant you'll more than likely feel a universal sense of connectedness with all women who have been pregnant before, especially your own mother. If your mother rejects you now or rejected you when you first came out and hasn't reentered your life, this pain can be overwhelming. This hurt may be intensified or restimulated by your own transitioning into motherhood, and these wounds can be very difficult to heal. Even if you were rejected 15 years ago, these wounds may reopen during pregnancy.

Telling Extended Family and Friends

It may also be a challenge to figure out how to tell extended family and friends. Many people in our lives appear to accept us and our sexual orientation, but for some heterosexuals, the idea of lesbians raising children nudges our "lifestyles" into the unacceptable. Pregnant lesbians seem to push more "primal buttons" than non-pregnant lesbians. To avoid having to witness any anticipated or unexpected negative responses from the people in our lives, it's becoming more and more popular for lesbians to announce their pregnancies via postcard. Akin to a birth announcement, some families send out a "We're having a baby" card. This form of mass announcement allows you to do the majority of your "coming out" about the pregnancy in one fell swoop.

Unexpected Responses

Some women experience the seemingly positive, although disconcerting, response of suddenly being brought back into the fold of their family or having an instant circle of friends as soon as they share the news about the pregnancy. It's as if some invisible barrier has been broken down when lesbians do something that heterosexual people can relate to.

Women share with us the mixed feelings that arise when their mother or sister suddenly communicates with them on a daily basis and sends them letters and baby clothes, whereas prior to pregnancy they only communicated on birthdays and holidays. Or how strange it is to instantaneously be invited to many more social gatherings than they were before because their straight friends feel they can now share with them in ways they could not before. It's also quite common to become the "lesbian poster-child family" for your friends or neighborhood, with everyone wanting to show off their lesbian friends who are having a baby so they can prove how liberal they are, even if their motivation is subconscious.

Although these responses may be touching, they can also feel infuriating. These responses can be especially poignant if your partner isn't included in the lavished attention, or if the past homophobia of these same people isn't even mentioned because you've now become "acceptable."

How to Address Homophobic Reactions

At some point in time most lesbians encounter a directly homophobic response to the news that they're pregnant. It can be startling to excitedly share your news and have people not know what to say. It's confounding to realize that these people to whom you've been out for so long have been judging you the whole time. Their response may be silence or a simple "Oh" followed by a change of subject. Or it may come as a homophobic diatribe blasted at you. All of these responses are difficult to deal with. When someone reacts negatively to the news of your growing family, it's hard to imagine what continued place they'll hold in your life. Their response puts them into an entirely new category. Thus, you feel not only the pain of their response, but also the pain of losing these people as trusted members of your life.

It may be necessary to give these friends or relatives the ultimatum that if they can't leave their criticisms out of their interactions with you, you'll discontinue the relationship. As painful as leaving a meaningful relationship is, continuing to expose yourself—and eventually your children—to homophobia on a regular basis is not only painful but also self-hating and disempowering for your kids. Although most relatives and friends can agree to disagree and not discuss it, there's no denying the altered place they now hold in your life. Sometimes it becomes easier just to let that person out of your life than to have to pretend their judgment and rejection aren't really there simply because you've agreed not to discuss it.

Homophobic responses usually feel like they come out of the blue, and you're rarely prepared for them. If you're in public and someone you don't know discredits your life—as may well happen at least once during your pregnancy, and certainly during your parenthood—you have two choices: directly call them on their homophobia or swiftly leave the scene. If the negative response comes from someone you know, it's important to be brave enough to cut them off and not let them continue. This can be done with statements such as the following, which you can practice ahead of time:

- "I hear you have a strong opinion on the subject of lesbians having children. However, I/we are very excited about our family and are not asking for your opinion."
- "Please don't criticize my life. I have made my choices from love. If you can't accept this, I'd prefer that you keep your feelings to yourself."

These statements will stop most people in their tracks and help them realize the inappropriateness of their reaction. Some, however, will continue on. If they must, and you've been direct, then to maintain your integrity you must leave the conversation by walking away or hanging up the phone. It takes courage to confront someone's homophobia midstream, but the only way we will make this a safer world for ourselves and our children is to do just that.

There may be times when you feel comfortable and confident discussing someone's concerns about your family. This is always your choice. You can choose with whom you have such conversations, and you get to decide when enough is enough. Having someone respectfully discuss their questions is a completely different scenario than having someone attack your family. Nonetheless, it's important to remember that you're not obligated to educate anyone about the validity of your family; you can say this to them and remind them that you don't ask them to justify their choices to you. Likewise, there's the option of saying you don't want to address their concerns but are willing to give them a referral, such as PFLAG, where their concerns can more appropriately be addressed.

Telling the World That Your Partner Is Pregnant

Your pregnant partner has the luxury of deciding how much to reveal to any person at any given time when she tells them she's pregnant. When you tell the world you're becoming a parent, however, you inherently come out each time. If you haven't directly discussed your home life and sexual orientation with everyone in your life, the announcement of the pregnancy will often be an official coming out as well.

Each nonbiological mother chooses to navigate this issue differently. We encourage you to resist the urge to keep silent out of fear or discomfort. In choosing to become a parent, you've chosen to take on society's homophobia and claim your right to parenthood. Pregnancy allows you the opportunity to become confident in your coming-out process, so that by the time your child is born you will be better equipped to be a lesbian family.

Telling the people you work with is important, even though many nonbirth moms think that not discussing the pregnancy at work is also an appropriate decision. We disagree. How will you advocate for yourself to get maternity leave when your baby is born if management doesn't know your partner is pregnant? How will you investigate whether the baby can join your insurance plan if your employer doesn't know you're having a baby? How will you take time off when your child is sick if they don't know you're a mother?

Granted, perhaps you have good reason to believe that if you came out you would lose your job or suffer irreparably. If this is the case, you may want to investigate how important it is to you to continue working at that job. Could you get a job where you could be an out parent? These are personal decisions, yet ones that should not be overlooked.

As a nonbiological mother, you may feel negated if your partner chooses not to disclose that she is partnered and parenting with you, her loving partner. How do you think she (and your child) would feel if you didn't acknowledge them in your worlds?

Whereas "passing" may have worked for you in the past as the safest way of avoiding awkward moments, it may now serve to undermine your family unit. Give this thought and attention. We must do everything we can to strengthen our personal relationships so that they make it through the challenges of early parenting. Taking pride in your family is one of the strongest steps you can take to do just that.

Still, it isn't always easy or comfortable to constantly be asked, "What do you mean you're having a baby? You're not pregnant! Are you adopting?" Having to always explain that your partner is pregnant can feel like a lot of work when all you're trying to do is share your joy about the pregnancy.

If coming out in this way makes you uncomfortable, consider practicing what you're going to say. Likewise, try coming out about the pregnancy to people you encounter but don't know in everyday life. For example, when you're buying ice cream try mentioning to another customer that your partner is pregnant and try to strike up a casual conversation about it. Does he or she have kids? Did anyone he or she knows have the same ice-cream craving during pregnancy that your partner/wife has? Situations like these are perhaps safer settings where you can attempt to become more comfortable and familiar discussing your family.

Telling People That Your Partner Is Pregnant When You Were Unable to Conceive

If you haven't been able to conceive or maintain a pregnancy yourself, it can be emotionally agonizing to tell others that your partner is pregnant. Telling people can often be followed by holding back (or breaking into) tears about how you yourself couldn't get pregnant. You may have not kept everyone up-to-date on the progress of your own infertility struggles, so when they hear that your partner is pregnant they may be confused and ask what happened. Thus, sharing the news of the pregnancy also means sharing the news that you were unable to conceive or hold a pregnancy yourself. In many instances this means unexpectedly being more emotionally vulnerable than you had wished with any particular person. This can make telling people very poignant and sometimes heart-wrenching.

Likewise, if you're having a hard time telling people—or even entertaining the idea of telling people—of the pregnancy and your partner is ready and eager to let everyone know, this can put a strain on your relationship. She is undoubtedly less conflicted about the pregnancy and being public about the news. Although she'll most likely understand your feelings and be supportive, she may also want you to let go of your feelings and fully share in the newness of this pregnancy. Talk about and share your feelings compassionately and respectfully. Clear the air as soon as possible so that resentment and anger don't color your experience of pregnancy. If necessary, seek joint or individual counseling to resolve this issue.

How to Handle the Barrage of Personal Questions

As a pregnant lesbian, you will more than likely face numerous personal—and sometimes inappropriate—questions when you share your news with others. It's helpful to prepare yourself so that you won't feel so taken aback when they arise. Sometimes you may feel the subject is none of their business. Remember, you're under no obligation to answer personal questions. To maintain your integrity it's important to answer only the questions that feel appropriate and to have pre-established responses to questions that are hostile or invasive. Commonly posed questions include:

- How is it possible for you to be pregnant?
- Did you mean to get pregnant?
- What does your partner think about this? (implying that you were having an affair with a man and accidentally got pregnant)
- Did you use a sperm bank?
- Don't you know that sperm banks are dangerous and only down-and-out men looking for fast money go there?
- What if you have a boy? How are you going to raise a son?
- Tell me all about your donor.

• Did you have sex or use a turkey baster?

• How can you live with the guilt of inviting such discrimination into your child's life?

• Don't you think it's unfair to have a child when you know that lesbian relationships don't survive and that your child will live in a broken home?

Knowing that personal questions will come your way allows you to explore for yourself and with any relevant family members how you'd like to respond. For example, many families don't want to give out any information about their donors. By doing so, they feel it misdirects the focus from a female-parent family to a traditional heterosexual model. When you're asked questions about the donor, a pat reply such as "We're keeping that information to ourselves" or "The identity of the donor isn't what is important to us about our child" will often stop further questioning.

Deciding for yourself how much is appropriate to share is a personal choice. Once again, it will probably be most helpful to check in with your body's response when you're answering questions. Notice when you feel tight, defensive, or nervous. This may indicate that you're sharing more than what's comfortable for you.

Coming Out as a Single Mother

Single lesbian mothers are caught in a very interesting place. Many women have chosen single motherhood because they haven't found a suitable partner and their biological clock is ticking. Others want to be parents and have no intention of partnering. Still others had relationships that dissolved during their pregnancy. The majority of single lesbian mothers we've worked with fit into the first category.

Even today, single motherhood carries a cultural stigma. Although in the U.S. women aren't officially allowed to marry other women, partnered parents are often held in greater regard than single ones. Although there are millions of single mothers of all sexual orientations in our country, rampant stereotypes surround them. The prejudice and discrimination faced by single mothers of any sexual orientation is often just as great or sometimes greater than the discrimination faced by partnered lesbians. Many people are willing to accept that a couple, of any gender, is more equipped to raise a child than a single woman is.

Single mothers by choice are often given a hard time initially by friends and family who can't understand why anyone would want to parent on their own. When you tell people you're pregnant and that you'll be a single mother, you'll face a variety of responses from outrage to pity. It's common to have to repeatedly assert that you're a single mother by choice—if you are—and that you're sharing positive, joyous news.

If you're a single lesbian, the additional overlay of homophobia colors the responses of others. It's your choice whether to disclose your sexual orientation in any given situation. If you're not out—and plan to stay closeted—you may answer these personal questions more evasively than if you're out or planning to come out. Numerous single mothers-to-be have expressed that the greater issue is that they're single rather than that they're lesbian or bisexual.

Lesbians With Surprise Pregnancies

A number of lesbians every year get pregnant unintentionally. These conceptions predominantly occur when lesbian-identified women have sex with men. A surprise pregnancy for a lesbian usually comes as a complete shock. Because it's so completely unexpected, it can feel overwhelming. Apart from the shock, there's also the recovery from denial. When you aren't planning to get pregnant and if you barely realize it's a possibility, it's easy to deny the symptoms of pregnancy until you're quite far along. If this is the case for you, it may not be an option for you to terminate the pregnancy even if you would have chosen to do so. Therefore, a small but significant number of lesbians each year find themselves not only with surprise pregnancies, but also unwanted pregnancies.

When you have a surprise pregnancy that you intend to continue, everything in your life turns around. This includes trying to elicit support from friends and family members. The stress of discovering that you're suddenly going to be a mom is compounded if you aren't out and/or if your circle of friends is judgmental of lesbians who have sex with men. Nonetheless, finding support is crucial. Resist the urge to keep the pregnancy a secret until you've sorted everything out. It may take the entire pregnancy to feel you have a grip on your life changes. If you find that your identity, circle of friends, and body are all changing too rapidly for you to keep up, be sure to seek counseling.

Most lesbians take years preparing to be a parent. When you're suddenly dropped into it, you may feel paralyzed by the enormity of the endeavor. It helps to know that you're not alone. We see a number of lesbian-identified women each year who unintentionally get pregnant and choose to continue the pregnancy. There are many of you out there.

Pregnancy as a Time of Physical and Emotional Transformation

Pregnancy is an amazing opportunity for personal growth. It has been said that the "inner work" possible during pregnancy is equivalent to three years of therapy. As the body undergoes a radical metamorphosis, so do you on your journey to becoming a parent. The physical and hormonal changes of pregnancy provide a natural time to deepen and explore all of your relationships. Commonly explored relationships include those with your partner, your body, and your mother. These relationships are explored by all pregnant women, and are thus universal themes of pregnancy. For lesbian and bisexual women, however, there are usually specific twists to these themes. In the following sections, we'll discuss common physical and emotional changes that arise during pregnancy as well as issues that are specific to lesbian couples.

Life as a Pregnant Dyke

It isn't always easy to maintain a sense of lesbian visibility as a pregnant mother. In fact, your pregnancy can easily consume your queer visibility and identity. Because you've joined the club of pregnant women, you may often be assumed to be straight. As the nonpregnant mom, you often maintain your queer visibility but are invisible in terms of the pregnancy. If you're bisexual and partnered with a man, you're perceived as straight. And if you're a single pregnant woman of any sexual orientation, you're usually assumed to be straight. These assumptions often come equally from within the queer community and outside of it.

These same transformations and questioning of our queer identity may happen inside ourselves because we no longer have the same identity markers to depend upon. Our identities change as we become parents, and there may be an awkward period while we try on a variety of self-projections until we find a balance between our motherhood and lesbian identity. Internally it's not so much a question of what our sexual orientation is, but rather how we continue to express our queer identity while pregnant.

For example, many women we meet during preconception have a specific image of what a mom looks like, and it's usually quite different from their "hip dyke" self-perception. Women often face some outward overhauls as they try to reconcile these two images. Many women strive for "mommy hair" or a more feminine style of dress in order to feel they're ready to be a mother. Usually, over time each woman finds her own comfortable style, but there are often some comical interpretations along the way.

Many of these issues of gender, motherhood, and sexual orientation are highlighted if you're butch. If you've always felt most comfortable expressing yourself with "masculine" traits and appearances, blending an incredibly female body experience/feminine cultural experience with your butch identity can be a challenge.

Body Changes and Their Accompanying Emotions

Breast Growth

For some women, the rapid rate of breast growth during pregnancy feels overwhelming and alienating. If you've always prided yourself on not needing to wear a bra, suddenly having large breasts can make you feel like you're living in someone else's body. You may feel overly feminine or overly sexualized simply by having larger breasts. This early physical transformation is true preparation for the tremendous changes your body will undergo throughout the pregnancy and birth experience. Staying connected to your body and trying to embrace these changes will ultimately make pregnancy, birth, and nursing much more pleasurable experiences for you.

I Have to Wear *What?!*

It can be equally challenging as a pregnant lesbian to find appropriate clothes. Maternity clothes are usually very feminine. If you're accustomed to wearing more butch or "masculine" attire, it can feel awkward to have to purchase feminine clothes that don't reflect your self-perception. Likewise, continuing to dress in the same fashion as prior to pregnancy means wearing oversize clothes that fit your growing belly, which can make you feel dumpy instead of pregnant. Suspenders and low cut pants are often a good option in lieu of maternity pants.

If you're frequently mistaken for a man when you're not pregnant, it may feel very surreal to still be mistaken for a man now that you are or feel so obviously pregnant. Likewise, if you often pass as a man to the general public and enjoy it, you may be discouraged if you no longer pass anymore. Maintaining a butch persona throughout pregnancy inherently questions the outside world's stereotypes, and possibly your own, of what it means to be a pregnant woman.

The unexpected flip side to the challenging issue of butch pregnancy clothing is that the impact of being pregnant, whether hormonal or cultural, may cause you to gravitate toward clothes more feminine than you ever would have considered wearing while not pregnant. To start sporting dresses and leggings may throw your identity for a loop if these are radically different from your nonpregnant attire. Occasionally, however, you may not even notice the stylistic differences that are so obviously apparent to your partner and friends.

If you dress "femme" while pre-pregnant, maternity clothing styles have broadened sufficiently in the last few years that you probably won't have a huge problem finding clothes that suit you during pregnancy if you have a sufficient budget. Many of us find maternity clothing costs untenable, especially since we don't wear them that long. Thus, we borrow clothes from relatives and friends. The older styles in general were often very desexualized and "little girl"-like. No matter how you usually dress, invest the time, money, and creativity necessary to obtain one basic outfit that fits you well and doesn't drive you crazy stylistically—it's important to your self-esteem and body image. Most women by the end of pregnancy are down to wearing the same one, two, or possible three outfits every week.

Maternity clothes, in all sizes and styles, can now be found at many online retailers. See the resource list at the end of this chapter for more information.

Adapting to Physical Limitations

As with most pregnant women, there will probably come a time when you're no longer able to do the activities you've always been able to do, whether it's opening a jar, lifting a heavy object, balancing yourself on a ladder, or having sex in a certain position. With these limitations your identity may be thrown for a loop. Many women deeply enjoy their ability to lead active and athletic lives. Many feel that their competency and strength have marked their lesbianism and have helped them create an identity that feels empowered and comfortable. Having to work with the concept of physical limitations may often be confused with being "weak."

The crisis part of this shift seems to lift when you're able to recognize that you're not weak, but rather you're *pregnant*. Your identity as strong and capable in a physical sense is superseded for a brief interlude by the strength and capacity to grow and nurture a baby. Ultimately, you'll gain a broader respect for yourself and your body by acknowledging the qualities needed to grow a baby—but perhaps not without a few stumbling blocks along the way.

The physical changes during pregnancy are tremendous, and they are the most apparent transformations that accompany pregnancy. Adjusting to your body changing shape every day for month after month, however, isn't always easy to do. We've discussed the inevitable breast changes, clothing challenges, and physical limitations that are a large part of the adjustment of being pregnant. But your inner relationship to a radically different body shape is also a major part of pregnancy.

Many women think they're going to love the physical changes of pregnancy. In actuality, they usually experience a mixed bag of emotional responses to these changes. No longer knowing your body and its limitations can feel disturbing on a core level. One mom recently expressed to us her utter panic when she realized she could not even walk down the block without getting winded. She was previously accustomed to riding her bike 50 miles at a time and then going dancing that same night. The complete reversal of what she could depend on from her body shook her deeply. Women are often vaguely aware that they'll grow emotionally and spiritually during pregnancy, but rarely are they aware what this growth may demand of them.

Your Changing Body and Feeding

As we mentioned in Chapter 7, during pregnancy and postpartum, food is love. A pregnant mother feeds her baby directly from the food that she eats, as does a nursing mother. Feeding yourself so much quality food is a full-time job. It can be difficult to maintain this level of food preparation and intake all on your own, and the effort is magnified if you're experiencing morning sickness.

If you're single and don't have roommates, you'll need to figure out how to feed yourself when you're too hungry or sick or tired to cook. This is where friends can pitch in easily. They can drop off prepared food. Have Tupperware on hand to freeze meals and just leave one or two fresh portions out to eat. Most pregnant women won't eat the same thing three times in a row, so making a big pot of stew that will last you the next four days will no longer be the most successful way to cook for yourself. If you need to forgo spending money on fancy baby items to make way for expensive, healthy, prepared food, do it. Your baby is made from what you eat, and you'll feel loved and nourished if you feed yourself well.

If you're partnered, a large part of your partner's responsibility and joint commitment to the pregnancy is to help feed you. This isn't an easy job, since pregnant women are especially choosy about what and when they want eat.

If, however, the nonpregnant partner fails to do her part in keeping her partner well fed, the pregnant mom is likely to feel unloved. In fact, low blood sugar may spur many of the fights you may have during pregnancy. Thus, if your pregnant partner is being unreasonable but persistent, feed her before she blows her top. Often her desperation stems from a nutritional depletion, and things won't look so bad on a full stomach.

It isn't easy to realize that so much depends on your ability to feed your partner. This is especially so if she's the one who has usually prepared household meals. But just as she has the baby in her body and is lending her life energy constantly to growing the baby, whether or not she's in the mood to do so right then, you need to try your best to keep her well fed—whether or not you're in the mood to do so.

Sexual Abuse, Eating Disorders, and Body Issues

Rapid weight gain and body changes often trigger past eating disorders and sexual abuse traumas as well as overall negative self-esteem body image issues. Our culture seems to hold less respect for pregnant women's privacy than other people's. As a pregnant woman, you'll probably hear many comments from strangers, family, and friends about your size and weight gain. You'll receive not only unsolicited advice and unsolicited disclosures of others' experiences, but also direct judgment and criticism. It's common to be told in the same day that you're both too big and too small, regardless of how average your weight gain and growth may be. In fact, we've never worked with any client who was able to completely avoid a barrage of feedback from random people about her size. In this way society's true obsession with size becomes fully apparent. Thus, it's no surprise that old weight and size issues may reappear for you, even if you've done a lot of work to resolve them. In fact, some pregnant women with strong anti-fatphobia attitudes are surprised to recognize their own issues about weight and size and body image that they may never have felt. Surprise!

The reemergence of issues of sexual assault and abuse may come as more of a surprise, especially if you thought you had safely put these issues away. Still, the hormones of pregnancy, coupled with common underlying pregnancy feelings of being out of control, bring these issues to the surface for some women. Because these are past issues, it may take some time for you to recognize the emotional impact they may have on your pregnancy. It's helpful to be on the lookout if you think these issues could come up again for you and to seek counseling if necessary.

Often being aware of, naming, or expressing these feelings to someone is all that's needed to keep these issues at bay. Some women, however, feel as if they're being flooded with past traumatic memories or unable to maintain their healthy eating habits. If this is the case for you, remember to have compassion for yourself *and* to seek necessary support. If these issues arise, we've found that it's best to assume that they'll remain an active presence throughout nursing as well.

Emotional Changes

Increased Emotional Instability: Feeling Crazy

Exhaustion, discomfort, and nausea are the physical underpinnings of the cacophony of hormones and emotions that mark the first trimester of pregnancy. Many pregnant women express feeling scared and overwhelmed by the sheer intensity of all their feelings. Although some women are more sensitive to these hormones, and some are more prone to emotional expression from the start, every pregnant woman has elevated emotions. The altered mental and emotional state brought on by pregnancy hormones is almost impossible to describe to a nonpregnant person. Often the pregnant woman finds it difficult to recognize how "abnormal" she is feeling and acting. This level of emotional instability can make you and everyone around you feel like you're on an emotional roller coaster every day.

Usually, you and your loved ones grow more adjusted to the whole experience as you move into the second trimester, and your hormones will ease up a bit. Nonetheless, a fair amount of emotional volatility continues throughout the entire pregnancy. If having such strong emotions sweep over you triggers panic, anxiety, depression, or past trauma, you may consider seeking therapy. Sometimes this emotional instability can prove too much for a relationship or work environment, so without hesitation seek support if you need it.

Although the stereotype of the crazy pregnant woman is just that—a *stereotype*—the emotional swings during pregnancy can be wild and unsettling. If you know you tend to have significant mood swings when you're not pregnant, you may want to plan ahead for the kinds of support you may need during this time.

Control

If you've always prided yourself on your emotional stability, or if you've been the rock in your relationship while your partner has been more emotional, you may be in for quite a surprise. Being at the mercy of your emotions can make you feel out of control. When you find yourself crying over dog food commercials or because you wanted lasagna and not a casserole for dinner, you may no longer recognize yourself.

Feeling weepy and easily overwhelmed, as well as more physically limited than usual, can make you feel like a "helpless female." This usually feels quite scary for a woman who's always considered herself in control. Pregnancy helps you recognize how much being in control is an illusion. Maintaining control is crucial to many women's sense of safety; in fact, it's a coping skill learned much earlier in life when "out of control" times were perhaps truly dangerous. Being pushed by your pregnancy to accept new truths about yourself and the interdependency you share with others can feel overwhelmingly unfamiliar. The gift of this lesson is that parenting involves intimate daily interaction with another being, and therefore can't and shouldn't be solely in our control. Any new awareness and accommodation to feeling out of control will ease your transition to motherhood.

Self-Centeredness

Pregnancy, although in many ways readily visible, is for the most part a very internal process that requires considerable personal reflection. You may feel like you're never alone in your own body and thus start to develop a full relationship with the one inside you. You have an evolved instinct to put the needs and presence of your baby first, and your body has an evolved capacity to make you feel its pregnancy needs are undeniable. The combination of the two can make you appear self-centered to the rest of the world, and this isn't actually unhealthy.

Many nonpregnant partners, however, feel tried by how everything revolves around the pregnant woman: where she wants to go, what she does or doesn't want to eat, what she does or doesn't want to do. Many nonpregnant moms also feel like they've lost their partner. The pregnant woman may appear to be interested in nothing other than herself and her growing body and baby. When this happens, the nonpregnant partner may feel unappreciated and invisible. Add this invisibility to her inevitable societal invisibility, and it's easy for her to doubt what her role in this whole process is.

These feelings of having lost one's partner are certainly heightened in lesbian relationships where the partners have a strong level of "merge." To have one's role in the relationship replaced by the baby can leave the nonbiological mom feeling left out in the cold. What's hard to accept is that the pregnant mom usually doesn't even realize just how self-centered she is during pregnancy, or how this level of self-centeredness can transform into the same level of nurturing capacity to the baby. In fact, the pregnant woman can feel unsupported and unrecognized for all of the work she's doing, wanting the nonpregnant partner to put out more emotionally for her, regardless of whether she's capable of reciprocating.

This dynamic takes a lot of integrity to navigate as both of you are becoming mothers and have strong needs from each other. If you're the nonbiological mom, you may feel this whole situation is more than you bargained for. You may feel exhausted, unappreciated, clung-to, bossed around, or ignored. Furthermore, your best friend and lover to whom you'd normally turn for support is the cause of the trouble. Get some support just for you. There are beautiful, incredible experiences to be had while sharing a pregnancy, and acknowledging the challenges in no way denigrates the miraculous aspects, so don't feel guilty expressing your feelings about the difficulties that may arise.

This is the emotional reality of the first trimester and usually at least part of the second trimester. Some couples get a reprieve during the second trimester when they feel like they can reconnect again. Other couples, however, don't feel they reconnect until the baby is a few months old.

Mother Issues

Many lesbians are alienated from their mothers simply because of their sexual orientation. This may stem from the news of the pregnancy or may be a reality they've lived with throughout adulthood. Regardless, every pregnant woman seems to have a primal need for her mother. This need and longing seem equally strong whether your mother is dead or if she's your daily confidante. If you're adopted, you may find yourself revisiting your desire to know more about your birth mother. There just seems to be something about becoming a mother that triggers a woman's need for her own mother.

The pain of not being able to make the kind of emotional contact with your mother that you long for can be indescribable. It tends to cut to the quick of all of the abandonment issues each woman carries within. This unexpected need for a mother's love can often cause women to reach out to their estranged mothers at this time. Although some women are well received when they choose to do this, many are painfully rejected again.

If you're partnered and one of you has an involved mother, she can act as a surrogate mother to the other. However, if she refuses, or even fails to recognize your partner as part of the family, the pain will only be magnified. She may be willing to step into this role for you if you take the initiative to directly invite her to do so and tell her exactly what you appreciate about what she does or can do that would feel motherly.

Some women find that it's most helpful to spend time in quiet introspection exploring what qualities they're looking for from their mother. Once they've come up with these qualities—be they unconditional love or a warm, understanding embrace—it's easier to work to fill the need. It can be helpful to ask for those behaviors or qualities from a partner or friend.

For example: Joanne finally got pregnant. She and her partner Deborah had been trying for more than two years to conceive. Deborah was in contact with her family on a regular basis, but they lived across the country. Joanne hadn't seen her own mother in 15 years. During pregnancy Joanne felt an almost desperate need to contact her mother. But she knew that to do so would be self-defeating. One day she and Deborah sat down and made a list of all of the things Joanne felt she was missing by not having a mother. Deborah encouraged Joanne to be as specific as possible. Her list—after a good cry—looked like this:

- delicious, warm brownies made from scratch
- nighttime back rubs as I fall asleep
- hugs that let me know everything will be OK
- someone to cook for me without me feeling I have to reciprocate
- approval and unending excitement that we're having a baby

When Joanne had completed the list, she and Deborah looked at it together. Joanne felt much better being able to name what was missing for her. Just making the list had been painful yet cathartic. Deborah realized that although she would never be Joanne's mother—nor did she want to be—there were things she could do to help Joanne fill certain emotional gaps. Deborah got the recipe for the special brownies from Joanne's sister and baked them on a regular basis. She also gave Joanne nightly back rubs. As often as possible she swept Joanne into her arms and said reassuring things. And she took over more of the meal preparation. Joanne and Deborah asked Deborah's mother to help with the cooking when she flew out after the baby's birth and to express a great amount of approval and excitement to Joanne specifically on the phone whenever she called.

These things, of course, weren't a replacement for Joanne's mother, but they did allow Joanne to feel unconditionally loved and to further heal the pain of losing her mother. Deborah and Joanne found that an active approach to healing Joanne's emotional wounds was best. It brought them together even more closely as a couple and invited Deborah's mom more fully into the grandmother role, which she herself found reassuring.

Donor, Sperm, and Coparent Issues

At some point in the second or third trimester, women usually revisit their donor/coparent choices. If you used a known donor's sperm or plan on coparenting, you may find yourself revisiting whatever choices or options you had for legal protection of your parenting autonomy. You may be surprised by feeling threatened, in a way you hadn't previously, by the idea of having any contact with the donor or coparent. Don't' worry, this feeling is perfectly normal. First, you may be developing your protective mothering instincts. Second, if you're the one who's pregnant, you're probably beginning to realize that your 24-hour-a-day physical relationship with your baby is going to change at the birth. Most women face this with a great deal of relief, but also with a fear of not being able to protect the baby adequately on the outside, and loss of the constant intimacy now shared with the baby. The baby's new relationships with others that begin to develop at the moment of birth can get mixed up with the mom's impending feelings of loss, and therefore feel threatening. It's helpful to reread any journal writing you've done or any part of a contract you wrote with your coparent(s) that reminds you of the reasons you chose to create life in the way you did.

On the other hand, if you're coparenting it's common to feel as if the coparents aren't helping out during pregnancy and to resent the idea that they'll show up at the day of birth to start partaking in all the fun. They may not realize which kinds of help would benefit you now during pregnancy. They may not have yet realized that paying for a house cleaner for you or shopping for you or paying for prenatal massage is in fact caring for the baby. It seems a hard leap for people to make, especially those who haven't been around many babies or pregnant women. Remind your coparents of any agreement you made along these lines or spell it out for them very specifically now. Often women have secret thoughts along the lines of *They think they just get to show*

Limor Inbar-Hansen, Indelible Images

up at the birth after they said they were too busy to attend the childbirth preparation class and too busy to help feed me. Make sure to start the parenting relationship off well by being extra clear in your communication. Often we think we're being heard more clearly than we truly are, so express yourself whenever you need to.

If you've chosen to use sperm from an unknown donor, a number of issues may arise now that the baby seems more "real": What will s/he look like? Did we choose the right donor? Are we sure we made the best choices about the ethnicity of the donor? Talk out the issues once again as they arise, even if you spent a great deal of preconception time deciding carefully. You probably had very good reasons for making your decisions, but fears don't disappear by being ignored. Voice them and rediscover your trust.

Emotional Themes of Single Motherhood

The beginning of pregnancy can often be challenging for single women, as it is a time requiring great support when neither the support team nor the "asking for help" skills have yet been refined. It may help to know that for many women the first trimester of pregnancy is the absolute hardest, with great improvement often arriving around 10 weeks after conception. In the interim, call every person who has ever offered to help and solicit them to pitch in, even if you're not sure what they could do for you. They might be more clearheaded than you and come up with lovely offers. Often the hormone changes at first carry feelings of aloneness, isolation, and abandonment. You may feel these more acutely if you live alone. Or you may feel secure because you've developed many skills and resources for both enjoying alone time and creating connections when you need to. Good for you if you have. If you haven't, here are some aspects of pregnancy that seem particularly difficult and are just the places to ask for help.

You'll probably want one or a few special people with whom you can regularly share all the subtle details of your exciting great time of change. Choose one or two of them and ask if they'll be your companions in the adventure—they might be who you call at 7 A.M. when you first feel the baby kick, or who you call at 10 P.M. when you can't sleep because of heartburn. We also encourage all pregnant women to keep a journal. Pregnancy is a time of amazing intuition; later you'll want to be able to recall the insights you had. You need a variety of ways in your life to express and receive acknowledgement of the beautiful work you're doing growing your baby.

Nighttime

Nighttime can feel particularly lonely for many pregnant women. You may be up in the middle of the night with insomnia, nausea, or heartburn. Hormones exacerbate fears and worries, and these can loom in the dark of night when you feel it's too late to call anyone for support. If you experience this, be gentle with yourself. Have a warm bathrobe by your bed and a space heater if you need to feel cozy when it's cold. Be willing to get out of bed, make yourself some food and a warm drink, read a bit of a comforting book, or even take a warm bath instead of lying in bed feeling miserable. Prepare anything you may need for this special 3 A.M. time and place it within reach. It's a magical time to experience that most of us in regular life don't have the opportunity to be conscious for.

Avoiding Isolation

If you become too tired to do anything but work and sleep, let your friends know that they'll have to make an extra effort to maintain their friendships with you and to help you not fall into the self-defeating cycle of isolation: "I haven't seen my friend because life has been consuming. I can't call her now just to ask for help." Let your friends know you really want and need to spend time with them and explain that the time you spend probably needs to be a bit different than usual. They could show up after work with a meal to share with you, and then tuck you into bed by 8. They could socialize with you at the Laundromat, or in your kitchen as they help you prepare food on the weekend to freeze for weekday dinners. You may need to do your socializing in these ways so that you can get things done, connect with people, and still get as much sleep as you need (which is as much as possible).

In general, you'll find that your focus will be quite introspective: You'll probably want less and less to be in big loud groups. You'll probably be content to spend many minutes watching birds feed outside, letting your mind wander. This is the beautiful inward journey of pregnancy. It's essential to leave spaces of unstructured time in your life that permit this to happen.

Work During Pregnancy

You may feel under particular pressure to not call in sick to work when you'll be the sole financial provider for your baby. The time to think about budget and financial considerations is when you've just eaten and slept well the night before, not when you're throwing up at 6 A.M. Most women find working while pregnant is sometimes fine, sometimes fulfilling, and sometimes utterly exhausting. If you absolutely must work full-time, you'll find ways to organize the other parts of your life to let that happen. Getting a lot of sleep on the weekends and going to bed early during the week will be crucial. You'll probably do less socializing, and your house may not be as clean as you'd like. You may not get every closet on your list organized before the baby comes, and that's OK.

Asking for Help

During your insemination process, you may have already done the hard work of learning to ask for help. If you haven't, now's your chance. Sometime—and probably a number of times—in your child's first few years, you'll have to ask for help, whether it's carrying the stroller off the bus or tending to your child's needs when you have the flu. Does it seem impossible to ask friends for these levels of support? In reality, you're probably more hesitant to ask than they are to accommodate. You may have friends who feel that if you couldn't do it all on your own, you shouldn't have chosen to become a parent. These people will probably not remain your friends for long, and although it will be a sad loss, the loss is truly theirs. You'll find that you have other friends who are thrilled by your pregnancy. Whether they know very much or very little about children, they'll tell you they're excited to welcome your new child into the world. These people would love to help you, if you specifically tell them what you need.

As soon as you're pregnant and parenting, you may feel that the help you need is obvious and if anyone wanted to do it they would. This is simply not true. People who aren't parents often have no clue about parenting. They just need to be told. Because of this, some of your best help will probably come from other moms, especially single moms, who have the most to juggle yet know the most about how to support you. Get involved in a support group for pregnant and new moms. People in these groups are your best source of after-hours support, because they're used to being woken up in the middle of the night. You may be surprised, but people often feel blessed by the opportunity to help, as long as they have some idea of what you need.

Queer Community vs. Community of Mothers

Many pregnant lesbians experience a loss of friends in the gay community. Many feel their gay community has been replaced by a community of other parents. In most areas of the country, lesbian parents are still few and far between. This is certainly not the case in metropolitan areas or other smaller gay communities. But, at least for now, it remains true for most of the country. When you become a parent your priorities change, how you spend your time changes, and what you have the time and energy to do changes. As a result, you'll probably seek support and friendship from parents with children the same age as your own.

When you become pregnant these shifts begin to take place. As your need for rest increases and your desire to focus on "all things baby" increases, many of your non-parent friends may drift away. Although this is a natural process, it's still painful. Likewise, you can feel arbitrarily thrust into a community of heterosexual parents, unsure whether either of you want each other. It takes time to develop new friendships. Although in her book *Lesbian Mothers* Ellen Lewin documents that the priority for lesbian parents often shifts from having lesbian friendships to parent friendships, most lesbians would never consider straight parents to be a replacement for their queer friends. These are not interchangeable communities. Both serve specific needs.

If you find yourself outgrowing your queer community or if your queer community isn't child friendly and thus has left you, try to make contact with other lesbian and gay families in your area. For some this is easier than others. Actively making contacts during pregnancy, when you have more time than you would with a new baby, is a fruitful project to undertake.

Connecting with other gay and lesbian families can be accomplished by placing an ad in a local gay and lesbian newspaper or putting up a notice on a billboard at a bookstore or community center. Be persistent in your search. It can seem as if there are no other lesbian parents in your area, but more than likely there are. Even in our haven of lesbian parents in the San Francisco Bay Area, we've encountered many women in our groups who didn't know a single lesbian parent before coming into the group. Many lesbians we meet don't even know other lesbians. This isolation needs to be broken. Meeting other gay and lesbian parents is a good way to start to get more comfortable in coming out. The more people you ask, the greater the chances you have of finding gay and lesbian parents. Finding other queer parents is essential not only to your own comfort and well-being, but also for the comfort and well-being of your children.

Partner Issues

If you're partnered, your transformations during pregnancy will undoubtedly include your relationship with your partner. Change isn't always easy. In fact, more often than not it's downright stressful. If you are two women planning to have children together, it's important to look at the big picture. You'll need to make the health of your relationship a priority, as the universal stresses of pregnancy and the first year of life with a baby are tremendous. Add to that the pressure of internal and external homophobia, and you'll see that you're going to need to actively affirm your love for each other regularly in order to strengthen your relationship. There's a tendency for couples to give in to the stress of this time and break up because of it. Get support if you're nearing the point of breakup. If you felt your relationship was strong enough to sustain having children, then it probably is. We don't advocate staying together at all costs—being true to yourselves is the most important thing you can model for your children. Nonetheless, couples who make it through the baby's first year often regain what was fulfilling about the love relationship. By then life will usually have settled into a familiar pattern, and you'll be thinking about your next child instead of breaking up.

Some couples find that the growth changes during pregnancy help strengthen their relationship. They say they have never felt closer, that their love seems to blossom exponentially. Their sex life is great. Their physical intimacy is deeper than ever. These women only have the physical aches and pains of pregnancy to deal with. These are the lucky couples.

Most couples—of all sexual orientations—have much more on their plates than just pure pregnancy bliss. Although they may be thrilled to be pregnant, the intensity of change goes hand-in-hand with their excitement.

When One Partner Is Ambivalent About the Pregnancy

It's difficult to weather the emotional and practical demands of pregnancy when you're in a relationship in which only one of you is excited about becoming a parent. In these situations it's usually, although not always, the pregnant mom-to-be who is more excited and the nonpregnant mom-to-be who is ambivalent. Both of you need to provide room for the ambivalent partner to grow into motherhood. Pregnancy often becomes more exciting as it becomes more noticeable, which can lead to a deepening interest in the entire process for both partners.

Many pregnant women, however, realize this ambivalence isn't working for them as they'd hoped it would. Perhaps they assumed that once pregnant, they would see that their partners had come around, but they haven't yet. Or perhaps they realize that for them it's too painful to deal with a lack of commitment to the most consuming thing they've ever done and what will soon be the most important aspect of their life. In these situations, unfortunately, breakups are not uncommon.

Where Did the Romance and Physical Intimacy Go?

Many women experience intense morning sickness and other discomforts during pregnancy. The loving, active, nurturing partner can suddenly be replaced with a napping, uncomfortable, vomiting partner who goes to bed each night at 7. This is all a normal part of pregnancy, yet it doesn't often gel with the romantic notions of creating a baby together.

Some couples are able to maintain an intimate physical closeness throughout pregnancy. They mutually enjoy the body changes of the pregnant mom-to-be and love to snuggle and hug and are constantly physically close. Other women feel like being touched during pregnancy is the last thing on earth that they want. They need to sleep with a variety of pillows in order to feel comfortable, and they're alternately hot or physically uncomfortable, so although they might want physical intimacy, their personal comfort precludes their desire or ability to be physically close. This can be emotionally difficult for the nonpregnant mom who wants to maintain the physical closeness but feels rejected in her attempts to do so.

Sex

Most pregnant women don't want to have sex during the first trimester. They may be concerned about triggering a miscarriage or simply feel too sick and tired to have sex. Many pregnant women do have a strong sex drive during the second trimester of pregnancy, especially as increased blood flow increases vaginal and breast sensitivity.

On the other hand, some women don't want to have partner sex during pregnancy, as it triggers too many emotions for them. Sometimes women are too physically uncomfortable to want to have partner sex and are not with their partners during the few hours of the day when they feel good. In addition, some women are turned off by their pregnant partner's new body or don't think it's "right" to have sex when pregnant or with a pregnant woman.

Still, these same women may lead an active sex life with themselves through masturbation. This can be disconcerting if you're the one who wants partner sex and your partner is content with solo sex.

Physical Changes and Concerns

It's common for the pregnant woman not to be able to achieve orgasm. She may experience much sexual pleasure but physiologically be unable to achieve climax. Likewise, some women find that their breasts and clitoris are so sensitive that they can become overstimulated quite quickly. And some have painful—though not dangerous—contractions when they orgasm, thus abruptly concluding the rendezvous. The painful, crampy feeling that occurs in the uterus when pregnant women experience an orgasm is a type of contraction. The uterus has many kinds of contractions that serve different purposes. The contraction felt during orgasm, although uncomfortable, is nothing to worry about and usually lasts a few minutes before relaxing.

If a woman shows signs of preterm labor or is at high risk for preterm labor due to factors in her medical history, she'll be made aware of this by her health care provider and be educated about the signs of preterm labor. Most women in this situation are told to refrain from sexual activity. If the care provider is uncomfortable discussing lesbian sexuality, he or she might be vague about some details. In this case, you'll need to clarify by asking directly. Usually the activities to avoid if the pregnant woman is at increased risk for preterm labor are: penetrative vaginal or anal sex that stimulates the cervix directly (the wall between vagina and rectum is thin), nipple stimulation that causes the release of uterine-contracting hormones, and, especially, semen getting on the cervix, since it contains cervix-softening prostaglandins. For a woman without specific preterm labor risks, none of these sexual activities will put her at risk for premature labor.

Some women get yeast infections more easily during pregnancy. If this is the case for you, be careful to avoid using lubricant with glycerin, which may encourage yeast growth. Many women have extra vaginal secretions when they're pregnant and don't need as much lube. These clear white secretions are normal and aren't a sign of infection as long as they're not itchy, bubbly, foul smelling, yellowish green, or brownish. Once a woman has given birth, hormone changes related to breastfeeding will often cause her not to lubricate as much. At this point many women keep lubricant handy, depending on the sexual activities they enjoy.

Some pregnant women get herpes outbreaks more frequently than they did before pregnancy. If you fall into this category, try to notice if there's any correlation between friction or irritation of the skin and your outbreaks. In addition, women sometimes get purple swollen varicose veins in their labia and vagina during pregnancy. These should be treated gently with minimal touch or friction. Since pregnancy increases the chance of bladder infection, it's a good habit to urinate after sex so that you'll wash any bacteria out of the urethra that may have found their way up. Natural remedies and prevention tips for yeast, herpes, vaginal varicosities, and bladder infections can all be found in the pregnancy books listed at the end of Chapter 16.

At the end of pregnancy, when the baby's head is low in the mother's pelvis, penetrative sex needs to be gentle, especially with dildos. Myths about avoiding oral sex during pregnancy are unfounded; what should be avoided is blowing air forcefully into the vagina. In addition, breast milk may drip from the nipples when a pregnant woman is aroused. This is no reason for concern. It's an amazing thing!

Remember that the sexual spectrum is broad. What you desire sexually may change from month to month. You may feel awkward about not being able to physically get comfortable in your familiar positions if you're used to always being a top or a bottom. You'll need to get creative with your ever-growing pregnant belly and ever-changing hormones!

Nonmonogamy and Dating During Pregnancy

If you're single and dating, or partnered and nonmonogamous, there are some things to consider during pregnancy. First, it's crucial to remember that practicing safer sex is important before, during, and after pregnancy. This is especially true during pregnancy as any infection that you contract can have an impact on your pregnancy as well as the birth and potential health of your baby. Second, whereas you may have been comfortable with casual sex before, many women find that during pregnancy they're no longer able to have sex without forming a strong emotional bond with their sex partner. Third, many pregnant women in nonmonogamous relationships become very insecure and want their partners to at least temporarily be monogamous during pregnancy. In fact, many nonpregnant partners don't want their pregnant lover being sexual with others while she's carrying their baby. Be sure to check in with each other's feelings about nonmonogamy during this time so that you'll both be as sexually respectful and responsible as possible.

Affairs

Just as with heterosexual couples, numerous women who are monogamously partnered with women become aware that their partner is having sex with someone else at the end of the pregnancy. Sometimes nonpregnant partners stray out of fear of the huge commitment and intimacy before them, and sometimes they do it out of a need to receive attention instead of give it. This is a painful time for all concerned if it disrupts the trust in the relationship just before birth of the baby—which is a heightened time of emotional need for the pregnant woman. It also raises concerns about risks of sexually transmitted diseases if communication and honesty aren't practiced. Get some counseling if any of the above issues seems more than you can deal with by yourselves.

Pregnancy as Preparation for Birth

Pregnancy provides you with a daily opportunity to prepare for birth. As you learn to surrender to your body, you prepare to give birth. As you learn to ask for help from friends or a partner, you prepare to give birth. As you work with the numerous discomforts of pregnancy, you prepare for birth. As you come to love the growing baby, you prepare for birth. As you adapt to the constant presence of the baby in your life, you prepare for birth. Birth is the crowning experience of pregnancy, yet it's only the beginning of the journey you've been wanting for so long. In the following chapter we explore specific lesbian issues pertaining to birth and new motherhood.

Resources

Books
The Pregnancy Journal: A Day-to-Day Guide to a Happy and Healthy Pregnancy,
     A. Christine Harris, Chronicle Books, 1996

Online Maternity Clothing Retailers
From Here to Maternity
www.fromheretomaternity.com

imaternity
www.imaternity.com

Mothers in Motion, Inc. (sells maternity workout apparel)
www.mothers-in-motion.com

Mothers' Online Thrift Shop (sells gently used mother and baby goods)
www.motshop.com

Pickles & Ice Cream Maternity Apparel
www.picklesmaternity.com

That Glow
www.thatglow.com

Web Sites and Periodicals
About: Pregnancy & Birth (offers advice, personal stories, news, and a "belly gallery"!)
www.pregnancy.about.com

Childbirth.org (lists resources for all cycles of pregnancy and birthing)
www.childbirth.org

ePregnancy.com (offers articles, news, and messages boards)
www.epregnancy.com

Having a Baby Today (16-page newsletter emphasizing the miracle of birth. Log
onto www.havingababytoday.com for more information.)

Midwifery Today (A thorough and thoughtful magazine about natural birth. Log onto
www.midwiferytoday.org or call (800) 743-0974 for subscription information.)

Chapter 18 Preparing for Birth

Birth is amazingly universal, regardless of the mother's sexual orientation. Preparing for birth as a lesbian, bisexual, or single woman is similar, although not identical, to preparing for birth as a partnered heterosexual. This chapter pays specific attention to the unique aspects of the experience for lesbian, bisexual, and single women within the context of the deep transformations that lie ahead.

The end of pregnancy is a complex time. Most pregnant women are physically uncomfortable, with numerous aches and pains throughout the day and night. Although some women still enjoy being pregnant at the end of pregnancy, many are ready to no longer have to navigate their ever-growing body. The discomforts of the end of pregnancy allow women to look forward to the next phase of the process: giving birth.

Most pregnant women become very introverted during the final months of pregnancy, not realizing how consumed they are with their bodies and their growing baby. This preoccupation often leads to a desire for quiet introspection. When time permits, a pregnant woman may realize she's spent the past two hours staring off into space. On the outside, nonpregnant partners experience this phase of pregnancy as a departure from the external world and thus a departure from any meaningful interactions that don't revolve around the baby.

Unfortunately, most women don't have the option to stop working as early as they'd like. Most pregnant women would be thrilled to stop working around the sixth month of pregnancy. In fact, many report feeling uninterested in their job from the early months of pregnancy. Due to financial realities, however, women don't usually stop working until two weeks before their due date, and many work right up until the time they go into labor.

Working during the last month of pregnancy doesn't always allow sufficient time to emotionally prepare for birth. And if a pregnant woman is partnered, work schedules don't often provide built-in time to prepare together for the big event. In this chapter we cover ways in which you and your partner can prepare for birth together and as individuals in spite of leading busy lives.

Childbirth Education

We recommend that every mom giving birth for the first time take a formal childbirth education class. These classes provide a wonderful opportunity to educate yourself about the labor and birth process. The first step for a childbirth education class is to find one suited to your needs.

At Maia we teach childbirth education classes specifically for lesbian and bisexual women. Just to be able to bask in the glow of a room full of pregnant lesbians is an amazing experience for all who attend. We know that in most areas you may not even get to meet another pregnant lesbian. If you live in a town or city with a significant lesbian population, consider placing an ad asking other pregnant lesbians if they'd like to form a class with you. It's not difficult to find a childbirth educator who's willing to teach a group of women who have already gathered together.

When looking for a class, there are a number of things to keep in mind. In general, we recommend looking for private classes taught by childbirth educators rather than classes at hospitals. A private instructor will usually have a more holistic, integrated approach to birth that includes a greater emphasis on teaching you pain-management techniques and ways to avoid unnecessary medical technology. If you have difficulty locating such a teacher or class, contact local midwives for suggestions and referrals.

When you've found out about available classes, it really pays to do some screening on the phone. Come out about your family structure in your conversation and ask the teacher whether she has any experience working with lesbians. Likewise, whether you're partnered or not, ask whether she regularly has single women in her classes. You may also want to ask about the ethnic diversity of her classes. Pay attention and take notes on how she responds to these questions. Her comfort level will have everything to do with your comfort level in the class. Keep calling instructors until you've reached one who has at least an open respect for all family structures.

If you're having trouble locating such an instructor, or the idea of being the only single mother or lesbian mother/couple in the class is intimidating, or you don't feel comfortable coming out in this kind of group environment, we encourage you to find an instructor who's willing to provide private classes just for you. Most childbirth educators offer private classes upon request. A good childbirth education class should help you feel much more educated and prepared for your birth. These classes are often emotionally provocative and can help you determine your hopes and dreams for the birth experience. Besides attending a comprehensive childbirth education class when preparing for birth, it's helpful to explore the following issues.

Processing the Conception

When preparing to give birth, spend some time reflecting on the conception of your baby. How do you feel about the entire conception process? For women who became pregnant quickly and easily, there might not be much to reflect upon except gratefulness. If your conception journey was long and arduous, however, many painful feelings may still be lingering. In fact, even though your pregnancy is almost over, you may still be traumatized from the conception process. Trauma doesn't disappear overnight. Depending on the particulars, this trauma can last for years. The intersection of feelings about conception or previous pregnancy loss and feelings about your current pregnancy can be multifaceted and overpowering. Fears, self-doubt, and feelings of inadequacy left over from an extended conception period can undermine your trust in your body. This impacts how you feel about your ability to birth your baby. Likewise, if one partner in a couple was unable to conceive or hold a pregnancy and now the second partner is ready to give birth, this can retrigger the nonpregnant mom's feelings of inadequacy, resentment, or envy that she isn't the one who's about to have the baby.

This is a fruitful time to explore individually and as a team what impact the conception process or previous pregnancies still have on you and in what ways it might influence how you feel about giving birth. By exploring these feelings you may be able to release some of their unconscious hold on you.

Empowered Birth

The fact that women are able to give birth is truly amazing. It's miraculous that live human beings, nurtured from our blood, come forth from our bodies. Our culture, however, doesn't always revere women's innate power to create and bring forth life. If it did, society probably wouldn't be so misogynist or anti-child. Unfortunately, modern-day birth practices, which have developed within the context of our culture's view toward women, often leave women feeling disconnected from their bodies and traumatized by the entire experience.

When we educate ourselves and take birth back into the hands, bodies, and hearts of women, where it belongs, birth takes on an entirely new meaning. It's a life transition, an initiation on all levels. Women are trained to believe that birth will be too painful to withstand and are encouraged to consider pain relief through drugs. As midwives, we've seen hundreds of women amaze themselves as they discover that, with support and knowledgeable assistance, they can give birth without the help of drugs or machines. When they discover they can do this, they feel they've been given the gift of themselves. Their self-respect soars, and they begin motherhood on sure footing.

Nonpregnant partners helping and witnessing their pregnant partners consciously giving birth have a greater respect for life, their own role in the family, and the power of their partner. This shared experience also strengthens familial bonds.

Our goal for you is to experience the power of birth and for the birth of your baby to be one of the greatest events of your life. Your birth may take place in your home, a local birth center, or a hospital. You may use no medications to help with the pain; you may use many. You may give birth vaginally; you may have a cesarean section. Regardless as to what the outside appearances of your birth may be, we want you to firmly realize that you're the one who brings forth life.

Claiming your right to bring forth life onto the planet, rather than have your baby "delivered" is much more than just semantics. It takes education and trust. Claiming this power is definitely a lesbian and feminist thing to do, but often it seems harder for lesbians to claim than for heterosexual women. Perhaps this can be traced back to the conception/preconception periods in which lesbians and single women are routinely seen in the infertility clinics simply due to their lack of access to sperm. This pathologizing of our bodies right from the start can subtly or blatantly undermine our trust in our bodies. Making our conceptions medical events rather than intimate life experiences lays the groundwork for a medicalized birth.

This way of thinking about our own bodies is often carried over to the birth process where we can naturally assume that we are "high risk" due to having gone through a medicalized conception. As midwives, we've heard numerous women explain that they would strive for a natural birth or choose to give birth at home but that this pregnancy was so hard to achieve that they can't risk anything during the birth of their child. This fear-based attitude is erroneous and keeps women from educating themselves about the actual facts and statistics. It provides them with the false sense of security that somehow abdicating responsibility for their birth experience makes it inherently safer. These fears may stem from the belief that since their intuition and opinions seemed to have had no positive affect on their ability to conceive, their intuition and opinions have no purpose in helping them secure a positive birth experience. See page 394 for an explanation of the benefits and safety of home birth.

Empowered birth cannot happen if you fully abdicate your role in the process. By necessity, empowered birth is about the inner responsibility each woman has for educating herself about the pros and cons of routine procedures and for forming preferences about how she would like her birth to proceed, barring complications. This is empowered birth, and you have the power to actualize it.

Birth Vision

Although birth doesn't always look or feel the way you hope or expect, it's valuable to spend time clarifying your vision for the birth of your child. You may want to review your answers to the birth vision exercise in Chapter 17. Or you may wish to do the exercise again now from a new perspective closer to giving birth, before reading what you wrote in early pregnancy. In any event, creating a current birth vision is important.

If you're partnered, this exercise is best done individually and then as a team. Creating a concrete vision with as many details as possible is one way of claiming your power. This doesn't mean your birth will turn out exactly according to your vision. It does mean, however, that you've devoted the time and energy to examine what your heart's desire is in regard to the birth of your baby. It's highly valuable for all pregnant women to engage in this exercise prior to giving birth. It's especially valuable if you're partnered so that as a team you can visualize what's important to you in bringing your new baby into your family and the world.

Exercise

Take some time in quiet introspection or meditation, focusing on the perfect birth of your baby. Allow yourself to fully experience whatever feelings or images arise. It doesn't matter what you see or feel or how that pertains to the choices or outside world; simply allow this vision to be just that—a vision. Notice how you feel during the labor. What helps you feel more comfortable? Where are you? What time of day is it? Who's with you? Are there smells or sounds that you're enjoying, that help you to relax? If you're partnered, where is she? Do you feel connected and close? Is this feeling important to you? If you're single, be sure to notice who's with you. Do you feel supported and safe? When you've spent the time to fully allow yourself to experience these feelings, write them down on paper.

If you're the partner of the birthing woman, do this same exercise, focusing on the labor and birth from your position. What does your partner's ideal labor and birth look and feel like to you? Ask yourself the same questions the birthing mom asks herself.

When you've completed this exercise, share your vision with your partner and/or birth team. Which of these elements do you imagine will be easy to create? Which will be harder but worth striving for, and which will have to remain in the realm of your vision or be symbolically represented in other ways?

Common Partner Issues During the Last Months of Pregnancy

The discomforts, work schedules, and hormonal upheavals during the last months of pregnancy can create rifts between partners at a time when they'd like to feel closest. Though this is a common dynamic, it's often quite painful to feel emotionally distanced during such an important time of your life. Part of the rift comes from each partner's distinct separation of roles.

At the end of pregnancy, the nonpregnant partner often confronts the "provider" issues that fathers-to-be usually face. It can be stressful for the nonpregnant mom to embrace the traditional expectations of the father to provide financially for the family. Although this may not be the expectation within your own family, the nonpregnant partner will undoubtedly embrace this expectation to some extent as a way of providing additional security to the birthing mother. Because on average a woman's earning capacity is still much less than a man's, this stress can be great.

Nonpregnant partners may also feel an overwhelming compulsion to complete projects before the birth of their child. They're just fulfilling their own need to nest and provide for their pregnant partners a safe place to have a baby. To the pregnant mom, who often just wants time and attention with her partner, these projects may seem irrelevant. Each partner has different needs to fulfill to prepare for the arrival of their baby. These needs, however, are often conflicting because the pregnant mom is more inwardly focused and the nonpregnant mom is often concerned with the practical "outer" elements of life. An understanding of the separation of duties at this time can help ease frustrations or fears that the nonbirth mom doesn't want to be involved.

Feeling Left Out

The end of pregnancy is often emotionally challenging for the nonpregnant mom, due to so much focus being placed on the pregnant mom. Feeling left out of the attention lathered on pregnant women can spur feelings of disconnection and isolation. Many nonpregnant partners wonder what their role will be in their baby's life. Will the baby love them? Will they share the connection that biological mother has? Will they always feel like the third wheel? Will they love their baby as much as if they had given birth? When their role is overlooked by strangers—and family and friends—their fears of exclusion may become heightened.

These feelings may be conscious or subconscious. Often the nonbiological mother-to-be finds ways to confirm her unimportance in the family by excluding herself; she may make herself very busy or start arguments with the pregnant partner. It's important in a lesbian partnership to discuss the nonbirth mom's feelings and to do everything possible to encourage her to feel and be included. The slights of well-meaning people can seem subtle to the unobservant eye; when the slights are daily, however, they add up and may cause a great deal of resentment and pain.

Approaching parenting inclusion as a team is the only way to combat societal neglect of the nonpregnant mom. For example, although baby showers are often traditionally given only for the biological mom, in two-parent lesbian families there are two moms. Make sure the shower focuses equally on both mothers.

The language you use to discuss the baby, pregnancy, and birth set the tone for others. For example, if you're in public together and someone asks when your baby is due, you might say, "Carrie and I are ready for this baby anytime now" (while touching Carrie). This includes a partner more than just saying, "My due date is next week!"

As the pregnant mom, you can easily get so consumed with the baby and your pregnancy that your partner can feel like she's not a part of the experience. Take the time to explore her feelings and to encourage the team aspect of the pregnancy and reaffirm your desire to have children with her. Do what you can to help your partner feel more secure about her role and importance to you. You both will feel closer if you take the time to imagine what it's like to be in the other person's shoes and care for each other from that place of love.

Encourage Intimacy

Despite the various obstacles, encouraging intimacy throughout pregnancy is crucial to maintaining a healthy relationship with your partner. Therefore, it's important to do small things to help the two of you feel connected. For example, a nightly back or foot rub exchange is a nice connecting activity. Many couples claim they're too busy for such things; however, it's essential to find at least 10 minutes a day to connect as partners. If you can't find the time and make it a priority to spend a few minutes together now, before the birth of your child, how will you find time for each other after the baby arrives?

During the massage exchange the two of you can share your thoughts and feelings about the pregnancy, upcoming birth, or parenthood. Try to center your conversation on something "baby focused." Making each other a priority will help you ease into the birth experience together in the spirit of intimacy. In addition, make it a point to ask each other for what you need and what feels good, what could feel better, and what kind of touch doesn't work for you. These tactile and verbal communication skills are helpful tools for achieving intimacy and connection during labor. Remember, birth is potentially a time of great intimacy between a pregnant woman and her partner. If you enter the birth feeling alienated from each other, it's more difficult to achieve this intimacy during labor. Conscious preparation is usually necessary for most couples.

Single Moms

When entering the last months of pregnancy as a single mom, many women are faced with the enormity of their decision to birth and parent on their own, which can make them feel isolated. Although feeling alone is generally not the governing theme for pregnancy up to this point, as your body gets bigger and it's harder to do things for yourself, it's easy to become jealous and resentful of partnered pregnant women. This is often highlighted when taking a childbirth education class, as the classes are usually full of couples.

Commonly Asked Questions About Labor

• **How long does labor last?**

There's no formula for labor length. In fact, it is quite variable from woman to woman. There does seem to be some correlation between the length from your mother and/or sister's first birth to your own—especially if they were very fast labors. On average, a woman's first labor lasts anywhere between 11 and 24 hours. Some, however, may last as short as 5 hours and some as long as three days. The healthier you are during pregnancy, and the more prepared you are emotionally for the experience, the greater your ability to relax will be. Relaxation (and physical movement) are the keys to effective labor progression.

• **What are the stages of labor?**

Labor is typically divided into three stages. During the first stage, your cervix thins and opens. In the second stage you actively push the baby out. During the third stage you birth the placenta. For most women the first stage, when dilating contractions occur, is much longer than the second stage. On average, a first-time mother will spend two hours actively pushing her baby out.

• **How painful will it be?**

We will not try to fool you here. Labor hurts! Many women find, however, that there are no appropriate words in our vocabulary to describe this kind of pain. Some feel that although they have never experienced anything more intense or compelling in their lives, the sensation is not what they would call pain. There are numerous distinctions between the pain of labor and other kinds of pain we are familiar with. First, most pain is from injury or disease; during labor, this isn't the case. So in effect it is the good pain of hard work.

Second, there is a great reward at the end of the pain, which also has no corollary to most forms of pain. And third, the pain is intermittent. For most of labor the time spent between contractions—the time not hurting—is much longer than the length of the actual contractions, the time spent in pain. This point is significant. You can mentally prepare for labor in many ways, such as learning relaxation, practicing meditation techniques, and remembering to place your attention on the blissful time between contractions rather than fearing future contractions.

• How long will I be sore afterward?

Once again, there is great variability from woman to woman. With lots and lots of rest during the first week after giving birth, however, there should be very little remaining pain if you gave birth vaginally. Any vaginal pain will be limited after the first week to that of the continued healing of any sutures you may have. Some women have painful hemorrhoids for the first few weeks after the birth of their child. Even if you are no longer sore, it will take a good five to eight weeks for you to feel like your old self.

If you gave birth by cesarean section, the healing process is much longer. Some women experience significant physical discomfort up to three weeks later. Have compassion for yourself; you just had major abdominal surgery and gave birth to your baby and are sleep deprived and learning to be a mother. As soon after the surgery as possible enlist support from friends and family. This is essential if you are a single parent.

Thus, preparing for birth and making it through the end of pregnancy are often one and the same. You'll need to enlist the help and support of people who love and care about you. You'll need to think about which of your friends or family members you'd like to be with you while you give birth. This same person/people should be willing to attend your childbirth education classes with you.

A single mom we worked with recently enlisted her friends to come over at the end of her pregnancy to help her clean her apartment. It was getting to be too big of a job for her to do on her own, yet she was having strong nesting urges for an immaculate environment. Likewise, in addition to forming her birth team, she had her church and friend community create a postpartum support plan for her. This plan included a list of people who took turns bringing food to her every day for the first week and then every second or third day for the next three weeks. Each person who brought food would stay for 30 minutes to help around the apartment doing small chores, washing clothes, or taking care of the baby while she showered. She had people lined up to spend the night at her apartment every night for the first week if she wanted it. This plan was completed in the beginning of her ninth month so that she could relax and get ready to give birth without worrying about how she would manage postpartum.

Pre-Birth Preparation for Coparents

Sometimes women choose to invite their male coparent(s) to the birth. If this is Share your vision with each person who will be attending the birth so that everyone can be aligned with the spirit of your vision. We've found that it's essential to discuss, in advance, your birth philosophy with your coparents. Likewise, it's important to spell out how decisions will be made during the birth: whether you'd like their participation or whether their role will be that of observing, nondecision-making participants. Without this discussion, unnecessarily tense moments may arise during the birth.

For example, say you come to a point where you're ready for an epidural and have requested one, but your coparents feel drugs are harmful to the baby. If you haven't specified that you're making these decisions and that their role is to support you through the process no matter what, they may feel it's appropriate to inundate you with their opinion that you're doing damage to the baby. This can lead to open hostility at a time when harmony and unity are of utmost importance for all involved—especially the baby.

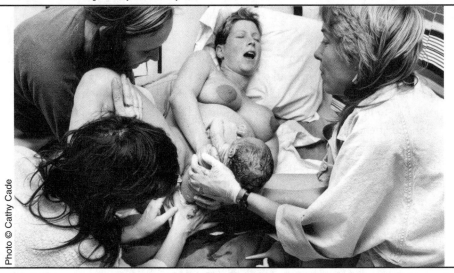

Photo © Cathy Cade

If you anticipate your birth philosophies to be radically different from those of your coparent(s), you may consider not asking them to the birth but rather inviting them to see the baby soon after the birth. You're not obligated to invite your coparent(s) to the birth. In fact, in our experience as midwives, if a birthing mother isn't entirely comfortable with her choice of birth attendants, no matter who they are within the family, labors that are longer, harder, and more complicated may result.

One lesbian family we know whose donor is an active coparent explained to him that they weren't inviting him to the birth, just as he had not invited them to his ejaculation. When put in such graphic terms, the donor immediately understood why they didn't want him present.

The Big Event

Preparing for Labor

Labor and birth are tremendous, life-changing experiences. After giving birth, many women express that they've never done anything more powerful in their lives. Many nonbirthing parents express awe when they recall the birth of their children, saying that it was one of the most amazing events of their lives. In the following section we cover some of the issues that are specific to lesbian and single women giving birth.

From the hormonal research being conducted on the differences between lesbians and heterosexual women and birth, it seems that lesbians (and we would say single women as well), especially older lesbians, have prolonged pregnancies and labors. Our midwifery experience concurs with this research, while denoting a difference between women who are more practiced at letting go and those who maintain a high level of control in other aspects of their lives as well as their labors. The two factors that seem to reduce the tendency for these longer labors are: taking herbs prenatally to help the uterus be ready and preparing emotionally well in advance for letting go. There are many ways to herbally prepare for labor. If this is of interest to you, you may wish to read Susun Weed's *Wise Woman's Herbal for the Childbearing Year.* (See the resource list at end of Chapter 16.) No matter what you choose, the herbal tea we recommend you take preconceptionally should be taken every day during your pregnancy as wonderful preparation for labor. See Chapter 8 for preparation information.

Labor and birth involve a tremendous amount of letting go. Giving in to the sensations of labor and letting the contractions move through your body without fear or resistance are key to experiencing a straightforward labor and birth. It has been our repeated experience that many independent, autonomous lesbians, bisexual, and single women have a difficult time surrendering their control to the process of labor. This emotional theme of needing to be in control seems common for our communities. Perhaps this is largely due to the fact that in order to be a lesbian parent, or a single parent by choice, you must be an inwardly strong woman who feels ready to confront the judgments of the outside world. Women of such strength have often cultivated this strength in the face of great opposition. Experiencing birth, where strength is equated with total surrender into the unknown, often runs counter to the survival skills that have guided many women up until this point.

Thus, one of the best forms of preparation for labor is to practice letting go, surrendering, and asking for help. On a daily basis during pregnancy it's vital to cultivate these skills. You can do this through the simple act of finding an inner sanctuary of quiet, calm, safety. You can do this by asking a friend for a back rub or by taking a nap at work. In any event, it's important to practice the skills of letting go, surrendering, and asking for help.

Cesarean Birth

Cesarean births, or C-sections, are quite common for hospital-planned deliveries in the United States, encompassing up to 30% of births. Many factors contribute to this rate of surgical birth, and some insightful texts have been written addressing the issue. C-sections may be planned in a variety of cases, including, for example, for a larger baby that is presenting knee or butt down instead of head down. In this case, the C-section is usually scheduled and performed before the onset of labor. Sometimes a C-section is performed once labor has begun but has gotten stuck without progressing despite any other interventions tried. This is usually not an emergency. Occasionally, but not often, an emergency C-section is performed for reasons such as severe fetal distress or separation of the placenta before birth. Each of these situations can look somewhat different, feel somewhat different, and necessitate different levels of postpartum help.

A planned C-section usually will be the easiest to recover from, because a woman will not be exhausted from labor. Unless a cesarean is a real emergency, spinal or epidural anesthesia is almost always used, meaning you'll be awake for the procedure although you won't feel any pain. This means you can see your baby immediately and will be out of the recovery room and able to hold him or her fairly soon.

Also, most operating rooms now invite the partner to be present (if she self-identifies as partner, not just as friend) to sit by the head of the birth mom, talking to her, meeting the baby, and then going to the nursery with the baby until everyone can reconnect in a postpartum room. If you are the nonpregnant partner, you do not have to watch any of the surgery if you not want to. A curtain will be put up that hangs over the birth mom's chest to block your view. If the baby is doing fine, he or she will have a brief initial exam on the warming table in the operating room, then be wrapped in blankets and given to you to bring over to your partner. Her arms will be tied down to the operating table with IV's and blood pressure cuffs. You'll need to touch and talk to the baby, putting your pinky finger in its mouth if he or she wants to suck until you all reunite. The baby will recognize your voice and be comforted by you!

If you're having a nonemergency cesarean part of the way through labor, it will look similar to the above description. The baby is born within 10 minutes of the actual start of the surgery, but it will take 30–45 minutes to sew in the stitches to close up the incision. Usually, the entire process, including waiting for the room to be ready, waiting for the anesthesiologist to arrive, and the like, takes a fair while. You may still be feeling contractions the entire time. Stay focused and present, talking out loud with your support team about all the feelings you might be experiencing: frustration that you're stuck in labor, fear of surgery, relief to be almost done, excitement to meet your daughter or son.

Emergency Cesareans: If you have an emergency C-section birth, it will be done usually less than 20 or 30 minutes from the time the decision is made. You'll probably be given general anesthesia, which makes you completely go to sleep, because it works faster. In this case, your partner, if you have one, almost certainly will not accompany you into the operating room. When you come out you'll probably be quite groggy for up to four hours in the recovery room before you hold your baby and nurse.

In this case, it's wonderful for your partner or support person to go to the nursery and sit with the baby until you're all together in the postpartum room. If an emergency C-section must be performed, give explicit permission for your partner, friend, or family member to be allowed in the nursery. The nursery may ask you to choose just one person to have this privilege. If you have an emergency C-section, you may feel a lot of concern for your own health or the baby's health in the few minutes while you await the surgery. Breathe deeply and slowly, and go deep inside to connect with the baby, letting the infant know that he or she will be born very soon.

Recovery: It's normal to need a lot of extra postpartum help, to have good days and bad days as you recover, and to experience a whole slew of emotions on top of the usual new-motherhood emotions. Much helpful information is available for women who give birth by cesarean. Many women take a long time to sort through their birth experiences, no matter what the birth looks like. This is especially true for women who give birth by cesarean. All births are sacred, no matter where or how they occur.

Studies of the brain and neural pathways suggest that humans automatically respond to any given situation in the ways that are most familiar and most frequently used. Thus, unless you cultivate new responses to pain, fear, and the unknown, you'll slip into your trained responses. If you regularly practice creating new responses, you'll be more able to access these responses during labor. This is just like exercising a muscle: If your muscles aren't in shape, your stronger muscles must compensate for the weaker muscles. So, your best preparation for birth is to strengthen your muscles of surrender.

Emotional preparation also involves coming fully to terms with your decision to parent. Keeping the baby inside your body helps delay the inevitable: that you're going to be a mother. If you're still holding onto strong levels of internal homophobia or concerns about your donor choice, or worries about being a single parent, it's worth your time to process, process, process. This will not only help you become more comfortable with your choices, but also will likely help you shorten your labor time and not go too far past your due date.

Home Birth

If you're planning a home birth, you've most likely chosen a midwife who's familiar with and supportive of your family structure. If you're partnered, your midwife has undoubtedly encouraged the two of you to freely express yourselves as intimately as you wish. If you're single, she's probably helped you devise a postpartum support plan and encouraged you to invite a friend or family member to be your birth partner.

Because women often choose home birth for the comfort factor and have found midwives with whom they're comfortable, there's usually no context for homophobia to arise. It's important, however, to explore these issues, since there's always the possibility that you'll have to be transported to a hospital. So be sure to read the following section and discuss the pertinent points with your midwife.

Birth Center Birth

Birth centers are usually small operations with a few midwives and/or several doctors. So once again, although there isn't the same assurance that the staff is totally familiar and comfortable with your family situation, it's quite likely that every staff member has been briefed on your situation and is prepared to have you in the center. As a result, it's unlikely that you'll encounter any virulently homophobic staff members. Some uneducated employees, however, may unknowingly offend you. Read the following section on hospital birth for suggestions.

Hospital Birth

A hospital is by far the most common and complex birth environment for lesbians. In a hospital setting our families have to navigate many unique issues. This is primarily because there are so many people involved whom you've never met. You can prepare for some things in advance, but most must be dealt with in the moment.

Preparation

As a part of your prenatal care, cover with your practitioner in detail who's in your family, what each person's role will be in the birth, and what their titles are. Once you feel comfortable with your doctor or midwife's understanding of your family, find a way for the other practitioners in the medical group to also share an understanding of your family situation. This can be done by scheduling prenatal appointments with the other practitioners and by typing up a "cheat sheet" that spells everything out for your provider to include with your chart. This enables whoever works with you, if they look at your chart, to have a basic understanding of and be able to use the appropriate language for your family.

The Benefits of Having a Labor Coach

We highly recommend that anyone planning a hospital birth use a professional labor coach, also called a doula. A labor coach is a professional birth attendant, a woman you hire to stay with you throughout your labor and birth. She has many functions, one of which is being your personal advocate in the hospital.

Having a trained professional who loves birth allows you and your partner or birth team to focus on the birth, knowing that your advocate will be working on your behalf to help you have the birth of your choice. A labor coach usually meets with you once prior to the birth to review her skills and your birth vision. Then during labor she'll either meet you at your home or the hospital and remain with you the entire time. It's emotionally satisfying to have a labor coach at the birth for numerous reasons. She'll advocate for your wishes medically, support partners and friends emotionally, and offer nonmedical suggestions to reduce pain and increase effective contractions. Nurses and hospital staff are often helpful, but they aren't with you throughout the process; usually, they just drop in on you from time to time.

Another benefit to having a labor coach is that she can act as your filter. She can ensure that hospital staff members have familiarized themselves with your family structure. She can ask for a new nurse if you have a nurse with whom you feel uncomfortable. She can come out for you to new staff during a shift change. She can be your buffer. If you want her to have this role, however, you must specify this ahead of time in detail and ask whether she is comfortable and able to do so. It is, of course, most helpful, but not necessary, if she has worked with other lesbian families in the past.

Labor Itself

Be sure to bring a few copies of your family cheat sheet to the hospital at the time of birth. One of these can be attached to the outside of your door, another to your labor chart. These will be visual cues for the staff to familiarize themselves with your family prior to coming in contact with you. You'll also want to bring copies for the pediatric department and the postpartum ward.

Remember, you're a consumer who is hiring the hospital and staff to provide a service for you. Therefore, you're the one with the power. It's important to remember

Preparing for Birth Legally

How to protect your family legally is a dynamic topic with changes in legislation and court precedents occurring frequently. It's also a topic that varies significantly from state to state. We refer you to the National Center for Lesbian Rights (contact info listed at the end of this chapter) for the most recent information. Here we give a brief overview of preparations to consider.

Durable Power of Attorney: Everyone should have one of these, including information on your preferences concerning life-extending measures and organ donation, but most importantly who will make decisions about your medical care if you're incapacitated. This is especially crucial for gay and lesbian couples, who aren't recognized as spouses or partners in almost every state, and therefore don't have visitation or decision-making rights guaranteed without this document. Though it's highly unlikely that giving birth will incapacitate you, we recommend that you fill out this simple document for peace of mind and bring a copy with you to the hospital if that's where you're giving birth. You don't necessarily need to see a lawyer for this; sample documents can be found online, and now most hospital admitting offices have them as well.

Birth Certificates: If you're partnered, the nonbiological mother's name will be added after a second-parent adoption is completed, if you have this option available and choose it. Currently, there are only two parent spots on a birth certificate. Some women see if they can get their name put in the "father" box, but this doesn't enhance their legal parental recognition in any way. In fact, if you decide to complete the second-parent adoption process, your lawyer will probably be ask you to refrain from doing this until the process is complete. Each state sets its own policy for what can be entered in the "father" box. Some of the options in your state may be: unknown, withheld, — ,DI (for donor insemination), AI (for alternative or artificial insemination), or the father's name.

•

this, because if at any point you feel or experience homophobia from any member of the hospital staff, you can ask for a replacement. Usually, in these situations both you and the person in question will feel relieved.

We've heard of women who gave birth at a hospital where they hadn't met the doctor ahead of time claim that lesbianism was their religion and that they must only work with a female doctor. Although this doesn't guarantee a lesbian-friendly doctor, it does eliminate the possibility of having a male doctor if that prospect is uncomfortable for you.

Second-Parent Adoption: Although logically this process of securing legal recognition for a nonbiological parent should be similar to stepparent adoption, which is fairly straightforward, it's instead awkwardly modeled on traditional adoptions. Therefore, it usually requires home visits from the state social worker, counseling for all parties, a lawyer, a court visit, and numerous fees (which may be a few thousand dollars). Depending on your area, these may all be a friendly formality or they may be quite nerve-wracking. If the donor is known, he must sever his paternal rights and responsibilities as part of this process. The final legal statement entitles the nonbiological parent to full and equal legal recognition as the birth parent. Many partnered women choose to go through this process to obtain legal parental rights for the nonbiological mom. This is especially important for her when dealing with schools, medical providers, homophobic grandparents, or airlines, in terms of having decision-making authority. It also protects her claim to custody in case of a break up. This process cannot be completed before the child is born and can take up to nine months to complete. It's recognized by state statute in Connecticut, District of Columbia, Illinois, Massachusetts, New York, New Jersey, and Vermont. It's also recognized in scattered counties in numerous other states such as California, where women have hired lawyers and filed cases successfully. As domestic partnership and civil union laws change in each state, the process may soon become much simpler in some states.

Uniform Parentage Act: This is a recent legal precedent in some counties in California, Massachusetts, and a few other states. It's a simple court order that acknowledges both the biological mom and nonbiological mom as legal parents based on their intent to be legal parents. In some places it can be completed before the birth of the baby. In some places it can be completed with a couple who has conceived using sperm bank or known-donor sperm. It hasn't been challenged in court yet, and a lawyer is needed to help you with the process.

Coming Out

If you're the partner of a woman in labor, it's important for both of you to come out to each relevant person who enters your hospital room. When you're looking forward to the baby's birth, this can seem like overkill, but in the moment you'll understand the importance. If a nurse, anesthesiologist, or doctor is going to be providing you with care, they should understand who's a part of your family. Otherwise they'll only direct the conversation to the laboring mom and assume that you are her sister, friend, etc. If you don't come out, they'll ask you to leave whenever they perform routine procedures. You'll be excluding your partnership from the experience. If you take the initiative and introduce yourself and your partner to each person who enters the room, there will be little room for confusion. Having everyone understand the nature of your relationship opens up the freedom for intimate expression. Although you can certainly be physically and emotionally intimate without explanation, we often feel more uncomfortable and inhibited if we don't come out.

Physical Intimacy

Holding and being held, giving back rubs, looking deeply into someone's eyes while breathing through more difficult contractions, and other kinds of physical intimacy are all meaningful parts of labor—as are terms of endearment, loving hugs, and hand holding in the silence between contractions. If you're not out or feel uncomfortable with public gestures of affection, you and your partner may withhold such intimate expression—but to do so only hurts you both. To hold back out of fear of others' judgments is both understandable and sad. Remember, this is the birth of your baby. This is your mutual entrance into motherhood. This is your experience.

If you anticipate that expressing physical intimacy in the hospital may be hard for you, you may want to spend time before the birth practicing being more intimate in public. Use this time as preparation. If you usually don't hold hands or hug in public, push yourselves to try to do so in places that feel safe. Labor support involves a lot of touch and kind, loving words. You'll both feel much closer if you're able to share this form of intimacy during the birth of your baby.

Nonpregnant Partner Issues

When your partner is giving birth, it's a tremendous event to witness and share. It is not, however, always easy to see your partner in so much pain. In fact, many nonpregnant moms-to-be find that they wish that their laboring partners would take pain medication just to give *them* a break! It's important to discuss in advance your philosophies surrounding pain medication and other important topics so that you're able to work as a team. If you, the nonpregnant partner, are "pro pain relief" and she wants a "natural" birth, you must find a way to respect her desires and support her through the contractions. The same holds true if she's "pro pain relief" and you're invested in a "natural" birth. The woman in labor should make the ultimate decision about what level of pain she's willing to endure. If you do have a philosophical difference here, you may need to do some concerted personal growth work surrounding letting go and allowing the pregnant mom her birth experience. This can be especially difficult if you plan to give birth in the future or if you had hoped to give birth but were unable to conceive or sustain a pregnancy.

Sometimes seeing your partner in so much pain, or seeing how out of control she feels, or seeing various tubes and monitors attached to her body, can trigger personal sexual abuse issues. Although this can be surprising, it's actually a common experience. Birth can also be painful to witness as it becomes more and more medicalized. Some birthing women or partners of birthing women see many of the procedures as dehumanizing and even humiliating.

Some birthing women and some female partners find that the birth of their child resembled more of a rape than a joyful experience. If this is the case for you, you may need to do some fast growth work during the labor and immediately postpartum. If you're the nonbirthing partner, these feelings are usually best kept from your laboring partner. As hard as it may be to not share with her, at this time and during the vulnerable postpartum period it isn't appropriate for her to take care of your abuse issues. If you realize this may become an issue for you, it's best to take a proactive approach. First, seriously consider hiring a labor coach and informing her of your abuse background. Second, enlist the support of a friend whom you can call or ask to be at the birth—if only in the waiting room—so that you'll have someone to talk to if you need to work through your feelings during the birth. If you assume you'll just stuff your feelings down and tough it out, you won't be fully present for your baby or your partner.

When the Baby Is Actually Being Born

When it's time for the baby to be born, everyone in the room is usually very excited. Make sure you have a spot where you feel included in the experience—whether that means holding your partner up as she pushes, holding one of her legs and being able to both look into her eyes and watch the baby emerge, or helping to catch the baby. Often many people enter the birth room at the last minute; don't let this overwhelm you to the point where you feel excluded. Assert yourself into a your desired position so that you feel you are an integral part of the birth.

We've noticed that many lesbian couples plan that the nonbirth mom will be the first to hold the baby when he or she is born. This is a special touch they feel will increase their bonding. Numerous women who give birth instinctively need to hold the baby right away. Then, when they're ready to let go, they hand the baby into the arms of the other mother. You may want to discuss these options together ahead of time.

Should I Use Pain-Relief Drugs During Labor?

Once again, this decision is a very personal one. Our experience as midwives, however, leads us to believe that women can make it through labor without pain relief should they desire. But many women ask "Why would I want to?" There are many reasons, but one of the most significant is that your baby will enter the world drug free. Although babies supposedly are not affected by the drugs women are offered in labor, that is not actually the case. It's more accurate to say that there don't seem to be any long-term negative side effects for a child whose mother is given medications during labor. (Although numerous studies seem to bring that into question as well.)

For anyone who has attended births, it is easy to tell the difference between the alert and present babies born without medication and those who are more sedated from the pain relief medicine temporarily circulating in their bodies. Many babies whose mothers received pain medicine are slower to nurse. They may need the time to work the medication out of their body first.

And equally important, many women feel tremendously empowered by giving birth without pain relief. This sense of power carries over into motherhood.

Other women have no desire to challenge themselves to a duel with labor pain. If this is the case for you, and you feel you are informed about the drugs available, by all means use them. With appropriate prenatal preparation and adequate labor support, however, pain medication may not be necessary. Using pain relief is not bad, but it's best avoided unless you really need it. Resist the urge to use it out of fear. Educate yourself about your options so that you will be able to request the best form of pain relief for you, if you do decide to choose it.

Other Proven Forms of Pain Management

• Hire a professional labor assistant. The skills,.knowledge, and experience of a woman trained to support women in labor has been documented to reduce the need for pain medication and to shorten the average length of labor.

• Hypnotherapy or hypnobirthing are great forms of pain management practiced in pregnancy that greatly reduce labor pain. Some recent statistics suggest that self-hypnosis during labor can shorten labor time by up to one third.

• Ninety percent of women find that massage and directed touch relieves pain and provides vital sustenance to continue through labor without pain medicine.

• Taking baths and showers tends to make the pain much more manageable for most women. It also provides a wonderful means of connection and intimacy for mother and partner.

• Practice and try relaxation and breathing techniques.

• Practice aromatherapy during your labor.

Take a Healthy Approach to Pain Medicine

• Do not medicate before you experience painful contractions just because you're afraid of how much pain you might be in later. Take each contraction as it comes. If a contraction truly feels unmanageable and you want drugs, we recommend that you change position and/or get into the shower or bath. If after three more contractions in a new position you still want drugs, then go ahead.

• Establish a word or phrase ahead of time with your support team that means you really do want drugs. This way you can feel free to say anything you want about drugs during your labor in your pain, and your team will know whether you're just venting or whether you actually want to receive pain medication.

• If you absolutely know you don't want to be offered pain relief—and you are giving birth in a hospital or birthing center—have this written clearly in your chart. Then, when you're in labor, have your support team remind the staff not to offer you pain relief. It is much better to ask for pain medication yourself than to feel as though it is constantly being offered to you like candy.

If your baby needs to go to the nursery or the pediatric station in the room, it's best if the nonbirth mom accompanies the baby through all times of separation from the birth mother. If you're the nonbirth mother, you'll provide a reassuring presence and voice that your baby will recognize. Spend this time talking out loud or singing to your child. Your partner will manage without you. Although it may be hard to separate from your partner at this time, this will be a very significant bonding time with your baby, and your voice will guide the baby through all of these new experiences.

To prepare in advance to accompany the baby to the nursery, make sure you have drawn up your legal papers beforehand and have brought them to the hospital with copies, and that you've received the appropriate identification bracelets from the nurse that allow you to enter the nursery as a parent.

Coparents and Known Donors

If you choose to invite your coparents or known donor to the birth, discuss openly and honestly what you'd like their roles to be and how you'd like them to identify themselves to the staff. Just as it's important to discuss this with your care providers, it's even more important to discuss this with the men themselves. Often women, especially partnered lesbians, don't want the donor or male coparents to receive the primary attention from the hospital staff. Because our culture is heterosexually biased, it feels natural for people to refer to a baby in relation to its biological parents. Thus, everyone must focus on your true family model in order for something other than the standard "mother and father" assumptions to arise.

Be specific about how you'd like the men to interact with others at this time of

Water Birth

Most home-birth midwives, and some hospitals and independent birth centers, offer women the option of giving birth in water. Water can greatly relieve the pain of labor. Many women experience the pain as being up to 50% less intense when in a tub or shower. When a woman is submersed in a tub or hot tub, the effects of gravity are different, enabling a greater range of motion with much less exertion. In our own births we have used water and can attest to its remarkable powers. We recommend using water as a pain management and relaxation tool for all women in labor.

Some women choose to go one step farther and actually give birth to their babies in water. When women give birth in water they report experiencing much less pain. Also, there's usually less vaginal tearing and rarely the need for episiotomy. It is felt that giving birth in water is less traumatic for the baby. When babies are born into warm water, often they are much more relaxed and do not cry when they are first born.

joy and vulnerability. The nonbirth mom can feel especially vulnerable now, so it's vital to support her role as primary parent. Discussing possible scenarios in advance as a team will help prevent any misunderstandings later on.

Single Mothers

As mentioned, it's best if a single mother has at least one close friend or family member who's committed to being her birth partner. When setting up such a commitment, it's essential to clarify that this person will be available regardless of time of day or day of week. If s/he does have time restraints, you'll need to arrange for a backup person. Make sure this person understands that you'll probably also want them to stay for the first few hours after the baby is born. In fact, whether you give birth at home or in a birth center or a hospital, it's best to have friends who are willing to stay overnight with you the first week.

Although no one ever wants to have a cesarean section, it's always a possibility and therefore should be planned for ahead of time. If you do end up requiring a C-section, you may need around-the-clock support for the first week or even two weeks after the birth. This may include the time when you're in the hospital as well. If you plan to have the baby with you 24 hours a day rather than keep him or her in the nursery after a cesarean birth, you'll absolutely need companionship because you'll need help lifting your baby to your breast.

It can be emotionally agonizing to think of asking for that much support as a single mom. It's much easier, however, to plan for these events in advance rather than to scramble for the support you need when you're most vulnerable. Contingency plans are essential. In the event of a difficult birth or a cesarean, many women have a backup plan for a long-distance friend or relative to be on standby to fly in and stay for a week and help out during this time of need. It's by no means admitting failure if you need to ask for help. It's best to plan ahead so that you're already prepared.

In Conclusion

The experience of childbirth can encompass every physical sensation and emotion that humans are capable of feeling. It can be an incredibly challenging and incredibly triumphant at the same time. See our resource list below for excellent books on the general emotional and physical experiences of birth for the baby, the birth mom, and the partner. If you're partnered, explore and plan all the ways you can do the beautiful work of staying connected as lovers and as a family during the birth. Whether or not you're partnered, organize adequate support for yourself and anyone else in your family so that you can focus on being fully present for the amazing power of this experience.

Resources

Books

The Birth Partner: Everything You Need to Know to Help a Woman Through Childbirth,
Penny Simkin, Harvard Common Press, 1989

Birth Reborn, Michel Odent, Birth Works, 1994

*Birth Without Violence: The Book That Revolutionized the Way We Bring Our Children
Into the World*, Frederick Leboyer, Inner Traditions International Ltd., 1995

Birthing From Within, Pam England and Rob Horowitz, Partera Press, 1998

Easing Labor Pain: The Complete Guide to a More Comfortable and Rewarding Birth,
Harvard Common Press, 1992

*Gentle Birth Choices: A Guide to Making Informed Decisions About Birthing Centers,
Birth Attendants, Water Birth, Home Birth, Hospital Birth*, Barbara Harper,
1994

*Mothering the Mother: How a Doula Can Help You Have a Shorter, Easier, and
Healthier Birth*, Marshall H. Klaus, Phyllis H. Klaus, and John Kennell,
Perseus Press, 1993

Natural Birth, Toi Derricotte, Firebrand Books, 2000

Reclaiming the Spirituality of Birth: Healing for Mothers and Babies, Benig Mauger,
Healing Arts Press, 2000

Organizations

National Center for Lesbian Rights
870 Market St., Suite 570
San Francisco, CA94102
(415) 392-6257 or (415) 392-6257
www.nclrights.org

Web Sites

Hypnobirthing: A Celebration of Life
www.hypnobirthing.com

Water Baby: All About Waterbirth
www.waterbirthinfo.com

Chapter 19 Welcome to Motherhood!

Can you even believe it? You're finally a mother! After all your dreams, plans, and attempts to get pregnant, after the long pregnancy and the labor and birth, your much-loved baby is here. Congratulations! Most women spend their pregnancies thinking of birth as a culmination rather than a beginning. With such a focus on getting pregnant, being pregnant, and giving birth, many new parents aren't prepared for the reality of being a parent. Postpartum—and by that we loosely mean the first three months of your baby's life—is challenging for all new parents. For lesbian parents it can be a particularly stressful time, especially for the nonbirth mother. The personal challenges of postpartum are unique to each family, influenced by family structure, amount and quality of community support, financial stresses, challenges of the birth experience, and the difficulty of learning breastfeeding, to name just a few. Despite the wide variation of personal factors, many common issues arise during this time.

The postpartum period is amazingly rich: full of new love, new identities, little sleep, and more hormonal changes than you may have expected. Little is written, taught, or acknowledged about this special time. In this chapter we describe some of the issues that arise for most women, as well as experiences specific to lesbian and bisexual women and their families. Each family will find creative solutions and support for their particular challenges beyond what we have the space to suggest here. Often, however, just reading a description of something similar to your own experience can help you feel less isolated and reassure you that no matter how difficult your challenge, you need not feel any shame or embarrassment or failure in asking for help.

When Can We Get Back to Normal?

You may only have a few other women's stories against which to measure your own experiences, since modern medicine doesn't recognize or educate about the complexity of the postpartum experience, nor do most pregnancy books. In fact, Western culture is unique in not embracing the first 40 or so postpartum days as a sacred period in which mothers require special help, nurturance, and support. The dominant myth that women in agrarian cultures give birth in the fields and go right back to hoeing is based in part on observations by U.S. soldiers of women during war, and European observations of women whose traditional practices had been destroyed by colonialism or slavery.

In reality, although women remain active through pregnancy and early labor in most cultures, the birth itself and the postpartum period are respected as an extraordinary time of family life. In most cultures, families are protective of the birth mother-child unit, not requiring regular daily tasks and activities from the mother until about six weeks postpartum. Within that six weeks, mothers are traditionally massaged, fed special diets, allowed to rest, kept warm, and exempted from cooking and cleaning. Babies are held and massaged, and both mother and child are kept inside and away from drafts and strangers (and foreign germs).

The modern-day "super woman" image many women aspire to involves greeting multiple visitors, keeping house, and losing weight, all while getting to know the baby, learning to nurse, adjusting to being a new mother, and healing from birth. Often, this also involves returning to work full-time outside the home within weeks of birth, leaving the baby in the care of nonfamily members. Many aspects of this "super woman" role deny the birth mother's physical and emotional needs as well as the needs of the baby, the other parent, and siblings.

Moving through the physical and emotional transformations of birth requires and deserves patience, care, and attention. It doesn't make sense to try to return immediately to business as usual, because bringing a new person into the family isn't an everyday experience. Becoming a mother isn't an everyday occurrence in your household either, whether or not you gave birth. New rhythms, routines, and communications need to evolve, and the way to discover and integrate the ones that best suit your particular family is to give yourselves space to explore, experiment, feel, and heal. You'll find a new sense of "normal" over time, step by step. Some steps take a few weeks; some take a number of months.

The First Couple of Weeks

The first days may seem an endless blur, because day and night don't feel much different to the baby—and therefore to you. This time period is magical yet challenging. You'll do almost nothing else than eat, sleep, nurse, and take care of your baby's needs. In the midst of these wonderful tasks you'll encounter a wide range of emotions, which are heightened by hormones and lack of sleep.

In addition, your body's physical changes during the postpartum period may surprise you. Healing from birth takes time and gentle nurturing. Although birth is not an illness, it's a huge transformation involving an amazing amount of physical exertion and occasional medical intervention. Each woman heals differently, at a different pace. Each family gels differently, at a different pace. Patience and trust are much needed throughout the postpartum period.

Limor Inbar-Hansen, Indelible Images

Rest in Bed the First Week to 10 Days

We strongly recommend spending the first week almost entirely in bed. This advice takes many American women by surprise because of our culture's lack of respect for the postpartum period. In our practice, we've seen that women who spend the first week resting adequately and focusing without distraction on themselves, each other if they're partnered, and their babies have fewer breastfeeding problems, a lower risk of postpartum infection, and less postpartum depression. Try to eliminate any need to leave the house the first week. Besides resting and bonding, when the baby is new you have to sleep—as much as possible—when he or she sleeps.

This rest period is especially important for coupled lesbian families, as it lets the family relationships solidify within the home before you all move out into the world together. These relationships are so new and emotional at first that they need special nurturing; they won't get this nurturing if everyone is distracted and exhausted. The nonbirth mom especially needs a lot of time and recognition within the family unit and the partnership to ease any fears and insecurities she may have about her role.

If you're partnered, either of you may find it difficult to just be with each other and the baby and feel all the feelings of new motherhood. A common response at first is to feel as though you might go stir-crazy or need to run away. Using activities to escape feeling emotions usually doesn't resolve anything; it just sets you up for postpartum depression.

You're in the liminal newness of motherhood, and it feels unstable emotionally, hormonally, and perhaps physically. Be gentle and patient with yourself. Over time you'll get to know your new self with the same deep familiarity you may have been used to previously. Instead of engaging in your previous activities right now, just sit with your feelings, write in a journal, or do some artwork that allows your feelings to arise.

Visitors and Support

If you've asked others to help out once you give birth, now is the time to get that help. They should be bringing food or helping to do a load of laundry or dishes if they have 20 minutes. They might hold the baby while you take a shower. They might stay with you for a couple of hours so your partner or you can catch up on sleep. If your guests aren't actively helping out, they should probably limit their visits, if at all, to 10 minutes. Unfortunately, a classic dynamic we see all too often is when a guest comes to socialize and hold the baby, focusing all their attention on the baby and the birth mom, while the nonbirth mom ends up feeling like a hostess/servant. Remember, if you're partnered, you both are new mothers, and your guests should reflect that by providing support to you as a family.

Without adequate help and adequate acknowledgement of her primary parenting role, it's easy for the nonbirth mom to feel that all she does is cook, clean, run errands, and help out, but not truly parent. The nonbirth mom may resent her partner for treating her like the helper and herself like the "real" mom, or may feel resentful of others who see her in this way. If she's doing all of this in addition to working full-time, she may experience her own unique form of exhaustion that compounds all of her emotions. Whether or not the birth mom graciously thanks her, she should know that she's doing an essential part of parenting with all her logistical support as well as the direct love and caring she gives the baby. This extreme division of labor usually changes over time.

If you're the nonbirth mom, when your friends and family stop by, ask them to go ahead and heat up the food they've brought and feed it to both of you. Let them know that, like the birth mom, you're in bed or on the sofa because you're also doing the night shifts. Ask good friends to do any out-of-the-house family errands that would otherwise take you away from home at first, even if these errands are not birth/baby-specific. In these ways, you can also receive support during this great time of love and transition.

Single-Mom Support

If you're single, remember the great postpartum support plan of action you created and be sure to activate it. If you haven't organized help, delegate this task to a good friend who likes to organize. All you need to do is give a list of names and phone numbers to her or him, and don't be shy. Your friend will ask others to organize meals, help with housekeeping, shopping, and help you and the baby heal and nurse.

Body Changes

A woman undergoes tremendous physical changes in the postpartum period. Even if women have prepared themselves by reading or researching, they often have forgotten, in the intensity of the birth, that they're not yet done with the physical aspects of the motherhood journey. Many women don't recognize their vulvas after they give birth, and can become quite upset the first time they look with a mirror or touch themselves. Their partners may have the same response. Don't fear! The swelling will recede, skin tags from hemorrhoids or stitches will shrink, and normal muscle tone will return.

Your pregnancy hormones will drop rather suddenly after birth, producing a variety of symptoms. These usually occur in the first two to five days, sometimes lasting through day 7. The most notable two symptoms are that your breast milk will fully come in—which may be uncomfortable and make breastfeeding temporarily difficult—and you may feel especially weepy and overwhelmed. Back to our mantra about limiting visitors during this tumultuous period: Spend time alone with your partner or a good friend and the baby while getting over these hurdles until the milk comes in all the way.

Breastfeeding Challenges

Breastfeeding can almost always be successful if you have adequate support. If you have a difficult time, call other moms who have nursed, La Leche League (see the resource section at the end of this chapter), or a lactation consultant. Call sooner rather than later. Some nipple pain is normal, but intense and frequent pain means you need some help. Trouble getting the baby to latch on, or concerns about not producing enough breast milk, can be alleviated with some experienced advice and enough support. Support for a breastfeeding woman means being encouraged with confidence and patience on the part of others around you. It means that others bring you food and drink so that you have all the calories you need and are well hydrated. There's much more to say about the physical and emotional pleasures and challenges of nursing than we have room for here. Please see the resource list at the end of this chapter.

Dealing With Upsetting Aspects of the Birth

Birth can sometimes leave a woman feeling raw and traumatized. Many women have to open their hearts and souls to give birth, confronting some of their biggest physical challenges in life and the accompanying emotional changes. In the midst of this they may be touched disrespectfully or invasively by care providers they have or have not met previously. Sometimes the birth goes in directions a woman would have rather avoided. Sometimes the "hugeness" of birth can feel shocking, no matter the details. Often birth stirs up old memories of times that felt painful, out of control, shameful, vulnerable, adrenaline-filled, or frightening. And sometimes during birth we learn things about ourselves that are poignant.

If you're the partner of someone who gave birth, you may also have these responses. You may have doubts about the adequacy of the support you provided. You may feel great pain or disempowerment about not being able to fix or rescue your partner from the challenging aspects of her experience. It's crucial that you too get to acknowledge all of your feelings so that they don't create a rift between you and your partner. Your partner is healing from giving birth and processing her own journey and is therefore probably not the best person with whom to do all of your emotional work. However, both of you taking responsibility for working through your own birth feelings, and sharing with each other where appropriate, will bring you together as a couple even more deeply.

Whether you're the birth mom or the nonbirth mom, find the safe places and people in your life with whom you can do this emotional work. Not all friends will be open, supportive listeners. Find those who are and take the time you need to tell and retell your story. Ignoring the trauma of birth is hard on our self-esteem. As queer parents in particular, you need to start out your parenting with high self-esteem to weather the inevitable stresses that arise especially for single moms and/or lesbian moms.

To approach this healing, be gentle with yourself about your birth experience. Let yourself feel any and all the emotions you need to. You may feel angry or sad about the smallest details as well as the largest. Give yourself permission to feel it all, but find compassion for yourself when you might instead reach for shame or self-blame. You may need to make peace with decisions you made that in retrospect don't seem ideal. Welcome to parenthood! Claim all the powerfulness and good work you did in labor as well as the hard parts, so that you don't tell your story to yourself wholly as a victim. Feel as much love for yourself as you do for your baby. You're as perfect as the child you made! You have all the time in the world to slowly unravel this birth story and all it has to teach you. Don't rush through it!

Sibling Bonding

If you already have children, it's important to focus on the process of sibling bonding. In queer families, our children may or may not be biologically related. You may be acquainting a much older child from a previous heterosexual marriage with your new baby or you may be introducing siblings with different birth mothers or even more part-time siblings who live primarily with other parents. In any event, it's important to foster their bonds and connections with each other. This is usually quite easy and natural to do.

It's important to make sure, if the first child/children were not birthed by this newest baby's birth mother, that they don't feel like they become stepchildren to her now. In other words, the mother who just gave birth needs to be aware of including her existing children in her bond with the new baby. The biological connection between the current birth mom and the new baby can seem consuming and alienating to the other children and cause them to question their own relationship with this mom. This is a subtle but incredibly essential piece to keep an eye on for family harmony. The focus on biology from the outside world can sometimes underscore the feelings the older children may be having. For example, if visitors are constantly exclaiming about how *now* that she's a mother she understands this or that, the older kids can wonder why *they* did not make her a mother previously. Be aware that all siblings are sensitive to being displaced, and this added dynamic makes it extra necessary to provide constant reassurance of the invaluable role of each member of the family.

Partner Issues

Vulnerability

It's important to understand that the emotional backdrop for new motherhood for all involved is *vulnerability*. In fact, looking back, most parents realize that they've never in their lives felt more vulnerable. Although in heterosexual families a man certainly experiences monumental emotional changes as he becomes a father, his role is clearly culturally established, and there's built-in recognition from peers about what it's like to have a wife postpartum and to live with a new baby.

For lesbian two-parent families, the birth mom and baby are equally vulnerable as those in heterosexual families, but the nonbirth mom is just as vulnerable. Because she has no legal or culturally recognized role, she can feel completely and utterly vulnerable in all ways. Thus, there's no one person in the family holding a clear sense of self, and therefore emotional stability, to ground the family as a whole.

If you're the nonbirth mom, you may feel quite vulnerable from the lack of public recognition of your parenting role. Others may ignore your role and your feelings, especially during the initial postpartum period. Innocuous questions such as "How was the birth?" or "How are you feeling?"—if only posed to the birth mother—can certainly leave you feeling excluded. When your emotions are so tender and new, especially from lack of sleep, the most well-meaning people relegating you to the invisible can feel heartbreaking. This is only compounded if your legal parenting status is unclear or unrecognized. Discuss your feelings and your experiences with your partner. Despite her best intentions, she too may exclude you in ways she doesn't recognize, which only heightens your feelings. With good communication she can be your most ardent supporter.

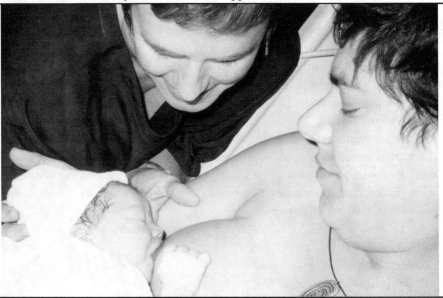

Out in public after your first few weeks at home, nonbirth moms are often assumed to be the child's grandmother, even when this is an inappropriate guess based on your age. It speaks to the extreme lack of openness straight culture has to perceiving family outside of rigid norms. Being mistaken in your role with the child may continue for sometime, especially if you don't share the your child's last name. As your child grows older, he or she and you together will find ways of identifying or introducing yourselves that feel true and clear about your vital mother role, leaving less room for guesswork on others' parts.

Your partner who just gave birth may be feeling a newfound connection with the other women in her life, both family and friends, who have shared the experience of birth. This divide may be especially painful to you if you tried unsuccessfully to get pregnant before she did. Seek help from someone other than her on this one. Honor your experiences as different but equal. She has had a unique physical experience that she needs the opportunity to hold and reflect on.

If every postpartum woman, whether birth mom or not, could hold the awareness and compassion for the extreme vulnerability of each other in the postpartum period, weathering this time would be a lot easier.

Fear of Intimacy

You may have never loved anyone as much as you love your baby. How wonderful and special to have your heart feel so full and open—and how terrifying! If you realize that this much love could be lost should anything happen to your child, you'll probably feel some panic. You may imagine this in the form of sickness, injury, or the death of your baby, or as the loss of your baby if you don't have guaranteed legal parenting rights. You may even feel trapped, realizing it's too late to stop loving this deeply; you developed this deep love in pregnancy or the first time you held the baby and couldn't deny it if you tried. In this situation most women find some resolution by looking deeply into any spiritual beliefs they have that allow them a sense of trust or faith in something larger or higher than themselves.

This process is important to recognize in a couple situation because either parent can experience it, and the response can often include pulling back emotionally from the partner. This pulling away can simply be a response to a fear of deep intimacy or it can come from the unfamiliarity of feeling so close to more than one person. When you recognize this, talk and share so that neither of you takes the other's reaction personally, but can instead support the other to remain embodied and closely connected.

The Nonbirth Mom's Feelings About Breastfeeding

If you're the nonbirth mother, you may feel many mixed emotions about your partner breastfeeding. You may feel jealous that the baby is so intimately connected to a part of your lover's body that she had previously shared only with you. This is normal. If many visitors and family want to hold the baby at first, their time with the baby comes out of the time you spend with your baby, because the baby's nursing time isn't negotiable. Therefore, it's reasonable for you to be protective with your time holding the baby. Understand that initially while your baby is awake it will probably almost exclusively be breastfeeding. And although at first the baby will be spending many more hours asleep than awake, a number of those hours will probably be spent sleeping on your partner's breast. In time the baby will space out his or her nursings and be awake for longer stretches. Meanwhile, the first eight weeks or so can easily seem like an eternity of waiting to have more contact with the baby, especially if you felt that as soon as the baby was born you'd be able to begin a 50/50 relationship. The 50/50 concept is a set-up for frustration for two reasons. The first is that in reality the parenting effort both of you will put out is about 200/200. Secondly, each of your 200% will look different from the other's because of the biology of breastfeeding. This does change over time, even though you may not be able to see that far ahead with confidence.

I Feel Excluded/I've Lost My Partner

Many nonbirth moms feel that the birth mom has gained someone to love in the form of the baby, while the nonbirth mom has lost the love of someone, namely her partner. The birth mom and baby may appear an inseparable and whole dyad, complete unto themselves. Fathers feel this way as well, but they at least have their own socially accepted and unique title/role.

Nursing a baby, especially at first, can so saturate a birth mother's need for human touch that it may replace all the adult opportunities for physical intimacy and snuggling. Try to recognize this and don't internalize it as rejection. If you feel threatened, it's much better to acknowledge these feelings by discussing them rather than building up resentment that shows itself in other less healthy ways.

This is an important time for you both to stay connected to the idea that you made the baby together out of love and that you love each other through the baby—and also adult to adult. You may only have 30 seconds here or there to express your love for each other, but try to do it every day, whether by saying "I love you" or by acknowledging each other in other special ways. Give each other a lot of positive feedback and appreciation, whether it's about each other as mothers, lovers, or just as wonderful people.

Bonding

The nonbreastfeeding mom may have many concerns about her own bonding with the baby at first in the absence of the breastfeeding connection and within the time limits that breastfeeding imposes. She may have strong fears that the baby won't need or recognize her. This may be compounded by the birth mom's attitude toward sharing the baby. Many people don't realize that mothering instincts, driven most likely by hormones, compel many women to keep their newborns within hearing and seeing range. Indeed, feeling that the baby is too far away or gone for too long is very excruciating. If your partner just gave birth and is feeling this short psychic umbilical cord, she may seem to be acting irrationally by not allowing you to take the baby outside or even into the front room of the house. This attitude has little to do with her trust for you and more to do with her inexplicable emotional needs.

These deep intuitive parenting senses may seem exaggerated and unnecessary now, but women who can stay open to them will be developing a most useful parenting tool. You all may have to laugh at the ridiculous aspects while still trying to honor these instincts because you don't want to close off or distance yourselves from the place they originate. The nonbirth mom will develop her own maternal intuition in time as well. The birth mom would do well to try to communicate exactly how she feels, including the partner in her experience whenever possible. Be very conscious about allowing the nonbirth mom to develop her own style of parenting and providing space for her to figure out how to mother the baby on her own. You may be tempted to interpret the baby's cries or quick to correct her, but try to resist impulses such as these so that she can develop her own parenting style and problem-solving intuition.

One aspect of parenting that is often particularly challenging is comforting a crying baby. Regardless of the reason the baby started to cry, a nursing mom can often comfort the baby at the breast, while a non-nursing mom or coparent will have other ways to comfort the baby. The non-nursing mom may feel she is inadequate because the baby is so easily comforted at the breast. Babies are directly and passionately expressive of their feelings. Try to relax your shoulders, take three or four deep breaths, and while you physically hold the baby, energetically hold some safe space around it as well. That way, your child can feel whatever he or she needs to feel without being "fixed" or silenced. If your baby is crying for reasons other than hunger, everyone needs to be patient and supportive of the non-nursing mom's ability (and that of coparents as well) to develop her own connection with the baby, including a variety of ways to be with the baby when he or she is crying.

In general, each parent will need her own time and style of bonding with the baby. Sometimes because of living arrangements or the number of parents, each may feel he or she isn't getting fair share. It's helpful to remind everyone before the birth that the baby will primarily be with the nursing mom at first. Each parent is essential for the other roles s/he provides, even if they don't all involve one-on-one time with the baby. Nonetheless, there's plenty to do with the baby while the breastfeeding mom rests, including diapering, bathing, massaging, and holding it so the nursing mom or one of the other parents can nap. Over time, bonds will form organically. Each parent will have his or her own unique way of understanding the child and responding; the baby will recognize each parent's voice and style of touch. This may be hard to remember and trust in the beginning, but be patient and you'll be rewarded with beautiful parent/infant relationships.

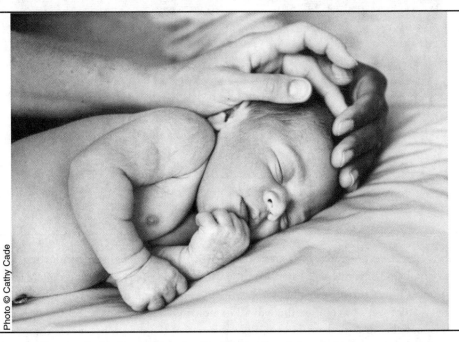

Photo © Cathy Cade

If you're the birth mom in a family situation involving multiple parents, you may have agreed to a fairly specific structure of sharing in the care of the new baby before you became pregnant. Now that you're in the reality of new motherhood, this structure may be perfect or may feel wildly inappropriate. Renegotiate, if you need to, in light of this new awareness. Parenting arrangements need to be dynamic, changing to accommodate new needs and awarenesses as they arise. To discuss new or different plans than you had previously doesn't mean you negotiated in bad faith; it means you now have a much more realistic view of your unique new parenting reality and can more accurately represent both your own needs and what you perceive your baby's needs to be.

The Next Weeks and Months

Returning to Work

This topic warrants thorough discussion since work arrangements may greatly influence the structure and quality of family life. Sexism and the inherent lack of respect for children in our culture unnecessarily limit our options. Usually, state disability will reimburse the birth mom a portion of her regular salary from up to four weeks before the due date to six weeks after the baby's birth (eight if birthed by cesarean). The Family and Medical Leave Act allows a mother up to 12 weeks of unpaid leave to care for her child. Some workplaces offer a longer paid maternity leave than six weeks. Others offer the option of taking more time off unpaid. Still others expect you back at work six weeks postpartum. If you're partnered, your partner should inquire about her company's maternity and paternity leaves to see which she may qualify for or prefer to use—believe it or not! Many progressive companies are recognizing new mothers who haven't given birth, through awareness of domestic partner families and families formed through adoption. Don't let your own homophobia prevent you from exploring and obtaining the most leave time you can both for emotional security and depth of bonding.

You may choose to go back to work when your leave runs out, or sooner. You may choose to stop working entirely for six months, one year, or longer. You might try to job-share, reducing your hours to part-time and asking your workplace to hire someone for the other hours. Perhaps you can work from home or telecommute part-time. Some workplaces are amenable to your having the baby there at least part-time until he or she starts to crawl, although you should realize that you'll work more slowly and less efficiently this way. Perhaps you and your partner or coparents can arrange your schedules so that you don't have to hire a child care provider. Once the birth mom's milk supply is well-established—at six to eight weeks after birth—she may choose to return to work and express milk so that the nonbirth mom can stay home with the baby. Or perhaps you're single and must work full-time relatively soon after you give birth in order to keep your job security or pay the bills.

Explore as many creative child care and work options as possible, daring to ask your boss for arrangements they may not usually offer, just to have the options that best suit your family. Good child care is difficult to find and isn't subsidized, so we often have to settle for something less than ideal. Nonetheless, listen to your heart. If your situation doesn't feel right, go back to the drawing board. Ask other parents about local resources or arrangements they may have discovered.

Second-Parent Nursing

If you intend to share breast-feeding with the birth mom, you'll probably find that the only information available is for adoptive moms. This isn't entirely relevant to you, because you won't be the only one breastfeeding. Nonetheless, read through any available adoptive nursing information and integrate it with the information we provide here.

Many women want to share in the breastfeeding experience for the unique bond it can create with the baby or for the physical experience of nursing. Some women have heard that enough nipple stimulation can cause their bodies to produce breast milk, even if they haven't recently given birth. This can occur, although in most cases women nursing in this way won't produce enough milk to be the sole nutritive provider for the baby. Nursing, however, doesn't have to meet all of a baby's caloric needs to be fulfilling. Nursing also provides comfort and connection, even if you don't produce breast milk. Babies have an intrinsic need to suck that is often greater than their need for milk. In other words,

they love to suck, even if they're not hungry. They won't only suck on a pacifier or a pinky finger in these situations; they often will latch on and nurse a non-lactating person's breast, even if it's differently shaped or sized than their birth mom's breast. With this in mind, read on and then think carefully about what your particular interest in nursing entails so that you can decide as a family how to approach breast-feeding. Don't be surprised if the mom who gave birth has different questions and concerns. You should both learn as much as possible to start the conversation.

The birth mom needs to establish a good milk supply and breast-feeding technique with the baby, since the nutritive value of her milk will be primary for the baby. She should nurse exclusively "on demand" for the first six weeks of the baby's life. After this, a mother can begin to share feedings. Therefore, the nonbirth mom may wish to begin preparing her breasts a few weeks after the baby's birth, when things begin to settle a bit.

Breast Pumps

Moisten your nipples and start slowly pumping with a breast pump. This will help increase the elasticity of the nipples and areola and get you used to the feeling of nursing. Electric pumps such as the Medela Lactina work best because you can double pump (pump on both sides simultaneously) which will increase the levels of prolactin in your body.

There's some controversy about using the breast pump to stimulate milk production. Some feel it's unwise to prepare with a pump because it will distract you from the experience at hand and because the slight amount of milk produced, if any, can discourage you easily and lead you to give up. If you choose to pump anyway, start pumping a few weeks before latching the baby on, three times per 24-hour period gradually increasing to 8 times per 24 hours. Pump three minutes on each side gradually increasing to six minutes per side.

Hormones

Some doctors prescribe hormones to stimulate breast-milk pro-duction. These hormones, however, haven't undergone much clinical testing, and there are a number of drawbacks to using them. For starters, they're expensive and not always effective, and they may cause undesired side effects. In addition, the use of these hormones requires physician supervision and is not advisable for women with low blood pressure or depression. As an alternative, many women take safe and gentle herbs to boost their breast-milk production. These include borage, fennel, fenugreek, milk thistle, and motherwort.

Supplemental Devices

The supplemental device is a small container filled with breast milk or formula with attached tubes that are taped to the mother's breast. The milk flows down the tubes from the container, which is hung around the mom's neck, and into the baby's mouth as it sucks on the nipple. You can fill the device with breast milk expressed from the lactating mother.

Postpartum Depression

Many different theories look to specific hormonal, physiological, or emotional causes of postpartum depression. The unique combination of all the above is, of course, relevant to each woman suffering this hardship. The brain biochemistry of some women is deeply affected and perhaps imbalanced once the surging hormones of birth drop off suddenly and are replaced by breastfeeding hormones. Lack of sleep and frequent low blood sugar can feel destabilizing mentally and lead to feeling blue or overwhelmed. Always germane are the psychosocial issues we've described that come to bear during the postpartum period: old memories of trauma or abuse, past birth issues, how you were or were not loved as an infant, and isolation or lack of support through a very challenging time of transition involving your most core identity. Many women feel periods of blueness, sadness, or even surges of grief, anger, or fear in the postpartum period.

Clinical depression, however, is usually more constant and can move from "low" feelings to general apathy, sleep disturbance, lack of caring for or about the baby or yourself, loss of appetite, and a downward spiral of isolation. Please reach out for help if you have these signs and they're not disappearing. Please seek assistance if you're the partner or friend of someone with these symptoms. Call a local counseling hotline, ask your midwife or obstetrician for a referral, or even ask for a referral from your local hospital's labor and delivery unit.

The nonbirth mom isn't immune to depression herself. She faces similar new parenting stresses and lack of sleep, as well as often having to return to work before she's ready. She has many roles to balance—with very few roles models—as she finds her way through issues that both mothers and fathers experience culturally. She too may need support and counseling.

Postpartum Sex

When your body may be ready to have sex often has little bearing on when you're emotionally ready to have sex. It's safe to resume vaginal penetration and/or oral sex as soon as the birth mom's postpartum bleeding has completely stopped. When bleeding stops, the uterus has closed and healed and is no longer at risk for infection by germs that may enter the vagina. This can happen anywhere from two to six weeks after giving birth. Before the bleeding has stopped, women can get in a well-cleaned bathtub with plain water or water and specific herbs that speed up the healing process (called sitz herbs), but should avoid putting anything in the vagina or on the vulva, including fingers, swimming-pool water, vibrators, and tampons.

After a woman gives birth vaginally, the inside of her vulva is different than it was before. All of the folds inside the vagina were stretched to capacity and then reshaped themselves once the baby was born. Nerves that received pressure may take up to six months to regrow, and after they do, many women experience new and different areas of vaginal sensation. Newly healed tissue is very sensitive. Initially, it may feel too sensitive for any stimulation, but eventually it may feel pleasantly extra sensitive. Each time we give birth vaginally, our vaginas change significantly, and we get to explore them anew when we are ready. If you had a cesarean birth, you may also feel changes in your vagina if you labored to the extent that the baby's head came low into your pelvis.

As a result of these changes, our internal markers of pleasure often have changed, leading to feeling new and vulnerable about sex. Don't count on liking or desiring the same kind of touch or sexual stimulation as you did prior to pregnancy and birth. Sometimes it's frightening or upsetting that nothing feels familiar. Instead, try to think of sex as a new opportunity for exploration and variation of pleasure. Postpartum sex is about rediscovery. Therefore, you'll need to be extra sure to communicate verbally what feels good and what doesn't. If you're breastfeeding, the new hormones will suppress some of your estrogen production. This means you may not self-lubricate as much when you're sexually aroused as you did previously. If your partner counts on your vaginal wetness as a sign of your pleasure, she may be confused, and so may you. This may no longer be a reliable marker of sexual arousal. So use extra lubricant if you need it and communicate to your partner that you're turned on!

Some women like to have a lot more vaginal penetration after they've given birth because it's more comfortable than it was previously or their vaginas are more sensitive now. Other women feel exactly the opposite. Still others may enjoy penetration but need it to be much slower or gentler. Breastfeeding moms and nonbirth moms alike often feel as if the birth mom's breasts are no longer a sexual object: They've become functional and sacred for the sole use of the baby. Although this is true for many women, others experience newfound sexual sensitivity in their breasts and enjoy nipple or breast contact tremendously. Most women will leak milk, especially early on, when sexually aroused. Check out how sexual breast contact feels for you before deciding to avoid it all together.

Although the physical aspect of sex after childbirth is difficult for many women, the emotional side is often just as challenging. Just because a woman has healed physically doesn't mean she has emotionally. If the birth involved trauma or vaginal tearing, it may take quite some time before the birthing woman is ready to have anyone—including herself—touch her vulva. This body/emotional reconnection may take many months to complete. In fact, the desire to resume sexual contact often does not occur before deep emotions about the birth begin to be resolved.

Likewise, the nonbirth mom can also have issues that arose during the birth that make it difficult to resume being sexual again. Sometimes just watching your partner go through so much pain is hard to let go of. Any intimate contact can bring you to that memory, possibly bringing up sadness, anger, helplessness, or even guilt. Having witnessed vaginal trauma such as tearing, episiotomy, or suturing can be enough to quell the libido for some time. Sometimes having watched your partner's vulva stretch so widely and have a baby emerge from what used to be her "honey pot" may put you in too much awe to touch it. If during labor you watched many people touch her vagina—especially if they did so roughly or nonconsensually—either you or she may feel as if it's not hers anymore for herself or for you. You may have just as much healing to do as she has, and the things you find difficult may be entirely different from her experience. Talk about this, if not with your partner then with others, including your midwife or a counselor if you need to.

Many women feel uncomfortable with their bigger bodies after they give birth, which affects their ability to perceive themselves as sexually desirable or their desire to be naked. Body image, self-esteem, and libido go hand in hand for many women. Being able to talk about this openly with your sexual partner can help to relieve any shame or negative feelings.

Some nonbirth moms find that after childbirth they're no longer sexually attracted to their partner since they see her as a mother instead of a lover. Sometimes birth moms feel the same way. They're too exhausted and consumed with breastfeeding to even think about sex. Prolactin, the nursing hormone, can really dampen sex drive, although sex drive usually resumes for all involved at some point during the first year after childbirth. Often for the birth mom it coincides with either her nursing hormones dropping as the baby eats more solid food or experiencing lifestyle changes that allow her to spend more time alone replenishing her reserves, so that she feels more capacity to share her body not only with the baby but also with her partner. Although partnered lesbians may spend some time with their sexual desires out of sync with each other, they'll eventually match up. However, finding time and energy logistically as well as emotionally to make love while parenting is a whole new ballgame. Take it when and where you can, and in the interim remember that there are many nonsexual ways to express physical intimacy and nurturing with each other. If, however, either mom is delaying any sexual expression more than 10 months postpartum it may be a good time to seek therapy to help resolve the underlying issues.

Sex and Single Moms

Most single moms are content with solo sex for a long while after giving birth. The length of time that this feels complete varies widely from woman to woman. Many single women don't have the time or energy to date at all in the first year postpartum and feel just fine about that. Some don't want to have sex with anyone until they've met someone who could potentially be a long-term partner, whereas other single moms are much more interested in casual sex since they're not presently able to even think about putting energy into a potentially long-term relationship. Dating nonparents usually involves a lot of explaining and educating before you can both share similar expectations of the type and schedule of time you'll have together. Dating other parents can be logistically challenging, although potentially more emotionally supportive.

Resources

Books

After the Baby's Birth: A Woman's Way to Wellness, Robin Lim, Celestial Arts, 1991

The Breastfeeding Book: Everything You Need to Know to Nurse Your Child From Birth Through Weaning, Martha Sears and William Sears, Little Brown & Co., 2000

The Continuum Concept: In Search of Happiness Lost, Jean Liedoff, Perseus Press, 1986

Eat Well, Lose Weight While Breastfeeding: The Complete Nutrition Book for Nursing Mothers, Including a Healthy Guide to the Weight Loss Your Doctor Promised, Eileen Behan, Villard Books, 1992

How Weaning Happens, Diane Bengson, La Leche League International, 2000

Infants and Mothers: Differences in Development, T. Berry Brazelton, Delacorte Press, 1994

Nursing Mother, Working Mother: The Essential Guide for Breastfeeding and Staying Close to Your Baby After You Return to Work, Gale Pryor, Harvard Common Press, 1997

The Mother's Guide to Sex: Enjoying Your Sexuality Through All Stages of Motherhood, Anne Semans and Cathy Winks, Three Rivers Press, 2001

Natural Family Living: The Mothering Magazine *Guide to Parenting*, Peggy O'Mara and Jane McConnell (eds.), Pocket Books, 2000

Nursing Your Adopted Baby, Kathryn Anderson, La Leche League, 1983

The Queer Parent's Primer, Stephanie A. Brill, New Harbinger, 2001

Touchpoints: Your Child's Emotional and Behavioral Development, T. Berry Brazelton, Perseus Press, 1994

The Womanly Art of Breastfeeding, Gwen Gotsch and Judy Torgus, Penguin, 1997

You Are Your Child's First Teacher, Rahima Baldwin, Celestial Arts, 2000

Breastfeeding Products and Baby Supplies

Ameda Breastfeeding Solutions

www.ameda.com

BH Pump Center
www.bhpumpcenter.com

Little Koala Breastfeeding Products and Baby Supplies
www.littlekoala.com

RightOnMom.com
www.rightonmom.com

Organizations
COLAGE (Children of Lesbians and Gays Everywhere)
3543 18th St., #1
San Francisco, CA 94110
(414) 861-5437
www.colage.org

International Board of Certified Lactation Consultants
7309 Arlington Blvd., Suite 300
Falls Church, VA 22042-3215
(703) 560-7330
www.iblce.org

La Leche League International (contact main office for local chapters or consult your local phone directory)
1400 N. Meacham Rd.
Schaumburg, IL 60168-4079
Phone (847) 519-7730
www.lalecheleague.org

Nursing Mothers Counsel
For local chapter information call (650) 599-3669 or visit www.nursingmothers.org.

Web Sites
Single Young Moms' Mailing List
members.tripod.com/~SingleMoms

SingleMOMZ: The Site by Single Moms for Single Moms
www.singlemomz.com

Parting Words...

Amidst all the awkward changes, diapers, and sleepless nights, you'll find moments stretching into hours of pure ecstatic love. You'll hold your baby while he or she sleeps, watching your child inhale and exhale, and your heart will feel full of compassionate love. You might catch the way your baby's breath quickens at the sound of your voice when you enter the room or how your baby's eyes stare into yours when you bring your face near, and you realize at that moment your child loves you just as fully. If you're partnered, you might see the tenderness with which your partner holds the baby, and you'll feel the adoring love you have for her well up in your heart, realizing you've embarked upon a miraculous journey together. You might find yourself in a moment feeling fully present and competent as you care for your child or reflecting on the pride you have at growing and birthing your baby, and you'll realize you have a newfound deep unconditional love for yourself.

This deep sense of love and joy can be found many times a day in parenting. It's from this place that you'll renew your monumental parenting patience when it runs low. Sometimes we do a funny process of limiting how much happiness or joy we feel, whether we're afraid to lose that joy because we don't trust that it's sustainable or because we don't feel we deserve that much joy and love. Joy and love are our birthrights. They're the deep rewards of parenting. Soak them up.

As midwives who have helped thousands of lesbian, bisexual, and heterosexual women create family, we feel it's safe to say that the people who spend the most time *prior to parenting* clarifying their intentions, goals, and expectations from each family member are the families who start parenting on the strongest footing. They are also the families who have the greatest chances of staying together through the daily challenges of parenting. Conception, pregnancy, and birth are truly just the beginning steps of the lifelong journey of parenting. It is hard to imagine that birth is just the beginning when you have come so far to get to the point of giving birth! Clarity in this part of the journey, however, carries over to deeper confidence and clarity in the second half of your life: actual day-to-day parenting.

We hope that this book has allowed you to feel that the path to pregnancy, birth, and parenthood is a little clearer, easier, and more accessible. We also hope it has guided you through the many decisions you as a lesbian, bisexual, or single woman of any orientation, have to make in order to become parents—thereby helping you identify your own unique path to parenthood. And most of all, we hope that this book has allowed you to recognize, value, and celebrate the love that you have to share with a baby. Keep growing that love from the inside out—this is your greatest gift to your children.

Although there are many struggles we each face when we choose to parent in a predominantly heterosexual culture, once we become parents we realize that those struggles—when addressed consciously and with compassion—just help to lay a solid foundation for our family. Remember to take the time to congratulate yourself for being one of the pioneers of intentional parenting outside of traditional heterosexual relationships/marriage. When times are rough, slow down and appreciate the internal and external struggles you face and applaud your bravery to become a parent in the midst of these challenges. When you're feeling alone, keep in mind that there are *millions* of us already out there parenting our children with pride and love, and millions of women just like you, on the verge of becoming parents. You are not alone.

So wherever you are in the process, check in with yourself to make sure that you're coming from a place of love and confidence as you create the foundation for your parenthood. Nourish yourself and your relationships as you nourish your body—the future home for your baby—and as you nourish your baby-to-be. Take the time you need to firmly feel that the decisions you're making are the right ones for you.

As you read these last words, some of you will be awaiting the imminent birth of your baby, and some of you will have read this book cover to cover before even beginning to inseminate. Regardless of where you are in the process at this moment, we hope that all of the information we have shared with you has been both informative and inspirational. Take what you have learned and share it with others.

The experience and wisdom you gain from your path to pregnancy will start you off way ahead of the game. The challenges of parenting still await you, but you are well prepared. Honor how far you have come and take a deep breath…the joy you have so dearly been wanting is awaiting you.

So we send you off on your adventure with well wishes. Whether you're at month 10 or year 10 of your journey at the time of reading this, just pondering parenting or due in two weeks, we hope you find your joy and love at each step of this daunting and rewarding experience. The intention of the book has been to provide as much information as possible about the wide diversity of experiences and choices lesbian, bisexual, and single women have, and encourage women to take this information and make their own true and unique best decisions. Our goal in presenting the topics holistically is to encourage women to value the connections between their emotional, physical, and spiritual selves throughout conception, pregnancy, and birth, and to find ways to feel comfortable and safe in their bodies. We wish you great happiness amidst all the challenges queer parenting (in fact any parenting) includes, and we know you'll raise your children with great love and pride. Good luck!

Photo © Cathy Cade

Glossary

For more detailed information on specific terms and concepts (some of which may not be listed here), consult the index.

Assisted Reproductive Technology (ART): Usually refers to the process of in vitro fertilization, although it also refers to placing an egg and sperm surgically together in the uterus or fallopian tube.

Basal body temperature (BBT): The lowest temperature of the body on a particular day, usually early in the morning immediately upon awakening. Women monitor their BBT as a method of tracking fertility and predicting their day of ovulation.

Biological father: A man whose sperm was involved in a child's conception. Does not necessarily imply parental involvement.

Chem panel: A blood chemistry test that assesses someone's overall health. Most laboratories print out a range of normal values next to the test results so it's fairly easily to see when a result is abnormal.

Chlamydia: A bacteria that can infect the reproductive tract, urethra, lungs, and eyes. It is most often sexually transmitted. It can create scar tissue, causing infertility, and often does not produce any symptoms. It can also be transmitted from mother to infant during birth.

Clomid: The brand name of clomiphene, a drug taken in pill form at the beginning of the cycle to stimulate ovulation.

Coparent: A term with many definitions. Usually refers to an adult who shares parenting responsibilities but isn't romantically involved with the birth mother, or to an adult who shares parenting responsibilities but isn't the primary parent. The verb *coparent* means to parent together.

Corpus luteum: The gland formed by the ruptured follicle following ovulation.

Cytomegalovirus (CMV): A virus to which many of us have been exposed at some point in our lives. It usually will only make you sick if your immune system isn't working well. Getting an active CMV infection while pregnant can cause birth defects such as central nervous system damage, brain damage, and hearing loss.

Double ovulation: When ovulation occurs more than once a cycle, often seven to 10 days apart.

Doula: Another name for a labor coach or postpartum care provider, a professional nonmedical birth and postpartum attendant who helps the entire family practically and emotionally.

Egg donor: A woman who takes fertility drugs to mature a large number of eggs, which are retrieved with a minor surgical procedure and combined with sperm during in vitro fertilization. The embryo is then placed in the uterus of another woman who wishes to parent. Usually, women who are older and have few healthy eggs left are encouraged to consider using an donor's eggs if they have fertility challenges.

Egg health: Refers to whether or not the egg is able to respond to the hormone message from the brain that tells it to mature and ovulate.

Estradiol: One form of estrogen, produced by the ovaries, that can reveal information about a woman's level of fertility.

Estrogen: A hormone that stimulates the development of female secondary-sex characteristics.

Fertile mucus: A substance, produced by the cervix, that serves as a natural filtration system and allows healthy, well-formed sperm into the cervix.

Fertility drugs: Medications that induce the ovaries to produce many eggs. Except for clomiphene, all are administered by injection.

Folic acid (or folate): One of the B vitamins. Key in the formation of the baby's neural tube, which becomes the spine. Women are encouraged to take a folic acid supplement during preconception, as the neural tube forms in very early pregnancy.

Follicle-stimulating hormone (FSH): Hormone produced in the pituitary gland in the brain that triggers the follicles in the ovary to mature eggs so they can be ovulated.

Follicular phase: The first half or so of the menstrual cycle, from the first day of the menstrual period to the point of ovulation.

Fresh sperm: Sperm that has just recently been ejaculated and will be used for insemination immediately without freezing.

Frozen sperm: Sperm that has been cryogenically frozen at a sperm bank or fertility clinic and is thawed before insemination.

Genetic testing: May refer to blood tests that check for genetically inherited diseases in a man or a woman, such as cystic fibrosis, Tay-Sachs disease, or sickle-cell anemia. May also refer to various tests such as amniocentesis done during pregnancy to diagnose chromosomal abnormalities of the fetus, such as Down's syndrome or any of the aforementioned diseases.

Go-between: Someone who works with a woman to screen a sperm donor to some extent and maintains the confidentiality of both parties by picking up and dropping off the donated semen.

Gonorrhea: A contagious inflammation of the genital mucous membrane caused by a sexually transmittable bacteria. It can be transmitted from mother to infant during birth.

Human chorionic gonadotropin (HCG): The main pregnancy hormone produced by the embryo. This is the hormone that pregnancy tests check for. When given mid cycle by injection, it can stimulate the body to ovulate, just as LH does.

Hysterosalpingogram (HSG): A series of X rays taken after opaque dye has been placed in the uterus through a tube in the cervix in order to diagnose a number of irregularities, particularly tubal blockage.

Identity-release donor: A sperm donor from a sperm bank who has authorized the bank to release his identifying information to the child upon his or her request as an adult.

In vitro fertilization (IVF): Conception that occurs in a laboratory with an egg retrieved surgically from the uterus.

Initial hormone tests: Tests a woman may undergo before inseminating to check if her hormone levels are optimal for conception.

Internalized homophobia: Shame, self-doubt, guilt, or not feeling deserving of first-class treatment because of a lesbian, gay, or bisexual orientation.

Intracervical insemination: Often a fancy word for vaginal insemination, although sometimes it refers to finding the cervix by using a speculum and then depositing the semen right at the opening of the cervix, instead of injecting in the back of the vagina without the use of a speculum.

Intrauterine insemination (IUI): A method of insemination that involves washing the sperm to separate it from the semen, then placing it directly into the uterus with a sterile plastic tube that is passed through the cervix.

Known donor: A sperm donor whose identity is known, or a sperm donor obtained through a sperm bank whose identity will be released to the child upon his or her request as an adult.

Luteal phase: The second half or so of the menstrual cycle, from the point of ovulation to the day before the next menstrual period.

Luteinizing hormone (LH): Hormone produced in the pituitary gland in the brain that triggers ovulation. Ovulation predictor kits test for LH surges.

Menopause: A physiological state women go through as their ovaries run out of eggs and their hormones change in response. Women may menstruate regularly for a number of years with very decreased fertility due to having few eggs left before the onset of menopause.

Midwife: A traditional birth attendant. Almost always a woman, she may practice at home or in the hospital and be trained holistically or medically from a variety of educational models; she may also be a nurse. A midwife provides complete prenatal and postpartum care, and offers education and support to the entire family. Most women in the world, historically and currently, give birth with a midwife in attendance, not a physician. World Health Organization statistics show that on average the best birth outcomes occur at home with a midwife in attendance. Statistics in the United States reflect this as well.

Myco/ureaplasma: Bacteria that can be found in the reproductive tracts of women and occasionally men. They do not cause any symptoms but are suspected of increasing a woman's risk of miscarriage. They both can be transmitted sexually but are easily treated with oral antibiotics.

Nonbiological mother: A woman who is not biologically related to her child. Usually used to identify the partner of the birth mother. This term is not preferred by most women, who usually just call themselves "mother" or use a more positive term that does not identify them solely by what they are not.

Ovulation: The release of the mature egg from the ovary.

Pituitary gland: Gland located in the brain. This is the site of production of many reproductive hormones including FSH and LH.

Preconception counseling: Education and support on any of a variety of topics, including fertility awareness, nutritional needs, pre-pregnancy, avoidance of birth-defect-causing substances are common topics. Lesbian and bisexual women often also receive information on sperm donors, legal issues, insemination methods, and many other issues specific to them.

Premature ovarian failure: When a woman runs out of eggs to ovulate and experiences menopause at a relatively very early age.

Progesterone: A hormone that is produced in either the ovary or the placenta. It has many roles, one of which is to "tell" the uterus to maintain its fertile lining in the second half of the cycle in case an embryo is on its way to implant in it.

Prolactin: A hormone made in the pituitary gland that is best known for its role in stimulating breast milk. High levels of prolactin can inhibit ovulation.

Prostaglandins: Natural chemicals essential to the working of the muscle in the ovary to release the egg.

Quarantine: Sperm banks often hold a donor's sperm for six months, after which they repeat his tests for sexually transmitted diseases. If the tests are negative at that time, the sperm is released from quarantine. This process increases the accuracy of the testing, as some infections take weeks to months after exposure to show up on a test yet are transmittable immediately.

Reproductive endocrinologist: Professional term for an infertility specialist, an obstetrician gynecologist who has specialized training in causes of infertility, reproductive hormones, and infertility treatment technologies.

Rugae: The folds of the vaginal walls.

Second-parent adoption: A legal process available in some states that gives full parenting rights to a nonbiological mother in a lesbian partnership.

Semen analysis: A test, known by many people as a sperm count, that examines many other components of semen than just the number of sperm.

Thyroid: Large endocrine gland located at the base of the neck that produces the hormones thyroxine and triiodothyronine.

Unknown donor: A sperm donor who will always remain anonymous.

Vaginal insemination: Method of insemination in which the semen is deposited via a small syringe into the back of the vagina so it can swim into the uterus. Sometimes the syringe is held in place by a cup placed over the cervix.

Yes donor: See identity-release donor.

Index

About the Photographers

Cathy Cade lives in Oakland, Calif. She has been photographing lesbian mothering for more than 30 years and is the birth mother of two sons conceived by donor insemination. She is the owner of Cathy Cade: Personal Histories, Photo Organizing, and Photography. One of her specialties is pregnancy nudes.

Limor Inbar-Hansen, who has been photographing since the early 1980s, received the Eddie Adams Photographic Award while in her first year at the New England School of Photography. Ms. Inbar-Hansen quickly became a contributor to magazines such as *Time* and *Newsweek*, and worked with world-renowned photographers Donna Ferrato ("Living With the Enemy," *Aperture*) and Philip Jones-Griffiths (Magnum Photos). As a member of Impact Visuals Photo Agency, Ms. Inbar-Hansen concentrated on photographing the exquisite in everyday life. Her photos of gay and lesbian families, as well as her documentation of social and political events, have been exhibited in the United States and the Middle East.

Jean Weisinger is a self-taught African American photographer based in Oakland. She has traveled to Africa, Cuba, India, Mexico, Jamaica, Australia, New Zealand, Europe, and throughout the U.S. Ms. Weisinger has exhibited her work in one-person and selected group exhibitions in the U.S., Cuba, Africa, and India. Her photographs have appeared in numerous films, books, and a wide range of publications, as well as on posters, post cards, and in calendars. Her photographs are in collections throughout the world. Ms. Weisinger's vision is to travel around the world and to document the people of the earth. She believes that her photographs embrace the true spirit of people's hearts.